# Europeanization and Globalization

## Volume 3

**Series editors**
Nada Bodiroga-Vukobrat
Rijeka, Croatia

Siniša Rodin
Luxembourg, Luxembourg

Gerald G. Sander
Ludwigsburg, Germany

T0414185

More information about this series at http://www.springer.com/series/13467

Vesna Tomljenović • Nada Bodiroga-Vukobrat • Vlatka Butorac Malnar • Ivana Kunda

Editors

# EU Competition and State Aid Rules

Public and Private Enforcement

 Springer

*Editors*
Vesna Tomljenović
General Court of EU
Luxembourg, Luxembourg

Nada Bodiroga-Vukobrat
Faculty of Law
University of Rijeka
Rijeka, Croatia

Vlatka Butorac Malnar
Faculty of Law
University of Rijeka
Rijeka, Croatia

Ivana Kunda
Faculty of Law
University of Rijeka
Rijeka, Croatia

ISSN 2366-0953 ISSN 2366-0961 (electronic)
Europeanization and Globalization
ISBN 978-3-662-56909-2 ISBN 978-3-662-47962-9 (eBook)
https://doi.org/10.1007/978-3-662-47962-9

Printed on acid-free paper

This Springer imprint is published by Springer Nature
The registered company is Springer-Verlag GmbH, DE
The registered company address is: Heidelberger Platz 3, 14197 Berlin, Germany

# Preface

The effective enforcement of competition and state aid rules is one of the keys to the successful economic development and stability of the EU internal market. While the Commission plays the central role in the application of EU state aid rules, the situation is somewhat different when it comes to the application of EU competition rules. Following the entry into force of Regulation 1/2003, national enforcers have been given the authority and duty to apply EU competition rules in all cases affecting trade between Member States. Consequently, proper and uniform application across Member States is one of the biggest challenges in this area of law. The novelties are many as it is an ever-changing body of law constantly being adapted to new market situations. We are witnessing a proliferation of decisions and judgments at both the EU and national levels, continuously reshaping the landscape of competition law. Legislative activities are not lagging behind either. One of the most recent developments concerns the adoption of the Directive on Antitrust Damages Actions, which has created as many opportunities as obstacles.

Against this backdrop, an international conference was organised to provide a platform to discuss recent case law and legislative developments in the separate but related areas of competition and state aid law. We succeeded in bringing together a unique gathering of EU judges, academics and professionals who provided outstanding contributions at what became the fourth Petar Šarčević international conference: 'EU Competition and State Aid Rules: Interaction between public and private enforcement'. The conference, held on 9 and 10 September 2015 in Rovinj, Croatia, was organised by various Croatian and foreign institutions: the Croatian Comparative Law Association (CCLA); the Institute for European and Comparative Law (IECL) of the Faculty of Law, University of Rijeka, Croatia; the Fridtjof Nansen Institute, Norway; the Jean Monnet Inter-University Centre of Excellence Opatija, Croatia; the Croatian Competition Agency (CCA); and the Croatian Judicial Academy.

This book is the direct result of the named conference. Impossible as it is to discuss all recent developments in a single volume, the book focuses on selected issues related to the enforcement of competition rules on one hand and state aid rules on the other. The book's 14 chapters are arranged into four parts. The first part is devoted to the role of courts in the public enforcement of competition law at the EU and national levels. The second part deals with selected challenges of the public enforcement of EU competition rules before the Commission. Selected issues on private enforcement of EU competition rules are tackled in the third part of the book. The fourth part examines the most challenging issues related to the enforcement of state aid rules.

We are particularly grateful and honoured to be able to present in this volume contributions from several judges and legal secretaries of the General Court of the EU, including the President of the General Court of the EU, the Honourable Judge Marc Jaeger. There are no persons better placed to discuss the role of the courts in the enforcement of competition rules than those involved in the decision-making process. Each member of the General Court of the EU provided meaningful, hands-on and essential insight into the topic covered. Their generous support and involvement in the entire project would not have been possible had it not been for one of the editors, Professor Vesna Tomljenović, as we still like to call her, who became the first Croatian Judge at the General Court of the EU in 2013, after an academic career of nearly three decades at the Faculty of Law, University of Rijeka, Croatia. Of course, we extend our deepest appreciation to all our authors, whose enthusiastic collaboration and expertise make this book a valuable contribution to the practice and science of competition and state aid law.

As editors, we hope you will enjoy reading this book as much as we enjoyed preparing it, and we are confident that it will serve you as a valuable source of information and insight.

Luxembourg, Luxembourg                                          Vesna Tomljenović
Rijeka, Croatia                                          Nada Bodiroga-Vukobrat
Rijeka, Croatia                                                       Ivana Kunda
Rijeka, Croatia                                          Vlatka Butorac Malnar
July 2017

# Contents

# Contributors

**Dubravka Akšamović** Faculty of Law, University of Osijek, Osijek, Croatia

**Marc Barennes** General Court of the European Union, Luxembourg, Luxembourg

**Nuria Bermejo** Faculty of Law, Autonomous University of Madrid, Madrid, Spain

**Ludovic Bernardeau** General Court of the European Union, Luxembourg, Luxembourg

University of Paris-Nanterre, Nanterre, France

**Vlatka Butorac Malnar** Faculty of Law, University of Rijeka, Rijeka, Croatia

**Nicola Chesaites** Quinn Emanuel Urquhart & Sullivan, LLP, London, UK

**Anca D. Chirita** Durham University, Durham, UK

**Edita Čulinović Herc** Faculty of Law, University of Rijeka, Rijeka, Croatia

**Mihail Danov** University of Leeds, Leeds, UK

**Marc Jaeger** General Court of the European Union, Luxembourg, Luxembourg

**Viktor Kreuschitz** General Court of the European Union, Luxembourg, Luxembourg

**Silvère Lefèvre** General Court of the European Union, Luxembourg, Luxembourg

**Marijana Liszt** Posavec, Rašica & Liszt Law Firm, Zagreb, Croatia

**Jasminka Pecotić Kaufman** Faculty of Economics and Business, University of Zagreb, Zagreb, Croatia

**Siniša Petrović**  Faculty of Law, University of Zagreb, Zagreb, Croatia

**Ana Pošćić**  Faculty of Law, University of Rijeka, Rijeka, Croatia

**Miro Prek**  General Court of the European Union, Luxembourg, Luxembourg

**Alexandr Svetlicinii**  University of Macau, Macau, China

# Reviewers

**Hana Horak**
Faculty of Economics, University of Zagreb, Zagreb, Croatia

**Nina Tepeš**
Faculty of Law, University of Zagreb, Zagreb, Croatia

# Part I
# The Role of Courts in Public Enforcement of EU Competition Rules

# 25 Years of the General Court: Looking Back and Forward

Marc Jaeger

**Abstract** In this article, the author, the President of the General Court of the European Union since 2007, reflects on the past, current and future EU judicial architecture. The first part of the contribution focuses on the structural evolutions that the General Court has gone through, achieving revolutionary solutions as to how the way cases are dealt with can be improved. However, the success story of this jurisdiction has led to an increase in its workload, creating a worrying backlog. Therefore, the second part addresses the various solutions implemented to tackle this problem, from the entry into force of new procedural rules last July to the foreseeable impact of the structural reform that will double the number of judges of the General Court.

## 1 Introductory Remarks

25 Years of evolution, 25 years of revolution, 25 years of production – no one would contest the fact that it would be hard to sum up these years in a few pages. It might seem to be rather daring to sketch 25 years of transformation in the judicial landscape of the EU and to envision how bright its future can be in a contribution so limited in space. However, just because the task seems impossible does not mean that it should not be undertaken. This has actually been the motto of the General Court since its establishment and its spirit for 25 years.

This article follows my contribution on the occasion of the 4th Petar Šarčević International Scientific Conference entitled 'Rethinking the role of the General Court – EU competition and state aid rules: interaction between public and private enforcement', which took place in Rovinj (Croatia) on 9 April 2015. I would like to thank Mr. Vivien Terrien for his precious assistance in writing this article, which reflects the situation as at 7 May 2015. It thus gives an updated view of my contribution 'The EU General Court: institutional aspects and perspectives', published in French in "Cours du Master international Droit de l'UE", vol. 4 "Le Tribunal de l'UE", Sofia 2014. All views expressed are strictly personal and are solely the responsibility of the author.

M. Jaeger (✉)
President, General Court of the European Union, Luxembourg, Luxembourg
e-mail: Marc.Jaeger@curia.europa.eu

© Springer-Verlag Berlin Heidelberg 2017                                                      3
V. Tomljenović et al. (eds.), *EU Competition and State Aid Rules*,
Europeanization and Globalization 3, https://doi.org/10.1007/978-3-662-47962-9_1

**Remember the Past to Foresee the Future**  An anniversary represents the perfect occasion to reflect on the past and also to consider directions to be followed in the near future. However, before looking ahead and playing as fortune teller regarding the architecture that the European Union judiciary may take (see Sect. 3), one should always look back to measure the distance covered so far, the achievements, the result of all these bricks patiently fashioned and put together to build a coherent and efficient judicial structure: the General Court (see Sect. 2).

## 2  The General Court: A Look Back

'In souls nobly born, valour does not depend upon age.'[1] Already in its early years, the General Court demonstrated the key role it could play in a mature EU judicial system. Its hard work and thorough and well-founded analysis were acknowledged, and the court saw its scope of action increased. Not only was its solid first-instance level (see Sect. 2.1) affirmed, but it also saw unprecedented and creative judicial developments (see Sect. 2.2).

## 2.1  From 'Specialised' to 'General': The Recognition of an Essential First-Tier Court

The recognition of the need to add a true first-tier level to the EU judicial system did not occur in a day but occurred in stages. The founding idea was far from the current structure of the General Court. At first, the EU legislators envisaged a specialised body limited in terms of subject matter and the nature of its parties (see Sect. 2.1.1). Experience and success led to the reshaping of this entity to give to rights holders a new interlocutor that could dedicate its time to hear all types of complex factual and legal complaints (see Sect. 2.1.2).

### 2.1.1  A Specialised Court: Subject Matter and Parties

Most of the time forgotten, often overlooked, in its first years, the General Court was the first specialised court of the European Union. Not only were its competences restricted to a limited number of fields, but the nature of potential claimants was also circumscribed to very specific categories of applicants.

---

[1]P Corneille, Le Cid, Act II, Scene II (personal translation).

**Specialised in Terms of Subject Matter** In 1986, the Single European Act[2] established the foundations of this court. Adding Article 168a to the EEC Treaty, Article 11 of the Single European Act stated:

The EEC Treaty shall be supplemented by the following provisions:
'Article 168a

1. At the request of the Court of Justice and after consulting the Commission and the European Parliament, the Council may, acting unanimously, *attach to the Court of Justice* a court with jurisdiction to hear and determine *at first instance*, subject to a right of appeal to the Court of Justice on points of law only and in accordance with the conditions laid down by the Statute, (. . .) classes of action (. . .)' (emphasis added).

Behind this provision, the EU legislator's intention was to relieve the Court of Justice. This had become overloaded with dense factual cases, and it no longer had time to examine them in detail[3] as its primary task resided in interpreting EU law, which meant focusing all its resources on ruling on points of law. Hence, the idea arose of creating a first instance tribunal to deal with such complex cases.[4] However, from the outset, this option was subject to conditions and limitations. Article 11 of the Single European Act specified:

---

[2]Single European Act [1987] OJ L169/1. The Single European Act was signed on 17 February 1986 in Luxembourg (by Belgium, Germany, Spain, France, Ireland, Luxembourg, the Netherlands, Portugal and the United Kingdom) and on 24 February 1986 in The Hague (by Denmark, Italy and Greece). It entered into force on 1 July 1987.

[3]From the ECJ's establishment, the duration of proceedings regarding direct actions increased significantly from 8.5 months in 1970 to 24 months in 1988.

[4]See, in this sense, the fourth, fifth and sixth recitals of Council Decision No 88/591/ECSC, EEC, Euratom of 24 October 1988 establishing a Court of First Instance of the European Communities [1988] OJ L 319/1:

Whereas, in respect of actions requiring *close examination of complex facts*, the establishment of a second court will improve the judicial protection of individual interests;

Whereas it is necessary, in order to maintain the quality and effectiveness of judicial review in the Community legal order, to *enable the Court to concentrate its activities on its fundamental task of ensuring uniform interpretation of Community law*;

Whereas it is therefore necessary to make use of the powers granted by (. . .) Article 168a of the EEC Treaty (. . .) and to transfer to the Court of First Instance jurisdiction to hear and determine at first instance certain classes of action or proceeding which *frequently require an examination of complex facts*, that is to say actions or proceedings brought by servants of the Communities and also, (. . .) so far as the EEC Treaty is concerned, by natural or legal persons in competition matters, (. . .) (emphasis added).

The EEC Treaty shall be supplemented by the following provisions:
'Article 168a

1. At the request of the Court of Justice and after consulting the Commission and the European Parliament, the Council may, acting unanimously, attach to the Court of Justice a court with jurisdiction to hear and determine at first instance, subject to a right of appeal to the Court of Justice on points of law only and in accordance with the conditions laid down by the Statute, *certain classes of action or proceeding* (. . .)' (emphasis added).

Accordingly, when the Council adopted the birth act of the General Court—at that time called the Court of First Instance of the European Communities or referred to by its acronym, CFI – in 1988, it was specified that in substance this new court:

shall exercise at first instance the jurisdiction conferred on the Court of Justice by the Treaties establishing the Communities and by the acts adopted in implementation thereof:

(a) in *disputes between the Communities and their servants* (. . .);

(c) in actions brought against an institution of the Communities (. . .) [in relation] to the implementation of the *competition rules applicable to undertakings*.

(. . .)[5] (emphasis added).

Therefore, the Court of First Instance became the only EU jurisdiction to look at the facts and law of competition and staff cases and, consequently, the first specialised judicial body in the EU.

**Specialised in Terms of Parties**  Initially, the Court of First Instance's jurisdiction was limited not only to specific fields of law but also to a specific type of litigation. Article 11 of the Single European Act specified:

The EEC Treaty shall be supplemented by the following provisions:
'Article 168a

1. At the request of the Court of Justice and after consulting the Commission and the European Parliament, the Council may, acting unanimously, attach to the Court of Justice a court with jurisdiction to hear and determine at first

---

[5]Council Decision No 88/591/ECSC, EEC, Euratom of 24 October 1988 establishing a Court of First Instance of the European Communities [1988] OJ L319/1, Article 3(1). This text also transfers competences regarding actions introduced by undertakings and associations in the field of levies, production, prices, cartels and mergers within the framework of the ECSC Treaty. Note also that Article 3(3) set a two-year period (from the start of the CFI's operation) to review, 'in the light of experience, including the development of jurisprudence', whether this transfer of competence could not also concern 'actions brought against an institution of the Communities by natural or legal persons (. . .) and relating to measures to protect trade within the meaning of Article 113 of that Treaty in the case of dumping and subsidies'.

instance, subject to a right of appeal to the Court of Justice on points of law only and in accordance with the conditions laid down by the Statute, certain classes of action or proceeding *brought by natural or legal persons. (. . .)'* (emphasis added).

Article 3 of Council Decision 88/591/ECSC, EEC, Euratom, indicated as follows:

1. The Court of First Instance shall exercise at first instance the jurisdiction conferred on the Court of Justice by the Treaties establishing the Communities and by the acts adopted in implementation thereof:

(c) in actions brought against an institution of the Communities *by natural or legal persons* (. . .) [in relation] to the implementation of the competition rules applicable to undertakings.

2. Where the same natural or legal person brings an action which the Court of First Instance has jurisdiction to hear by virtue of paragraph 1 of this Article and an *action for compensation for damage* caused by a Community institution through the act or failure to act which is the subject of the first action, the Court of First Instance shall also have jurisdiction to hear and determine the action for compensation for that damage (emphasis added).

Therefore, the CFI's stand was restricted in terms of audience since both the Single European Act and the 1988 Council decision circumscribed the nature of litigants who could have their case trialled before the General Court solely to natural or legal persons. Only such plaintiffs could have their claims heard by the CFI. This new court was thus specialised. First, it was restricted to legal actions seeking the annulment of an EU act, pursuing a failure to act by EU institutions and attempting to obtain damages as compensation for a violation committed by these institutions. Second, such actions had to be introduced by natural or legal persons.

Considering all the above, an intermediary conclusion can be asserted: as far as one can look back into the General Court's past, one will find a court specialised in classes of action introduced by individuals (including civil servants) and companies when dealing with competition matters or the EU Staff Regulation. This landscape would soon take a completely different shape (see Sect. 2.1.2).

### 2.1.2  General Court: Subject Matter and Parties

The first 10 years of operation of the CFI would be decisive in determining this new court not as a specialised judicial body, as intended at the beginning, but as an unavoidable link within the EU judicial chain, whose jurisdiction would cover all fields of law and whose bar would be more open than initially thought.

**General in Terms of Subject Matter** Less than 4 years after its start, the Court of First Instance was given the competence to rule on all types of action brought by natural and legal persons, i.e. with no limitation regarding the field of law concerned. Article 1 of Council Decision 93/350/ECSC, EEC, Euratom,[6] states:

Decision 88/591/ECSC, EEC, Euratom is hereby amended as follows:

1. the following shall be substituted for Article 3(1):
   'The Court of First Instance shall exercise at first instance the jurisdiction conferred on the Court of Justice by the Treaties establishing the Communities and by the acts adopted in implementation thereof (. . .):
   (a) in disputes as referred to in Article 179 [EU staff cases] of the EEC Treaty (. . .);
   (c) in actions brought by natural or legal persons pursuant to the second paragraph of Article 173 [action for annulment], the third paragraph of Article 175 [action for failure to act] and Articles 178 [action for damages] and 181 [compromissory clauses] of the EEC Treaty;

2. paragraphs 2 and 3 of Article 3 are hereby repealed; (. . .) [indications added].

The 1993 Council decision realised a blunt transfer of competences from the Court of Justice to the Court of First Instance that transformed the latter from a specialised court into a general court in terms of subject matter.[7] In EU judicial history, 8 June 1993 should be regarded as a red-letter day. On this day, the EU first-tier court became—and still is—the sole and unique interlocutor for individuals and the business world. Only before this tribunal can points regarding the facts and law of cases introduced by these litigants be examined, discussed and trialled. Today, with the exception of EU civil servants, the General Court is and remains *the* court of the EU people and companies active on EU territory.

**General in Terms of Parties** Almost a decade would be necessary to move to the next stage – a new age for the Court of First Instance, which would shed its skin of a court solely for 'persons', whether natural or legal. Article 11 of the Single European Act expressly excluded any other type of litigant from the CFI's jurisdiction:

---

[6]Council Decision No 93/350/ECSC, EEC, Euratom of 8 June 1993 amending Decision 88/591/ECSC, EEC, Euratom establishing a Court of First Instance of the European Communities (93/350/Euratom, ECSC, EEC).

[7]Article 3 of Council Decision 93/350/ECSC, EEC, Euratom postponed the empowerment of the CFI in the field of trade protection measures (dumping and subsidies) to a later date and made it dependent upon the adoption of a specific decision by the Council. Accordingly, Council Decision 94/149/ECSC, EC of 7 March 1994 amending Decision 93/350/Euratom, ECSC, EEC amending Decision 88/591/ECSC, EEC, Euratom establishing a Court of First Instance of the European Communities [1994] OJ L 66/29 fixed the entry into force as 15 March 1994.

The EEC Treaty Shall be Supplemented by the Following Provisions:
'Article 168a

1. At the request of the Court of Justice and after consulting the Commission and the European Parliament, the Council may, acting unanimously, attach to the Court of Justice a court with jurisdiction to hear and determine at first instance, subject to a right of appeal to the Court of Justice on points of law only and in accordance with the conditions laid down by the Statute, certain classes of action or proceeding brought by natural or legal persons. *That court shall not be competent to hear and determine actions brought by Member States or by Community Institutions (. . .)*' (emphasis added).

In other words, litigation initiated by Member States, for instance, was the Court of Justice's private turf. However, in 2001, the Treaty of Nice broke this taboo by opening the CFI's courtroom to certain types of action brought by Member States.[8] Article 31 of this treaty, consolidating the 1993 Council decision at the highest EU normative hierarchy, states:

Article 225 [ex-article 168a] shall be replaced by the following:
'Article 225

1. The Court of First Instance shall have jurisdiction to hear and determine at first instance actions or proceedings referred to in Articles 230, [ex-article 173] 232, [ex-article 175] 235, [ex-article 178] 236 [ex-article 179] and 238, - [ex-article 181] *with the exception of (. . .) those reserved in the Statute for the Court of Justice.* The Statute may provide for the Court of First Instance to have jurisdiction for other classes of action or proceeding. (. . .)' [indications added] (emphasis added).

Annexed to this treaty, the Protocol on the Statute of the Court of Justice specifies in Article 51:

*By way of exception* to the rule laid down in Article 225(1) of the EC Treaty (. . .), *the Court of Justice shall have jurisdiction in actions brought by the Member States*, by the institutions of the Communities and by the European Central Bank (emphasis added).

Thus, it could be considered that, despite the general terms used in the new Article 225 of the EC Treaty, due to the express exception laid down in Article 51 of the Statute of the Court of Justice, there were no changes as to the nature of applicants who could introduce an action before the Court of First Instance. This would overlook Declaration 12, annexed to the Treaty of Nice, on Article 225 of the Treaty establishing the European Community, which clearly indicates as follows:

---

[8]Treaty of Nice [2001] OJ C 80/1.

The Conference calls on the Court of Justice and the Commission to *give overall consideration as soon as possible to the division of jurisdiction* between the Court of Justice and the Court of First Instance, *in particular in the area of direct actions*, and to submit suitable proposals for examination by the competent bodies as soon as the Treaty of Nice enters into force (emphasis added).

This call was well received, and the Council adopted Decision 2004/407/EC, Euratom of 26 April 2004 amending Articles 51 and 54 of the Protocol on the Statute of the Court of Justice, Article 1 of which provides:

Article 51 of the Protocol on the Statute of the Court of Justice shall be replaced by the following:
'Article 51

By way of derogation from the rule laid down in Article 225(1) of the EC Treaty (. . .), jurisdiction shall be *reserved* to the Court of Justice in the actions referred to in Articles 230 and 232 of the EC Treaty (. . .) when they are brought *by a Member State* against:

(a) an act of or failure to act *by the European Parliament* or *the Council*, or *by both* those institutions acting jointly, *except for*:

   – decisions taken by the Council under the third subparagraph of Article 88(2) of the EC Treaty [State aid];
   – acts of the Council adopted pursuant to a Council regulation concerning measures to protect trade within the meaning of Article 133 of the EC Treaty [dumping];
   – acts of the Council by which the Council exercises implementing powers in accordance with the third indent of Article 202 of the EC Treaty;

(b) against an act of or failure to act *by the Commission under Article 11a of the EC Treaty* [enhanced cooperation].

Jurisdiction shall also be *reserved* to the Court of Justice in the actions referred to in the same Articles when they are brought *by an institution of the Communities* or by the European Central Bank *against an act of or failure to act by the European Parliament, the Council*, both those institutions acting jointly, or *the Commission*, or brought by an institution of the Communities against an act of or failure to act by the European Central Bank' [indications added] (emphasis added).

In other words, the EU legislator decided to empower judges of the Court of First instance to hear cases filed by Member States against the Commission (except in enhanced cooperation) and against the Council when one of its acts adopted in the field of State aid, trade protection measures (dumping) or one of its acts by which it exercises implementing powers is at stake. At the beginning of the new millennium, the idea of what used to be a specialised court thus vanished, and the CFI put on new clothes: a court dealing, more or less, with all EU topics for all direct actions at first instance.

## 2.2 From First Instance Court to General Court

After the 'specialised' nature that was given to the CFI by the fairies bent over its cradle, the second characteristic that the CFI was blessed with at its creation was the 'first instance' stamp it could affix to its judgments (see Sect. 2.2.1). However, following the example of the first 10 years, the new millennium would leave its mark on the CFI's history by amending this last characteristic (see Sect. 2.2.2).

### 2.2.1 First Instance Court: General and Specific

No real need seems to exist in this contribution to dedicate too much time or space to the well-known competence inherent in the lower court to review decisions at first instance. The generally understood first instance judicial review power enables this court to examine grounds based on errors of fact or errors of law. The question that has occupied, and still occupies, most of the actors implied in litigation proceedings at this level concerns the standard of review applied by judges when dealing with cases introduced before them. This article does not, and actually cannot, have the objective of analysing such a question. However, a less commented aspect of the 'first instance' level might be worth briefly mentioning. The evolution of the EU legal system has indeed brought to the first instance court two different types of decision to be reviewed: those adopted by an institution that are directly challenged and those that go through a quasi-judicial procedure before being allowed to be reviewed by the EU first-tier court.

**General First Instance** The 'first instance' notion at the EU level should not be confused with other types of first instance court that can be found in a variety of Member States' judicial systems. The CFI has mainly been conceived as a judicial review court. In other words, it does not hear from one party the incriminating elements found by a prosecutor and from the other the exculpatory ones in order to try a case. Its task consists of examining the legality of a decision adopted by an EU institution. Basically, it reviews an administrative procedure to ensure judicial protection. Thus, the EU lower court mainly applies a legality review standard that focuses on the external and internal legality of the contested decision. As a result, it represents the first court to be involved in the process of confirming or infirming the challenged act.

As an illustration of these general first instance proceedings, one can look at the treatment by the General Court of antitrust cases where, for example, a Commission decision sanctioning a company for its involvement in a cartel is challenged on the grounds of violation of the right of defence during the pretrial phase and violation of Article 101 TFEU due to a wrong finding concerning an agreement between competitors based on a false interpretation of the facts. Points of fact and law are contested at first instance, where the judges are in charge of exercising a legality review and, in some instances, full jurisdiction.[9] On appeal, the Court of Justice can only rule on legal points raised by one of the parties with regard to the lower court's judgment.[10]

Other examples may be taken from all subject matters for which the first-tier tribunal is competent, for example Council decisions taken in the field of restrictive measures, such as asset-freezing sanctions imposed on banks involved in financing Iranian nuclear activity, which are reviewed concerning facts and law at first instance by the General Court and which represent the third-largest subject matter in cases introduced (more than 7%) and completed (more than 8%) in 2014.[11]

**Specific First Instance** If the 'first instance' notion at the EU level is usually well known in the EU public sphere in terms of its general meaning, as described above, awareness of this notion going beyond the review of mere decisions adopted following purely administrative procedures is less common. Interestingly, the judicial review at first instance also concerns decisions adopted by quasi-judicial bodies. A relevant illustration is given by the most common type of case introduced before the General Court: intellectual property cases, most of them being EU trademark cases.[12] Litigation in this field concerns decisions adopted by the Office for Harmonization in the Internal Market (Trade Marks and Designs) (hereinafter OHIM), created in 1994. However, unlike Council or Commission decisions, before being challenged before the General Court, OHIM decisions are reviewed by the first instance department, which took the decision, and then by the OHIM Boards of Appeal.[13]

Similar systems have been put in place since then. In 2007, the European Chemical Agency (ECHA) was founded. This deals with the control of chemical

---

[9]On the standard of review applied in competition law cases by the General Court, see Jaeger (2011a, b)

[10]See Article 58(1) of Protocol (No 3) on the Statute of the Court of Justice of the European Union, annexed to the Treaties, as amended by Regulation (EU, Euratom) No 741/2012 of the European Parliament and of the Council of [2012] OJ L 228/1, and by Article 9 of the Act concerning the conditions of accession to the European Union of the Republic of Croatia and the adjustments to the Treaty on European Union, the Treaty on the Functioning of the European Union and the Treaty establishing the European Atomic Energy Community [2012] OJ L 112/21.

[11]See Court of Justice of the European Union, Annual Report 2014, pp 183 and 185, available via Curia    http://curia.europa.eu/jcms/upload/docs/application/pdf/2015-04/en_ecj_annual_report_ 2014_pr1.pdf. Accessed 30 Apr 2015.

[12]See Council Regulation (EC) No 207/2009 of 26 February 2009 on the Community trade mark [2009] OJ L78/1, and Commission Regulation (EC) No 2868/95 of 13 December 1995 implementing Council Regulation (EC) No 40/94 on the Community trade mark [1995] OJ L 303/1.

[13]See Office for Harmonization in the Internal Market. https://oami.europa.eu/ohimportal/en/ appeal. Accessed 30 Apr 2015.

substances pursuant to the Regulation on Registration, Evaluation, Authorisation and Restriction of Chemicals (REACH).[14] Certain ECHA decisions can be appealed before the ECHA Board of Appeal.[15] These decisions can then be challenged before the General Court, which examines them as a first instance tribunal.

Finally, as a reaction to the financial crisis, new measures to stabilise and improve financial markets have been taken. The new supervisory framework for financial regulation in Europe came into force in January 2011.[16] This framework put in place three new European Supervisory Authorities (ESAs) for the financial services sector: the European Banking Authority (EBA) based in London, the European Insurance and Occupational Pensions Authority (EIOPA) in Frankfurt, and the European Securities and Markets Authority (ESMA) in Paris. Certain decisions of these three authorities can be appealed before a joint body of the ESAs called the Joint Board of Appeal.[17] In turn, the Joint Board of Appeal's

---

[14]Regulation (EC) No 1907/2006 of the European Parliament and of the Council of 18 December 2006 concerning the Registration, Evaluation, Authorisation and Restriction of Chemicals (REACH), establishing a European Chemicals Agency, amending Directive 1999/45/EC and repealing Council Regulation (EEC) No 793/93 and Commission Regulation (EC) No 1488/94 as well as Council Directive 76/769/EEC and Commission Directives 91/155/EEC, 93/67/EEC, 93/105/EC and 2000/21/EC.

[15]See European Chemicals Agency. http://echa.europa.eu/regulations/appeals. Accessed 30 Apr 2015.

[16]Regulation (EU) No 1092/2010 of the European Parliament and of the Council of 24 November 2010 on European Union macro-prudential oversight of the financial system and establishing a European Systemic Risk Board [2010] OJ L331/1; Council Regulation (EU) No 1096/2010 of 17 November 2010 conferring specific tasks upon the European Central Bank concerning the functioning of the European Systemic Risk Board [2010] OJ L331/162; Regulation (EU) No 1093/2010 of the European Parliament and of the Council of 24 November 2010 establishing a European Supervisory Authority (European Banking Authority), amending Decision No 716/2009/EC and repealing Commission Decision 2009/78/EC [2010] OJ L331/12; Regulation (EU) No 1094/2010 of the European Parliament and of the Council of 24 November 2010 establishing a European Supervisory Authority (European Insurance and Occupational Pensions Authority), amending Decision No 716/2009/EC and repealing Commission Decision 2009/79/EC [2010] OJ L331/48; Regulation (EU) No 1095/2010 of the European Parliament and of the Council of 24 November 2010 establishing a European Supervisory Authority (European Securities and Markets Authority), amending Decision No 716/2009/EC and repealing Commission Decision 2009/77/EC [2010] OJ L331/84; Directive 2010/78/EU of the European Parliament and of the Council of 24 November 2010 amending Directives 98/26/EC, 2002/87/EC, 2003/6/EC, 2003/41/EC, 2003/71/EC, 2004/39/EC, 2004/109/EC, 2005/60/EC, 2006/48/EC, 2006/49/EC and 2009/65/EC in respect of the powers of the European Supervisory Authority (European Banking Authority), the European Supervisory Authority (European Insurance and Occupational Pensions Authority) and the European Supervisory Authority (European Securities and Markets Authority) [2010] OJ L331/120.

[17]See European Banking Authority. http://www.eba.europa.eu/about-us/organisation/joint-board-of-appeal. Accessed 30 Apr 2015; European Securities and Markets Authority. http://www.esma.europa.eu/page/board-appeal. Accessed 30 Apr 2015; European Insurance and Occupational Pensions Authority https://eiopa.europa.eu/Pages/About-EIOPA/Organisation/Board-of-Appeal/Board-of-Appeal.aspx. Accessed 30 Apr 2015. See also the Rules of Procedure of the Board of Appeal of the European Supervisory Authorities, available via European Banking Authority.

decisions can be challenged before the General Court, which examines them as a first instance tribunal. It should also be said in passing that the General Court is competent to review decisions taken by the European Central Bank in the context of the Single Supervisory Mechanism (SSM)[18] and the Single Resolution Mechanism (SRM).[19]

The development of EU agencies and bodies has reinforced this specific notion of 'first instance'. Still, this judicial review is of a 'first instance' nature: facts and law are under the control of the first-tier tribunal, judgments of which are subject to appeal proceedings limited to points of law before the Court of Justice. The first instance nature of the EU lower court was such an intrinsic characteristic of this court that it was even reflected in its name until 2009. However, the Treaty of Lisbon changed its appellation, and the underlying reasons justifying this modification were far from being cosmetic, flippant or devoid of purpose (see Sect. 2.2.2).

### 2.2.2 General Court: Appellate and Interpretative

With the entry into force of the Treaty of Lisbon on 1 December 2009, the Court of First Instance became the General Court. It is 'General' when the evolution of its competence is taken into consideration, as described above. The early years of a specialised court dealing with competition law matters and EU staff cases have long gone. However, a first instance court it was, and a first instance court it is. One could thus wonder whether this tribunal could not have been named the General Court of First Instance if the purpose was to better reflect the fact that in terms of subject matter this court has slowly been invested of wider competences than had once been foreseen. The reason for the abandonment of the 'first instance' qualification has to be sought elsewhere. Indeed, such a characterisation would have been outdated and misleading, with the appellate and interpretative features of that court being overlooked.

---

http://www.eba.europa.eu/documents/10180/15733/1_Rules_of_Procedure.pdf/6f607767-8d00-464a-8448-4f730671d7bc. Accessed 30 Apr 2015; the Guidelines to the Parties to Appeal Proceedings before the Joint Board of Appeal of the European Supervisory Authorities, available via European Banking Authority. http://www.eba.europa.eu/documents/10180/15733/2_Guidelines_to_the_Parties.pdf/6ecd4b5f-9504-4d18-9f7e-19205ffd12a7. Accessed 30 Apr 2015.

[18]Council Regulation (EU) No 1024/2013 of 15 October 2013 conferring specific tasks on the European Central Bank concerning policies relating to the prudential supervision of credit institutions [2013] OJ L287/63; Regulation (EU) No 1022/2013 of the European Parliament and of the Council of 22 October 2013 amending Regulation (EU) No 1093/2010 establishing a European Supervisory Authority (European Banking Authority) as regards the conferral of specific tasks on the European Central Bank pursuant to Council Regulation (EU) No 1024/2013 [2013] OJ L 287/5.

[19]Regulation (EU) No 806/2014 of the European Parliament and of the Council of 15 July 2014 establishing uniform rules and a uniform procedure for the resolution of credit institutions and certain investment firms in the framework of a Single Resolution Mechanism and a Single Resolution Fund and amending Regulation (EU) No 1093/2010 [2014] OJ L 225/1.

**Appellate Court**  One of the reasons for the name change is that the nature of the control exercised by this lower court is no longer exclusively of a first instance kind. For more than 10 years now, the General Court has also been an appellate court. Signed on 26 February 2001, the Treaty of Nice entered into force almost 2 years afterwards on 1 February 2003. Article 31 of this treaty specifically indicated:

Article 225 shall be replaced by the following:
'Article 225

(...)

2. The Court of First Instance shall have jurisdiction to hear and determine actions or proceedings brought against decisions of the judicial panels set up under Article 225a.

Decisions given by the Court of First Instance under this paragraph may exceptionally be subject to review by the Court of Justice, under the conditions and within the limits laid down by the Statute, where there is a serious risk of the unity or consistency of Community law being affected. (...)' (emphasis added).

In addition, Article 32 of the same treaty inserted a new provision, Article 225a, to the Treaty establishing the European Community, stating:

The Council, acting unanimously on a proposal from the Commission and after consulting the European Parliament and the Court of Justice or at the request of the Court of Justice and after consulting the European Parliament and the Commission, may create judicial panels to hear and determine at first instance certain classes of action or proceeding brought in specific areas. (...)

Decisions given by judicial panels *may be subject to a right of appeal on points of law only* or, when provided for in the decision establishing the panel, a right of appeal also on matters of fact, *before the Court of First Instance.* (...)[20] (emphasis added).

In allowing the creation of judicial panels to hear and determine at first instance certain classes of action or proceeding brought in specific areas and whose decisions are challengeable before the CFI, this treaty gave to the CFI an appellate jurisdiction. 'Specific areas', however, had to be identified. Declaration No 16 on Article 225a of the Treaty establishing the European Community, attached to the Treaty of Nice, gave a clear indication as to the first subject matter that should be treated by such a judicial panel by specifically stating as follows:

The Conference asks the Court of Justice and the Commission to prepare *as swiftly as possible* a draft decision establishing a judicial panel which has

---

[20]Treaty of Nice [2001] OJ C 80/1.

jurisdiction to deliver judgments at first instance on *disputes between the Community and its servants*[21] (emphasis added).

Staff cases were thus nominated as the perfect candidate for a transfer and to be taken over from the CFI's competence and allocated to such a specialised court. Accordingly, on 2 November 2004, the Council adopted Decision 2004/752/EC, Euratom establishing the European Union Civil Service Tribunal (hereinafter CST), considered as an improvement in the operation of the Community courts' system.[22] The Council decided to attach the CST to the CFI and to limit appeals of CST decisions before the CFI to points of law only 'in the same conditions as those governing appeals lodged at the Court of Justice against decisions of the Court of First Instance'.[23]

From this moment, the appellate nature that used to be the privilege of the Court of Justice became a shared feature between two courts in the EU judicial structure. This new role was quickly endorsed by the CFI, which heard its first ten appeals in 2006 and reached a record figure in 2013 of 57 appeals. If a period of adaptation was probably needed at the beginning—the duration of proceedings for this new type of case increasing from 7.1 months in 2006 to 18.3 months in 2011—efficient treatment of such cases was rapidly put in place, and the duration of proceedings drastically dropped to 12.8 months in 2014. Compared to the 14.5 months needed by the Court of Justice to deal with its appeals, the results of the General Court could be seen as truly remarkable.[24]

Considering the above, it should be stated that the exclusive 'first instance' nature of the General Court belongs to history and that the Council, by creating this judicial panel, along with the willingness of the EU legislator expressed in the highest norms of EU law, improved the functioning of the entire EU court architecture.

**Interpretative Court** However, not only is the General Court today a court of appeal like the Court of Justice; it can also be an interpretative court, another feature that is normally inherent to the definition of the Court of Justice. In this regard, it should be recalled that the Single European Act expressly excluded preliminary rulings from the CFI's competences.[25] Article 11 of this act clearly indicated:

---

[21]Treaty of Nice, Declaration on Article 225a of the Treaty establishing the European Community [2001] OJ C 80/1.

[22]Council Decision No 2004/752/EC Euratom of 2 November 2004 establishing the European Union Civil Service Tribunal, [2004] OJ L 333/7, second recital and Article 1.

[23]Council Decision No 2004/752/EC Euratom of 2 November 2004 establishing the European Union Civil Service Tribunal, [2004] OJ L 333/7, eighth recital.

[24]The indicated figures are available in the annual reports of the Court of Justice of the European Union, which can be found via Curia http://curia.europa.eu/jcms/jcms/Jo2_7000/. Accessed 30 Apr 2015.

[25]Single European Act [1987] OJ L169/1, Article 168a, para 1.

The EEC Treaty shall be supplemented by the following provisions:
'Article 168a

2. At the request of the Court of Justice and after consulting the Commission and the European Parliament, the Council may, acting unanimously, attach to the Court of Justice a court with jurisdiction to hear and determine at first instance, subject to a right of appeal to the Court of Justice on points of law only and in accordance with the conditions laid down by the Statute, certain classes of action or proceeding brought by natural or legal persons. *That court shall not be competent* to hear and determine actions brought by Member States or by Community Institutions or *questions referred for a preliminary ruling* under Article 177. (...)' (emphasis added).

However, 15 years, later the EU legislator, having seen the development of the EU first-tier tribunal as described above, decided to reach certain conclusions quite opposite to the initial approach laid down in the Single European Act. Indeed, the Treaty of Nice inserted a provision in the Treaty establishing the European Community allowing, under certain circumstances, the General Court to take up the role of an interpretative jurisdiction.[26] Article 31 of this treaty specifically indicated:

Article 225 shall be replaced by the following:
'Article 225

(...)

3. The Court of First Instance shall have jurisdiction to hear and determine questions referred for a preliminary ruling under Article 234, in specific areas laid down by the Statute.

Where the Court of First Instance considers that the case requires *a decision of principle* likely to affect the unity or consistency of Community law, it may *refer the case* to the Court of Justice for a ruling.

Decisions given by the Court of First Instance on questions referred for a preliminary ruling may exceptionally be *subject to review by the Court of Justice*, under the conditions and within the limits laid down by the Statute, where there is a *serious risk of the unity or consistency of Community law* being affected' (emphasis added).

Therefore, since 2001, the General Court should have been sharing with the Court of Justice not only appellate jurisdiction but also interpretative competence: this is its design, at least as planned by the highest EU legislator.[27] However, the prerequisite condition for empowering the judges of the EU lower court with this

---

[26]Treaty of Nice [2001] OJ C 80/1, Article 225.

[27]Treaty of Nice [2001] OJ C 80/1, Article 225, para 3.

new competence rests in the prior determination of these 'specific areas'. As explained above, such a task has been carried out in the context of the partial transfer of the appellate jurisdiction where the same wording was used. In this regard, specific areas were limited to disputes between the EU and its servants. In stark contrast, the identification of specific areas where the EU first-tier tribunal would be competent to hear and determine questions referred for a preliminary ruling has never been undertaken. Although no declaration was attached to the Treaty of Nice calling for swift action to create this new power, as done by Declaration 16 for appellate jurisdiction, it should, however, be noted that, first of all, Declaration 14 on Article 225(2) and (3) of the Treaty establishing the European Community provided for an evaluation mechanism for the execution of this new role:

> The Conference considers that when the Council adopts the provisions of the Statute which are necessary to implement Article 225(2) and (3), it should *put a procedure in place to ensure that the practical operation of those provisions is evaluated no later than three years after the entry into force of the Treaty of Nice* (emphasis added).

In addition, the allocation of an interpretative role to the General Court did not mean that the Court of Justice would face the risk of losing its privilege to interpret EU law at last instance. Indeed, even in these specifics fields, the Court of Justice would not lose its entire competence since, on the one hand, when a case calls for a landmark decision that could affect the unity or the coherence of EU law, the General Court can forward it to the Court of Justice, while on the other hand, the General Court's judgments on preliminary rulings can be reviewed by the Court of Justice. This latter safeguard is the same as the one set for the appellate jurisdiction—namely, the possibility for the Court of Justice to review a decision adopted by the General Court that could lead to a serious risk to the unity or the consistency of EU law. However, such a procedure would obviously delay the ultimate response awaited by the national judge who introduced the preliminary reference. Therefore, a very practical requirement was laid down in Declaration 15 dedicated to this competence, indicating as follows:

> The Conference considers that, in exceptional cases in which the Court of Justice decides to *review a decision of the Court of First Instance* on a question referred *for a preliminary ruling*, it should act under an *emergency procedure* (emphasis added).

The implementation of this second partial transfer of competence was a priori seen as something that would soon be realised. However, the reason for the fact that until now it has stayed only in the realm of possibility should not be sought in the difficulty of identifying specific areas. Indeed, one of the fields that would appear to be a natural candidate is intellectual property. The experience gained by the General Court in this legal domain is tremendous because of the volume of cases it has to deal with every year. The true obstacle to the execution of this transfer may actually be found in the fact that in the last few years the General Court has experienced a historic increase in the number of cases introduced, which has directed attention more towards modifications of working methods and procedure and ultimately to reflection on far-reaching structural reform.

Over 25 years, the nature of the first-tier tribunal has radically changed. However, all these modifications have a common feature in that they have all led to an addition of competences: more types of topic to rule on, more types of litigant to take care of and more types of request to deal with. This evolution is undoubtedly a sign of recognition of the good work provided by the General Court to the EU people. However, this has to be qualified by examining two sets of figures: first, 253 cases were introduced in 1995 and 912 last year; second, in the last 15 years (1999–2014), the duration of proceedings increased from 12.7 months to 23.4 months on average.

It would be a shame if the success story of the General Court eventually turned into a failure to answer the need for efficient justice in the EU. Birds of ill omen have predicted such a future. However, to avoid this terrible prophecy, measures have been taken. Some of them should be implemented in the coming months, while others are still under discussion. Having looked back at the past of the General Court, the time has come to look ahead at the shape the that General Court might soon display (see Sect. 3).

## 3   The General Court: A Look Ahead

Two important events with a substantial impact on the operation of the General Court have occurred. First, adopted on 2 May 1991, the General Court's rules of procedure have been amended several times, notably to take into account the various enlargements of the EU and to absorb the new competences transferred from the Court of Justice. However, a real need to comprehensively revise these rules became apparent in the last few years, especially in order to increase judicial efficiency. Therefore, after some intense work, the General Court welcomed its new rules of procedure in July this year (see Sect. 3.1). Second, and in parallel with this procedural reform, structural reform seemed to be necessary due to worrying figures concerning judicial activity. However, both the content and method relating to this reform have triggered much controversy and debate that explain the ongoing state of this modification (see Sect. 3.2).

### 3.1   A Fresh Look at the Rules of Procedure (2015)

At the beginning of 2012, the General Court decided to launch a wide review of its rules of procedure. After two and a half years, this process came to an end, the

Council approving the revised text drafted with the agreement of the Court of Justice on 10 February 2015, pursuant to Article 254(5) TFEU. The new rules of procedure were scheduled to enter into force on 1 July 2015.[28] Among them, two broad categories can be distinguished for the sake of presentation: rules intended to improve the coherence (see Sect. 3.1.1) and those intended to improve the efficiency (see Sect. 3.1.2) of the EU judicial system.

### 3.1.1   New Rules of Procedure to Improve Coherence

Coherence is one of the objectives sought by the adoption of the new rules of procedure. To achieve this aim, first the structure of the current rules had to be adapted to the numerous modifications they had been subject to for 25 years. Second, the rules in themselves had to be simplified in the light of lessons drawn from internal practice and external comments.

**Adaptation** Two types of adaptation were necessary. First, normative inflation had led to the addition of provisions without there being an overview of the structure in order to insert these modifications in the most understandable way. Consolidation was thus needed. Second, the General Court is one part of the entire EU judicial system. Other parts of this organisation had experienced modifications over the years that had had consequences for the EU lower court's structure. Harmonisation was thus needed.

**Consolidation** As described above, the General Court's 25 years of existence have seen numerous structural developments. This evolution has been accompanied by many procedural modifications, and consequently numerous amendments to the rules of procedure have enabled procedures to be adapted and improved according to the needs and developments encountered by the EU lower court. However, insiders unanimously observed that this piecemeal process had reached its limit, and a serious restructuring of the original text needed to be undertaken. The new rules of procedure therefore not only put in order previous amendments but also arrange the provisions in such a way as to adapt them to the reality of proceedings. In this regard, a clear distinction between the different classes of action to be heard and determined by the General Court is made. Looking at the actual state of litigation before the General Court, three main categories stand out: direct actions, proceedings relating to intellectual property rights and appeals. Instead of having one title dedicated to 'procedure', another to a 'special form of procedure' and then two more on 'proceedings relating to intellectual property rights' and on 'appeals against decisions of the European Union Civil Service Tribunal', the new structure, as to forms of action, is principally articulated around three titles with inner coherence. These separate 'direct actions', 'proceedings relating to intellectual

---

[28]Rules of procedure of the General Court [2015] OJ L 105/1.

property rights' and 'appeals against decisions of the Civil Service Tribunal'. All relevant rules are now assembled within each block.

**Harmonisation**  On 11 August 2012, the European Parliament and the Council adopted Regulation (EU, Euratom) 741/2012 amending the Protocol on the Statute of the Court of Justice of the European Union and Annex I thereto,[29] and on 25 September 2012 they adopted the new rules of procedure of the Court of Justice, which entered into force on 1 November 2012.[30] Several modifications had an impact on the procedure of the General Court. Therefore, to ensure consistency in the procedural provisions governing proceedings brought before the Courts of the European Union, the new rules of procedure of the General Court bear the consequences of these amendments. First, they give practical effect to the changes to the Statute relating to the creation of the position of vice-president of the General Court. In this regard, Article 9 of the new rules of procedure specifies, *inter alia*, the method of electing the vice-president, while Article 11 of these rules states her or his responsibilities. Second, they incorporate the provisions adopted by the Court of Justice, taking into account the specific nature of direct actions between a natural or legal person or a Member State on the one hand and an institution of the Union on the other. For instance, Article 2 of the new rules of procedure specifies the purport of these rules in an identical way as was done in Article 2 of the rules of procedure of the Court of Justice adopted in 2012.

**Simplification**  After 25 years of operation, a meaningful assessment regarding the usefulness and intelligibleness of certain rules could be efficiently conducted. The result of this process has led the General Court to simplify its rules of procedure both in terms of the mandatory requirements directed to the parties and in terms of the terminology used in the wording of its rules.

**Usefulness**  The new rules of procedure clarify certain requirements that apply in the context of the General Court's proceedings in trying to simplify several rules. For instance, Article 51 of the new rules of procedure now clearly lists all formal documents that have to be produced by the representatives of legal persons governed by private law. Similarly, some anachronisms have been deleted from the new version of the rules. For example, Article 52 of the new rules of procedure relating to privileges, immunities and facilities applicable to the parties' representatives no longer mentions the rule governing foreign currency allocation to agents, advisers and lawyers for the performance of their duties.

Taking into account the true objective sought when imposing certain procedural requirements, the simplification process has sometimes led to an effort to specify some of these rules. This was the case, for instance, for those concerning the lodging and service of procedural documents, the formalities for procedural documents, their content and the time limit for submission of such documents. For

---

[29]Regulation (EU, Euratom) 741/2012 amending the Protocol on the Statute of the Court of Justice of the European Union and Annex I thereto [2012] OJ L 228/1.

[30]On this topic, see Gaudissart (2012), p. 603.

instance, Article 72 of the new rules of procedure no longer refers to the possibility of lodging documents using 'other technical means of communication available'. Instead, this provision indicates that the electronic lodging of documents is possible via 'the method referred to in the decision of the General Court adopted pursuant to Article 74'. In other words, the e-Curia system, put in place by the decision of the General Court of 14 September 2011,[31] supersedes all other electronic means, and the lodging of documents by e-mail is no longer considered useful.

**Intelligibleness** In reviewing its rules of procedure, the General Court paid particular attention to the terminology used to phrase provisions. Indeed, it was observed that over the course of successive amendments, the rules of procedure have sometimes used several different terms to denote the same concept. There was thus an unnecessary risk of generating divergent interpretations or initiating different constructions where the same and identical meaning should have prevailed. In this regard, the new rules of procedure now employ a single and unique term to qualify a concept that is repeated at different places within the document. For instance, Article 1 of the new rules of procedure gives more definitions than the previous version. Among them, the notions 'General Court', 'party' and 'representatives of the parties' are straightforwardly explained to avoid any ambiguities as to the entity or the person concerned when these terms appear to designate those responsible for the adoption of a decision or the provisions of a document.

Moreover, the new rules of procedure have been produced with a view to rationalising the terms used in the various language versions of a document. Indeed, variations were spotted when one read the General Court's rules of procedure in different language versions. In this context, it should be recalled that the rules of procedure are published in the Official Journal of the European Union and are authentic in all 24 official languages of the EU. Article 227(1) of the new rules of procedure specifically underlines this principle.

As mentioned above, there was a strong belief in the need to profoundly review the General Court's rules of procedure. However, it would not have generated such feeling if it had been triggered solely by the need to improve coherence. The revision also pursued the objective of improving judicial efficiency, responding to the urge to put in place more reactive procedures (see Sect. 3.1.2).

### 3.1.2 New Rules of Procedure to Improve Efficiency

Efficiency ranks high in the list of objectives pursued by the General Court in the review process of its rules of procedure. To increase the degree of efficiency, proceedings first have to be as smooth as possible. However, when this court faced unexpected procedural questions, it could not turn to its rules of procedure to swiftly respond to them, thus running the risk of slowing down the entire

---

[31]Decision of the General Court of 14 September 2011 on the lodging and service of procedural documents by means of e-Curia [2011] OJ C 289/9.

treatment of a case. The new rules of procedure therefore had to enhance the level of procedural certainty by inserting provisions that would at least make sure that situations that had not been tackled in the previous version would be part of this new one. Second, to increase the degree of efficiency, proceedings have to be as fast as possible. For more than 7 years now, a series of internal measures has been relentlessly adopted in order to accelerate case treatment by the General Court. The new rules of procedure had to take their share of this work and participate in the progress of this court towards securing the right to benefit from effective justice at the level of the General Court. All provisions thus had to be thought over in order to revamp the procedures to make them work more swiftly.

**Filling the Gaps** Not all situations can be anticipated when drafting rules of procedure, and the General Court has been confronted with unforeseen issues. In order to provide solutions to procedural situations that have not yet been addressed in the rules of procedure, the new text adds provisions to that effect. For instance, circumstances in which a case may be reassigned were not specified in the previous rules of procedure. The revised version provides in Article 27:

1. *If the Judge-Rapporteur* is prevented from acting, the President of the competent formation of the Court shall notify the President of the General Court, who shall designate a new Judge-Rapporteur. If the new Judge-Rapporteur is not attached to the Chamber to which the case was first assigned, the case shall be heard and determined by the Chamber in which the new Judge-Rapporteur sits.

2. In order to *take account of a connection between cases* on the basis of their subject-matter, the President of the General Court may, by reasoned decision and after consulting the Judge-Rapporteurs concerned, reassign the cases to enable the same Judge-Rapporteur to conduct preparatory inquiries in all the cases concerned. If the Judge-Rapporteur to whom the cases have been reassigned does not belong to the Chamber to which the cases were first assigned, the cases shall be heard and determined by the Chamber in which the new Judge-Rapporteur sits.

3. *In the interests of the proper administration of justice*, and by way of exception, the President of the General Court may, before the presentation of the preliminary report (. . .), by reasoned decision and after consulting the Judges concerned, designate another Judge-Rapporteur. If that Judge-Rapporteur is not attached to the Chamber to which the case was first assigned, the case shall be heard and determined by the Chamber in which the new Judge-Rapporteur sits.

4. Before designating the Judge-Rapporteur as provided in paragraphs 1 to 3, the President of the General Court shall seek the views of the Presidents of the Chambers concerned.

5. Where the composition of the Chambers has changed as a result of a decision of the General Court on the assignment of Judges to Chambers, a case shall be

heard and determined by the Chamber in which the Judge-Rapporteur sits following that decision, unless the deliberations have commenced or the oral part of the procedure has been opened (emphasis added).

As can be seen from the wording of the above provision, the great level of detail attached to this new rule was a result of the past experiences that the General Court had faced in situations when it had had to reassign cases. It now provided an explicit legal basis in three types of events (the judge being prevented from sitting, the identification of a connection during proceedings, reallocation to ensure efficient treatment) that might lead to the need to designate a new reporting judge and consequently to reassign the case within the court.

Another illustration can be found in reading Article 91(b) in combination with Article 92(3) of the new rules of procedure. Article 91(b) specifies former Article 65 in stating:

Without prejudice to Articles 24 and 25 of the Statute, the following measures of inquiry may be adopted:

(. . .)

(b) *a request to a party for information or for production* of any material relating to the case; (. . .) (emphasis added).

Article 92(3) adds:

3. A measure of inquiry referred to in Article 91(b) may be ordered *only where* the party concerned by the measure *has not complied with a measure of organisation of procedure previously adopted* to that end, *or where expressly requested* by the party concerned by the measure and that party explains the need for such a measure to be in the form of an order for a measure of inquiry. The order prescribing the measure of inquiry may provide that inspection by the parties' representatives of information and material obtained by the General Court in consequence of that order *may take place only at the Registry and that no copies may be made* (emphasis added).

Therefore, the latter provision fills the gap regarding the action to be taken after a document has been produced pursuant to a measure of inquiry ordered by the General Court.

**Improving Swiftness** Since 2007, the General Court has never stopped questioning its working methods and putting in place internal reforms. All my mandates as President of this court have been directed at improving efficiency in dealing with cases introduced before the General Court. This is the priority I have set.[32] To achieve the objective of decreasing case backlogs, the duration of

---

[32]See, for instance, Bodoni (2007), Croft (2011), Lambote (2015).

proceedings has to be reduced as much as possible while maintaining the high quality of judgments. The average duration of cases completed in 2014 fell by 3.5 months (from 26.9 months in 2013 to 23.4 months in 2014), that is to say, a change of more than 10%, returning to the figures recorded a decade ago.[33] This positive figure was the result of many measures that it was possible to implement immediately by optimising available resources. Among them, one could mention the possibility of ruling on intellectual property cases without a hearing[34]; the clarification of the role of interveners in such cases[35]; the reorganisation of the court into eight chambers, and then nine in September 2013, with three judges; the creation of a specialised chamber to deal with appeals against CST decisions; the implementation of a monitoring system regarding the respect of internal deadlines; the reform of writing methods, especially for reports of hearings, judgments and orders; the introduction of more flexibility in allocating cases due to the existence of a connection; or the development of new technologies in the daily exchange of documents.

To consolidate and continue the General Court's efforts to maintain its capacity to deal with cases within a reasonable time and in accordance with the requirements of a fair trial, as laid down in the second paragraph of Article 47 of the Charter of Fundamental Rights of the European Union, the new rules of procedure also had to give concrete expression to a need for increased judicial productivity. In this regard, one should welcome the revised version of the rules of procedure since they participate in the constant endeavour to improve the efficiency of the General Court. Among the relevant measures that could be mentioned in this context, attention should in particular be given to three categories.

First, the new rules of procedures include measures aimed at reducing the number of steps within a procedure. For instance, Article 181 establishes, as a principle, a single round of pleadings in intellectual property cases, removing the usual second round of written exchanges between the parties. It states:

(...) the written part of the procedure shall be *closed after* the submission of the *response of the defendant* (...) (emphasis added).

As explained above, the ability of the General Court to rule without an oral part had been introduced before the revised version of the rules of procedure. However, this possibility was limited to intellectual property cases. Article 106 extends this option to the procedure in direct actions by removing the automatic need to hold a hearing:

---

[33]See the Court of Justice of the European Union, Annual Report 2014, p 123, available via Curia http://curia.europa.eu/jcms/upload/docs/application/pdf/2015-04/en_ecj_annual_report_2014_pr1.pdf. Accessed 30 Apr 2015.

[34]Amendments to the Rules of Procedure of the Court of First Instance of the European Communities [2008] OJ L 179/12.

[35]Amendments to the Rules of Procedure of the Court of First Instance of the European Communities [2009] OJ L 184/10.

1. The procedure before the General Court shall include, in the oral part, a hearing arranged either of the *General Court's own motion* or *at the request* of a main party.

2. Any request for a hearing made by a main *party must state the reasons* for which that party wishes to be heard. It must be submitted within three weeks after service on the parties of notification of the close of the written part of the procedure. That time limit may be extended by the President.

3. *If there is no request* as referred to in paragraph 2, the General Court may, if it considers that it has *sufficient information available* to it from the material in the file, decide to rule on the action *without an oral part* of the procedure. In that case, it may nevertheless later decide to open the oral part of the procedure (emphasis added).

If in the case of direct actions the submission of a reasoned request from a main party is sufficient to oblige the General Court to hold a hearing, it should be noted that Article 207 of the new rules of procedure allows the General Court to disregard such a request and rule without an oral part in appeals:

1. The parties to the appeal proceedings *may request* an opportunity to state their case in a hearing. Any such request *must be reasoned* and be submitted within three weeks after service on the parties of notification of the close of the written part of the procedure. That time limit may be extended by the President.

2. On a proposal from the Judge-Rapporteur, *the General Court may*, if it considers that it has sufficient information available to it from the material in the file, *decide to rule on the appeal without an oral part* of the procedure. It may nevertheless later decide to open the oral part of the procedure (emphasis added).

Second, the new rules of procedure also include measures aimed at accelerating the decision-making process. For instance, Article 19 delimits for the first time in a single provision the competences of the presidents of chambers, the general rule being that these presidents exercise their powers after hearing their reporting judges. The idea behind this novelty is to transfer certain decision-making powers of the chambers to the presidents of chambers, keeping in mind, however, that the president of a chamber may refer any decision falling within her or his remit to the chamber itself. Article 83(3) provides an illustration of the emphasis put on the more proactive role of the president of a chamber in conducting proceedings:

1. The application initiating proceedings and the defence may be supplemented by a reply from the applicant and by a rejoinder from the defendant unless the General Court decides that a second exchange of pleadings is unnecessary because the contents of the file in the case are sufficiently comprehensive.

2. Where the General Court decides that a second exchange of pleadings is unnecessary it may authorise the main parties to supplement the file in the case if

the applicant presents a reasoned request to that effect within two weeks from the service of that decision.

3. The President shall prescribe the time limits within which those procedural documents are to be produced. *He may specify the matters to which the reply or the rejoinder should relate* (emphasis added).

In the same spirit, the new rules of procedure tend to increase the number of circumstances in which a ruling is to be given by means of a simple decision. For instance, Article 144(4) substitutes the requirement to decide by reasoned order on an application to intervene lodged by a Member State or an institution, as requested by former Article 116(1), with a simple decision from the president of the chamber. One of the most striking examples of the willingness to accelerate the decision-making process is found in Article 132 of the revised rules of procedure, which allows the General Court to expedite a case considered to be manifestly well founded:

Where the Court of Justice or the General Court has already ruled on one or more questions of law identical to those raised by the pleas in law of the action and the General Court finds that the facts have been established, it may, after the written part of the procedure has been closed, on a proposal from the Judge-Rapporteur and after hearing the parties, *decide by reasoned order* in which reference is made to the relevant case-law to declare the action *manifestly well founded* (emphasis added).

Last, but far from being the least of the measures aimed at seeing a real growth in swifter decision-making procedures, the new rules of procedure expand the scope of application of provisions relating to a single judge. Article 29 states:

1. The following cases assigned to a Chamber sitting with three Judges may be heard and determined by the Judge-Rapporteur sitting as a single Judge where, having regard to the lack of difficulty of the questions of law or fact raised, to the limited importance of those cases and to the absence of other special circumstances, they are suitable for being so heard and determined and have been delegated under the conditions laid down in this Article:

(a) *cases referred to in Article 171* (. . .); [intellectual property cases]

(. . .)

3. *The decision relating to the delegation* of a case to the single Judge *shall be taken*, after the main parties have been heard, *by the Chamber* sitting with three Judges before which the case is pending. Where a Member State or an institution of the Union which is a party to the proceedings objects to the case being heard and determined by the single Judge the case shall be maintained before the Chamber to which the Judge-Rapporteur belongs [indications added] (emphasis added).

This provision shows that actions brought against decisions of the Boards of Appeal of the OHIM or of the Community Plant Variety Office (hereinafter, CPVO) and concerning the application of the rules relating to an intellectual property regime may, from now on, be subject to the single-judge procedure. Moreover, it follows from the third paragraph of Article 29 of the new rules of procedure that, unlike in Article 51(2) of the previous version of the rules of procedure, unanimity is no longer required to decide on the transfer of the case to a single judge, a majority in a three-judge chamber being sufficient.

Third, the new rules of procedure finally include measures aimed at limiting potential delaying attempts and unnecessary added complexity to procedures. For instance, an application to intervene often creates lengthy difficulties in the treatment of the main action. The revised rules of procedure thus remove the possibility of intervening after the 6-week period starting from the publication in the Official Journal of the European Union of the notice indicating, *inter alia*, the lodging of an application initiating proceedings. This type of intervention, which was limited to the submission of observations at the stage of the oral procedure and only based on the report for the hearing, now belongs to history. Moreover, Article 142 clarifies the rights conferred on interveners. More specifically, the first paragraph of this provision clearly indicates:

1. The intervention shall be limited to supporting, in whole or in part, the form of order sought by one of the main parties. *It shall not confer the same procedural rights* as those conferred on the main parties and, in particular, *shall not give rise to any right to request that a hearing be held.* (...) (emphasis added).

These additional explanations are an attempt to achieve a better understanding of the role of the intervention, hence the specifications within the revised text, whenever it is relevant, of the exact scope of the intervener's rights. Lastly, Article 144 limits the possibility of requesting confidential treatment of certain information or documents. More precisely, it makes clear that only the main parties can request such treatment with regard to interveners. This modification aims at eliminating the massive and time-consuming work that the General Court had to undertake when dealing with confidentiality claims from interveners towards some or all other parties.

The setting of shorter legal time limits in the new rules of procedure than those previously prescribed for requests for hearings contributes to avoiding undue delay in the duration of proceedings. As seen above, Article 106(2) fixes a 3-week period to submit a request for a hearing. Pursuant to Article 191 (which specifies that, save certain exceptions, provisions governing direct actions are applicable to proceedings relating to intellectual property rights), this deadline also concerns such requests in the context of actions against decisions of the OHIM or CPVO Boards of Appeal. The new rules of procedure thus bring about a reduction in the period within which these requests may be filed since under former Article 135a, a 1-month period was given to parties.

Finally, the new rules of procedure lead to a simplification of the default procedure. In this regard, it should be noted that unlike former Article 122, Article 123 of the revised text no longer envisages the possibility of holding a hearing in this procedure. Moreover, it does not allow for any preparatory inquiry either. Lastly, it does not leave any room to the defendant, which cannot intervene and should be served any procedural documents. All these measures thus protect the General Court from frivolous or superfluous procedural steps.

Internal measures and procedural reform have been undertaken to tackle the backlog faced by the General Court. However, such actions, which are not only necessary but indispensable, are not sufficient if not accompanied by a greater modification. Therefore, as far back as 25 September 2009, on the occasion of the celebration of the 20th anniversary of the General Court, I raised the alarm over the backlog and called for a reform of the structure of the General Court.[36] On the basis of statistics concerning judicial activity, disturbing trends could be identified, and the time had come to initiate wide-reaching structural reform (see Sect. 3.2).

## 3.2 An Appealing Look to Get an Appealing Look

Since my appeal for support for reform in 2009, there has been a fundamental debate on the architectural structure of the Court of Justice of the European Union. Worrying figures have been presented, analysed and monitored. Although the ways of addressing the issues are diverse and controverted, a common conclusion is at least shared among all stakeholders: the General Court will not be able to face an augmentation of the number of cases introduced and treat them in compliance with the right to have an efficient judicial remedy with its current organisation. A solution has to be found, and efforts made in this sense resulted in a first proposal that did not manage to win the support of the EU legislator (see Sect. 3.2.1). A second proposal is currently being examined; however, the journey that this reform has embarked on shows that the path is full of pitfalls (see Sect. 3.2.2).[37]

### 3.2.1 Structural Reform: Rise and Fall

To structurally reform the General Court, the intervention of the EU legislator is necessary. Indeed, as explained in detail below, two possibilities are envisaged: the setting up of a specialised court and an increase in the number of judges. The first option has been allowed since the Treaty of Nice and has been confirmed by the

---

[36]Jaeger (2009).

[37]On the chronology of events related to the reform, see the MLex case file Amendment to Court of Justice Statute. Available via MLex http://www.mlex.com/EU/Content.aspx?ID=145077. Accessed 30 Apr 2015.

Lisbon Treaty. Article 257 TFEU provides for the combined action of the European Parliament and the Council, pursuant to ordinary legislative procedure, to establish specialised courts attached to the General Court to hear and determine at first instance certain classes of action or proceedings brought in specific areas. The Commission, after consultation with the Court of Justice, or the Court of Justice, after consultation with the Commission, has to initiate the procedure. The second option requires a modification of the Statute of the Court of Justice since its Article 48 states that the General Court shall consist of 28 judges.[38] Therefore, the procedure laid down in Article 280 applies. Accordingly, such an amendment can only be made by the European Parliament and the Council, acting pursuant to the ordinary legislative procedure, at the request of the Court of Justice, after consultation with the Commission, or at the proposal of the Commission, after consultation with the Court of Justice.

**Two Ways** It should be recalled that Article 19 of the Treaty on European Union states:

1. The Court of Justice of the European Union shall include the Court of Justice, the General Court *and specialised courts*. It shall ensure that in the interpretation and application of the Treaties the law is observed.

Member States shall provide remedies sufficient to ensure effective legal protection in the fields covered by Union law.

2. The Court of Justice shall consist of one judge from each Member State. It shall be assisted by Advocates-General.

The General Court shall include *at least* one judge per Member State (emphasis added).

Therefore, this provision, on the one hand, provides that the Court of Justice of the European Union shall include specialised courts and, on the other hand, establishes that the General Court shall include at least one judge per Member State. From this provision, two different ways of answering the problems faced by the General Court were derived: (1) the transfer of some of its competences at first instance to a specialised court, as was done with the Civil Service Tribunal, and (2) an increase in the number of judges.

**Specialised Court** Regarding the addition of a specialised court to the General Court, it should be noted that in 2009 a discussion took place as to the possibility of creating such a jurisdiction to deal with intellectual property cases. Among the advantages of this option, two should be specifically mentioned in the context of the

---

[38] As last amended by Article 9 of the Act concerning the conditions of accession to the European Union of the Republic of Croatia and the adjustments to the Treaty on European Union, the Treaty on the Functioning of the European Union and the Treaty establishing the European Atomic Energy Community [2012] OJ L 112/21.

quest for a more efficient EU judicial system. First, it should be stressed that higher productivity, due to economies of scales, can be expected when cases are examined by judges having specific expertise in the field. From both quantitative and qualitative points of view, such a specialised court would be of real interest. Second, the chosen field (i.e., intellectual property cases) is well circumscribed (three subject matters are concerned (trademarks, models and designs, plant varieties) that rarely have a horizontal impact on other fields of EU law), homogeneous (three-quarters of these cases are *inter partes*, rarely involving interveners or raising new legal issues) and quantitatively massive. For the past 10 years, the volume represented by this subject matter within the number of cases introduced before the General Court has increased immensely: from 98 cases in 2005 to 295 in 2014. In 2014, this type of case accounted for more than 32% of the total number of introduced cases, more than 33% of the total number of completed cases and 34% of the total number of pending cases. Moreover, it should be noted that with regard to the total number of challenged decisions in this field, only 16% were appealed before the Court of Justice. The number of cases transferred and the number of potential appeals against decisions of this specialised court before the General Court can thus be assessed with a high degree of certainty.

**More Judges** With more judges, the General Court's strike force would undoubtedly be amplified. However, drawbacks could result from this option. It would seem to be important to point out two of them with regard to the impact of such options on the efficiency of EU proceedings. First, every 3 years, the General Court experiences an unstable period due to the partial renewal of judges' mandates. Multiplying the number of judges would increase the disturbance factor linked to this element. Second, such an increase would automatically require more resources to coordinate the work within the General Court. Likewise, more resources would be necessary at the level of the Court of Justice. Due to the expected increase in output, more appeals would be filed before the Court of Justice, whose staff though would remain constant. In this regard, it should be noted that the duration of proceedings regarding appeals only decreased last year. Indeed, although in 2014 it amounted to 14.5 months, the trend for the past few years has been entirely different: 14 months in 2010, 15.1 months in 2011, 15.2 months in 2012 and 16.6 months in 2013.

Both of these options (i.e., a specialised court and an increase in the number of judges) were seriously considered, sometimes with supplementary ideas such as an increase in the number of legal secretaries (aka *référendaires*, who assist judges in case treatments) or even a combination of the two main options (although in a time of financial crisis, budgetary issues had to be taken into consideration and a choice between the two was more reasonable, at least as a first step). On 22 December 2009, the General Court produced an analysis concluding in favour of a specialised court in intellectual property cases.

**Attempts** However, on 28 March 2011, the Court of Justice chose the second option consisting of increasing the number of judges. Its proposal to modify the

Statute of the Court, sent to the European Parliament and the Council, entailed the appointment of 12 additional judges to the General Court.[39]

**First Series of Attempts** The proposal was first discussed under the Hungarian presidency of the EU. Questions were raised, *inter alia*, with regard to the costs of the reform, estimated at approximately 13 million euros, the relevance of preferring a separate intellectual property tribunal, the geographical distribution of the 12 new judges, the justifications underlying the specific figure given for additional judges and the consistency of rulings across the restructured court.

Discussions continued under the Polish presidency of the EU, focusing on the costs involved with the addition of 12 judges and the manner of their appointment. In October 2011, the European Commission adopted a formal position in favour of plans to add 12 new judges to the General Court, though advocating the creation of at least two new specialised chambers within the court to deal with subjects that give rise to 'a large volume of litigation'.[40] In November 2011, Germany proposed that six of the 12 new judges should be permanent, the appointment of the other six being subject to a rotation system.

Denmark took over at the beginning of the year 2012, warning, however, that reaching an agreement on how to increase the number of judges at the General Court during the Danish-led presidency of the EU would be 'extremely difficult'.[41] The Danish presidency nevertheless proposed a lottery system for selecting the 12 extra judges as a temporary measure. The scheme was supposed to be in place for 6 years until governments found a lasting solution to the problem. The compromise failed to garner support.

**Second Series of Attempts** In July of the same year, the Cypriot presidency reopened discussions with the aim of further exploring other possibilities, such as the addition of a different number of judges (five, six, eight, nine, eleven, fourteen or fifteen) or an increase in legal secretaries. After many debates, the idea of having nine extra judges who would sit for two terms if coming from a large EU Member State and one term only if from a small Member State was put on the table. Confronted with opposition, a last-minute proposal was offered consisting of two parallel rotation systems for nine additional judges, depending on their geographical origin: one system for four judges coming from large Member States appointed for two successive mandates and another for five judges from small Member States nominated for a single mandate. However, the proposition did not align governments' views.

---

[39]Council document 8787/11 of 7 April 2011. Available via European Council, Council of the European Union http://data.consilium.europa.eu/doc/document/ST-8787-2011-INIT/en/pdf. Accessed 30 Apr 2015.

[40]Commission opinion on the requests for the amendment of the Statute of the Court of Justice of the European Union, presented by the Court, COM(2011) 596 final, 30.9.2011. Available via European Parliament http://www.europarl.europa.eu/meetdocs/2014_2019/documents/juri/dv/com_com%282011%290596_/com_com%282011%290596_en.pdf. Accessed 30 Apr 2015.

[41]Rego (2011).

On 1 January 2013, Ireland assumed the EU rotating presidency. However, it decided to focus on other topics related to judicial efficiency (such as modifications of the procedural rules) and not to make the structural issue of the General Court a priority. At that time, talks were deadlocked.

In mid-2013, Lithuania held the EU presidency. It made a fresh attempt to resume talks and go ahead with structural reform by proposing a plan to double the number of judges, i.e. from 28 to 56, over the next two decades (i.e., by 2032). In the event that during this process it became clear the General Court had reached an appropriate size, the appointment procedure could be stopped, and any Member States left without a second judge would then see their additional candidate rotated into the existing group. This idea found little favour among EU governments and was abandoned.[42]

When Greece started its 6-month slot in the EU presidency seat in 2014, it had another proposal for appointing additional judges, which came directly from the President of the Court of Justice. The new plan was to have nine candidates to be screened by the Article 255 panel, four would be in office until 2016 and the tenures of the remaining five would last until 2019, allowing the expiry of judges' terms to be spread over two consecutive replacement periods. In addition, the panel's reserve list would include an additional five to nine candidates, ranked in order of merit, who could cover any appointments that might be needed before the next selection procedure. Finally, the proposal guaranteed that there would never be more than two nationals of the same Member State at the General Court.[43] Although the EU governments then agreed to pursue a plan to add nine judges, and the European Parliament Committee on Legal Affairs approved this plan, the Member States still failed to reach an agreement on the appointment system amid concerns from smaller countries that their nationals would not be represented.

At the 22nd Annual Intellectual Property Law & Policy Conference, held on 24 April 2014, at Fordham University School of Law in New York City, Court of Justice Judge Rosas, president of the rules of procedure's committee, announced that the reform initiative seemed dead.[44] The proposal had stalled over how the additional judges would be designated to ensure a fair distribution among the EU Member States. At the Council of Bars and Law Societies of Europe's conference on 'The Future of the European Union Courts', held in Brussels on 28 April 2014, Court of Justice Vice-President Lenaerts confirmed that the reform process had failed; that he would accept, under certain conditions, 'Jaeger's solution';[45] and that EU governments should consider novel solutions such as creating specialised courts and reforming the appeal procedure.[46]

---

[42]Croft and Newman (2013).

[43]Croft and Newman (2014a).

[44]Croft and Nylen (2014).

[45]Seytre (2014).

[46]Newman (2014).

At the same event, I stressed the fact that all these talks at the Council had resulted in a big waste of time and energy, that other solutions were possible and had been discussed and that everyone had to draw conclusions about who should take responsibility for this fiasco. If my words were harsh, they were nonetheless well weighted. In addition to the reminder that I addressed to EU legislators to conduct impact assessments on litigation before creating any new agencies or giving new competences to existing bodies whose decisions would ultimately be challenged before the General Court, I urged them to hear the ideas that had been concretely formulated to reform the structure of this court. On 3 September 2014, the Italian Presidency of the Council sent to the Court of Justice an invitation letter to present new proposals in order to facilitate the task of securing agreement within the Council on the procedures for increasing the number of judges at the General Court (see Sect. 3.2.2).

### 3.2.2 Structural Reform: Rebirth or False Dawn?

On 24 September 2014, the Court of Justice announced that it would put on the table a new proposal demanding 28 more judges.[47] On 13 October 2014, the Court of Justice moved to propose to the Council to double the number of judges of the General Court,[48] taking into consideration the fact that 'the Greek Presidency of the Council in the first half of 2014 concluded that, while the Court of Justice would have to consider other options, any solution involving fewer Judges than the number of Member States, and, consequently, requiring a choice to be made between Member States, would encounter the same difficulties as those which, in recent years, have prevented agreement from being reached in the Council'.[49] Although the EU legislative procedure regarding this proposition is still ongoing, certain observations can already be made.

**New Proposal** According to the Court of Justice's new proposition, the doubling of the number of judges of the General Court should take place in three phases. In the first phase in 2015, 12 additional judges would be appointed to provide the General Court with the immediate reinforcements it calls for. In the second phase in 2016, the Civil Service Tribunal would be rolled into the General Court. This would increase the number of judges by seven and would include the transfer to the

---

[47]Croft (2014a).

[48]See Council document 14448/1/14, 20.11.2014. Available via European Council, Council of the European Union http://data.consilium.europa.eu/doc/document/ST-14448-2014-REV-1/en/pdf. Accessed 30 Apr 2015.

[49]Document entitled Response to the invitation from the Italian Presidency of the Council to present new proposals in order to facilitate the task of securing agreement within the Council on the procedures for increasing the number of Judges at the General Court, annexed to the letter from the President of the Court of Justice of the European Union to the Chairman of Coreper, dated 13 October 2014. Available via European Council, Council of the European Union. Accessed 30 Apr 2015.

General Court of first-instance cases relating to the EU civil service. Where a national of a Member State performs the judge's duties at the CST, that Member State would have the opportunity to propose her or his appointment as a judge of the General Court, provided that it did not participate in the first stage. Finally, in the third phase in 2019, nine additional judges would be appointed.

**Council Level** At the meeting of EU government representatives held in Brussels on 7 November 2014, concerns were raised about the cost of this proposal, which amounts to 22.9 million euros and represents a 6.6% increase in the total budget of the Court of Justice of the European Union.[50] On 11 December 2014, the EU ambassadors agreed in principle on the new proposal to double the number of judges, albeit with a reduced number of legal secretaries assigned to each judge (two instead of three) in order to help reduce costs. However, the Italian presidency ended without striking a deal on how judges in each phase would be appointed.[51] In January 2015, after assuming the EU presidency for 6 months, the Latvian government took over negotiations, aiming to reduce the cost of reform and find a satisfactory system for all EU Member States to appoint judges in the initial stage. As far as the latter was concerned, the risk was that the last stage would not be implemented due to financial reasons, which would leave some Member States without a second judge. In March, the EU governments agreed on a lottery system to designate the first Member States to appoint an additional judge in the initial phase, the other Member States following according to the list of EU presidencies. In addition, the cost of the reform was cut to 14 million euros through administrative savings, the court having to reallocate its existing staff.

**European Parliament Level** This agreement now has to be backed by the European Parliament. A lively discussion is currently going on before the EP commission in charge of legal affairs concerning how to choose the way of reforming the functioning of the General Court. On 22 April 2015, the person in charge of steering the proposal through this institution invited judges from the EU courts to speak to members of parliament.[52] On 28 April 2015, I presented the view of the General Court based on my position already expressed in 2009. First, other judges had the opportunity to contribute to the discussion by giving their personal opinions, and then the member of parliament responsible for this file declared that 'the legitimacy of doubling the judges [had become] extremely contestable and could easily become a very dangerous symbol of EU mismanagement of funds'.[53] After that, the Court of Justice issued a press release supporting its proposal.[54] At the time of writing, the legislative procedure is still in progress. Once this

---

[50]Croft (2014b).

[51]Croft and Newman (2014b).

[52]Newman (2015a).

[53]Newman (2015b).

[54]Court of Justice of the European Union, Press Release, Reform of the EU's court system, No 44/15 of 28 April 2015.

commission reaches a decision, the European Parliament will still have to vote on the proposal.

**Difficulties Ahead?** Although not yet adopted, if this reform passes, it is clear that it will have an impact on the institution and the General Court itself.

**Impact on the Institution** As far as the institution is concerned, the General Court returns as the court of first instance for litigation for civil servants, while the Court of Justice returns as the appellate court for this litigation.[55] Back to square one then? In fact, the problems identified back in 2009 when the General Court envisaged that the addition of a number of judges (see Sect. 3.2.2) might become even more pronounced as a result of the doubling of the number of its judges. How will the Court of Justice ensure the unity and consistency of EU law when appeals flow from the General Court's increase in output? In the Court of Justice's opinion, the implementation of the review procedure has proved somewhat complex. Would it not be easier to revamp this procedure instead of reorganising the three EU courts' structure?

Unuttered ideas float in the air concerning how to deal with the risk of being overburdened. A filtering system with the common law procedure of leave to appeal might be put in place. A new transfer of competences from the Court of Justice might be envisaged, as recently revealed through a press release published on 28 April 2015. However, while the possibility of transferring interpretative competence has expressly been foreseen since 2001, the Court of Justice does not seem to be willing to operate such a transfer. Indeed, one of the reasons put forward to support its reform proposal is explicitly the need for the Court of Justice to be the one and only court responsible for ensuring uniform interpretation of the law.

Finally, such a huge increase in the number of judges would have unavoidable consequences for the entire administrative staff of the institution. More cases handled would mean more procedural decisions and hence an increased workload for the Registry. More decisions mean more translations and hence an increased workload for the lawyer-linguists and, more generally, the directorate-general for translation. More decisions mean more hearings and hence an increased workload for interpreters and, more generally, for the directorate-general for interpretation.

**Impact on Jurisdiction** Concerning the impact of the reform on the General Court, it should be recalled here that every 3 years, the General Court undergoes periods of disturbance due to the partial renewal of its members. My recurrent call for stability through the reappointment of their judges by Member States or, at least, for an early indication of their intentions in this regard was echoed by the Council of Bars and Law Societies of the European Union (CCBE) in a letter

---

[55]Compare Court of Justice of the European Union, Press Release, The President of the Court of Justice presents the Council of Justice Ministers with a number of proposals and ideas on the future of the judicial system of the European Union, No 36/99 of 28 May 1998 with Skouris (2008).

dated 26 March 2013.[56] The doubling of the number of judges renders inevitable a profound change in the General Court's working methods. The proposed reform makes necessary a certain degree of specialisation and rationalisation in case allocation to reporting judges. The topic regarding the introduction of a certain degree of specialisation of the General Court has been discussed for a long time. In substance, the idea is that allocating cases to specialised chambers within the General Court would assist with the quality of decision-making and speed up the throughput of cases. At this time, the specialisation of the chambers is a work in progress, and there is fruitful discussion among the members of the General Court. Coordination to maintain and guarantee the coherence of case law will also be a challenge with a court that is twice as big.

History teaches attentive observers that certain trends may be sound. The development of the General Court is outstanding in this sense. It shows that a specialised judicial body may turn into a general one when needed and that additional levels may be necessary to address specific needs. The General Court went from revolution to evolution and then from evolution to devolution. Despite its obvious achievements, to some extent proved by the fact that the General Court can be considered a victim of its own success, will it return to be a purely and exclusively first instance court 25 years after its establishment?

Case law gives abundant examples of the fact that judges are far from being almighty. They are rightfully dependent on the willingness of the EU legislator, the sole representative of the EU people. Sometimes the only possible way to change a situation that is, in the eyes of the law, inconsistent with what one would expect from a fair legal system is to call for legislative modification. This action does not belong to the judge, who can only draw the attention of the legislator. Moreover, it has to be acknowledged that the General Court does not have the decision as to its future in its own hands. It has done everything that could possibly have been done to make itself heard. It is now up to the EU legislator to decide wisely.

## References

Bodoni S (2007) Jaeger, new EU court head, says priority cutting case backlog. Bloomberg, 10 October 2007. Available via Bloomberg. http://www.bloomberg.com/apps/news?pid=newsarchive&sid=ayYfhR7ueZyw. Accessed 30 Apr 2015

Croft L (2011) Court General: the view from the bench. MLex Magazine (6) July-September

Croft L (2014a) EU court will demand 28 more judges in new proposal. MLex Insight, 24 September 2014

Croft L (2014b) EU states raise budget concerns about 28 new judges. MLex Insight, 10 November 2014

---

[56]President E Tsouroulis' letter regarding the appointment of Judges to the EU Courts, 26.3.2013. Available via CCBE http://www.ccbe.eu/fileadmin/user_upload/NTCdocument/260313_EN__EU_Repsp1_1364893059.pdf. Accessed 30 Apr 2015.

Croft L, Newman M (2013) Proposal to double EU court judges to 56 finds little support. MLex Insight, 2 October 2013

Croft L, Newman M (2014a) EU high court moves to unblock talks over appointing new judges. MLex Insight, 7 January 2014

Croft L, Newman M (2014b) EU governments home in on deal to double judges at EU court. MLex Insight, 11 December 2014

Croft L, Nylen L (2014) Push for more EU judges is 'dead', Rosas says. MLex Insight, 25 April 2014

Gaudissart M-A (2012) Le refonte du règlement de procédure de la Cour de justice. Cahiers de droit européen (CDE) 3:603–669

Jaeger M (2009) Is it time for reform? The Court of First Instance of the European Communities is celebrating its 20th anniversary. Available via Curia. http://curia.europa.eu/jcms/jcms/P_52392/. Accessed 30 Apr 2015

Jaeger M (2011a) Standard of review in competition cases: can the General Court increase coherence in the EU judicial system? In: Today's multilayered legal order: current issues and perspectives, Liber Amicorum, in honour of Arjen WH Meij, Zutphen, Paris

Jaeger M (2011b) The standard of review in competition cases involving complex economic assessments: towards the marginalisation of the marginal review? J Eur Competition Law Pract 2(4):295–314

Lambote S (2015) Adopter le réflexe du droit de l'Union européenne. Legimag (9) March

Newman M (2014) EU states could tweak rules to streamline court appeals, senior judge says. MLex Insight, 28 April 2014

Newman M (2015a) EU judges should give testimony on court overhaul, lawmaker says. MLex Insight, 23 March 2015

Newman M (2015b) EU judges dismiss plan to revamp General Court as 'yesterday's solution'. MLex Insight, 29 April 2015

Rego AR (2011) Agreement on General Court reform by June 'extremely difficult,' Danish presidency official says. MLex Insight, 28 December 2011

Seytre D (2014) Communication, information et réformes à la cour. Le Jeudi, 22 May 2014

Skouris V (2008) The Court of Justice and the challenges of the enlarged European Union. ERA Forum 9(1):99–108

# The General Court as the EU Competition Court?

**Miro Prek and Silvère Lefèvre**

**Abstract** Competition litigation has been at the centre of the General Court's jurisdiction since its creation. Yet it now solely constitutes a minority of the applications introduced. Even though the statistical importance of competition law has decreased in its overall workload, it is argued that, in view of the extent of the review it can exercise over the Commission's decision in this field, the General Court remains the best-placed forum to deal with this type of litigation.

## 1 Introduction

A strong link between competition law and the Court of First Instance (later to become the General Court) existed at the date of its creation since competition law was one of the two areas of jurisdiction that was transferred to the newly established court by Council Decision 88/591.[1] However, the increasing number of types of areas of litigation transferred to the General Court—which makes it 'general' not only in name but also in reality—meant that competition litigation is less and less the centre of its daily activity, as shown in Table 1. This relative loss of importance of competition litigation is also a consequence of the process of decentralisation of EU competition law, which has led to competition disputes being more frequently dealt with in national fora with the assistance of the Court of Justice.

---

This paper is a formalised version of speeches given at the 4th Petar Šarcevic Conference on Competition and State Aid which took place in April 2015.

[1]Together with Civil Service litigation. Council Decision 88/591/ECSC, EEC, Euratom of 24 October 1988 establishing a Court of First Instance of the European Communities [1988] OJ L 319/1, as amended by Council Decision 93/350/ECSC, EEC, Euratom of 8 June 1993 [1993] OJ L 144/21.

M. Prek (✉) • S. Lefèvre
General Court of the European Union, Luxembourg, Luxembourg
e-mail: Miro.Prek@curia.europa.eu; Silvere.Lefevre@curia.europa.eu

© Springer-Verlag Berlin Heidelberg 2017
V. Tomljenović et al. (eds.), *EU Competition and State Aid Rules*,
Europeanization and Globalization 3, https://doi.org/10.1007/978-3-662-47962-9_2

**Table 1** New cases introduced before the General Court 2010–2014

| New cases : nature of proceedings | 2010 | 2011 | 2012 | 2013 | 2014 |
|---|---|---|---|---|---|
| State aid | 42 | 67 | 36 | 54 | 148 |
| Competition | 79 | 39 | 34 | 23 | 41 |
| Intellectual property | 207 | 219 | 238 | 293 | 295 |
| Other direct actions | 207 | 264 | 220 | 275 | 299 |
| Appeals | 23 | 44 | 10 | 57 | 36 |
| Appeals concerning interim measures or interventions | 1 | 1 | 1 | – | – |
| Special forms of procedure | 77 | 88 | 78 | 88 | 93 |
| Total | 636 | 722 | 617 | 790 | 912 |

Source: Registry of the General Court, Annual Reports

Moreover, the introduction of the commitment procedure (Article 9 of Regulation 1/2003[2]) also plays an important part in this 'statistical' loss of importance of competition litigation for the General Court. Indeed, in non-cartel areas, commitment decisions are much more numerous than prohibition decisions based on Article 7 of Regulation 1/2003. This is demonstrated in Fig. 1:

Yet it would be too extreme to answer in the negative the question raised by the title of this presentation. In view of its jurisdiction over questions of facts and of law, the General Court can, alone, lead a process for which the national courts and the Court of Justice need to cooperate through the preliminary ruling procedure. In other words, if competition law constitutes less the heart of its daily activity than it used to, the General Court remains the best-placed forum, in the European Union, to resolve competition disputes. This is even more so in view of its 25 years of experience in this field, which, when analysed, demonstrates a clear trend towards an ever-increasing level of scrutiny of the Commission's decision in this field. This trend will be highlighted below in three directions: the gradual loss of importance of the 'marginal standard of review', the move towards the greater use of the General Court's 'unlimited jurisdiction' and a stronger emphasis on protection against the arbitrary exercise of the Commission's investigatory powers.

---

[2]Council Regulation (EC) No 1/2003 of 16 December 2002 on the implementation of the rules on competition laid down in Articles 81 and 82 of the Treaty [2003] OJ L 1/1. Article 9: Article 9— Commitments: '1. Where the Commission intends to adopt a decision requiring that an infringement be brought to an end and the undertakings concerned offer commitments to meet the concerns expressed to them by the Commission in its preliminary assessment, the Commission may by decision make those commitments binding on the undertakings. Such a decision may be adopted for a specified period and shall conclude that there are no longer grounds for action by the Commission [. . .]'. Such a procedure is not deemed appropriate when the Commission intends to impose a fine. See recital 13 of Regulation 1/2003.

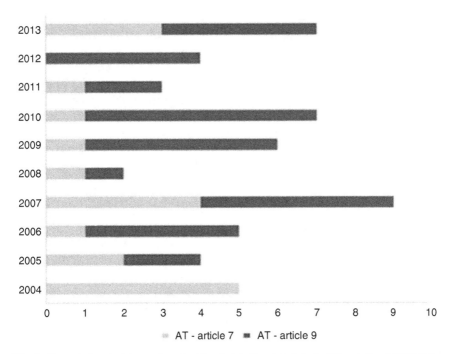

**Fig. 1** Commission decisions adopted under Article 7 and Article 9 of Regulation 1/2003 (May 2004–December 2013) – excludes cartels (Source: European Commission, Competition Policy Brief, 2014/3, p 3)

## 2 The 'Marginal Standard' of Review Marginalised

On the basis of a settled case law, which finds its origin long before the creation of the Court of First Instance, a 'limited review' is carried out in relation to aspects of the Commission's decisions that involve 'complex economic matters' in the course of the application of Articles 101(1),[3] 101(3),[4] 102[5] TFEU or when assessing the compatibility of a proposed merger.[6] The Court limits itself to verifying whether the relevant rules on procedure and on the statement of reasons have been complied with, whether the facts have been accurately stated and, finally, whether there has been any manifest error of assessment or misuse of powers. Since the General Court may only annul the Commission's legal appraisal of the facts when faced with errors on the part of the Commission of a certain dimension, reference is made to a

---

[3]Case 42/84 *Remia and Others v. Commission* ECLI:EU:C:1985:327.

[4]Joined Cases 56/64 and 58/64 *Consten and Grundig v. Commission* ECLI: EU:C:1966:41.

[5]Case T-65/96 *Kish Glass v. Commission* ECLI:EU:T:2000:93, p. 64.

[6]Joined Cases C-68/94 and C-30/95 *France and Others v. Commission* ECLI: EU:C:1998:148.

'marginal standard of review', providing the Commission with 'a margin of appraisal'. Its importance should not be overestimated.

In the first place, it must be kept in mind that the existence of a margin of appraisal to the benefit of the Commission in competition matters only concerns one of the grounds of review, namely the infringement of the Treaties or any rule of law relating to their application. Even within the framework of this ground, a limited review is only carried out as an exception. The General Court normally undertakes a comprehensive review of whether the conditions of Article 101, Article 102 or the merger regulation[7] are met. This 'exceptional nature' of the marginal review was expressed as early as the *Remia* judgment of the Court of Justice inasmuch as it stated that

> although as a general rule the Court undertakes a comprehensive review of the question whether or not the conditions for the application of article [101](1) are met, it is clear that in determining the permissible duration of a non-competition clause incorporated in an agreement for the transfer of an undertaking the Commission has to appraise complex economic matters.[8]

In the second place, a margin of appraisal to the benefit of the Commission is no discretion in the true sense since it derives from the choice of the judiciary not to interfere with issues it considers too intricate to lend themselves to judicial scrutiny. Discretion in the stricter sense is the consequence of the will of the treaty makers or of the legislator to provide the Commission with a freedom of decision, the respect of which is demanded by institutional balance.[9] In that perspective, a margin of appraisal merely provides the Commission with latitude that can be reduced whenever the Court considers that it has sufficient knowledge to exercise a comprehensive review of its assessments, however complex they may be.[10]

In that respect, if key moments exist in the 'history' of competition litigation, year 2002 is certainly one of them. It could be argued that the series of merger decisions annulled that year was the consequence of an increase in the level of scrutiny carried out by the Court of First Instance, which, accordingly, led to a reduction in the scope of the marginal review.[11]

Even though it dismissed the appeal introduced by the Commission against the *Tetra Laval* judgment, the Court of Justice did not explicitly underline that the General Court was free to conduct a comprehensive review in areas held to be

---

[7]Council Regulation (EC) No 139/2004 of 20 January 2004 on the control of concentrations between undertakings [2004] OJ L 24/1.

[8]*Remia* (n 3), p. 34.

[9]On this question, see Bailey (2004), pp. 1337–1339. See also Fritzsche (2010), p. 361.

[10]In that sense, see the opinion of AG Cosmas in Case C-83/98 P *France v. Ladbroke Racing and Commission* ECLI:EU:C:1999:577, footnote 4.

[11]Case T-342/99 *Airtours v. Commission* ECLI:EU:T:2002:146; Case T-310/01 *Schneider Electric v. Commission* ECLI :EU:T:2002:254; Case T-5/02 *Tetra Laval v. Commission* ECLI:EU: T:2002:264.

complex, if it felt in a position to do so; it rather focused on the extent of the burden of proof that the Commission carries by stating that

> the Courts of the European Union must not refrain from reviewing the Commission's interpretation of information of an economic nature [; n]ot only must those Courts establish, among other things, whether the evidence relied on is factually accurate, reliable and consistent but also whether that evidence contains all the information which must be taken into account in order to assess a complex situation and whether it is capable of substantiating the conclusions drawn from it.[12]

It added that in relation to a 'prospective analysis', that is to say 'an examination of how a concentration might alter the factors determining the state of competition on a given market in order to establish whether it would give rise to a serious impediment to effective competition', it is necessary for the Commission 'to envisage various chains of cause and effect with a view to ascertaining which of them are the most likely'.[13]

In spite of a certain ambiguity in the language used, it appears that the Court of Justice endorsed the principle of a more in-depth review of the Commission's assessments in competition matters. The more recent judgments of the Court of Justice in relation to the review by the General Court of the legality of decisions imposing fines for violations of competition law are further evidence of that. It was indeed clearly stated that the General Court cannot use the Commission's margin of appraisal 'as a basis for dispensing with the conduct of an in-depth review of the law and of the facts'.[14]

This led Advocate General Mengozzi to underline that '[f]or several years the scope of the case-law on marginal review has been significantly reduced'.[15] In the same manner, in view of the language now used by the Court of Justice, as well as the actual review exercised by the General Court in practice, one can only approve the position expressed by President Jaeger of 'a marginalisation of the marginal review',[16] in which it is advocated that marginal review should be disconnected from considerations of complexity but, rather, solely linked with policy choices.[17]

---

[12]Case C-12/03 P *Commission v. Tetra Laval* ECLI:EU:C:2005:87, p. 39.

[13]Ibid, p. 43.

[14]Case C-389/10 *KME Germany and Others v. Commission* ECLI:EU:C:2011:816, p 129; Case C-386/10 *Chalkor v. Commission* ECLI:EU:C:2011:815, p 62. See also Case C-199/11 *Otis and Others* ECLI:EU:C:2012:684, pp. 59 and 61.

[15]Opinion in Case C-382/12 *MasterCard and Others v. Commission* ECLI:EU:C:2014:42, p. 119.

[16]Jaeger (2011), p. 299.

[17]Ibid. p. 310.

## 3 A Wide Conception of the Unlimited Jurisdiction of the General Court in Relation to Fines and Penalty Payments

Article 261 TFEU states that '[r]egulations adopted jointly by the European Parliament and the Council, and by the Council, pursuant to the provisions of the Treaties, may give the Court of Justice of the European Union unlimited jurisdiction with regard to the penalties provided for in such regulations'. Under Article 31 of Regulation 1/2003 and Article 16 of Regulation 139/2004, '[t]he Court of Justice shall have unlimited jurisdiction to review decisions whereby the Commission has fixed a fine or periodic penalty payment[; i]t may cancel, reduce or increase the fine or periodic penalty payment imposed'.

Article 261 TFEU, rather than an autonomous remedy, constitutes an extension of the powers normally vested in the General Court and is exercised in the course of an action for annulment.[18] By virtue of its unlimited jurisdiction, the General Court is not limited to the alternative of dismissing the application or annulling the contested decision but can also alter the amount of fines (or penalty payments) imposed.

There has been some debate as to the precise determination of the circumstances that may trigger the exercise by the General Court of its additional powers. One view was to consider that such powers can only be triggered once the General Court reached a conclusion as to the illegality of the decision.[19] In contrast to this narrow view, a wider conception was proposed, according to which although the exercise of unlimited jurisdiction takes place within the framework of an action for annulment, it can be exercised without any prior finding of illegality.[20] Thus, a mere finding that the level of fines is not appropriate in the circumstances of the case is sufficient to alter it. Once disconnected from the assessment of the legality of the decision, the powers of the General Court under Article 261 TFEU broaden considerably since they can be used for considerations of equity, such as the ability of an undertaking to provide a bank guarantee to secure the payment of the fine[21] or to correct an error of assessment in the calculation of the fines, which finds its origin in the undertaking concerned and thus has no bearing on the legality of the decision.[22]

The most recent case law of the Court of Justice gives strong indications that it favours a broad interpretation of the powers of the General Court under Article

---

[18]Order in Case T-252/03 *FNICGV v. Commission* ECLI:EU:T:2004:326, pp. 21–25. See also Case T-69/04 *Schunk and Schunk Kohlenstoff-Technik v. Commission* ECLI:EU:T:2008:415, p. 246; Case T-132/07 *Fuji Electric v. Commission* ECLI:EU:T:2011:344, p. 207.

[19]Case T-15/02 *BASF v. Commission* ECLI:EU:T:2006:74, p. 582.

[20]Case T-50/03 *Saint-Gobain Gyproc Belgium v. Commission* ECLI:EU:T:2008:252 and Case T-37/05 *World Wide Tobacco España v. Commission* ECLI:EU:T:2011:76. See Bernardeau and Christienne (2013), pp. 809/810.

[21]Case T-11/06 *Romana Tabacchi v. Commission* ECLI:EU:T:2011:560, pp. 282–286.

[22]Case T-217/06 *Arkema France and Others v. Commission* ECLI:EU:T:2011:251, pp. 247–280; see also Case T-322/01 *Roquette Frères v. Commission* ECLI:EU:T:2006:267, pp. 293–316.

261 TFEU since it mentions the possibility for the General Court 'in addition to carrying out a mere review of the lawfulness of the penalty, to substitute their own appraisal for the Commission's and, consequently, to cancel, reduce or increase the fine or penalty payment imposed'.[23] Such an approach is also more in line with 'fundamental rights' considerations. Indeed, in order to comply with Article 6 (1) ECHR, the imposition of fines by an administrative body such as the Commission (rather than by a court of law) must be coupled with an appeal 'before a judicial body that has full jurisdiction, including the power to quash in all respects, on questions of fact and of law, the challenged decision'.[24] In the European Union, this task belongs to the General Court on the basis of its jurisdiction under both Articles 261 and 263 TFEU. If it is unclear whether unlimited jurisdiction that is strongly tied to the legality of the decision matches such a definition and qualifies as full jurisdiction within the meaning of the ECHR, the wider conception certainly does correspond to the case law of the ECtHR. The *Menarini* judgment[25] is evidence of this. Even though it concerns in the first place the Italian system of enforcement of competition law, its findings are highly relevant for EU competition law, in view of the strong similarities existing between both systems. Indeed, the observation that it is sufficient for the relevant court to be able to control the facts and evidence and verify whether the administration made proper use of its powers and carried out a thorough analysis of the appropriateness of the penalty to qualify as a judicial body that has full jurisdiction is equally applicable to the General Court.

In the same manner, there is no doubt as to the compatibility of such a system of enforcement of competition law with Article 47 of the Charter of Fundamental Rights. The Court of Justice has underlined:

> [t]he review provided for by the Treaties [...] involves review by the Courts of the European Union of both the law and the facts, and means that they have the power to assess the evidence, to annul the contested decision and to alter the amount of a fine [; t]he review of legality provided for under Article 263 TFEU, supplemented by the unlimited jurisdiction in respect of the amount of the fine, provided for under Article 31 of Regulation No 1/2003, is not therefore contrary to the requirements of the principle of effective judicial protection in Article 47 of the Charter.[26]

---

[23]Joined Cases C-238/99 P, C-244/99 P, C-245/99 P, C-247/99 P, C-250/99 P to C-252/99 P and C-254/99 P *Limburgse Vinyl Maatschappij and Others v. Commission* ECLI:EU:C:2002:582, p. 692; Case C-3/06 P *Groupe Danone v. Commission* ECLI:EU:C:2007:88, pp. 61–62; *Chalkor* (n 14) p. 63.

[24]See for instance *Janosevic v. Sweden* App no 34619/97 (ECtHR 23 July 2002) p. 81.

[25]*A Menarini Diagnostics SRL v. Italy* App no 43509/08 (ECtHR 27 September 2011).

[26]See *Chalkor* (n 14), p 67; *KME Germany* (n 14), p. 133; and Case C-272/09 P *KME and Others v. Commission* ECLI:EU:C:2011:810, p. 106.

## 4 Better Protection Against Potential Arbitrary Use of the Commission's Investigatory Powers

Articles 20(4) and 18(3) of Regulation 1/2003 confer on the Commission the power to compel undertakings to submit to an inspection, as well as to provide the information it requests. Such powers, exercised in the initial (preliminary) phase of an antitrust procedure, are aimed at providing the Commission with the information that may lead to the opening of a formal procedure and are consequently of fundamental importance for the enforcement of competition law. Yet their utility cannot eclipse their potential adverse consequences on the undertakings concerned. Inspections are an intrusion in the private sphere of the undertakings, and Article 20 (4) of Regulation 1/2003 allows them to be conducted without judicial authorisation. The answer to a decision requesting information must not to be taken too lightly by the undertakings concerned since it may involve a heavy workload and involves fines or penalty payments if the answer is late, incorrect, incomplete or misleading.[27]

Equilibrium must, consequently, be found between, on the one hand, the need to provide the Commission with certain leeway when it searches for information about potential violation of competition law for which it does not (yet) have a clear picture and, on the other hand, the protection of the undertakings concerned against potential abuses in the exercise of these (heavy) powers. In the judicial review of such decisions, the control of compliance by the Commission with its duty to state reasons plays a central part and reflects the search for the above-mentioned equilibrium. While accepting the principle that this duty is lighter than in relation to other decisions, particular attention is paid to the presence in the contested decision of the elements listed in Articles 18(3) and 20(4) of Regulation 1/2003.

One such element is held as 'fundamental' for the protection of the undertakings concerned: the obligation on the part of the Commission to state the subject matter and purpose of the decision.[28] In the rationale of Articles 18(3) and 20(4), this specific obligation represents a limit against potential excesses by the Commission of its powers and allows for a judicial review of such decisions.[29] Thus, in the context of a decision requesting information, the Commission is limited to require the disclosure of information that may enable it to investigate putative infringements that justify the conduct of the inquiry and are set out in the request for information.[30] In the same manner, the information searched for and collected in an

---

[27]Article 23 (1)(b) of Regulation 1/2003.

[28]See for instance the judgment of 25 November 2014 in Case T-402/13 *Orange v. Commission* ECLI:EU:T:2014:991, p. 80, in relation to inspection decisions, and the judgment of 14 March 2014 in Case T-306/11 *Schwenk Zement v. Commission* ECLI:EU:T:2014:123, p. 29, in relation to decisions requesting information.

[29]See for instance Case T-339/04 *France Télécom v. Commission* ECLI:EU:T:2007:80, p. 57.

[30]See for instance Case T-297/11 *Buzzi Unicem v. Commission* ECLI:EU:T:2014:122, p. 28.

inspection must be relevant for the subject matter and purpose of the inspection.[31] Failure in this regard leads to an annulment of the challenged decision, as the recent judgment of the Court of Justice in *Deutsche Bahn* demonstrates,[32] with the consequence that the Commission is not allowed to use the information so collected.

Moreover, it can be deduced from a clear indication of what the Commission is looking for[33] that its investigatory powers were not used in a manner contrary to the prohibition of arbitrary or disproportionate interventions in the private sphere of undertakings.[34] Yet such a review based on the drafting of the decision might not be sufficient when doubts exist as to whether the Commission did not abuse its (heavy) powers by fishing for information rather than acting on reasonable suspicion.[35]

The recent case law of the EU courts addresses this difficulty by favouring an *in concreto* scrutiny of the elements that led the Commission to use its investigatory powers. Upon request from an applicant, the General Court may order the Commission to communicate such elements and ascertain whether they justified the use of its powers. While this possibility had been contemplated for a long time by the Court of Justice,[36] it is only recently that this scrutiny has been carried out, in relation to both inspection decisions[37] and decisions requesting information.[38]

In this respect as well, the more in-depth control conducted by the General Court appears in line with the requirements of Article 6(1) ECHR since the possibility of a search of premises without prior judicial authorisation—as contemplated by Article 20(4) of Regulation 1/2003—is conditioned upon the availability of an effective ex *post factum* judicial review.[39] There is no doubt that the actual verification of the evidence on the basis of which the Commission acted reaches the relevant threshold of review.

---

[31]See the opinion of AG Kokott in Case C-37/13 *Nexans and Nexans France v. Commission* ECLI: EU:C:2014:223, p. 62.

[32]Case C-538/13 P *Deutsche Bahn and Others v. Commission* ECLIR:EU:C:2015:404, pp. 57–71.

[33]See *Orange* (n 28) p. 90.

[34]See in relation to inspection decisions Case T-135/09 *Nexans France and Nexans v. Commission* ECLI:EU:T:2012:596, p. 40, and in relation to decisions requesting information Joined Cases T-458/09 & T-171/10 *Slovak Telekom v. Commission* ECLI:EU:T:2012:145, p. 81.

[35]Opinion of AG Kokott in *Nexans and Nexans France* (n 31) p. 43.

[36]Joined Cases 97/87 to 99/87 *Dow Chemical Ibérica and Others v. Commission* ECLI:EU: C:1989:380, p. 52; Case C-94/00 *Roquette Frères* ECLI:EU:C:2002:603, pp. 54–55.

[37]*Nexans France and Nexans* (n 34) pp. 72–94 and Case T-140/09 *Prysmian and Prysmian Cavi e Sistemi Energia v. Commission* ECLI:EU:T:2012:597, pp. 70–90.

[38]Case T-296/11 *Cementos Portland Valderrivas v. Commission* ECLI:EU:T:2014:121, pp. 42–61.

[39]See for instance *Harju v. Finland* App no 56716/09 (ECtHR 15 February 2011) pp. 40 & 44; *Delta Pekárny a.s. v. the Czech Republic* App no 97/11 (ECtHR 2 October 2014); *Vinci Construction and GMT génie civil et services v. France* App no 63629/10 & 60567/10 (ECtHR 2 April 2015).

## 5 Conclusion

The reader will probably have inferred from this brief presentation that we consider that the General Court not only is well placed to act as the competition court of the EU but also exercises an appropriate level of control over the Commission's decisions.

If limits to an effective judicial review in the field of competition law exist, they must be searched for elsewhere. In a context characterised by strong emphasis on the Article 9 procedure, it could be held to be of utmost importance that the General Court is in a position to verify whether such commitments are not too detrimental to the undertakings, their competitors or consumers.

In this respect, it must be observed that in its *Alrosa*[40] judgment, the Court of Justice put considerable constraints on the level of scrutiny that the General Court can exercise in Article 9 decisions since it prevents to a large measure an examination of the proportionality of such commitments. The (very) limited review imposed on the General Court may have led to the gates of the Article 9 procedure being opened slightly too wide. This is a situation that might have detrimental effects for all parties concerned.

## References

Bailey D (2004) Scope of judicial review under Article 81 EC. CML Rev 41:1327–1360

Bernardeau L, Christienne J-P (2013) Les amendes en droit de la concurrence: pratique décisionnelle et contrôle juridictionnelle du droit de l'Union. Larcier, Brussels

Cengiz F (2011) Judicial review and the rule of law in the EU competition regime after Alrosa. Eur Competition Law J 7(1):127–153

Fritzsche A (2010) Discretion, scope of judicial review and institutional balance in European law. CML Rev 47:361–403

Jaeger M (2011) The standard of review in competition cases involving complex economic assessments: towards the marginalisation of the marginal review? J Eur Competition Law Pract 2(4):295–314

---

[40]Case C-441/07 *Commission v. Alrosa* ECLI:EU:C:2010:377. On this judgment see Cengiz (2011), p. 127.

# The Enforcement of EU Competition Law by National Courts

Jasminka Pecotić Kaufman and Siniša Petrović

**Abstract** Regulation 1/2003 is the legal instrument that has probably brought about the most important changes in the history of the application of EU competition law. It has extensively altered existing procedures for the application of what are now Articles 101 and 102 TFEU. Its importance is indicated by the direct applicability of its rules in Member States by their national competition authorities and national courts. By providing explicitly for the possibility of national courts applying Articles 101 and 102, Regulation 1/2003 has promoted the private enforcement of competition rules. The authors, inter alia, discuss basic rules on cooperation between the European Commission, national competition authorities and national courts pursuant to Regulation 1/2003 and novelties in the Directive on Actions for Damages as regards enforcement of Articles 101 and 102 by national courts. In addition, taking into account the fact that basic procedural rules indispensable for the enforcement of competition rules by national courts are not harmonised, the authors point out limitations on harmonisation in terms of not only normative rules but also legal culture and legal traditions.

## 1 Introduction

The market economy is characterised by consumers' choices and by their decisive influence over what goods will be produced and what services will be provided. The 'invisible hand' states that if each consumer is allowed to choose what to buy while each producer or service provider is free to decide what to sell, the market itself will reconcile their respective choices by distributing production and prices at the level that is most favourable to each individual and consequently to the whole community. However, in making these choices, mistakes are inherent. After all, decisions on the various available options when making choices are ultimately made by

J. Pecotić Kaufman (✉)
Faculty of Economics and Business, University of Zagreb, Zagreb, Croatia
e-mail: jpecotic@efzg.hr

S. Petrović
Faculty of Law, University of Zagreb, Zagreb, Croatia
e-mail: sinisa.petrovic@pravo.hr

© Springer-Verlag Berlin Heidelberg 2017
V. Tomljenović et al. (eds.), *EU Competition and State Aid Rules*,
Europeanization and Globalization 3, https://doi.org/10.1007/978-3-662-47962-9_3

individuals who do not always act rationally. Thus, neither are the choices they make necessarily rational. Needless to say, more often than not, human actions are also driven by emotions that influence the final choice. In everyday life and interaction with other individuals, this is fortunate because otherwise the world would be more inhumane, to say the least. Nevertheless, from the economic point of view, the market economy is still the best system that society has achieved. Historical experience proves that economic systems that do not let individuals have the decisive say in making economic choices and thus make room for the market to regulate itself, but instead empower government officials to decide what will be produced at what prices and by whom, eventually fail or are worse off. Not only do such systems get it wrong in making choices; they also make the fundamental error of not allowing individuals to choose and make erroneous choices themselves. In the long run, these wrong choices would be beneficial to individuals since they would probably not make the same mistakes again. Hence, society would also be better off in due course as it might be expected that wrong decisions would be outnumbered by correct ones. More importantly, since individuals are those who make decisions for themselves, for better or for worse, they cannot blame others for their own failures.

In a market economy, the rules of competition law play a significant role with the aim of preventing the distortion of competition in the market. Competition law thus comprises rules that restrict the actions of undertakings that are considered to be detrimental to the general welfare of consumers, competitors, competition in general and society as a whole. Competition law is probably one of the most noticeable limitations on the contractual autonomy of undertakings. Hence, competition law may fundamentally limit the freedom of choice of undertakings and at first sight be perceived as a contradiction of the basic rules of a free market. Nevertheless, it is in effect a crucial element in preserving the free market in that the freedom of an undertaking is limited by the same freedom of other undertakings. Competition law only comes into play if and when the market freedom of these other undertakings is jeopardised by the actions of the former and it is imperative to restrict these actions and thus preserve general freedom on the market. Competition law should be applied only exceptionally when the invisible hand of the market itself is not sufficient to preserve market freedoms. Thus, competition law is a vital element in maintaining the free market.

## 2 The Aims of EU Competition Law

It has been argued, and rightly so, that generally speaking consumer welfare is the most important goal of competition law (Whish and Bailey 2011, p. 19 *et seq*). Arguably, it may be stated that the ultimate function of competition law is to bring benefits to consumers even if this is not always the most visible of its features. However, there might also be other objectives of competition law, such as the redistribution of wealth, the efficient allocation of resources, free competition, an open and competitive market, the competitiveness of industry and the economy in general, economic efficiency, the protection of competitors, protecting small and medium-sized enterprises, fighting unemployment, the equal development of all the regions within a market, and the prevention of takeovers of companies by foreign investors. In addition, the rules of competition law are applied as part of a particular industrial and economic policy (Lianos 2013) and may even serve the purposes of environmental policy. In making decisions in individual cases, competition authorities may take into account not only economic and industrial policy considerations but also social policy aspects, as well as environmental and cultural benefits (Witt 2014).

In the EU context, the goal of competition law is to help create and protect the internal market and to prevent its distortion. As defined by the European Court of Justice, competition rules are necessary for the functioning of the internal market, and 'the function of those rules is precisely to prevent competition from being distorted to the detriment of the public interest, individual undertakings and consumers, thereby ensuring the well-being of the European Union'.[1] The protocol (No 27) of the TFEU on the internal market and competition clearly states that the internal market, as set out in Article 3 of the Treaty on European Union, includes a system ensuring that competition is not distorted. Article 3 TEU clearly links competition law with the internal market, stating that the Union has exclusive competence in establishing the competition rules necessary for the functioning of the internal market. Likewise, Articles 101 and 102 unambiguously associate competition rules with the functioning of the internal market.[2] Thus, an analysis of the provisions of the TEU and the TFEU mentioning 'competition' or 'competition rules' supports the conclusion that competition law and the internal market are closely related and that the goal of competition law is to ensure the functioning of the internal market.[3]

---

[1]Case C-52/09 *TeliaSonera Sverige* ECLI:EU:C:2011:83, paras 21–22.

[2]Article 101/1 states: 'The following shall be prohibited as incompatible with the *internal market*: all agreements between undertakings, decisions by associations of undertakings and concerted practices which may affect trade between Member States and which have as their object or effect the *prevention, restriction or distortion of competition within the internal market*'. Article 102 stipulates: 'Any abuse by one or more undertakings of a dominant position *within the internal market* or in a substantial part of it shall be prohibited as *incompatible with the internal market* in so far as it may affect trade between Member States' (emphasis added).

[3]See e.g. Articles 119 and 120 on economic policy. According to Article 120, '(t)he Member States and the Union shall act in accordance with the principle of an open market economy with free competition, favouring an efficient allocation of resources'. As part of the provisions of the TFEU on the approximation of laws, appropriate measures may be adopted by the EU institutions in order to ensure that competition in the internal market is not distorted: 'Where the Commission finds that a difference between the provisions laid down by law, regulation or administrative action in Member States is distorting the conditions of competition in the internal market and that the resultant distortion needs to be eliminated, it shall consult the Member States concerned. If such consultation does not result in an agreement eliminating the distortion in question, the European Parliament and the Council, acting in accordance with the ordinary legislative procedure, shall issue the necessary directives. Any other appropriate measures provided for in the Treaties may be adopted.'

# 3  Regulation 1/2003: A New Source of Competition Law or the Necessary Means for the Enforcement of the Existing Law?

## 3.1  The Context of the Adoption of Regulation 1/2003

Regulation 1/2003[4] is the measure that has probably brought about the most important changes in the history of the application of EU competition law. This legal instrument extensively altered the existing procedures for the application of what are now Articles 101 and 102 TFEU. Its importance is indicated by the direct applicability of its rules in the Member States by their national competition authorities and national courts. In this way, the European Commission lost its monopoly on applying EU competition rules in their entirety.[5]

Several reasons influenced the adoption of Regulation 1/2003. The Commission believed that the 'competition culture'[6] in Member States had sufficiently developed to allow it to trust national competition authorities to apply European competition rules. Interestingly, its first day of application was 1 May 2004, the day of the accession of ten new Member States to the EU. This arguably indicated that the European institutions, especially the Commission, believed that the national competition authorities of these Member States would be ready to apply Articles 101 and 102 in their entirety, i.e. that they had become sufficiently prepared during the pre-accession period. By providing explicitly for the possibility of national courts applying Articles 101 and 102, the Regulation also promoted the private enforcement of competition rules. Another equally important reason for the adoption of Regulation 1/2003 was the Commission's desire to relieve itself of the burden of applying Article 101(3), which until then had required undertakings to request individual exemptions from agreements. It was precisely the above-mentioned development of a competition culture and the sufficient 'competition maturity' of undertakings that made it possible to pass on to them the burden of proof that the conditions for exemption from the prohibited agreements in Article 101(3) had been met. Thus, the Commission was given more room to concentrate on tackling the most serious breaches of competition law (Monti 2014).

It is now a well-established and an undisputed rule that Articles 101 and 102 TFEU have a direct effect on relations between individuals. Consequently,

---

[4]Council Regulation (EC) No 1/2003 of 16 December 2002 on the implementation of the rules on competition laid down in Articles 81 and 82 of the Treaty (OJ 2003 L1, 4.1.2003, p 1).

[5]Until the entry into force of Regulation 1/2003 (1 May 2004), the Commission had the sole power to apply Article 101(3) TFEU, which was granted to it under Art 9 of Regulation No 17: First Regulation implementing Articles 85 and 86 of the Treaty (OJ 13, 21.02.1962, p 204).

[6]For example, see para 1 of the Preamble of Regulation 1/2003.

room was made to enforce these rights before national courts.[7] Thus, the Regulation made it possible to decentralise the application of Articles 101 and 102. However, the question is whether the Regulation also ensures a sufficient level of harmonisation in the application of these rules in the Member States, both by national competition authorities and by national courts. This paper aims to answer this question. This will be done by looking at the purpose of Regulation 1/2003,[8] the aims of competition law as set out by the TEU and TFEU, the general principles of EU law and the procedural rules for the application of the Regulation.

## 3.2 Basic Rules on Cooperation Between the European Commission, National Competition Authorities and National Courts According to Regulation 1/2003

Regulation 1/2003 contains rules that are aimed at guaranteeing the effective application of the competition rules of the TFEU by the national competition authorities of the Member States and national courts. Very broadly speaking, these rules may be categorised into four groups: (i) rules regarding cooperation between the Commission and national competition authorities, (ii) rules on cooperation among national competition authorities, (iii) rules on cooperation between national courts and the Commission and (iv) rules providing for cooperation between national courts and national competition authorities:

(i) Regulation 1/2003 requires that the Commission and the national competition authorities of the Member States apply Community competition rules in close cooperation. For this purpose, the Commission is given a pivotal role in ensuring their effective and harmonised application. This is clear from the rule prohibiting national competition authorities, when they rule on agreements, decisions or practices under Articles 101 and 102 TFEU, from taking decisions that run counter to decisions adopted by the Commission. At the same time, national competition authorities are required to consult the Commission whenever they deem it necessary to achieve the stated goal of harmonised application. The Commission and the competition authorities of the Member States have the power to provide assistance to one another on any factual or legal matter, including the providing of confidential information. When acting under TFEU competition rules, national competition authorities have to inform the Commission in writing beforehand, or without delay afterwards, when commencing an initial formal investigative measure. If the

---

[7] Case C-453/99 *Courage v Crehan* ECLI:EU:C:2001:465, para 23.

[8] As stated in the Preamble of Regulation 1/2003 (para 1), 'In order to establish a system which ensures that competition in the common market is not distorted, Articles 81 and 82 of the Treaty must be applied effectively and uniformly in the Community'.

Commission initiates a procedure to adopt a decision in accordance with the provisions of Regulation 1/2003, the competition authorities of the Member States lose their competence to apply Articles 101 and 102 TFEU. The competition authorities of the Member States must inform the Commission no later than 30 days before the adoption of a decision requiring that an infringement be brought to an end or accepting commitments or withdrawing the benefits of a block exemption regulation. To this effect, national competition authorities have to provide the Commission with a summary of the case, the envisaged decision or, in the absence thereof, any other document indicating the proposed course of action. At the request of the Commission, the competition authority must make available to the Commission any other documents it holds that are necessary for the assessment of the case. The information supplied to the Commission may be made available to the competition authorities of other Member States.

(ii) In general, national competition authorities may also exchange between themselves information necessary for the assessment of a case that they are dealing with under EU competition rules, e.g. information concerning the commencement of an initial investigative measure that needs to be taken when applying EU competition rules by a national competition authority may be made available to the competition authorities of other Member States. In addition, national competition authorities may make available a summary of the case, the envisaged decision or, in the absence thereof, any other document indicating the proposed course of action to the competition authorities of other Member States.

(iii) As for the position of national courts in relation to the Commission when applying the articles of the TFEU on competition law, it is foreseen that they may ask the Commission to transmit to them information in its possession or its opinion on questions concerning the application of Community competition rules. On the other hand, Member States are obliged to forward to the Commission a copy of any written judgment of national courts deciding on the application of these provisions of the TFEU. When national courts rule on agreements, decisions or practices under Article 101 or Article 102 TFEU that are already the subject of a Commission decision, they cannot take decisions running counter to the decision adopted by the Commission. In this respect, the position of national courts with regard to the Commission is the same as the position of national competition authorities. Where it is required to safeguard the coherent application of Article 101 or 102 TFEU, the Commission, acting on its own initiative, may submit written observations to Member State courts. With the permission of the court in question, it may also make oral observations. National courts must also avoid giving decisions that conflict with a decision contemplated by the Commission in a procedure it has initiated. To this effect, the national court may assess whether it is necessary to stay its proceedings. By all means, national courts may request the Court of Justice of the EU to give preliminary rulings under Article 267 TFEU.

(iv) Concerning the relationship between national courts and national competition authorities, the basic rule states that the competition authorities of the Member States, acting on their own initiative, may submit written observations to their national courts on issues relating to the application of Article 101 or 102 TFEU and, with the permission of the court in question, may also submit oral observations to them. For the purpose of preparing their observations only, the competition authorities of the Member States may request the relevant court to transmit or ensure the transmission to them of any documents necessary for the assessment of the case. These powers of the national competition authorities are without prejudice to the wider powers to make observations before courts conferred upon the competition authorities of Member States under the laws of a particular Member State.

With respect to these rules, several comments may be made.

Firstly, the precedence of the Commission's decisions in the application of EU competition rules (Articles 101 and 102) is clearly provided for, which is basically a reflection of the previous state of affairs when the Commission had a monopoly on applying such rules. Although national competition authorities are encouraged to apply Articles 101 and 102, and the whole system envisaged by Regulation 1/2003 is aimed at a decentralised application of these rules, in cases when the Commission has already taken a decision, the decision is binding on national competition authorities. The Commission is also entrusted with a type of supervisory role over national competition authorities, either by stating its opinion or at least by being informed of pending cases before national competition authorities.

Secondly, it may basically be concluded that any obligation of a national competition authority vis-à-vis the Commission can simultaneously be regarded as a possible course of action towards other national competition authorities (e.g., supplying information on particular cases). This also reflects the Commission's primary role in the effective and coherent application of European competition law.

Thirdly, the position of the national competition authority of a Member State towards the national courts of that Member State is similar to the position of the Commission with regard to the possibility of submitting written and oral observations. However, while the Regulation unambiguously states that courts cannot take decisions running counter to a decision adopted by the Commission and that they must avoid making decisions that conflict with a decision contemplated by the Commission in a procedure it has initiated, the decisions of a national competition authority do not have such a binding effect on the national courts of the same Member State. It is possible that such rules are foreseen by national law, but the Regulation itself does not deal with the issue. Nevertheless, this obvious gap in ensuring the coherent application of European competition rules is, to a large extent, overcome by the Directive on damages.[9]

---

[9]Directive 2014/104/EU of the European Parliament and the Council of 26 November 2014 on certain rules governing actions for damages under national law for infringement of the competition law provisions of the Member States and of the European Union (Text with EEA relevance), OJ L 349, 5.12.2014, p. 1.

Fourthly, the Regulation does not specifically address the issue of whether the decisions of national competition authorities are binding on their national courts (Pecotić Kaufman 2012, p. 7 *et seq*).[10] It is only stated that the competition authorities of Member States may on their own initiative submit written observations to their national courts and submit oral observations with the permission of the court in question. The Regulation does not state anything about such a possibility for national competition authorities before the national courts of other Member States. Consequently, according to the provisions of Regulation 1/2003, national courts are bound only by the authority and persuasiveness of their respective national competition authorities.

# 4 Novelties in the Directive on Actions for Damages

This crucial aspect of the effect of decisions of national competition authorities is nevertheless dealt with explicitly by the Directive on actions for damages,[11] which obliges Member States to ensure that an infringement of competition law established by a final decision of a national competition authority or by a review court is deemed to be irrefutably established for the purposes of an action for damages brought before national courts under Article 101 or 102 TFEU or under national competition law. Thus, the final decisions of national competition authorities are binding on the national courts of that Member State. At the same time, it is important to note that the decisions of the national competition authorities of other Member States do not have the same effect. Member States only have to ensure that the decisions of the national competition authorities of other Member States may be presented before national courts as at least prima facie evidence that an infringement of competition law has occurred and, as appropriate, may be assessed along with any other evidence adduced by the parties.[12] While these rules are a significant step forward from Regulation 1/2003 by giving binding effect to the decisions of national competition authorities in cases before their national courts, it is obvious that when adopting the Directive, Member States were not ready to give such effect to the decisions of the national competition authorities of other Member States.

Recital 3 of the Directive basically repeats what is said in Recital 7 of Regulation 1/2003, i.e. that national courts have an essential part to play in applying competition rules and that they protect subjective rights under Union law, e.g. by awarding damages to the victims of infringements. However, the emphasis is now on the right

---

[10]The paper primarily deals with general enforcement issues in one country, but some points regarding the binding effect of decisions of competition authorities are valid for any Member State.

[11]Directive 2014/14/EU of the European Parliament and of the Council of 26 November 2014 on certain rules governing actions for damages under national law for infringements of the competition law provisions of the Member States and of the European Union (OJ L 349, 5.12.2014, p. 1).

[12]Article 9 of the Directive on actions for damages.

to compensation and the 'full effectiveness' of Articles 101 and 102 TFEU. Anyone can claim compensation before national courts for the harm caused to them by an infringement of these provisions. It is interesting to observe how the power to apply EU law in the area of competition law, especially Article 101, once in the domain of the Commission, is now dispersed throughout the EU via national courts. In this sense, we may call this a 'democratisation' in the application of EU rules. Many challenges arise in this context, particularly national judges being asked to know, understand and apply EU competition rules, and rule on complex cases such as damages actions arising from the infringement of competition rules. The question remains how effective justice and a level judicial playing field can be obtained throughout the EU taking into account so many differences, not only in a normative sense but also in terms of judicial traditions and customs, i.e. legal cultures and mentality. In many countries where the judicial system has suffered from a decades-long lack of normal democratic processes, so many challenges remain in providing effective justice in 'usual' cases that it is questionable what plaintiffs that have suffered harm from an infringement of competition law can achieve in starting such complex cases with national courts. However, the Directive on actions for damages in this sense gives not only an obligation for normative harmonisation but also an incentive for national judicial systems to provide effective judicial solutions in this regard. The Court of Justice has played an important part in establishing key principles that have been incorporated and elaborated upon in legislative acts such as Regulation 1/2003 and the Directive on actions for damages. Now, the focus has shifted from this highest instance to the numerous national judicial fora that will have to adjudicate in concrete cases where plaintiffs claim antitrust damages.

## 5  General Principles of EU Law Relevant to the Application of Competition Law

The exclusive competence of the EU to establish competition rules necessary for the functioning of the internal market[13] may be perceived as a metaphor of the importance that the EU institutions confer on competition law, particularly taking into account the economic origins of the EU and the consequent central role of the internal market. This is the reason why the EU institutions, most importantly the Commission, originally had a monopoly on applying Articles 101 and 102 TFEU.

With the adoption of Regulation 1/2003 and the decentralisation of the application of these rules, in order to ensure that competition law is appropriately applied not only by EU institutions but also by national competition authorities and national courts, the general principles of EU law are important: the primacy of European

---

[13] Article 3(1)(b) TFEU.

law, the principle of conferral, the principles of subsidiarity and proportionality, the duty to cooperate and the principle of effectiveness.

It is stated that in accordance with the well-established case law of the Court of Justice of the European Union, the Treaties and the law adopted by the Union on the basis of the Treaties have primacy over the law of Member States under the conditions laid down by the said case law.[14]

Under the principle of conferral, the Union acts only within the limits of the competences conferred upon it by the Member States in the Treaties to attain the objectives set out therein. Competences not conferred upon the Union in the Treaties remain with the Member States.[15]

Pursuant to the principle of sincere cooperation, the Union and Member States, in full mutual respect, assist each other in carrying out tasks that flow from the Treaties. The Member States take any appropriate measure, general or particular, to ensure the fulfilment of the obligations arising out of the Treaties or resulting from the acts of the institutions of the Union. The Member States facilitate the achievement of the Union's tasks and refrain from any measure that could jeopardise the attainment of the Union's objectives.[16]

Under the principle of subsidiarity, in areas that do not fall within its exclusive competence, the Union acts only if and in so far as the objectives of the proposed action cannot be sufficiently achieved by the Member States, either at the central level or at the regional and local levels, but can rather, by reason of the scale or effects of the proposed action, be better achieved at Union level. Under the principle of proportionality, the content and form of Union action do not exceed what is necessary to achieve the objectives of the Treaties. The institutions of the Union apply the principles of subsidiarity and proportionality as laid down in the Protocol on the application of the principles of subsidiarity and proportionality.[17]

Under the principle of effectiveness, Member States provide remedies sufficient to ensure effective legal protection in the fields covered by EU law.[18] The EU has for this purpose created an institutional framework that aims to promote its values, advance its objectives and serve its interests, those of its citizens and those of the Member States and ensure the consistency, effectiveness and continuity of its policies and actions.[19] Most straightforwardly, the Directive on actions for damages states that, in accordance with the principle of effectiveness, Member States must ensure that all national rules and procedures relating to the exercising of claims for damages are designed and applied in such a way that they do not render practically impossible or excessively difficult the exercise of the right to full compensation for

---

[14]Declaration 17 concerning primacy annexed to the final act of the intergovernmental conference which adopted the Treaty of Lisbon, signed on 13 December 2007.

[15]Article 5(2) TEU.

[16]Article 4(3) TEU.

[17]Article 5(3–4) TEU.

[18]Article 19(1) TEU.

[19]Article 13(1) TEU.

harm caused by an infringement of competition law. In addition, in accordance with the principle of equivalence, national rules and procedures relating to actions for damages resulting from infringements of Article 101 or 102 TFEU may not be less favourable to the alleged injured parties than those governing similar actions for damages resulting from infringements of national law.[20]

## 6 The Functioning of National Judicial Systems and the Application of Competition Law Rules in Practice: Pilot Field Study

In the context of decentralised application of competition rules in the EU, it becomes important how national judicial systems function, i.e. whether they are fit to apply these rules in an effective manner, providing legal certainty and ensuring consistency of EU antitrust rules as applied across the EU. In 2014, a pilot study commissioned by DG Justice[21] (Pilot field study on the functioning of the national judicial systems for the application of competition law rules) collected data on the functioning of national judicial systems in the application of EU competition law rules, in particular on the number of incoming, pending and resolved cases in which Articles 101 and 102 TFEU had been applied, as well as the duration/length of proceedings per instance. The views of a representative group of stakeholders (parties, practitioners and judges, and representatives of consumers, professionals and businesses) were also gathered, especially with regard to the efficiency, quality and independence of national judicial systems when applying EU competition rules. The study covered both cases of public enforcement and cases of follow-on private enforcement of competition rules further to decisions of the Commission or of national competition authorities (covering all instances of review).

It is clear from the study that the competent national courts for competition law vary among Member States, with most Member States providing for judicial review actions in two different instances and with some allowing judgment in a third instance. In addition, in some Member States (Portugal, Sweden, UK), specialised courts exist for dealing with judicial reviews, while in others (e.g., Austria, Bulgaria, Belgium) specific chambers have exclusive competence for ruling on competition law cases.[22]

In contrast with judicial review actions, Member States do not organise follow-on actions centrally, and neither do specialised or exclusive courts exist in the

---

[20]Article 4 of the Directive on actions for damages.

[21]Pilot field study on the functioning of the national judicial systems for the application of competition law rules. Available at http://ec.europa.eu/justice/effective-justice/files/final_report_competition_and_eu_28_member_states_factsheets_en.pdf. Accessed 4 July 2015.

[22]Pilot field study, pp. 11–12.

majority of Member States, with civil and commercial courts having competence over such cases, with all Member States providing for follow-on actions to be heard in at least two instances.[23]

The burden of proof varies in Member States, depending on whether the action is a judicial review or follow-on proceedings. As far as judicial reviews are concerned, in the majority of Member States the burden of proof is on the applicant, in the sense that they need to show an error in the decision of the national competition authority, while in other Member States the burden of proof is on the national competition authority, which has to show that there has indeed been a breach of competition rules. The level of proof can also differ among Member States. In contrast to judicial reviews, in follow-on actions, all Member States place the burden on the applicant to demonstrate that an action should be brought.[24]

The time frame for lodging judicial review cases varies between Member States. With regard to judicial review cases in the first instance, the time limitation varies from 14 days following the date of notification/publication of the decision (Bulgaria) to 75 days (Cyprus) following publication of the decision. In the second instance, it ranges from 14 days from the publication of the judgment (Bulgaria) to three months (Belgium) following the notification of the judgment. In comparison to other Member States, applicants in the UK have two years to file an action for judicial review. For follow-on cases, Member States apply general civil and commercial law provisions for the recovery of damages, with a time limitation for lodging claims in the first instance significantly longer than for an appeal in the second instance.

Interim measures in competition cases can be issued by the national competition authorities when undertaking an investigation, as well as by the competent court for dealing with judicial reviews and follow-on actions. Interim measures issued by courts in judicial review cases can be implemented in Member States in order to suspend the effects of a decision, with the suspension measure and conditions relating to its implementation varying among Member States.[25] In follow-on cases, injunctive relief is applied as an interim measure in all Member States, although different conditions apply among them for awarding injunctions (the urgency of the claim, the need to avoid imminent/irreparable harm and the need to protect a specific legal right).

For court hearings, Member States adopt varying practices depending on the instance of the case, as well as on whether the case relates to a judicial review or follow-on proceedings. For judicial reviews, oral hearings are not the norm in a small number of Member States where written submissions are used (Austria, Czech Republic, Denmark, Slovenia), while in the majority of Member States the judicial review process is a mixture of both written and oral submissions, with at

---

[23]Pilot field study, p. 16.

[24]Pilot field study, p. 21.

[25]Pilot field study, pp. 26–28.

least one hearing initiated in each instance. For follow-on actions, oral and public hearings are the norm in Member States.[26]

Provisions are in place in Member States for enforcing judgments relating to follow-on actions through enforcement measures, including compulsory enforcement through executory orders/deeds/writs, delays in execution of judgment, execution of judgment (e.g., payment) in part, writs of movables, writs of sale of land and writs of attachment.[27]

The Alternative Dispute Resolution (ADR) mechanisms existing in Member States are not specific to competition law matters, and the use of ADR in competition law cases varies significantly among Member States.[28] In some Member States, modes of alternative dispute resolution are generally available, but it is questionable as to whether ADR is really used.

The field pilot study gives a comparative analysis of the key features of competition law cases and the length of legal proceedings. Two different time spans have been chosen for data collection: data relevant for the period 1 May 2004 to 1 June 2013 (since the entry into force of Regulation 1/2003) and more recent data for the period 1 January 2008 to 1 June 2013. In the 2004–2013 period, a total of 1,044 Article 101 and 102 resolved cases were identified (each of these represents a judgment on the merits of a single instance). The total number of so-called full cases is 740. It is important to stress that the numbers do not include cases in which national competition authorities applied national competition rules having a similar purpose to that of Articles 101 and 102 TFEU but without applying in parallel the corresponding TFEU rules. The number of Article 101 cases is 738 (546 full cases), the number of Article 102 cases 247 (164 full cases) and combined 101 and 102 cases 59 (37 full cases). In most Member States (17), the majority of cases are based on Article 101 TFEU. In five Member States, cases were identified that concerned both Articles 101 and 102. In the 2008–2013 period, a total of 870 cases were identified (651 full cases), of which 629 are Article 101 cases (485 full cases), 199 are Article 102 cases (140 full cases) and 42 are Article 101 and 102 cases (29 full cases). In 17 Member States, the majority of cases concern Article 101, while in four Member States there were cases that jointly applied Articles 101 and 102.[29] The above figures show that it took several years after the coming into force of Regulation 1/2003 before judicial activity intensified in terms of the application of Articles 101 and 102 at the national level (more than two-thirds of all resolved national cases in the 2008–2013 period).

Between 1 May 2003 and 1 June 2013, the vast majority of cases identified concerned judicial review and/or public enforcement. This can in part be explained by the fact that follow-on cases are more difficult to identify.[30] Out of 1,044 total

---

[26]Pilot field study, p. 28.

[27]Pilot field study, p. 29.

[28]Pilot field study, pp. 29–30.

[29]Pilot field study, pp. 31–34.

[30]Pilot field study, p. 35.

cases (740 full cases), 208 were private enforcement (follow-on) cases (147 full cases) and 836 were public enforcement (judicial review) ones (593 full cases). Between 1 January 2008 and 1 June 2013, out of a total of 870 cases (651 full cases), 154 concerned private enforcement (follow-on) (125 full cases) and 752 were public enforcement cases (judicial review) (526 full cases). Particularly high shares of follow-on actions were identified in Austria, Finland, Germany, Sweden, the Netherlands and the UK.[31] The above results show that the proportion of private enforcement cases (follow-on cases) did not change when comparing the two periods (2004–2013 and 2008–2013), which seems to allow the conclusion that private enforcement did not intensify with time.

Analysis of the length of proceedings reveals that there is a great difference in nearly all Member States between the shortest and the longest judicial proceedings. The longest average duration of cases is reported in Finland, Denmark and Ireland, and the shortest average duration is for Austria, Bulgaria, Latvia and Lithuania. At the same time, the low number of relevant data for follow-on cases is statistically unreliable, so it is not possible to reach any conclusion.

In the majority of judicial reviews, the defendants were national competition authorities, while in follow-on actions the vast majority of defendants were large companies. In both judicial review cases and follow-on actions, the applicants were mostly large companies, followed by SMEs, while in some countries consumers or consumer associations were involved as applicants. These are not surprising results for both judicial review cases and follow-on action cases.

Information about the costs of proceedings could be retrieved from only 15 Member States. Costs include state and court fees, legal costs and other costs. As for the costs of state and court fees, the highest amounts are charged by courts in Germany, Hungary, France, Portugal and the Netherlands. The highest legal fees were those determined by courts in the UK, Sweden, Finland and Denmark.

Intervention by *amicus curiae* is extremely rare; the European Commission intervened in one case in each of Austria, Lithuania and Slovakia and three times in France, while a national competition authority intervened once in Belgium, twice in Lithuania and three times in Spain.[32]

The study also includes an analysis of feedback on the efficiency, quality and independence of the national judicial systems based on an online survey for parties involved in proceedings involving the application of EU competition law, an online survey for national judges competent in the application of EU competition law and an online survey for legal practitioners involved in proceedings before national courts involving the application of EU competition law.[33] Since the surveys were addressed to the addressees of competition law and those who are supposed to apply the law, it would definitely be interesting to know their views on some of the crucial issues regarding the application of EU law by the national courts. However, due to

---

[31]Pilot field study, p. 37.
[32]Pilot field study, pp. 73–74.
[33]Pilot field study, p 75 *et seq.*

the very low percentage of answers received in comparison to the number of surveys sent out, reliable conclusions cannot be drawn.

## 7 Lack of Harmonisation in Procedural Law for Enforcement

At the outset, it is important to stress that basic procedural rules indispensable for the enforcement of competition laws and their application by national courts are not only contained in European legal instruments designed specifically for competition law, foremost in Regulation 1/2003 and more recently in the Directive on actions for damages. Procedural rules are also part of the national laws of Member States, which are not harmonised to any great extent at the European level. This is specifically true for general procedural laws valid in civil and/or commercial proceedings, which are to a large extent the exclusive domain of Member States. The issues mentioned here are not an exhaustive list of differences between national laws, but rather they serve an illustrative purpose.

Regulation 1/2003 gives the Commission, acting on its own initiative, explicit power to adopt decisions ordering interim measures in cases of urgency due to the risk of serious and irreparable damage to competition. Similarly, national competition authorities may, acting on their own initiative or upon a complaint, make decisions ordering interim measures. However, the Regulation does not provide for specific preconditions for such decisions,[34] except a very general rule that such decisions shall be made in cases of urgency due to the risk of serious and irreparable harm to competition. Undoubtedly, standards in ordering interim measures are different in various Member States. True, it would be difficult to harmonise these standards since rules on interim measures are always on purpose very general to make room for discretion in ordering such measures, basing decisions on all the relevant circumstances.

Regulation 1/2003 establishes rules concerning the powers of the Commission and national competition authorities of Member States in acting before national courts. At the same time, it is expressly stated that these rules are without prejudice to the wider powers to make observations before courts conferred on the competition authorities of Member States by the laws of these states.[35] This latter provision obviously takes into account that Member States have different rules on this issue. The question is whether these different rules might cause different decisions in national courts due to the wider or narrower powers of the respective national competition authorities to bring actions before their national courts, irrespective of what kind of proceedings are involved, whether it is a review case of the decision of

---

[34] Article 5 of Regulation 1/2003.
[35] Article 15 of Regulation 1/2003.

a national competition authority or a stand-alone or follow-on action for damages initiated by a private party.

As far as the effects of the decisions of national competition authorities are concerned, it has already been mentioned that national courts are bound by the decisions of the Commission and by the national competition authorities of that Member State but not by the decisions of the national competition authorities of other Member States. The final decision of the latter may, in accordance with national law, be presented before national courts as at least prima facie evidence that an infringement of competition law has occurred.[36] These rules, in conjunction with possible different national rules regarding the involvement of the national competition authorities of other Member States before a national court, as explained above, may indeed result in different standards in the application of EU competition rules by national courts.

Unquestionably, the duration and costs of proceedings are ultimately important points that need to be taken into account when assessing whether an enforcement system is functioning and whether it is user friendly. The duration of proceedings differs significantly in various Member States, and consequently it is all about the speed of the justice served. Lengthy proceedings discourage parties from initiating them, and thus it is all about the decision in which forum to commence an action for damages, if there is an opportunity to make such a choice, depending on the appropriate national legislation and/or European legal instruments. In addition, long-lasting proceedings may significantly increase the costs that can be extremely high anyway. Costs entail not only court and state fees but also legal fees, which especially in competition cases may be significant. Hence, costs could also be considered as a 'business' limitation on the starting of actions by undertakings before national courts. In follow-on actions, this limitation is to some extent eliminated by the Directive on actions for damages requiring Member States to adopt provisions in their national legislation that give a binding effect to the final decisions of national competition authorities in proceedings before national courts establishing infringements of competition law.

On the other hand, it is even conceivable that undertakings may attempt to abuse their right to initiate actions before courts by relying on the foreseen length of proceedings and the subsequent costs for defendants that may not be in a position to bear them. In this case, it is possible that stand-alone actions are in themselves considered as abusive. The General Court concurred with the view of the Commission, confirming its position that 'in principle the bringing of an action, which is the expression of a fundamental right of access to a judge, cannot be characterised as an abuse' unless 'an undertaking in a dominant position brings an action (i) which cannot reasonably be considered as an attempt to establish its rights and can therefore only serve to harass the opposite party, and (ii) which is conceived in the framework of a plan whose goal is to eliminate competition'.[37]

---

[36]Article 9 of the Directive on actions for damages.

[37]Case T-111/96 *ITT Promedia v Commission* ECLI:EU:T:1998:183, para 30.

## 8    Further Harmonisation Needed?

Lack of full harmonisation of the national procedural rules of Member States for enforcement is not limited to competition matters but is omnipresent in other areas of law. The length of proceedings and their cost are definitely not issues that can in any way be confronted only from the competition law aspect. Their harmonisation would require overall substantive reforms in all Member States, and it is highly debatable whether Member States would be ready for such huge steps and the intrusion of European law into their exclusive domain in judicial proceedings.

Besides this, there are limitations on harmonisation not only in legal rules but also in legal culture (Koziol 2013, p. 303), legal tradition and probably even (legal) mentality.

On the other hand, the essentially negative effects of non-harmonisation are limited by the general principles of the application of European law and the general rules of European law regarding access to justice.[38]

The basic question is, however, whether further harmonisation is at all necessary or desirable. To address the issue in the correct manner, one has to bear in mind that the fundamental goal of competition law in the EU is to ensure the functioning of the internal market and to prevent the distortion of competition. In addition, the general principles of European law must be considered, and it must be determined if they make room for any further harmonisation of procedural rules. It is true that competition law issues are the exclusive competence of the Union, which would in itself be sufficient to uphold the view that further harmonisation is within the powers of EU institutions. Nevertheless, the further harmonisation we are referring to is not confined to issues related to competition law but encompasses comprehensive national procedural rules within the competence of Member States. Ultimately, the underlying point at issue is evaluating whether the principles of effectiveness and equivalence in the application of competition rules may be accomplished without further harmonisation.

Finally, even if the view is that further harmonisation is necessary as a principle, the problem might be what the legal basis for harmonising procedural rules could be since in accordance with the principle of national procedural autonomy, administrative and judicial procedures are the competence of Member States (Cseres 2010, p. 30 *et seq*). The basis for the harmonisation of procedural rules might be Article 114 TFEU, which empowers the European institutions to adopt measures for the approximation of provisions laid down by laws, regulations or administrative actions in Member States which have as their object the establishment and functioning of the internal market. Another possible basis might be Article 81 TFEU, which allows for the adoption of measures for the approximation of laws of Member States necessary for judicial cooperation in civil matters having cross-border implications, provided that these measures are necessary for the proper functioning of the internal market. In both instances, one would have to prove

---

[38]Article 47 of the Charter of Fundamental Rights of the European Union.

that the harmonising instrument was indispensable and that without its adoption the functioning of the internal market might be in jeopardy.[39]

# References

Cseres K (2010) Comparing laws in the enforcement of EU and national competition laws. Eur J Leg Stud (3)1:7–44

Koziol H (2013) Harmonising tort law in the European Union: Advantages and difficulties. Available via Elte Law Journal. http://eltelawjournal.hu/harmonising-tort-law-in-the-europe an-union-advantages-and-difficulties/. Accessed 13 June 2015

Lianos I (2013) Some reflections on the question of the goals of EU competition law, CLES Working Paper Series. Available via London's Global University. https://www.ucl.ac.uk/cles/ research-paper-series/index/edit/research-papers/cles-3-2013. Accessed 1 July 2015

Monti G (2014) Independence, interdependence and legitimacy: The EU Commission, national competition authorities, and the European competition network, EUI Working Papers, Law 2014/01. Available via European University Institute. http://cadmus.eui.eu/bitstream/handle/ 1814/29218/LAW_2014_01.pdf?sequence=1. Accessed 15 June 2015

Pecotić Kaufman J (2012) How to facilitate damage claims? Private enforcement of competition rules in Croatia: domestic and EU law perspective. Yearb Antitrust Regul Stud 7(5). Available via SSRN. http://papers.ssrn.com/sol3/papers.cfm?abstract_id=2277147. Accessed 10 June 2015

Whish R, Bailey D (2011) Competition law. Oxford University Press, Oxford

Witt A (2014) Public policy goals under EU competition law: Now is the time to set the house in order, University of Leicester School of Law Research Paper No. 14-09. Available via SSRN. http://papers.ssrn.com/sol3/papers.cfm?abstract_id=2407962. Accessed 9 June 2015

---

[39]E.g. Case T-526/10 *Inuit Tapiriit Kanatami and Others v European Commission* ECLI:EU: T:2013:215, paras 28, 29, 35.

# Judicial Review in EU and Croatian Competition Cases: The Procedure and Intensity of Judicial Review

**Dubravka Akšamović**

**Abstract** This article provides an overview of judicial review in competition cases in EU and Croatian competition law cases. It discusses the substantive standard of review, summarises the procedural issues in judicial review and summarises some of the key considerations relevant for potential applicants and parties in competition law cases.

## 1 Introduction

This article examines the procedural rules and standards of judicial review applied in EU and Croatian competition law cases. In the first part of the paper, the article will describe the results of detailed research on proceedings before the General Court in EU competition cases under the new rules of procedure adopted by the General Court in July 2015. The research supports the hypothesis that procedural safeguards are a perquisite for effective judicial protection of the litigant's rights in this forum. Procedural guarantees, together with the ability to go to court to vindicate substantive rights, constitute fundamental rights and call for unconditional enforcement. The new Rules of Procedure aim at speeding up proceedings, bring consistency and clarity in proceedings before the Court and thus improve the efficiency of the Court and strengthen the Court's capacity to deal with cases within reasonable time frames and in accordance with the requirements of a fair trial.

In the second part, the article will briefly reflect on judicial review in competition cases in Croatia. Competition law in Croatia is a recent development. Despite the successful implementation of this relatively new branch of law and a generally satisfactory enforcement policy, it seems that judicial review in competition cases does not follow European trends. In Croatia, only a small number of judicial decisions are available for study. Additionally, the success ratio in competition cases is rather low and far below the European average in the same type of cases.

---

D. Akšamović (✉)
Faculty of Law, University of Osijek, Osijek, Croatia
e-mail: daksamov@pravos.hr

© Springer-Verlag Berlin Heidelberg 2017
V. Tomljenović et al. (eds.), *EU Competition and State Aid Rules*,
Europeanization and Globalization 3, https://doi.org/10.1007/978-3-662-47962-9_4

Statistical analysis conducted in the EU shows that the success ratio against Commission decisions in competition cases is approximately 44.9%.[1] In a number of cases, the European Court has annulled or overruled Commission decisions, concluding that the Commission has committed a procedural error or come to the wrong conclusion based on incorrect findings of fact. This seems to prove that judicial review in EU competition cases is not 'a mere formal rubber stamping exercise'.[2]

Contrary to the trend in EU cases, it seems that judicial review in competition cases in Croatia is often purely a formality. The High Administrative Court, which is in charge of the judicial review of Croatian Competition Agency (CCA) decisions, has so far not demonstrated a serious ability to challenge CCA decisions based on rational and justified arguments. Thus, the High Administrative Court has not yet proven its ability to assert sufficient independent judicial authority to ensure effective judicial protection. In this sense, analysis of European court jurisprudence, new procedural principles and the standard of review in relation to competition law cases can be useful guidance for Croatian courts in defining or shaping their own standards of judicial review in competition law cases and providing fair, transparent and effective judicial protection for transactions affected by CCA decisions.

## 2 The Importance of Judicial Review in Relation to Competition Law Cases

Judicial review is of vital importance to any system respecting the rule of law. In connection with competition law cases, the enforcement structure of EU competition law, but also certain policy considerations, makes judicial review in this field of law essential.[3]

The European Commission is entrusted with broad, almost unlimited powers in relation to enforcement of EU competition law rules. The Commission conducts investigations and decides on opening proceedings, infringements and also fines. Thus, in the EU system, it is the mission of the courts to ensure that the Commission does not overstep the powers that it is entrusted with. EU courts must ensure that procedural due process is observed and that the underlying substantive principles of competition law are applied in a correct and consistent manner. The effectiveness of judicial review is even more important in view of the recent development of alternative enforcement procedures, which in general enable the Commission to forego full establishment of the infringement of competition rules while the parties waive part of their procedural rights. In such a context, allowing a full reconsideration of the sanctions and remedies imposed by the Commission is crucial for the Community legal order.[4]

---

[1]Tridimas and Gari (2010).
[2]Fox and Trebilcock (2012), p. 401.
[3]Geradin and Petit (2010).
[4]Van Beal (2011), p. 327.

Another function of judicial review and the European courts in connection with competition law concerns the implementation of competition policy. Competition laws are written broadly, and judicial precedent is a particularly important source of law in the interpretation of general treaties, norms and overall EU competition policy. Simultaneously, the courts ensure the consistent interpretation and application of treaty rules in light of their systematic function and legally defined goals and thereby ensure equal treatment and legal certainty in competition law enforcement at the EU level.[5] This aspect of judicial enforcement can be especially important to the newest EU Member States that have only recently enacted a competition law, such as Croatia.

The judiciary also brings a certain degree of flexibility to the implementation of competition law, thus enhancing the development of the law and the application of current economic thinking.[6] In enforcing competition rules, the Commission relies heavily on economic analysis. A large number of competition cases rely on *ex post* circumstantial evidence. For that reason, there is a great risk of error in Commission decisions with forward- looking application to developments in a particular market. For example, it might be extremely difficult to predict the growth of the market share of competing firms or to determine whether potential competitors will actually enter a market and thus influence the state of future competition in that market. In this sense, judicial review offers a crucially important opportunity to correct the adverse effect of misguided economic decisions on welfare.[7]

Finally, since competition law can directly interfere with fundamental rights,[8] it is the task of the courts to ensure that fundamental procedural rights, including privacy rights, the right to a fair and impartial hearing and other procedural rights, are sufficiently protected.

# 3 Types of Action and Legal Grounds for Judicial Review in Competition Law Cases

There are three main types of action before the EU General Court, each of which has its own characteristics: direct actions, actions in the field of intellectual property and appeals against decisions of the Civil Service Tribunal. Actions against Commission decisions in competition law cases fall into the category of direct actions. The Rules of Procedure define direct actions as those brought on the basis of Article 263 TFEU, 265 TFEU, 268 TFEU or 272 TFEU.[9] Commission decisions in

---

[5]Schweitzer (2012).

[6]Judicial Enforcement of Competition Law (1996) OECD, Paris, p 10. Available via OECD. http://www.oecd.org/daf/competition/prosecutionandlawenforcement/1919985.pdf. Accessed 3 Nov 2015.

[7]Geradin and Petit (2010), p. 12.

[8]E.g. see Geradin and Petit (2010), pp. 8–16.

[9]Rules of Procedure of the General Court [2015] OJ L 105/1. Article 1(2)(i).

competition cases are usually challenged by virtue of Article 263 TFEU. Article 263 of the Treaty allows the Court of Justice to review the 'legality of acts' of the EU institutions, other than recommendations or opinions, which are intended to produce legal effect vis-à-vis third parties. Actions brought under Article 263 TFEU are commonly referred to as actions for annulment. Through this action, the claimant requests the annulment of a Commission decision.

According to Article 263, the claimant can request an annulment of a Commission decision based on the following grounds: (a) lack of competence, (b) infringement of an essential procedural requirement, (c) infringement of the Treaties or of any rule relating to their application or (d) misuse of power. If the Court finds that the action for annulment is well founded, it declares the act concerned to be void.[10] This means that when the Court's decision turns on Article 263 TFEU, the Court has no authority to replace the Commission's decision with its own. It can annul the whole decision or only part of the decision. In the latter case, the Court, if it considers it necessary, states which of the effects of the decision that it has declared void shall be considered as definitive.

Unlike Article 263, whose main purpose is so-called control of legality, Article 261 of the Treaty gives the Court much broader powers in connection with Commission decisions concerning fines. According to Article 261 TFEU, the courts of the EU enjoy the discretion to cancel, reduce or increase the amount of fines or periodic penalty payments initially imposed by Article 261 TFEU and to replace the Commission's decision with their own.

The Treaty provisions establish goals and principles enabling judicial review of administrative decisions, including competition law cases. The goals and principles are stated generally. Thus, gap filling is often left to secondary legislation and to the jurisprudence of the Court. The most relevant source of secondary EU competition law for general competition law is Council Regulation 1/2003, particularly Article 31 of the Regulation. Article 31 of the Regulation is a copy of Article 261 of the Treaty. It gives the Court unlimited jurisdiction to review Commission decisions on fines. The same rule is contained in Article 16 of Council Regulation 139/2004 for fines imposed by the Commission in merger cases.

Finally, an important source of law in competition law cases is the European Court's jurisprudence. Since the European Court deals with institutional, procedural and substantive competition law issues, it is stated, with good reason, that the Court is the ultimate rule-maker in EU competition law cases. The whole system of judicial enforcement in competition cases is entrusted to two courts: the General Court and the Court of Justice. Whereas the General Court is responsible for reviewing at first and last instance the factual circumstances underlying a decision of the Commission in competition cases, the Court of Justice serves as the first and last level appeal court for General Court decisions. As mentioned in the introduction, the procedure before the General Court is regulated by the recently adopted General Court Rules of Procedure.[11] The following section will provide an

---

[10]Article 264 TFEU.
[11]Rules of Procedure of the General Court [2015] OJ L 105/1.

overview of the relevant steps of the procedure before the General Court in competition law cases according to the new rules.

# 4 Procedure Before the General Court According to the 2015 Rules of Procedure

The procedure before the General Court takes its inspiration from that followed by national courts. The General Court procedure constitutes a new, independent legal order of its own. Two factors, in particular, distinguish proceedings before the Court from those before national courts. Firstly, proceedings before the Court are governed by strict rules contained in European legislation (the Treaty, the protocol on the Statute of the Court and the Rules of Procedure). Secondly, proceedings before the Court are subject to rules on the use of language appropriate to a multilingual Community, a fact that influences the nature and the purpose of the procedure.

The procedure before the General Court is divided into two phases, written and oral. The written procedure is the core phase of procedure. The purpose of the written procedure is an exhaustive account of the facts, pleas and arguments of the parties and the forms of order sought. During the written procedure, the parties exchange procedural documents and present the defence. After the written procedure, the oral part of the procedure follows. An oral argument is not obligatory. The Court decides whether the procedure before the Court will include an oral hearing.[12]

The 2015 Rules of Procedure brought certain changes in connection with both the written and oral procedures before the General Court, in particular in connection with the service of documents, the length of written pleadings, replies and rejoinders, the modification of applications, the rules of confidentiality concerning documents during inquiry and others that will be addressed later in the text.

## 4.1 Commencement of the Written Procedure and Procedural Formalities

The written procedure starts with lodging the application at the General Court. The application must contain information about the applicant and the defendant, the subject matter of the dispute, a summary of the pleas in law on which the application is based, the evidence relied upon and the form of order sought by the applicant.[13]

---

[12] Article 106 of the Rules of Procedure of the General Court [2015] OJ L 105/1.

[13] Article 76 of the Rules of Procedure of the General Court [2015] OJ L 105/1.

It is important that the application is written clearly and that all the required documents are lodged. The General Court will reject as inadmissible an application lacking in precision or clarity[14] or where there is a lack of evidence or a failure to satisfy other formal requirements. For example, in determining whether an application was sufficiently clear and precise, the Court explained in *Fluorsid SpA and Minmet Financing Co. v. European Commission* that 'even though the applicants did not state expressly that their actions were in actual fact directed at two legally distinct decisions, addressed to two different legal persons respectively, the fact remains that it is sufficiently clear and precise from the application that the applicants sought to contest, and seek the annulment of those two decisions in so far as they adversely affected them'.

Article 263 TFEU establishes the parties' deadline for submitting an application. For cartel cases or merger decisions (acts requiring formal notice to the parties), the deadline is two months and ten days from the date of notification. This time limit is fixed, absolute and may not be extended.[15]

An application should not exceed 50 pages[16] (25 pages for the reply and the rejoinder). The limitation on the length of written submissions is aimed at preventing parties from lodging exceedingly long applications since often, particularly in cartel cases, applications exceed 300 pages, including annexes. Despite this limitation, the Rules of Procedure allow exceptions. The President of the General Court may authorise a party to exceed the maximum length of written pleadings in cases involving complex legal or factual issues. Cartel and merger cases regularly fall into this category.

According to the new Rules, an application can be lodged in one of the following ways: by e-curia, by fax or by post. An application by e-mail is no longer possible. A case is considered lodged when an application, drawn up by a lawyer,[17] is sent to the Registry. Parties in cartel and merger cases must be represented by an agent or lawyer. Parties that cannot afford a lawyer are entitled to apply for legal aid.

---

[14]See Order of 20 January 2012, T-315/10 *Groupe Partouche v. European Commission* ECLI:EU: T:2012:21.

[15]See T-404/08 *Fluorsid SpA and Minmet financing Co. v. European Commission* ECLI:EU: T:2013:321, para 53. See also T-291/04 *Enviro Tech Europe and Enviro Tech International v. Commission* ECLI:EU:T:2011:760, para 95.

[16]Article 75 of the Rules of Procedure prescribes that the General Court shall set, in accordance with Article 224, the maximum length of written pleadings. In a document published by the General Court called Practice Direction to the Parties, it is stated that depending on the subject matter and the circumstances of the case, the maximum number of pages for the application and defence shall be 50 pages. See: Practice Direction to the Parties adopted by the General Court [2007] OJ L 232/7, and the amendments to it (Amendments to the Practice Directions to Parties [2009] OJ L 184/8; [2010] OJ L 170/49; [2011] OJ L 180/52). However, the Rules of Procedure of the General Court in Article 75(2) prescribe that authorisation to exceed the maximum length of written pleadings may be given by the President only in cases involving particularly complex legal and factual issues.

[17]Article 43 of the Rules of Procedure prescribes that every pleading must be signed by the party's agent or lawyer, leaving no possibility for parties to lodge a pleading by themselves.

However, parties cannot represent themselves before the Court. Once an application has been properly lodged, the Registry will communicate a case number to the parties. The lodging of the application will appear on the Court's website within a few days of its complete filing with an indication of the case number and the names of the main parties (i.e., the applicant and defendant). A few months later, the main points of the action will be published in a notice in the Official Journal of the European Union.

An applicant must serve the application on the defendant. The defendant must file a response within two months of the date of delivery. After the defendant responds, the applicant may supplement the application by filing a reply. The defendant may also file a rejoinder, unless the General Court decides that a second exchange of pleadings is unnecessary because the filings are sufficiently comprehensive. In at least one recent cartel case (*Airfreight*), the General Court, having established that the case file was comprehensive enough to enable the parties to elaborate their pleas and arguments in the course of the oral procedure, in accordance with Article 47(1) of the Rules of Procedure, decided that a second exchange of pleadings was unnecessary. The General Court rejected the request for a submission of further documents to supplement the application for annulment and the defence under Article 47(1) of the Rules of Procedure and, in particular, to submit a reply to the Commission's defence. Finally, in connection with the above, it is important to add that the President of the Court may also specify the matters to which the reply or the rejoinder should relate.

The Rules of Procedure further prescribe that during the written procedure, parties are not entitled to introduce new pleas in law unless they are based on matters of law or fact that come to light in the course of the procedure.[18] Whether and when a particular matter constitutes a 'fresh issue' may be the subject of debate. For example, in *AKZO*, the point was made in the application that the case handler had acted *ultra vires* when he had warned AKZO in a telephone conversation that he would organise another dawn raid concerning a different product line if AKZO were to contest the statement of objections rather than settle the matter and pay damages to the plaintiff. In view of the fact that the Commission, in its statement of defence, was actually backing the conduct of its officials, AKZO made the argument in its reply brief that the Commission had committed a misuse of powers. The Court dismissed the argument because it considered it to be a fresh issue that had not come to light in the course of the written procedure.[19]

The parties must submit all the evidence they wish the court to consider in the first exchange of pleadings.[20] In exceptional circumstances, the main parties may produce or offer further evidence in support of their arguments, provided that the delay in the submission of such evidence is justified. When the parties have exchanged briefs, the written part of the procedure is closed. The judge-rapporteur

---

[18]Article 84 of the Rules of Procedure of the General Court [2015] OJ L 105/1.

[19]Van Beal (2011), p. 345.

[20]Article 85 of the Rules of Procedure of the General Court [2015] OJ L 105/1.

must prepare a preliminary report for the General Court. A preliminary report must contain an analysis of the relevant issues of fact and law raised by the action and explain whether and which measures of organisation or inquiry should be undertaken during the oral procedure. The judge-rapporteur will also propose to the Court whether to open the oral part of the procedure or not.

## 4.2 Oral Procedure

Once the written procedure has been completed, the Court will decide, based on the judge-rapporteur's opinion, whether to conduct an oral hearing. The new Rules of Procedure provide the Court with increased discretion to decide whether to conduct an oral hearing.[21] The General Court's current practice is to conduct oral hearings. However, according to Article 106(3) of the Rules of Procedure, the Court may decide to rule on a direct action without an oral part of the procedure: (a) if main party doesn't request hearing or (b) if the Court has sufficient informations available to decide based on the materials in the file.

The request for a hearing may be made by a primary party. The party requesting the hearing must state the reason for the request. A primary party's deadline to request an oral hearing is within three weeks after the servicing of the notification of the close of the written part of the procedure on the parties.[22] The General Court can also decide to hold an oral hearing on its own motion. There are at least two good reasons why an oral hearing is considered necessary before the General Court. For instance, in proceedings where there is only one round of written observations, the oral hearing provides the first and only opportunity for the parties involved to personally comment upon the written observations made by others. In addition, parties can clarify the forms of order sought, their pleas and arguments and the points at issue between them during an oral hearing.[23] They may also examine expert witnesses.[24] Second, a decision not to hold an oral hearing may also raise issues of a fundamental rights nature.[25] Article 6 of the European Convention on Human

---

[21] Article 87(3) of the Rules of Procedure states that the: 'General Court shall decide . . . whether to open the oral part of procedure'.

[22] Article 106(2) of the Rules of Procedure of the General Court [2015] OJ L 105/1.

[23] For more, see Rosas (2014).

[24] The ECJ raised an interesting point on parties' rights (requests) to examine witnesses in competition proceedings in Joined Cases C-239/11 P, C-489/11 P, C-498/11 P *Siemens v. Commission* ECLI:EU:C:2013:866. Siemens claimed under Articles 6(1) and 3(d) ECHR that it had the right to examine witnesses and that the General Court should have of its own motion given the opportunity to Siemens to question a specific witness. The Court of Justice confirmed that it is established in its jurisprudence that during the administrative procedure, the Commission is not required to afford the opportunity to examine witnesses. In addition, it is for the parties, not the General Court of its own motion, to request to examine incriminating witnesses. The right is also not absolute, as it is left to the General Court's discretion to grant or deny the request, which is compatible with Articles 6 and 3 ECHR.

[25] See Bernatt (2014).

Rights states that '[i]n the determination of his civil rights and obligations or of any criminal charge against him, everyone is entitled to a fair and public hearing within a reasonable time by an independent and impartial tribunal established by law'. In competition law cases, which apart from administrative law aspects (which are the predominant feature) also involve certain elements of criminal law,[26] there is a right of appeal on points of law only, which puts the onus on the organisation of an oral hearing before the General Court.[27] However, according to the Court's recent practice, an oral hearing is more often the rule than the exception.

### 4.2.1 The Course of the Oral Hearing

The Court will determine in advance the course of an oral hearing based on the judge-rapporteur's report deciding what measures of organisation and/or measures of inquiry it will take. In some cases, the parties may be asked before the hearing to provide more particulars of the forms of order sought by them and of their pleas in law in order to clarify obscure points or to examine in greater detail issues that have not been adequately explained.

The judge-rapporteur also prepares the Report for the Hearing to be sent to each party's lawyer or agent and to interested parties or other participants in the proceedings about three weeks before the hearing. After receiving the Report for the Hearing, the parties are invited to check the Report for errors. It must, however, be emphasised that the Report for the Hearing is, by its very nature, a report presented by the judge-rapporteur to the members of the Court and that it is for him to decide whether it needs to be amended.[28]

The oral proceedings are opened and directed by the president, who is responsible for the proper conduct of the hearing.[29] Parties may address the General Court only through their legal representative.[30] Before the hearing commences, the Court invites the parties' representatives to a brief meeting in order to settle arrangements for the hearing.[31] As a rule, the hearing starts with an oral argument from the parties'

---

[26]The European Court of Human Rights in its recent judgment in *Menarini Diagnostics S.r. l. v. Italy* (43509/08) considered that the fine imposed on an Italian company by the independent AGCM administrative authority and the *Consiglio di Stato* for unfair competition on the market for a diabetes diagnostic test was a criminal penalty, and that as a result the criminal limb of Article 6 (1) ECHR was applicable. See European Court of Human Rights, Information Note on the Court's Case-Law, August/September 2011.

Available via ECHR. http://www.echr.coe.int/Documents/CLIN_2011_09_144_ENG_894208. pdf. Accessed 5 Nov 2015. See further: Bellamy (2012), Forrester (2011), Lenaerts (2006).

[27]Rosas (2014), pp. 604–605.

[28]See Notes for the Guidance of Counsel, Court of Justice of the European Communities, 2009, p. 22. Available via Curia. http:/www.curia.europa.eu. Accessed 5 Nov 2015.

[29]Article 110(1) of the Rules of Procedure of the General Court [2015] OJ L 105/1.

[30]Article 110(2) of the Rules of Procedure of the General Court [2015] OJ L 105/1.

[31]Notes for the Guidance of Counsel, Court of Justice of the European Communities, 2009, p. 23.

representatives. As a general rule, the period initially allowed to each primary party is limited to a maximum of 20 min. An exception to this rule may be allowed by the Court in order to put the parties on an equal footing.[32] However, experience shows that the time allowed for oral arguments is generally sufficient.[33]

The oral argumentation of the parties' representatives is followed by questions from the members of the Court. The members of the Court frequently interrupt the parties' representatives when they are speaking in order to clarify points that appear to them to be of particular relevance. The hearing concludes, if necessary, with brief responses from those parties' representatives who wish to make them.

Once the oral hearing is closed, it can be reopened for two reasons. First, the oral part of the procedure is reopened upon the request of a primary party if during the hearing a quorum of the Grand Chamber is not attained or is lost.[34] Second, the oral part of the procedure may be reopened by order of the General Court (a) if it decides that it lacks sufficient information, (b) where the case must be decided on the basis of an argument that has not been debated between the parties, (c) where requested by a primary party that is relying on facts that are of such a nature as to be determinative but that it was unable to put forward before the oral part of the procedure was closed. Judges deliberate after the hearing. During deliberations, the judges agree on what the ruling for the case should be. The reporting judge is then responsible for drafting the judgment in due course and circulating it for confirmation to the other judges of the chamber of the case. After the hearing, the parties are informed of the date of the delivery of the judgment. Subject to the provisions of Article 60 of the Statute of the Court, the judgment is binding from the date of its service.

The General Court's decision is subject to appeal to the Court (ECJ). According to available statistics, approximately 30% of cartel cases have been appealed to the ECJ. As mentioned in the introduction, the success ratio against Commission decisions in competition cases before the General Court is rather high, around 45%. The success ratio of other cases appealed to the ECJ and decided upon is around 25%,[35] which is also not a negligible amount. These statistics also confirm that both courts, the General Court and ECJ, conduct serious and exhaustive reviews of Commission decisions.

---

[32]Notes for the Guidance of Counsel, Court of Justice of the European Communities, 2009, p. 25.

[33]Notes for the Guidance of Counsel, Court of Justice of the European Communities, 2009, p. 25.

[34]Article 113 of the Rules of Procedure in connection with Articles 23(3) and 24(3) of the Rules of Procedure.

[35]More accurate and complete data may be reviewed in Tridimas and Gari (2010). See also Cassels (2011); see further in Camesasca et al. (2013).

## 5   The Scope of Judicial Review in Competition Cases: Full Versus Limited Judicial Review

Probably one of the most controversial issues in connection with judicial review in competition law cases is the scope of judicial review. The problem arises in connection with the intensity of the judicial review of the substantive legality of the Commission's competition law decisions. The general approach, intrinsic to the classical concept of judicial review and which applies across all areas of Community law, is to the effect that the essential role of the judge is to control the 'legality' of the decisions of the administration.[36] In this sense, the question is what does 'control of legality' entail? Does control of legality, as prescribed in Article 263 of the Treaty, mean 'full judicial review' or 'limited judicial review'? Is the Court, based on Article 263 of the Treaty, entitled to re-examine the case on its merits? How fact intensive should judicial control be?

The scope of review problem to some extent also arises from the different powers exercised by the Court when it hears competition cases based on Article 263 or 261 of the Treaty. As mentioned earlier in the paper, there are two ways of challenging Commission decisions in competition cases: by virtue of Article 263 of the Treaty and by virtue of Article 261 of the Treaty. The general standard of judicial review under Article 263 of the Treaty is the so-called control of the *legality* of Commission decisions. According to the well-established case law, the Court has no power under Article 263 of the Treaty to substitute a Commission decision submitted for review with its own decisions or to substitute its own economic assessments for those of the Commission. Rather, if the action is well founded, the act concerned must be declared void. In this sense, the Court can only affirm or declare the Commission's decision void and cannot make a decision that directs a specific result. On the other hand, Article 261 of the Treaty gives the Court unlimited jurisdiction when deciding on fines. According to Article 261 of the Treaty, the Court can annul Commission decisions on fines, amend sanctions and increase or reduce them. Thus, when it comes to the appropriateness of the amount of the fine imposed, the EU courts exercise *de novo* review: they can amend the Commission's decision, assessing the factors taken into account differently when calculating the amount of the fine (the gravity and duration of the infringement).[37]

This dual approach with respect to the Court's powers in competition law cases in connection with the application of Articles 263 and 261 of the Treaty has revealed significant uncertainties regarding important dimensions of judicial review[38] concerning the application of Article 263 of the Treaty. It is not quite clear if the Court, based on Article 263 of the Treaty, is entitled to go beyond the 'formal' review of administrative decisions. Certain conclusions on the scope of

---

[36]Forwood (2009), p. 4.

[37]Bernatt (2014), p. 6.

[38]Schweitzer (2012), p. 2.

judicial review can be drawn from case law,[39] namely from cases such as *Ahlström Osakeyhtiö*,[40] *Rhône-Poulenc*[41] or the more recent decisions in *Tetra Laval*,[42] *Microsoft*,[43] *Menarini*[44] or *Posten Norge*.[45] However, it seems that a dilemma in connection with the extent or intensity of judicial review still exists and that 'the intensity of control [exercised by the EU courts over the Commission's decisions] varies depending on whether the Courts are reviewing the correctness of the facts, or the correct application of the law or the correctness of the Commission's appreciation of complex economic matters'.[46]

Questions of law are subject to full and comprehensive judicial review.[47] The European courts review whether the Commission's decision is based on a correct interpretation of EU competition law rules. This coincides with the Union courts' mandate to 'ensure that in the interpretation and application of the Treaties, the law is observed (Art. 19(1) TEU)'.[48] In this sense, the Commission enjoys no margin of discretion when it comes to the interpretation of EU law.

The principle of full judicial review also applies to the facts and to the application of the law to the facts.[49] As Judge Vesterndorf puts it: 'Control of primary facts by the CFI is intensive and . . . there is no margin for discretion on the part of the Commission. This is inherent in the nature of a control of the accuracy of facts. Either a fact is correct or it is not.'[50] The Court will examine whether the facts on which the Commission has based its decision are correct and complete, whether the facts have been accurately stated and whether there has been any manifest error of assessment. The Court also has to ensure that the Commission has respected its duty to state its reasons for a decision.[51] The result is that every year we see many Court judgments dissecting Commission decisions in minute detail.[52] However, it is generally accepted that certain limits exist in connection with the correctness of the Commission's appreciation of complex economic matters. The courts recognise that the Commission has expertise and experience in economic or technical matters. This means that it is not expected that the Court will conduct *de novo* reviews of complex economic analysis.[53]

---

[39]See: Ezrachi (2014), pp. 526–529.

[40]Case C-89/85 *Ahlström Osakeyhtiö and Others v. Commission* ECLI:EU:C:1988:447.

[41]Case T-1/89 *Rhône-Poulenc v. Commission* ECLI:EU:T:1991:56.

[42]Case C-12/03 P *Commission v. Tetra Laval* ECLI:EU:C:2005:87.

[43]Case T-201/04 *Microsoft v. Commission* ECLI:EU:T:2007:289.

[44]*Menarini Diagnostics S.r.l. v. Italy* [2011] ECHR 43509/08.

[45]Case E-15/10 *Posten Norge AS v. EFTA Surveillance Authority* [2012] EFTA Ct Rep 246.

[46]Geradin and Petit (2010), p. 19.

[47]See Schweitzer (2009). See also Ratliff (2009) and Laguna de Paz (2011).

[48]Schweitzer (2012). See also Schweitzer (2009) and Geradin and Petit (2010).

[49]Schweitzer (2009), p. 12.

[50]Vesterndorf (2007), p. 21.

[51]Ratliff (2009), p. 4.

[52]Ratliff (2009), p. 5.

[53]The situations that can be objectively considered complex economic matters have been the subject of several academic debates. See Laguna de Paz (2011). See also Bellamy (2012).

On the other hand, the Commission's possession of superior technical resources does not mean that the Court must decline to review the Commission's interpretation of economic or technical data. As stated in the *Microsoft* case, the 'Courts must not only establish whether the evidence put forward is factually accurate, reliable and consistent but also must determine whether that evidence contains all relevant data that must be taken into consideration in appraising a complex situation and whether it is capable of substantiating the conclusion drawn from it',[54] and '[t]he review of complex economic appraisal made by the Commission is necessarily limited to checking whether the relevant rules on procedure and on stating reasons have been complied with, whether the facts have been accurately stated and whether there has been any manifest error of assessment or misuse of powers'.[55] It thus seems clear that, in matters deemed to be 'complex economic assessments', the Court has so far accorded a degree of deference to the Commission.[56]

Legally, the Court is empowered to engage in fact-finding of its own in the course of its review. However, in most cases, the Court does not make use of that power. Instead, it carefully reviews the information in the files and inquires whether the facts adduced by the Commission are reliable, consistent and sufficiently meaningful in the light of the substantiated challenge by the applicant.[57] In some (or most) cases, such an approach will provide for a sufficient level of judicial protection. However, we should emphasise that in some cases, this may not be enough. If the Court is not involved in fact gathering and if it is looking at the same set of facts, then the Court can only second-guess the Commission's fact-gathering process and base its judgment on the known facts. Since judicial review (among other things) increases the legality of the administrative process and protects against arbitrariness, it would be more appropriate that the Court exercises full reviews and conducts *de novo* decision-making in competition law cases more frequently instead of limiting its review to checking on the correctness of the Commission's findings and conclusions.

## 6   Judicial Review in Croatian Competition Cases

EU law generally, but EU competition law in particular, has an important influence on the internal law of EU Member States. For Croatia, which is the newest EU member and which is still in the process of transformation from a non-market model to a market model economy, proper enforcement of competition law is particularly important. It might minimise private and even public abuse of power

---

[54]Case T-201/04 *Microsoft v. Commission* ECLI:EU:T:2007:289, para 89.

[55]Case 42/84 *Remia BV and Others v. Commission* ECLI:EU:C:1985:32, para 34. Cited also in Case T-201/04 *Microsoft v. Commission* ECLI:EU:T:2007:289, para 87.

[56]Bellamy (2012), p. 3.

[57]Schweitzer (2009), p. 13.

and anomalies regularly connected with the transition from one economic model to another.

Competition law in Croatia has existed since 1995. The Croatian Competition Agency (CCA), charged with implementing competition law and policy, was established in 1995. It started work in 1997 and since then has become the uncontested authority in the area of competition law enforcement to that extent that the role of the courts in this area of law is often overshadowed and marginalised compared to the role of the CCA. However, growing awareness about the importance of competition law and policy for the Croatian economy has resulted in the growing interest of scholars and practitioners in the effectiveness of judicial control in competition law cases. A discussion has emerged about whether the judicial review provided for in the Croatian legal system is broad and intense enough to ensure a sufficient degree of protection for private transactions, in particular the right to due process and a fair trial. In addition, it has also generally been accepted that an efficient judiciary and reliable and enforceable local law and procedures are perquisites for a healthy economy and for it to attract investment from both home and abroad.

The following paragraphs are dedicated to the procedure before the Croatian High Administrative Court in competition law cases, the effectiveness of judicial review and the standard of judicial review.

## 6.1   The High Administrative Court: The Main Judicial Instance in Competition Law Cases

Judicial control in competition law cases in Croatia is conducted by the High Administrative Court. The High Administrative Court is the highest judicial instance in administrative matters. However, in competition law cases, it has original jurisdiction in challenges to the Commission's acts. The jurisdictional authority of the High Administrative Court in competition law cases derives from two laws. The first is the Competition Act, which is *lex specialis* in competition cases and which regulates all the most important aspects of judicial review in competition cases before the High Administrative Court, such as grounds for review, types of CCA acts that can be challenged, *locus standi* (who can bring an action), time limits and standards of review. The second law from which the High Administrative Court derives its jurisdictional authority is the Administrative Disputes Act, which in competition cases is applied as the general law (*lex generalis*), regulates procedure before the Court, specifies the content of a complaint and governs the Court's decisions and remedies.

Proceedings before the High Administrative Court are of an administrative review nature. The administrative procedure in the Croatian legal system was initially modelled after French administrative law. Thus, as in French law, and now in EU law, the main focus of judicial review before the High Administrative

Court is 'control of legality'. However, in January 2010, the Croatian Parliament passed a new Administrative Disputes Act, which entered into force in January 2012. The enactment of the new law was just one of a series of measures aimed at modernising Croatian administrative law and the administrative judicature.[58] Although, according to the new Administrative Disputes Act, 'control of legality' continues to be the main aim of administrative procedure, the new act changed to a certain extent the scope and character of the adjudication of administrative disputes. New procedural rules prescribe the obligation of the Administrative High Court to conduct an oral hearing in the first instance, save in exceptional cases defined by law.[59] In addition, the new procedures allow the Court to independently determine the facts, which was not previously the case. In connection with competition law cases, this means that the High Administrative Court, which in competition cases acts as the first instance court, must conduct an oral hearing, which until now has rarely been the case. In competition cases, this rule may significantly contribute to the better protection of individuals' rights in administrative disputes. By enacting these changes, Croatia also harmonised its legislation with EU legal standards, in particular with Article 6 of the European Convention for the Protection of Human Rights.

## 6.2   Procedure Before the High Administrative Court in Competition Law Cases

Proceedings before the High Administrative Court start with lodging a claim. According to Article 67(1) of the Competition Act, there are four grounds for a claim: (1) misapplication or erroneous application of substantive provisions of competition law, (2) manifest errors in the application of procedural provisions, (3) incorrect or incomplete facts of the case and (4) an inappropriate fine and other issues contained in the decisions of the Agency. Besides the basis for the claim, the content of the claim and the standard course of proceedings are regulated by the Administrative Disputes Act. A claim as a legal remedy against a CCA decision must be lodged within 30 days of receipt of the decision.[60]

However, it is necessary to emphasise that not all CCA acts can be challenged. The CCA issues two types of acts in competition cases: decisions and procedural

---

[58]For more, see Koprić (2011), Đulabić (2014).

[59]Article 36 of the Administrative Disputes Act states that the Court may resolve a dispute with a decision without holding a hearing: 1. if the respondent acknowledges the statement of claim in full; 2. in a case where the adjudication is based on a final judgment rendered in a model dispute; 3. if the court establishes that a particular decision, action or administrative contract is defective so that it prevents an assessment of its lawfulness; 4. if the complainant disputes only the application of substantive law, if the facts of the case are indisputable, and if the parties in the complaint or in the response to a claim do not make a request to hold a hearing.

[60]Article 67(1) Croatian Competition Act.

orders. A CCA measure qualifies as a decision if it is intended to produce legal effects and brings about a distinct change in the legal position of the claimant. This would be, for example, a decision that levies a fine, a decision establishing an infringement or a decision imposing a remedy, such as an injunction. On the other hand, procedural orders are considered to be interlocutory and cannot be directly appealed. Article 67(2) of the Competition Act states that procedural orders can only be challenged when the CCA reaches a final decision on the merits of a claim, for example a decision that establishes an infringement of the Act and/or imposes fines.[61] Making a claim automatically imposes a stay on the effectiveness of the CCA decision.[62] It postpones the enforcement of the decision of the CCA until the High Administrative Court decides on the issue.

The Administrative Disputes Act prescribes strict rules regarding the contents of a claim (lawsuit). In addition to the standard elements that every claim must have, such as information about the parties and case, reasons for the lawsuit, etc., the claim (lawsuit) must include the direction and scope of the proposed annulment and, above all, the Administrative Disputes Act prescribes that it must be written in an understandable way. If the Court finds that the claim is not understandable, it will dismiss the lawsuit. On the other hand, if the Court finds that the claim is justified and that the other formal procedural requirements have been satisfied, such as time limits, *locus standi*, justiciability, etc., it will commence proceedings.[63]

Standing or *locus standi* is another issue that deserves closer examination since the Competition Act precisely defines who has *locus standi* and who can lodge a claim against a CCA decision.[64] According to the Competition Act, a claim against a CCA decision can be lodged by an injured party to the proceedings that is at least partly directly affected by the CCA decision (an undertaking or association of undertakings). A claim may also be filed by an interested third party that is not a party to the proceedings but that is granted certain procedural rights,[65] as defined in Article 38(3) of the Competition Act.[66] In competition cases, the claim is presided over by a panel of three judges.

---

[61] Article 67(1) of the Croatian Competition Act.

[62] Article 67(4) of the Croatian Competition Act.

[63] Articles 27–30 of the Administrative Disputes Act.

[64] Article 4(5) of the Act on Amendments to the Competition Act.

[65] This is the person who initiated the opening of proceedings before the Agency.

[66] Any of the following may initiate proceedings falling within the scope of the Agency: a natural person, professional association, economic interest group, trade group, consumer association, the Government of the Republic of Croatia, central administration authorities or local and regional self-governmental units. Proceedings are initiated by means of a written document, request, proposal, notice or complaint.

## 6.3 Extent of Judicial Review and Remedies in Competition Law Cases in Croatian Law

Once the claim has been brought, its effectiveness is inextricably linked to the intensity of the Court's review, that is to say, the extent of the review carried out by the Court. The extent of the review in competition cases in Croatia depends on two elements: (1) the contents of the claim and (2) the legal boundaries prescribed by the Competition Act. In connection with the first element, Article 31 of the Administrative Disputes Act prescribes that '[t]he Court shall decide within the boundaries of the claim, but is not bound by the grounds of the complaint'. This means that the Court has the authority to decide only on the issues that the claimant brought in its claim. Said in a different way, the Court is not entitled to address issues that the claimant did not raise in the claim. However, the Court is not bound by the grounds of the complaint.[67] In administrative proceedings in Croatia, (1) a claimant may ask the Court to annul a contested CCA decision because it is illegal, or (2) it may ask the Court to decide on the merits of the claim. If the Court establishes that a decision of the CCA is null and void, the Court adopts the statement of claim and declares the decision null and void.

On the other hand, if the claimant requests the Court to decide the claim on its merits, and if the Court finds the claim justified, it accepts the claim, nullifies the dispute decision and resolves the matter itself. This means that the Court's decision replaces the CCA decision. Unlike in EU law, the Court has the authority to substitute its decision for the Agency's in all infringement actions, not just with regard to fines as in EU law. However, so far, the High Administrative Court in Croatia has never made such a decision.

Concerning the scope or intensity of judicial review in cases other than competition cases, Article 33 of the Administrative Disputes Act empowers the Court to freely assess evidence and determine the facts. The Court must consider all the evidence offered in the process of adopting the disputed decision, by which it is not bound, as well as the facts that the Court established itself. From this, we may conclude that the High Administrative Court is in a position to conduct 'unlimited control of the legality' of contested decisions. However, Article 33 does not apply to competition because Article 68 of the Competition Act provides that '[t]he panel of judges of the Administrative Court of the Republic of Croatia shall discuss and decide on the basis of the facts presented in evidence during the proceedings'. Therefore, the Court is not entitled to determine new facts during court proceedings in a competition case. In addition, the plaintiff may not present new facts in

---

[67]For example, if the grounds for the claim are the misapplication or erroneous application of the substantive provisions of competition law and the Court finds that there have not been errors in the application of the substantive provisions of competition law, but on the other hand the Court finds that during proceedings before the CCA that the procedural rights of the parties have been infringed, the Court will annul the contested decision, but not for the reasons raised by the claimant, but for the reasons determined by the Court during proceedings. See: Đerđa and Šikić (2012), p. 195.

evidence but may propose new evidence relating to facts that have been presented in evidence during proceedings.[68] New facts may be presented only under the condition that the plaintiff demonstrates that such evidence could not have been obtained or the facts could not have been known at the time of the proceedings.[69] Consequently, the High Administrative Court in Croatia has much less power in connection with the intensity (or scope) of judicial review than the European Court. The European Court, as described earlier in this article, is entitled to conduct a full review of law and facts whenever it finds it necessary.

Another limitation in connection with the issue just addressed arises from the fact that there is no appellate review of High Administrative Court judgments because in competition cases, the High Administrative Court acts as a court of original jurisdiction. Under the current legislation, a party dissatisfied with a High Administrative Court judgment has no right to further recourse. The only legal remedy against a High Administrative Court judgment is to request the extraordinary examination of the legality of the final decisions of the administrative court or the High Administrative Court.[70] However, such a request cannot be lodged directly by the parties. A request for extraordinary examination of the legality of final decisions may be filed only by the State Attorney's Office of the Republic of Croatia within 6 months of the day the party receives notice of the final judgment.[71] This means that the parties in an administrative dispute must propose to the State Attorney's Office of the Republic of Croatia that it file a request for extraordinary examination of the legality of the final decision of the administrative court or the High Administrative Court. The State Attorney's Office may decide to file the request, but it may also decide not to file it. The State Attorney's Office of the Republic of Croatia may also file the request on its own initiative without waiting for a request. The request is filed with the Supreme Court of the Republic of Croatia, which in a panel composed of five judges decides on the request. If the Supreme Court of the Republic of Croatia adopts the request, it may annul the judgment and remand the case for a new decision or reverse the judgment.

# 7   Conclusion

Judicial review in competition law is of crucial and ever-increasing importance for the proper enforcement of competition law at both the European and national levels. The combination of the investigative, prosecutorial and decision-making powers in

---

[68] Article 68(2) of the Competition Act.

[69] Article 68(3) of the Competition Act.

[70] Article 78 of the Administrative Disputes Act.

[71] A request for extraordinary examination of legality is an interesting Croatian peculiarity in the Administrative Disputes Act. This is a remedy of last resort against a decision of the High Administrative Court which is 'proposed' by the State Attorney's Office to the Supreme Court of the Republic of Croatia. The Supreme Court has to decide on such an appeal. It is entitled to annul the judgment and remand the case for a new decision 'or reverse the judgment'.

the hands of the European Commission has to be compensated for by a sufficient level of judicial control of administrative decisions. Undertakings are entitled to expect a consistent approach in connection with the scope of judicial review and a fair and impartial judicial and/or administrative process, while the Court is under the obligation to apply the substantive competition law standards to the facts of a particular case fairly and in a predictable manner and to ensure procedural safeguards.

Analysis of the Court's jurisprudence shows that European jurisprudence has been in a state of constant change with respect to the issue of the appropriate standard of judicial review to be applied to competition cases, particularly in connection to the application of Article 263 of the Treaty. Although it is subject to debate whether the Court should conduct a full or restrictive control of the legality of a Commission decision, there is no doubt that the Court applies a demanding standard of review of Commission decisions, including with respect to issues of 'complex economic appraisals'.

We should expect the same or a similar approach from the national courts of EU Member States. However, contrary to the implementation of general competition law rules, where there is an obligation of Member States to harmonise legislation with the *acquis communautaire*, such an obligation does not exist in connection with judicial review. The standard of judicial review of administrative decisions at the national level (at least in Croatian law) is determined by national administrative law provisions. Thus, there may be significant differences in connection with procedure and the standard of judicial review in judicial proceedings before the EU courts and before the courts of Member States.

Analysis of Croatian legislation in connection with procedure before the High Administrative Court and the standard of judicial review in competition cases shows that the procedure before the High Administrative Court does not meet the standard of review applied by the European courts. The High Administrative Court of the Republic of Croatia reviews the same set of facts on which the CCA bases its decision. The High Administrative Court of the Republic of Croatia, contrary to the European courts, is not entitled to conduct a *de novo* review. This may be the most important (but not the only) reason for the low success ratio in competition cases before the High Administrative Court of the Republic of Croatia.

# References

Bellamy C (2012) ECHR and competition law post Menarini: an overview of EU and national case law. e-Competitions, No 47946, 5 July 2012. Available via Antitrust Writing Awards 2016. http://awa2013.concurrences.com/business-articles-awards/article/echr-and-competition-law-post. Accessed 5 Nov 2015

Bernatt M (2014) The compatibility of deferential standard of judicial review in the EU competition proceedings with Article 6 of the European Convention on Human Rights. Institute for Consumer Antitrust Studies Working Papers, Loyola University Chicago. Available via SSRN. http://papers.ssrn.com/sol3/papers.cfm?abstract_id=2447884. Accessed 13 Sept 2015

Camesasca P, Ysewyn J, Weck T, Bowman B (2013) Cartel appeals to the Court of Justice: the song of the Sirens? J Eur Competition Law Pract 4(3):215–223

Cassels J (2011) Appealing EU cartel decisions: prospects for success. Available via Fieldfisher. http://www.fieldfisher.com/publications/2011/11/appealing-eu-cartel-decisions-prospects-for-success#sthash.7Nr24Xho.dpbs. Accessed 15 Nov 2015

Đerđa D, Šikić M (2012) Komentar Zakona o upravnim sporovima. Novi informator, Zagreb

Đulabić V (2014) New wine in old wineskins: general administrative procedure and public administration reform in Croatia. Međunarodna revija za javnu upravu 12(2–3):183–197

Ezrachi A (2014) EU competition law: an analytical guide to the leading cases. Hart, Oxford

Forrester I (2011) A challenge for Europe's judges: the review of fines in competition cases. Eur Law Rev 36(2)

Forwood N (2009) The commission's more economic approach: implications for the role of the EU courts, the treatment of economic evidence and the scope of judicial review. European University Institute, Florence

Fox E, Trebilcock M (2012) The design of competition law institutions, global norms, local choices. Oxford University Press, Oxford

Geradin D, Petit N (2010) Judicial review in EU competition law: a quantitative and qualitative assessment. TILEC Discussion Paper, DP 2011-008

Koprić I (2011) Contemporary Croatian public administration on the reform waves. Godišnjak Akademije pravnih znanosti Hrvatske 2(1):1–40

Laguna de Paz JC (2011) Judicial review in European competition law. Available via University of Oxford, Faculty of Law. https://www.law.ox.ac.uk/sites/files/oxlaw/judicial_review_in_european_competition_law.pdf. Accessed 21 Sept 2015

Lenaerts K (2006) Some thoughts on evidence and procedure in European community competition law. Fordham Int Law J 30(5):1463–1495

Ratliff J (2009) Judicial review in EC competition cases before the European courts: avoiding *double renvoi*. European University Institute Robert Schuman Centre for Advanced Studies, 2009 EU Competition Law and Policy Workshop/Proceedings. Available via European University Institute. http://www.eui.eu/documents/rscas/research/competition/2009/2009-competition-ratliff.pdf. Accessed 15 Sept 2015

Rosas A (2014) Oral hearings before the European court of justice. Maastricht J Eur Comp Law 21 (4):596–610. Available via Maastricht Journal. http://www.maastrichtjournal.eu/pdf_file/ITS/MJ_21_04_0596.pdf. Accessed 1 Sept 2015

Schweitzer H (2009) The European competition law enforcement system and the evolution of judicial review. European University Institute, 2009 EU Competition Law and Policy Workshop/Proceedings. Available via European University Institute. http://www.eui.eu/Documents/RSCAS/Research/Competition/2009/2009-COMPETITION-Schweitzer.pdf.          Accessed 13 Sept 2015

Schweitzer H (2012) Judicial review in EU competition law. Available via SSRN. http://papers.ssrn.com/sol3/papers.cfm?abstract_id=2129147. Accessed 3 Nov 2015

Tridimas T, Gari G (2010) Winners and losers in Luxembourg: a statistical analysis of judicial review before the ECJ and the CFI 2001–2005. Legal Studies Research Paper No 59/2010. Queen Mary, University of London, School of Law

Van Beal I (2011) Due process in EU competition proceedings. Wolters Kluwer, Alphen aan den Rijn

Vesterndorf B (2007) The CFI: judicial review or judicial control. In: Baudenbacher C (ed) St. Gallen International Cartel Forum 2006: Neueste Entwicklungen in europaïshen und internationalen Kartellrecht, vol 7. Helbing & Lichtenhahn, Basel

# Enforcement of the EU Competition Rules in Lithuania: Application of the 'Effect on Trade' Concept in the Enforcement Practice of the National Competition Authority and Courts

Alexandr Svetlicinii

**Abstract** Following the decentralisation of EU competition law enforcement introduced by Regulation 1/2003, the national competition authorities (NCAs) of the EU Member States have become the primary enforcers of Articles 101/102 TFEU. At the same time, the enforcement records of the individual NCAs reported by the European Competition Network display substantial disparity in the number of investigations and envisaged decisions. Previous studies indicate that in several EU Member States, the proportion of EU cases in the overall workload of the NCAs remains low. The existence of the actual or potential effect on intra-Community trade produced by an anti-competitive practice serves as a jurisdictional criterion for the NCA to determine the applicability of EU competition rules in a given case. Therefore, the application of the 'effect on trade' concept by the NCAs and national courts can explain the disparity in the enforcement of EU competition rules by individual NCAs. The present paper provides a critical review of the enforcement practice of the Lithuanian Competition Council and Lithuanian administrative courts applying EU competition law, with special focus on the 'effect on trade' assessment that determines the applicability of EU competition rules. The incentives derived from this study can serve as a point of reference for other EU jurisdictions where the enforcement of EU competition rules by the NCAs displays similar patterns.

A. Svetlicinii (✉)
University of Macau, Macao SAR, China
e-mail: AlexandrS@umac.mo

© Springer-Verlag Berlin Heidelberg 2017
V. Tomljenović et al. (eds.), *EU Competition and State Aid Rules*,
Europeanization and Globalization 3, https://doi.org/10.1007/978-3-662-47962-9_5

# 1 Introduction: The System of Decentralised Enforcement of EU Competition Law

Synchronised with its enlargement wave of 2004,[1] the EU moved to decentralise the enforcement of EU competition rules, which had previously been enforced solely by the EU Commission, with judicial review of the EU Commission's decisions exercised by the European Court of Justice (ECJ).[2] The institutional reform was implemented through the adoption of Regulation 1/2003, which has recently celebrated its tenth anniversary.[3] By empowering national competition authorities (NCAs) and national courts to directly enforce Articles 101–102 of the Treaty of the Functioning of the European Union (TFEU),[4] Regulation 1/2003 has substantially increased the degree of enforcement of EU competition rules: after decentralisation, the majority of the infringement decisions sanctioning anti-competitive practices (anti-competitive agreements and abuse of dominant position) have been adopted by the NCAs rather than by the EU Commission.[5]

For the purpose of the consistent enforcement of EU competition rules by all Member States, Regulation 1/2003 has established the European Competition Network (ECN) consisting of the EU Commission and the NCAs of the EU Member States. Under Article 3(1) Regulation 1/2003, the NCAs must apply EU competition rules (Articles 101–102 TFEU) when anti-competitive practice 'may affect trade between Member States'.[6] Pursuant to Article 11 of Regulation 1/2003, the NCAs must notify the EU Commission regarding the opening of every new investigation and, consequently, the envisaged decision based on Articles 101–102

---

[1] The following ten countries became EU Member States on 1 May 2004: Cyprus, Czech Republic, Estonia, Hungary, Latvia, Lithuania, Malta, Poland, Slovakia, and Slovenia.

[2] See Ehlermann and Atanasiu (2002).

[3] Council Regulation (EC) No 1/2003 of 16 December 2002 on the implementation of the rules on competition laid down in Art 81 and 82 of the Treaty [2003] OJ L 1/1.

[4] Consolidated version of the Treaty on the Functioning of the European Union [2012] OJ C 326/47.

[5] According to the official EU statistics during the period 1 May 2004 – 31 March 2015, the NCAs carried out a total of 1675 investigations while the EU Commission during the same period investigated a total of 281 cases. See European Competition Network statistics. http://ec.europa.eu/competition/ecn/statistics.html. Accessed 23 Jan 2016.

[6] Regulation 1/2003, Article 3(1): 'Where the competition authorities of the Member States or national courts apply national competition law to agreements, decisions by associations of undertakings or concerted practices within the meaning of Article [101(1)] of the Treaty which may affect trade between Member States within the meaning of that provision, they shall also apply Article [101] of the Treaty to such agreements, decisions or concerted practices. Where the competition authorities of the Member States or national courts apply national competition law to any abuse prohibited by Article [102] of the Treaty, they shall also apply Article [102] of the Treaty.'

TFEU.[7] Thus, the 'effect on trade' serves as a jurisdictional criterion, which triggers the application of the EU competition rules.[8] The assessment of the existence (or absence) of the 'effect on trade' in each particular case remains the task of the individual NCA conducting the respective investigation.

Prior to the decentralisation of EU competition enforcement, the 'effect on trade' assessment had to be carried out by the EU Commission in order to justify the applicability of EU competition rules in particular cases. In the absence of a detailed regulation of this concept in the EU treaties, regulations and the EU Commission's soft law, the particularities of the 'effect on trade' assessment have been developed in the EU Commission's enforcement practice and in the ECJ's case law. In its early competition law jurisprudence, the ECJ adopted a broad interpretation of the 'effect on trade' concept, allowing the EU Commission to apply competition rules at a time when some Member States had not yet adopted the corresponding national competition legislation. One of the landmark cases in that respect was *Société Technique Minière*, where the ECJ held that an agreement was covered by Article 101 TFEU (ex-Article 81 EC) when it had 'an influence, direct or indirect, actual or potential on the patterns of trade between Member States'.[9] In *Compagnie Maritime Belge*, the ECJ emphasised that 'it is not specifically necessary that the conduct in question should in fact have substantially affected trade between Member States. It is sufficient to establish that the conduct is capable of having such an effect.'[10] The ECJ has also established certain presumptions for the 'potential effect' on intra-Community trade: 'A cartel extending over the whole of the territory of a Member State has, by its very nature, the effect of reinforcing the partitioning of markets on a national basis, thus impeding the economic interpenetration which the EC Treaty is designed to bring about.'[11] The ECJ also underscored that 'an effect on intra-Community trade is normally the result of a combination of several factors which, taken separately, are not necessarily decisive'.[12]

---

[7]Regulation 1/2003, Article 11: 'The competition authorities of the Member States shall, when acting under Article [101] or Article [102] of the Treaty, inform the Commission in writing before or without delay after commencing the first formal investigative measure... No later than 30 days before the adoption of a decision requiring that an infringement be brought to an end, accepting commitments or withdrawing the benefit of a block exemption Regulation, the competition authorities of the Member States shall inform the Commission. To that effect, they shall provide the Commission with a summary of the case, the envisaged decision or, in the absence thereof, any other document indicating the proposed course of action.'

[8]Cf Bailey (2009).

[9]Case 56/65 *Société Technique Minière v. Maschinenbau Ulm GmbH* [1966] ECR-389.

[10]Case T-24/93 *Compagnie Maritime Belge v. Commission, Court of Justice* [1996] ECR II-1201, para 201. See also Case 322/81 *Nederlandsche Banden Industrie Michelin v. Commission* [1983] ECR 3461, para 104; Case T-228/97 *Irish Sugar v. Commission* [1999] ECR II-2969, para 170.

[11]Joined Cases C-125/07 P, C-133/07 P, C-135/07 P and C-137/07 P *Erste Group Bank AG and others v. Commission* [2009] ECR I-8681, para 38.

[12]Joined Cases C-295/04 to C-298/04 *Vincenzo Manfredi v. Lloyd Adriatico* [2006] ECR I-6619, para 43.

In 2004, the EU Commission published its Guidelines on the 'effect on trade' concept with the purpose 'to give guidance to the courts and authorities of the Member States in their application of the effect on trade concept contained in Articles [101] and [102]'.[13] The EU Commission instructed the NCAs to assess 'separately in each case' whether the anti-competitive conduct is capable of affecting intra-Community trade, a 'jurisdictional criterion, which defines the scope of application of Community competition law'.[14] In its Guidelines, the EU Commission summarised the preceding ECJ case law concerning actual and potential effect on trade.[15] In addition, the EU Commission put forward certain quantitative criteria for the assessment of the 'appreciability' of the effect on intra-Community trade. According to the Guidelines, an agreement does not have an appreciable effect on intra-Community trade when two cumulative conditions are satisfied: (1) the aggregate market share of the parties on any relevant market within the Community affected by the agreement does not exceed 5%, and (2) in the case of horizontal agreements, the aggregate annual Community turnover of the undertakings concerned in the products covered by the agreement does not exceed 40 million euros.[16]

In line with its declared objectives, the EU Commission's Guidelines have provided the NCAs with certain guidance on the application of the 'effect on trade' assessment but did not achieve the intended coherence in its application for a number of reasons. First of all, the Guidelines are a soft law instrument that does not legally bind the NCAs. Second, the Guidelines have merely codified the ECJ's 'broad' interpretation concerning effect on trade, an interpretation that may no longer fit with the high degree of integration achieved within the EU internal market.[17] As a result, the NCAs have been left with a significant *de facto* margin of appreciation in determining the presence (or absence) of the effect on trade in each particular case. Since the early years of the decentralised enforcement of the EU competition rules, it has been noted that the ECJ's interpretation of the 'effect on trade' concept is largely broad and permissive, which should provide for the direct application of the EU competition rules by the NCAs in a wide range of cases.[18] It has been noted that the lack of clarity in applying the 'effect on trade' test has also contributed to the increased harmonisation of national (both substantive and procedural) competition rules with the EU competition rules. Otherwise, the parallel application of two distinct sets of rules in the same case would be an 'administrative nightmare'.[19]

---

[13]Commission Notice – Guidelines on the effect on trade concept contained in Articles 81 and 82 of the Treaty [2004] OJ C 101, para 3.

[14]Ibid, para 12.

[15]Ibid, para 34–43.

[16]Ibid, para 52.

[17]See Burnley (2002).

[18]See Wilks (2005), p. 445.

[19]See Mataija (2010), p. 97.

## 2   Application of the EU Competition Rules by the NCAs: The Decade of the Enforcement of Regulation 1/2003

The enforcement statistics summarised in Figs. 1 and 2 demonstrate the respective contributions of the NCAs of the EU Member States in the application of EU competition rules (based on the number of notified investigations and envisaged decisions).

These enforcement statistics demonstrate that during the first decade of Regulation 1/2003, the NCAs of the 'old' EU Member States notified the EU Commission a larger number of envisaged decisions under Articles 101–102 TFEU in comparison to the NCAs of the 'new' EU Member States.[20] According to the EU Commission, the existing divergences in enforcement are largely due to 'differences in the institutional position of NCAs and in national procedures and sanctions'.[21] However, the empirical data collected from the selected 'new' EU Member States provide a different picture: during the first decade of Regulation 1/2003, the NCAs of the 'new' EU Member States adopted a far larger number of decisions under national competition law in comparison to the decisions notified to the EU Commission under Regulation 1/2003.[22] Therefore, the divergent degree of enforcement of EU competition rules in those jurisdictions cannot be explained solely by the institutional or procedural constraints on the NCAs. The low proportion of EU cases in the overall workload of the individual NCAs should be linked to the application of the 'effect on trade' assessment, which precludes the application of the EU competition rules in the majority of the cases investigated by the selected NCAs. Such divergent application of the 'effect on trade' concept is possible due to a *de facto* broad margin of discretion exercised by the NCAs and the lack of effective procedural mechanisms that would permit the timely screening of the NCAs' decisions in order to review their application of the 'effect on trade' assessment.

The preceding research has revealed various approaches in the application of the 'effect on trade' assessment carried out by the individual NCAs. Some NCAs have followed a 'narrow' interpretation of the effect on trade and excluded the application of the EU competition rules due to the 'smallness' of the national market as part

---

[20]Statistics on the number of opened investigations and envisaged decisions notified by the NCA of each Member State to the European Commission under Article 11 Regulation 1/2003 between 1 May 2004 and 31 March 2015 are available at: http://ec.europa.eu/competition/ecn/statistics. html#2. Accessed 23 Jan 2016.

[21]European Commission, Communication from the Commission to the European Parliament and the Council. Ten Years of Antitrust Enforcement under Regulation 1/2003: Achievements and Future Perspectives COM (2014) 453, para 24, available at: http://ec.europa.eu/competition/ antitrust/legislation/antitrust_enforcement_10_years_en.pdf. Accessed 23 Jan 2016.

[22]See Botta et al. (2015). The covered jurisdictions include: Bulgaria, Czech Republic, Estonia, Poland, Romania, and Slovakia.

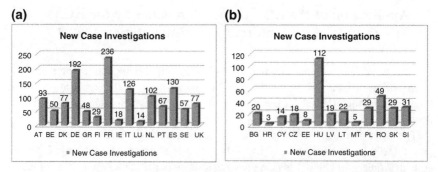

**Fig. 1** (**a**) 'Old' EU Member States; (**b**)'New' EU Member States. Source: http://ec.europa.eu/competition/ecn/statistics.html

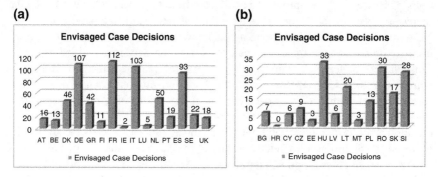

**Fig. 2** (**a**) 'Old' EU Member States; (**b**) 'New' EU Member States. Source: http://ec.europa.eu/competition/ecn/statistics.html

of the internal market of the EU.[23] Other NCAs have prioritised enforcement in high-impact cases (nationwide cartels and abuses of dominance), where the presence of the effect on intra-Community trade is more likely.[24] In other cases, the NCA has not included any 'effect on trade' assessment in its decisions, which makes it difficult to ascertain the factors considered by such an NCA.[25]

The present paper aims to supplement the existing research on this subject by studying the interpretation and application of the 'effect on trade' concept by the Lithuanian NCA and courts. In 2013, in response to a questionnaire of the ECN

---

[23]This approach has been identified in Bulgaria where the NCA has concluded on several occasions that the small share of the Bulgarian market in the EU internal market does not allow the finding of an 'appreciable' effect on trade even in cases where the anti-competitive practice has covered the whole of the national market. Ibid, p 1259.

[24]This is the case with the Romanian NCA. See Svetlicinii (2014).

[25]This is the case with the Polish NCA. See Botta et al. (2015), pp. 1262–1265.

Working Group on Cooperation Issues, the Lithuanian Competition Council (LTCC)[26] submitted that its national legislation was fully convergent with Article 3 Regulation 1/2003 concerning the parallel application of EU and national antitrust rules.[27] Given the relatively small size, openness and economic integration of Lithuanian markets within the EU internal market, it is expected that the existence of the effect on intra-Community trade would be present in multiple cases concerning anti-competitive agreements and abuses of a dominant position with national coverage. The ensuing sections of this paper will verify this initial assumption by analysing the practice of the LTCC and Lithuanian administrative courts engaged in judicial review of the LTCC's decisions.

## 3 The Enforcement Record of the Lithuanian Competition Council and Its First Decisions Under Regulation 1/2003

Between 1 May 2004 and 31 March 2015, the LTCC notified the EU Commission regarding 22 cases of opened investigations and 20 envisaged infringement decisions based on Articles 101–102 TFEU.[28] This enforcement record identifies the LTCC as the most active in the enforcement of EU competition rules amongst the NCAs of the Baltic states.[29] The present study has identified 20 LTCC decisions adopted by the LTCC during the 2004–2014 period, where the LTCC determined the applicability of EU competition rules on the basis of the 'effect on trade' assessment.[30] A comparison of this number with the total number of decisions on the merits adopted under national competition law[31] indicates that during the 2004–2014 period, the LTCC found the applicability of EU competition rules in 24% of all cases it had investigated. For example, in the field of cartel enforcement, during the period 2000–2012, the LTCC detected a respective infringement in 31 cases, out of which only in five cases was EU competition law (Article 101 TFEU or ex-Article 81 EC) applied.[32] The following review of the LTCC's decisional practice and the case law of Lithuanian courts reviewing the decisions of

---

[26]*Konkurencijos taryba* (Competition Council). http://kt.gov.lt/. Accessed 23 Jan 2016.

[27]ECN Working Group on Cooperation Issues, Results of the questionnaire on the reform of Member States (MS) national competition laws after EC Regulation No 1/2003 (22 May 2013). http://ec.europa.eu/competition/ecn/convergence_table_en.pdf. Accessed 23 Jan 2016.

[28]See European Competition Network statistics. http://ec.europa.eu/competition/ecn/statistics. html. Accessed 23 Jan 2016.

[29]The Estonian NCA has notified 8 opened investigations and 3 envisaged decisions; the Latvian NCA has notified 19 opened investigations and 6 envisaged decisions.

[30]See the Annex: Enforcement Practice of the Lithuanian Competition Council.

[31]See generally Gumbis et al. (2014). See also Fiala (2013), Virtanen (2000).

[32]See Bruneckiene et al. (2014), p. 265.

the LTCC will provide a better understanding of how the 'effect on trade' assessment is carried out in this Baltic jurisdiction.

The first case where the LTCC applied EU competition rules dates back to 2005 and concerns an abuse of dominant position on the market for automotive fuels committed by the crude oil refinery AB Mažeikių nafta.[33] According to the LTCC, the presence of the effect on trade was justified by the effect of discriminatory pricing on the trade flows of automotive fuels between the three Baltic states (Estonia, Latvia, Lithuania), which were identified as a relevant geographic market in that case.[34] It should be noted, however, that the LTCC's infringement decision was annulled by the Vilnius Regional Administrative Court[35] for a number of procedural deficiencies, including the failure to notify the envisaged infringement decision to the EU Commission as mandated by Regulation 1/2003.[36]

The Supreme Administrative Court[37] affirmed the annulment of the LTCC's decision but disagreed with the lower court on the interpretation of Regulation 1/2003.[38] The high court held that the failure to notify the envisaged decision to the EU Commission would not alter the substantive findings of the LTCC and, therefore, could not serve as a ground for annulment of the LTCC's infringement decision. Moreover, according to the Supreme Administrative Court, the LTCC's failure to comply with its procedural obligations under Regulation 1/2003 did not confer rights on the private parties in the challenge of the LTCC's decision.[39] Nevertheless, the Supreme Administrative Court annulled the LTCC's decision for the incomplete legal, economic and factual analysis of the case, including the definition of the relevant geographic market.

Following the annulment of its initial infringement decision in the *Mažeikių nafta* case, the LTCC undertook a repeated investigation and arrived at the same substantive conclusion: AB Orlen Lietuva (former AB Mažeikių nafta) had infringed Article 102 TFEU (ex-Article 82 EC) and its national equivalent by engaging in anti-competitive price discrimination on the market for ex-refinery sales of automotive fuels.[40] With regard to the definition of the geographic market, the LTCC narrowed it to the territory of Lithuania based on the volumes of sales, the specifics of transportation logistics, the limited capacity of storage facilities and Lithuanian sector-specific regulations.[41] The assessment of the effect on trade remained unchanged, and the LTCC repeatedly found the applicability of Article

---

[33]LTCC Decision Nr 2S-16 of 22 December 2005. See LTCC 22 December 2005.

[34]See Keserauskas (2005).

[35]*Vilniaus apygardos administracinis teismas*. http://www.vaateismas.lt/. Accessed 23 Jan 2016.

[36]Article 11(4) of the Regulation 1/2003. See Keserauskas (2007a). See also Keserauskas (2007b).

[37]*Lietuvos vyriausiasis administracinis teismas*. http://www.lvat.lt/. Accessed 23 Jan 2016.

[38]Judgment in administrative case A248-715/2008 of 8 December 2008.

[39]See Keserauskas (2008a).

[40]LTCC, Decision Nr 2S-31 of 16 December 2010. See LTCC 16 December 2010b.

[41]See Surblytė (2010).

102 TFEU. The LTCC's repeated decision was consequently upheld by the Vilnius Regional Administrative Court[42] and by the Supreme Administrative Court.[43]

The first decision where the LTCC applied Article 101 TFEU (formerly Article 81 EC) was adopted in 2006 and concerned the cartel on the paper market involving an information exchange scheme set up by the competitors.[44] As noted by former LTCC Chairman Dr Rimantas Stanikunas: 'On the basis of the findings of a complex investigation we have concluded the infringement not only of Article 5 of the Law on Competition prohibiting all agreements the object whereof is to restrict competition or restricting or intending to restrict competition, but also that of Article 81 of the EC which prohibits agreements and concerted actions between undertakings in the common market or part which may affect trade between Member States.'[45] In that case, the LTCC noted that cartels covering the whole territory of a Member State and foreclosing the entry of potential competitors from other Member States have an effect on intra-Community trade and should be prosecuted under both national and EU competition rules. The LTCC also found that the effect on trade was appreciable: the companies involved in the cartel occupied a significant portion of the national market, and the import volumes had been affected by their anti-competitive practices.[46]

The LTCC's assessment of the effect on trade in the *Paper Cartel* case was subsequently upheld by the Vilnius Regional Administrative Court.[47] While the appellants argued that the effect on trade could not be appreciable due to the fact that the information exchange between competitors had occurred only on a single instance, the court noted that the information exchange was related to imports of paper into Lithuania, and the effects of information exchange could last at least several months following its last occurrence. Subsequently, the Supreme Administrative Court undertook a more thorough scrutiny of the LTCC's assessment of the effect on trade. The court emphasised that 'appreciability' was a requisite criterion and could not be established hypothetically without taking into account the particularities of the case (the involvement of small and medium-sized undertakings, limited effects following Lithuania's accession to the EU, etc.).[48] As a result, the court annulled the LTCC's decision in the part establishing the applicability of Article 101 TFEU.[49] Interestingly enough, although the Supreme Administrative Court requested an *amicus curiae* opinion from the EU Commission under Article

---

[42]See LTCC 15 April 2011c.

[43]See LTCC 21 January 2013a.

[44]LTCC, Decision Nr 2S-13 of 26 October 2006, published in *Informaciniai pranešimai* Nr 87-843, 2006-11-17.

[45]LTCC 26 October 2006.

[46]See Keserauskas (2006), Seikyte (2006).

[47]See Keserauskas (2007c).

[48]Judgment in administrative case A502-34/2009 of 16 October 2009.

[49]See LTCC 16 October 2009.

15 Regulation 1/2003,[50] the Lithuanian court did not consult the EU Commission about the 'effect on trade' assessment.[51]

Goldammer and Matulionyté applauded the LTCC's decision in the *Paper Cartel* case, where the LTCC made a thorough assessment of the effect on trade, separating the period between and after 2004: 'All of the [LTCC's] more recent decisions... show a growing self-confidence, willingness and understanding concerning the application of EC law in the area of competition law. One can, therefore, observe a tendency towards ever-increasing application of EC law, in terms of both quality and quantity.'[52]

## 4 Finding the Effect on Trade in Cases of Horizontal Agreements Covering the Whole National Territory

The LTCC departed from its earlier approach to the 'effect on trade' assessment in cases of cartels covering the whole national territory two years later in a case concerning the exchanges of confidential information by dairy companies on the markets of the procurement of raw milk from farmers and various dairy products.[53] Although the market for the procurement of raw milk from farmers was oligopolistic with the four largest competitors accounting for up to 85% of the relevant market, the LTCC's infringement decision does not contain any 'effect on trade' assessment that would provide for the applicability of Article 101 TFEU. Thus, although the information exchange mechanism covered the whole national territory, and the market thresholds of the undertakings concerned significantly

---

[50]Article 15(1) of the Regulation 1/2003 provides that national courts may ask the EU Commission for its opinion on questions concerning the application of EU competition rules.

[51]See Opinion of the European Commission in application of Article 15(1) of Council Regulation (EC) 1/2003 of 16 December 2002 on the implementation of the rules on competition laid down in Articles 81 and 82 of the Treaty, Supreme Administrative Court of Lithuania, Administrative Case no A-502-337/2008. http://ec.europa.eu/competition/court/opinion_2002_uab_en.pdf. Accessed 23 Jan 2016. The paper cartel case is the second instance when the Lithuanian court requested an opinion of the EU Commission concerning the application of EU competition rules. The first instance occurred in 2005 when Vilnius Regional Administrative Court requested the EU Commission's opinion concerning the application of Article 102 TFEU in a case related to the public procurement regulations adopted by the municipality of Kaunas for the procurement of waste management services. See the Opinion of the European Commission in the application of Article 15(1) of Council Regulation (EC) 1/2003 of 16 December 2002 on the implementation of the rules on competition laid down in Articles 81 and 82 of the Treaty, Vilnius Regional Court, Case no 2-1068-52/05. http://ec.europa.eu/competition/court/kaunas_municipality_opninion_en.pdf. Accessed 23 Jan 2016. In its opinion, the EU Commission instructed the Lithuanian court on the assessment of the effect on trade in the light of the EU Commission Guidelines on that subject matter. See also Podgaiskyte (2014).

[52]Goldammer and Matulionyté (2007), p. 300.

[53]LTCC, Decision Nr 2S-3 of 28 February 2008.

exceeded those mentioned in the EU Guidelines,[54] the LTCC did not consider the potential effect on trade or its 'appreciability', which precluded the application of EU competition rules in that case.[55]

Furthermore, on appeal before the Vilnius Regional Administrative Court, the parties explicitly disputed the LTCC's national geographic market definition, demonstrating the existence of cross-border trade in raw milk between Latvia and Lithuania, which suggested that the relevant geographic market was at least multinational and covered at least two EU Member States. The court rejected these arguments, noting that the prices of dairy products in Lithuania were 12–22% lower than in the neighbouring countries.[56] The issue of the potential effect on trade was not addressed by the court either. When the parties moved to appeal the LTCC's decision before the Supreme Administrative Court, the latter disagreed with the Vilnius Regional Administrative Court on the issue of the anti-competitive nature of the information exchange but also did not consider the applicability of EU competition rules based on the 'effect on trade' assessment.[57] After a repeated investigation, the case was closed by the judgment of the Supreme Administrative Court due to the expiration of the limitation period.[58]

In 2010, with reference to the EU Commission Guidelines and the ECJ's case law, the LTCC again confirmed that agreements covering the whole territory of a Member State are usually capable of affecting trade between Member States by isolating the national market of the affected Member State.[59] On the basis of the 'effect on trade' assessment, the LTCC applied EU competition rules to the anti-competitive agreement on the market for third party liability insurance in the construction industry.[60] The LTCC's decision was upheld by the Supreme Administrative Court.[61] The court confirmed that the judiciary should undertake a comprehensive review of the NCA's application of EU competition rules in a given case. However, in the case of complex economic assessments, the Supreme Administrative Court limited the judicial review to the appraisal of procedural conformity, the statement of reasons, factual accuracy and manifest error of assessment.[62] It should be noted, however, that this approach was formulated by the court in relation to the substantive application of Article 101 TFEU (ex-Article 81 EC) and not in relation to the 'effect on trade' assessment, which determines the general

---

[54]EU Guidelines, para 52.

[55]See Keserauskas (2008b).

[56]See Keserauskas (2008c).

[57]See Keserauskas (2009).

[58]See Janciauskaite (2012).

[59]LTCC, Decision Nr 2S-33 of 23 December 2010, published in *Informaciniai pranešimai* Nr 100 (1)-1185, 2010-12-31.

[60]LTCC 27 December 2010d. See also LTCC 23 December 2010c.

[61]See LTCC 20 April 2012a.

[62]See Lurje (2012).

applicability of EU competition rules in cases investigated by the EU Commission or by the NCAs.

In another case concerning the resale price maintenance agreement between the supplier and the retailer on the market for frozen bakery products, the LTCC also followed the logic that the agreements covering the whole territory of Lithuania are by their nature capable of having an effect on intra-Community trade.[63] The LTCC noted that the retailer was present on the markets of several Member States (Latvia, Estonia, Bulgaria, Poland) where it was marketing the supplier's products.[64] A similar conclusion was reached by the LTCC in a case concerning a production limitation agreement concluded by the members of the Lithuanian Brewers Guild[65] since it covered the whole territory of Lithuania, and Lithuanian beer producers were also selling their products on the markets of other EU Member States.[66]

In 2012, the LTCC found an 'effect on trade' in a case concerning the online sales of tour packages where tour operators and an online platform operator conspired to fix the discounts offered to online customers.[67] Referring to the EU Commission Guidelines and the ECJ jurisprudence,[68] the LTCC noted that (1) the cartel covered the whole territory of Lithuania and (2) the tourism activity involved travel between Lithuania and other EU Member States.[69] On the basis of the above-mentioned factors, the LTCC applied EU competition rules in parallel with the national competition law. When the LTCC's decision was appealed before the Supreme Administrative Court, the court made a request for a preliminary ruling to the ECJ, seeking to clarify whether the participation of the tour operators in the computerised system for marketing the tourism packages amounted to their tacit approval of the price discount restrictions applied by that system.[70]

---

[63]LTCC, Decision Nr 2S-14 of 4 December 2014. The LTCC referred to Joined Cases T-213/95 and T-18/96 *Stichting Certificatie Kraanverhuurbedrijf (SCK) and Federatie van Nederlandse Kraanbedrijven (FNK) v. Commission* [1997] ECR II-1739, para 179.

[64]See also LTCC 8 December 2014g; LTCC 8 December 2014h.

[65]*Lietuvos aludarių gildija*. http://www.aludariai.lt/. Accessed 23 Jan 2016.

[66]LTCC, Decision Nr 2S-1 of 4 March 2014. It should be noted that although the LTCC established the infringement of Article 101 TFEU and its national equivalent, no sanction was imposed due to the 'legitimate expectations' of Lithuanian brewers who had previously submitted their agreement for review by the LTCC but had received no comment from the latter. On that basis, the LTCC formed a 'legitimate expectation' that the agreement in question was in compliance with competition rules, and the competition authority decided not to impose financial penalties on the undertakings concerned. See also LTCC 23 December 2013b; LTCC 4 March 2014b; Puksas (2014a).

[67]LTCC 7 June 2012c. See also LTCC 7 June 2012d.

[68]Case 311/85, *ASBL Vereniging van Vlaamse Reisbureaus v ASBL Sociale Dienst van de Plaatselijke en Gewestelijke Overheidsdiensten* [1987] ECR 3821.

[69]LTCC, Decision Nr 2S-9 of 7 June 2012. See also Mykolaitis (2012), Mencas (2012a).

[70]The Supreme Administrative Court formulated its questions to the ECJ as follows: '(1) Should Article 101(1) of the Treaty on the Functioning of the European Union be interpreted as meaning that, in a situation in which economic operators participate in a common computerised information system of the type described in this case and the Competition Council has proved that a system

## 5 Assessing Whether the Effect on Trade is 'Appreciable'

Due to the relatively small size of the Lithuanian national market as part of the EU internal market, it is reasonable to analyse the LTCC's assessment on how 'appreciable' the effect is on intra-Community trade in individual cases. In a 2011 case concerning a cartel on the market for orthopaedic products reimbursed under the state health insurance system,[71] the undertakings concerned referred to the EU Commission Guidelines[72] and argued that since the aggregate market share of the parties at the Community level did not exceed 5% and the aggregate annual Community turnover of the undertakings concerned did not exceed EUR 40 million, their agreement should not have any 'appreciable' effect on intra-Community trade.[73] The LTCC rejected this argument by pointing out that the market share of the undertakings concerned on the Lithuanian market was approaching 100% and the EU Guidelines provided that 'horizontal cartels covering the whole of a Member State are normally capable of affecting trade between Member States'.[74] The LTCC's decision was upheld by the Supreme Administrative Court.[75]

Similarly, in a 2012 infringement decision concerning vertical restraints in the market for cash handling and cash-in-transit services, the LTCC concluded that foreclosure of not less than 85% of the national market was sufficient to find an effect on intra-Community trade.[76] While the case was initially opened under both Articles 101 and 102 TFEU, the LTCC later based its infringement decision solely

---

notice on the restriction of discounts and a technical restriction on discount rate entry were introduced into that system, it can be assumed that those economic operators were aware, or must have been aware, of the system notice introduced into the computerised information system and, by failing to oppose the application of such a discount restriction, expressed their tacit approval of the price discount restriction and for that reason may be held liable for engaging in concerted practices under Article 101(1) TFEU? (2) If the first question is answered in the negative, what factors should be taken into account in the determination as to whether economic operators participating in a common computerised information system, in circumstances such as those in the main proceedings, have engaged in concerted practices within the meaning of Article 101(1) TFEU?' Request for a preliminary ruling from the Lietuvos vyriausiasis administracinis teismas (Lithuania) lodged on 10 February 2014—UAB Eturas and Others v. Lietuvos Respublikos konkurencijos taryba (Case C-74/14). See also LTCC 17 January 2014a.

[71]LTCC 20 January 2011a. See also LTCC 20 January 2011b.

[72]EU Guidelines, para 52.

[73]LTCC, Decision Nr 2S-2 of 20 January 2011, published in *Informaciniai pranešimai* Nr 7(1)-47, 2011-01-26.

[74]EU Guidelines, para 78.

[75]See LTCC 17 May 2012b.

[76]LTCC, Decision Nr 2S-15 of 20 December 2012f. See LTCC 20 December 2012e; LTCC 20 December 2012f. The LTCC's decision was subsequently annulled by the Supreme Administrative Court, which required the LTCC to assess whether the commitments offered by the undertaking concerned would be sufficient to exempt them from the liability for the competition infringement. After a repeated examination of the case, the LTCC arrived at the same conclusion – the parties had breached Article 101 TFEU and its national equivalent. LTCC, Decision Nr 2S-9 of 30 September 2014. See LTCC 30 September 2014e.

on Article 101 TFEU and its national equivalent.[77] The Supreme Administrative Court returned the case to the LTCC for an additional investigation.[78] It should be noted, however, that the court acknowledged the national dimension of the relevant geographic market and the long-lasting foreclosure of potential competitors that resulted from the anti-competitive practices. The LTCC's repeated investigation did not change its conclusion in relation to the existence of the effect on trade and the applicability of Article 101 TFEU.[79]

The relative smallness of the Lithuanian national market as an integral part of the EU internal market has not prevented the LTCC from finding a potential effect on intra-Community trade. In 2011, the LTCC applied EU competition rules in a case where an anti-competitive agreement concerned a shipping agency on the territory of the international port of Klaipeda.[80] In that case, the LTCC referred to the EU Commission Guidelines, which considered that 'even a port or an airport situated in a Member State may, depending on their importance, constitute a substantial part of the common market'.[81] Since the Klaipeda seaport[82] is the northernmost ice-free port on the eastern coast of the Baltic Sea, the most important and biggest Lithuanian transport hub, connecting sea, land and railway routes from east to west, the LTCC concluded that the potential effect on intra-Community trade was present.[83] The Vilnius Regional Administrative Court and the Supreme Administrative Court consequently reduced the amount of fines imposed by the LTCC but did not contest the LTCC's determination concerning the effect on trade and the applicability of EU competition rules.[84]

Similar considerations have prompted the LTCC to find the applicability of Article 102 TFEU in a case concerning a refusal to deal by the Vilnius International Airport,[85] which has effectively prevented a supplier of jet fuel for aircraft to access the relevant market.[86] The LTCC noted that Vilnius International Airport was the principal airport for international flights in Lithuania, with flights operated by airlines originating from different Member States and that higher fuel prices caused

---

[77]Mencas (2012b). The author questioned the LTCC's choice of the applicable competition rule given the fact that the case involved agreements between the dominant security company and several commercial banks, which sanction the banks if they decide to change their security service provider. Even though the LTCC concluded that the said agreements were not in the interest of the banks, it prosecuted all parties under Article 101 TFEU and its national equivalent.

[78]See Puksas (2014b); LTCC 8 April 2014c; Mencas (2014).

[79]See LTCC 30 September 2014f.

[80]LTCC 8 December 2011e. See also LTCC 8 December 2011f; Kačerauskas (2011).

[81]EU Guidelines, para 98.

[82]*Klaipėdos uostas*. http://www.portofklaipeda.lt/. Accessed 23 Jan 2016.

[83]LTCC, Decision Nr 2S-25 of 8 December 2011, published in *Informaciniai pranešimai* Nr 98(1)-962, 2011-12-14. See also Viederyte (2014).

[84]See LTCC 8 April 2014d; Puksas (2014c).

[85]*Vilniaus oro uostas*. https://www.vno.lt/. Accessed 23 Jan 2016.

[86]LTCC, Decision Nr 2S-23 of 6 November 2008, published in *Informaciniai pranešimai* Nr 91(1)-1180, 2008-11-28.

by anti-competitive practice may affect international travel between Lithuania and other Member States.[87] On that basis, the LTCC held that the specified abuse of dominant position had the potential to affect intra-Community trade.[88] The LTCC's findings were upheld on appeal by the Supreme Administrative Court.[89] In contrast, in three similar cases involving the abuse of dominant position by the Vilnius International Airport in the form of a refusal to deal and discriminatory treatment on the market for jet fuel supply, the LTCC, without a detailed explanation, found that Article 102 TFEU was inapplicable due to the absence of an appreciable effect on trade.[90]

## 6   Searching for a Consistent Approach to the 'Effect on Trade' Assessment

For the most part, the LTCC's decisions where the competition authority applies EU competition rules contain a relatively detailed assessment of the effect on trade, except for those cases where the LTCC has not found sufficient evidence to establish the existence of an infringement and has terminated the proceedings.[91] In almost all of its infringement decisions issued under EU competition rules, the LTCC has consistently held that the effect on trade could also be 'potential' and the LTCC, therefore, is not required to demonstrate the actual effects on trade stemming from the investigated anti-competitive practices. The LTCC's enforcement record indicates that the Lithuanian competition authority has taken an approach that anti-competitive agreements and practices covering the whole national territory are generally capable of affecting intra-Community trade by isolating the national market and preventing the entry of competitors from other Member States (this conclusion was reached in cases concerning various product markets: paper,

---

[87] See Keserauskas (2008d).

[88] See LTCC 6 November 2008.

[89] See LTCC 15 March 2010a.

[90] (1) LTCC, Decision Nr 2S-14 of 7 June 2007. See Keserauskas (2007d). In that case, an independent jet fuel supplier argued that Vilnius Airport had obstructed fuel supplies to its clients. The LTCC defined the relevant geographic market as local in scope, which precluded the finding of the applicability of Article 102 TFEU. (2) LTCC, Decision Nr 2S-24 of 5 November 2009; See Adomavičiūtė 2009; (3) LTCC, Decision Nr 2S-1 of 21 January 2010; See Keserauskas (2010). The case concerned the refusal to provide access to an 'essential facility' on the market for jet fuel supply to aircrafts. The LTCC briefly addressed the 'effect on trade' issue and concluded that due to the absence of an appreciable effect on trade between Member States Article 102 TFEU was inapplicable in that case.

[91] (1) LTCC, Decision Nr 1S-16 of 15 February 2013; (2) LTCC, Decision Nr 1S-55 of 18 April 2013; (3) LTCC, Decision Nr 1S-128 of 14 August 2014; (4) LTCC, Decision Nr 1S-190 of 22 September 2011; (5) LTCC, Decision Nr 1S-32 of 8 March 2012; (6) LTCC, Decision Nr 1S-58 of 18 April 2014; (7) LTCC, Decision Nr 1S-93 of 19 June 2014; See Surblytė (2014); LTCC 22 November 2011d; Moisejevas (2013), Juonys (2013).

insurance in the construction industry, frozen bakery products, beer). At the same time, there have been cases where a nationwide cartel was prosecuted exclusively under national competition rules (e.g., the raw milk and dairy products case). As demonstrated by the present study, the LTCC's enforcement record contains several instances of a divergent approach towards the 'effect on trade' assessment, while numerous cases contain no assessment at all, which makes it difficult to ascertain why the application of EU competition rules has been excluded by the LTCC in those cases.

In cases related to significant infrastructure units, which could be viewed as an essential facility in the course of international trade in goods and services, such as seaports and airports, the LTCC's practice includes diverging approaches as to whether the 'effect on trade' assessment should lead to the application of EU competition rules in such cases (compare the *Vilnius International Airport* cases). In relation to the 'appreciability' of the effect on trade, the LTCC has generally found the effects appreciable in cases where the undertakings concerned controlled a large portion of the relevant market (orthopaedic products, cash-related services).

There are also two types of cases where, unlike competition authorities of other Member States,[92] the LTCC has found no effect on intra-Community trade: decisions of the associations of undertakings covering the whole national territory and bid rigging at public tenders open for participation to undertakings from other Member States. In 2007, the LTCC found that the Chamber of Auditors[93] had infringed the national equivalent of Article 101 TFEU (ex-Article 81 EC) by adopting the recommended rates for auditing of the financial support received from the EU structural funds.[94] The Chamber of Auditors is a professional association established by the Law on Audit for the enforcement of the self-governance of individual auditors. In that case, the LTCC did not address the potential effect on trade that could be caused by the infringement in question, and the EU competition law was not applied. This was despite the fact that the LTCC had determined the relevant market to be the audit of EU structural funds in Lithuania, which implies that the whole territory of Lithuania was affected by the said anti-competitive decision of the professional association. The LTCC's decision was appealed before the Vilnius Regional Administrative Court.[95] Interestingly enough, the arguments of the parties evolved around the definition of undertaking under Lithuanian competition law and the possibility to apply the national equivalent of Article 101 TFEU (ex-Article 81 EC) to associations of undertakings.[96] While the applicability of Article 101 TFEU (ex-Article 81 EC) to the decisions of associations of undertakings had already been well settled in EU competition law practice, the LTCC had not applied EU competition rules in the given case, and the appeal

---

[92]See e.g. Svetlicinii (2014).

[93]*Lietuvos auditorių rūmai.* http://lar.lt/. Accessed 23 Jan 2016.

[94]LTCC, Decision Nr 2S-15 of 21 June 2007. See Keserauskas (2007e).

[95]Judgment in administrative case I-14-561/2008 of 14 February 2008.

[96]See Keserauskas (2008e).

focused exclusively on the interpretation of the national equivalent of Article 101 TFEU.

The second type of cases where the LTCC has enforced almost exclusively national competition rules is bid rigging in public procurement. For example, in 2008, the LTCC penalised several consulting companies for bid rigging in public tenders for consulting services supported by EU structural funds.[97] Although one can expect that such tenders would be open for participation to undertakings from other Member States and that the said bid rigging practices could preclude foreign competitors from entering the Lithuanian market, the LTCC's decision does not contain any analysis of the effect on trade and is based on the application of the national equivalent of Article 101 TFEU.[98] There have been several infringement decisions issued by the LTCC in cases involving bid rigging in public tenders, which are based exclusively on the national equivalent of Article 101 TFEU.[99]

# 7 Concluding Remarks

The Lithuanian Law on Competition expressly states that its objective consists in 'harmonising the law of the Republic of Lithuania and the European Union regulating competition relations'.[100] The Lithuanian competition law enforcement record shows that both the LTCC and the Lithuanian courts routinely refer to the EU legislation and case law in interpretation of the domestic competition rules, even in cases where the EU competition rules are not applied. As noted by Stanikunas and Burinskas, 'administrative courts of Lithuania rely on EU precedents even when only national competition law is being enforced'.[101] The authors conclude that 'copy-pasting' the EU competition rules into the national legislation 'largely helped to address the problem of uniform application of EU competition rules in Lithuania and helped comply with the so-called convergence rule established in Article 3 Regulation 1/2003'.[102]

At the same time, the selective analysis of the judicial review practice developed by Lithuanian administrative courts when reviewing the legality of the LTCC's decisions demonstrates that despite the thorough review of the facts (including the assessment of complex economic evidence such as the definition of the relevant market), the application of substantive competition rules (the concept of 'undertaking', an anti-competitive object and effect) and procedural norms (compliance with Regulation 1/2003), requests for *amicus curiae* to the EU Commission and

---

[97]LTCC, Decision Nr 2S-16 of 10 July 2008.

[98]See Adomavičiūtė (2008).

[99]See e.g. Surblytė (2009), Surblytė (2011).

[100]Law on Competition, No VIII-1099 of 23 March 1999, Article 1(3).

[101]Stanikunas and Burinskas (2014), p. 105.

[102]Ibid, 107.

requests for a preliminary ruling to the ECJ, the Lithuanian courts have largely paid relatively little attention to the jurisdictional criterion for the application of EU competition law—the effect on intra-Community trade. This can partly be explained by the fact that the appellants (the undertakings concerned) did not raise the issue of the application of EU competition rules based on the 'effect on trade' assessment carried out by the LTCC. This is despite the line of the ECJ's case law where the EU Court suggested that EU competition rules should be applied by the national courts *ex officio* as a matter of public policy.[103] Nevertheless, as summarised by Havelka, 'the signs that show that disregard for EU law or the incorrect application of Union law in national proceedings are nothing uncommon should not be ignored either'.[104]

As a result, the above review of the LTCC's enforcement practice and the jurisprudence of the Lithuanian administrative courts indicates that despite the harmonisation of substantive competition rules and frequent references to the EU Commission's soft law and enforcement practice, as well as to the ECJ case law, there are certain inconsistencies in the application of the 'effect on trade' concept, which reduce legal certainty as to the application of EU competition rules in the enforcement practice of the NCA. This is partly due to the system of notifications laid down by Regulation 1/2003, which leaves a *de facto* margin of appreciation to the NCAs in determining the existence of the effect on intra-Community trade in individual cases. Another reason for the remaining inconsistencies is the fact that Regulation 1/2003 requires the NCAs to notify their investigations and envisaged decisions only when the NCA has already determined the presence of an 'effect on trade' in a given case, which triggers the application of EU competition rules. In all other cases, including those where the NCA does not include any 'effect on trade' assessment in its decision based exclusively on national competition rules, the ECN does not receive any notification that would allow it to scrutinise the NCA's findings as to the effect on intra-Community trade.

**Acknowledgements** The author is grateful to Dina Lurje, Rimantas Stanikunas and Raimundas Moisejevas for their useful comments and suggestions. The author acknowledges the support from the Asia Europe Comparative Studies Research Project 'Competition Law and Policy in the Small Market Economies: Asian Challenges and European Experiences' funded by the Institute of European Studies of Macau Academic Research Grants 2014–2015.

---

[103]Case C-126/97 *Eco Swiss China Ltd v. Benetton International NV* [1999] ECR I-3055; and Joined Cases C-295/04 *Vincenzo Manfredi v. Lloyd Adriatico Assicurazioni SpA*, C-296/04, *Antonio Cannito v Fondiaria Sai SpA*, C-297/04, *Nicolo Tricarico v Assitalia SpA*, C-298/04 *Pasqualina Murgolo v. Assitalia SpA* [2006] ECR I-6619. See also Erecinski (2011).

[104]Havelka (2014), p. 156.

# Annex: Enforcement Practice of the Lithuanian Competition Council

Application of EU competition rules and national competition rules

| 2004 | | 2005 | | 2006 | | 2007 | | 2008 | | 2009 | | 2010 | | 2011 | | 2012 | | 2013 | | 2014 | | Ratio |
|---|---|---|---|---|---|---|---|---|---|---|---|---|---|---|---|---|---|---|---|---|---|---|
| EU | NC | EU | NC | EU | NC | EU | NC | EU | NC | EU | NC | EU | NC | EU | NC | EU | NC | EU | NC | EU | NC | EU/NC |
| 0 | 11 | 1 | 8 | 1 | 6 | 0 | 10 | 1 | 7 | 0 | 6 | 3 | 9 | 3 | 13 | 3 | 8 | 2 | 4 | 6 | 2 | 20/84 24% |

Application of Article 101 TFEU (ex-Article 81 EC)

|  | 2004 | 2005 | 2006 | 2007 | 2008 | 2009 | 2010 | 2011 | 2012 | 2013 | 2014 |
|---|---|---|---|---|---|---|---|---|---|---|---|
| Article 101 TFEU | – | – | 1 | – | – | – | 1 | 2 | 2 | 2 | 4 |
| National equivalent | 6 | 6 | 2 | 4 | 6 | 3 | 6 | 8 | 5 | 3 | 1 |

Application of Article 102 TFEU (ex-Article 82 EC)

|  | 2004 | 2005 | 2006 | 2007 | 2008 | 2009 | 2010 | 2011 | 2012 | 2013 | 2014 |
|---|---|---|---|---|---|---|---|---|---|---|---|
| Article 102 TFEU | – | 1 | – | – | 1 | – | 2 | 1 | 2 | – | 2 |
| National equivalent | 5 | 2 | 4 | 6 | 1 | 3 | 3 | 5 | 3 | 1 | 1 |

# References

Adomavičiūtė G (2008) The Lithuanian Competition Council fines three consulting agencies for collusive tendering in the market for consulting on projects supported by the EU structural funds (Eurointegracijos projektai, EIP Kaunas, EIP Vilnius). 10 July 2008, e-Competitions Bulletin July 2008, Art N° 57273

Adomavičiūtė G (2009) The Lithuanian Competition Council for the third time finds the State controlled airport guilty of abuse of a dominant position in operating airport facilities (Vilnius Airport/Baltic ground services). 5 November 2009, e-Competitions Bulletin November 2009, Art N° 57275

Bailey D (2009) Appreciable effect on trade within the United Kingdom. Eur Competition Law Rev 30(8):353–361

Botta M, Svetlicinii A, Bernatt M (2015) The assessment of the effect on trade by the National Competition Authorities of the 'new' member states: another legal partition of the internal market? Common Mark Law Rev 52:1247–1276

Bruneckiene J, Pekarskiene I, Soviene J (2014) The critical aspects of Lithuanian competition policy in relation to cartels. Procedia Soc Behav Sci 156:261–267

Burnley R (2002) Interstate trade revisited - the jurisdictional criterion for Articles 81 and 82 EC. Eur Competition Law Rev 23(5):217–226

Ehlermann C-D, Atanasiu I (2002) The modernisation of EC antitrust law: consequences for the future role and function of the EC courts. Eur Competition Law Rev 23(2):72–80

Erecinski T (2011) When must national judges raise European law issues on their own motion? ERA Forum 11:525–529

Fiala T (2013) (Publication Review) Competition law in Lithuania. Eur Competition Law Rev 34 (6):342–343

Goldammer Y, Matulionyté E (2007) Towards an improved application of European Union law in Lithuania: the examples of competition law and intellectual property law. Croat Yearb of Eur Law Policy 3:307–330

Gumbis J, Juonis M, Slepaite L, Kacerauskas K (2014) Competition law in Lithuania. Wolters Kluwer Law & Business

Havelka L (2014) Escaping the trap: the simplified application of EU law. Croat Yearb Eur Law Policy 10:131–158

Janciauskaite I (2012) The Supreme Administrative Court annuls decision on exchange of commercial information by dairies due to expiration of the limitation period (Dairies). 21 June 2012, e-Competitions Bulletin June 2012, Art N° 57286

Juonys M (2013) The Supreme Administrative Court of Lithuania draws the limitations of the Competition Authority's discretion to close the investigation under the Rules of Procedure (Viasat). 5 March 2013, e-Competitions Bulletin March 2013, Art N° 57283

Kačerauskas K (2011) The Lithuanian Competition Authority assesses the possibility of de facto termination of the agreement under Art 101 of the TFEU (Lithuanian ship agents). 8 December 2011, e-Competitions Bulletin December 2011, Art N° 57284

Keserauskas S (2005) The Lithuanian Competition Authority fines the national oil refinery for abuse of dominant position under Art 82 EC (Mažeikių nafta). 22 December 2005, e-Competitions Bulletin December 2005, Art N° 426

Keserauskas S (2006) The Lithuanian NCA fines members of the paper cartel (Schneidersöhne Baltija). 26 October 2006, e-Competitions Bulletin October 2006, Art N° 12705

Keserauskas S (2007a) The Vilnius District Administrative Court annuls the NCA's first Art 82 EC case in Lithuania on both legal reasoning and procedural grounds and, inter alia, for not having informed the EC Commission, in an excessive fuel prices case (Mažeikių nafta II). 28 June 2007, e-Competitions Bulletin June 2007, Art N° 13786

Keserauskas S (2007b) The Lithuanian Constitutional Court rules on the first Art 82 EC case on alleged excessive fuel prices (Mažeikių nafta). 31 January 2007, e-Competitions Bulletin January 2007, Art N° 13296

Keserauskas S (2007c) The Vilnius District Administrative Court upholds the NCA's decision in the first Art 81 EC case in Lithuania (Paper Wholesalers). 7 June 2007, e-Competitions Bulletin June 2007, Art N° 13971

Keserauskas S (2007d) The Lithuanian Competition Authority fines the State-controlled airport for abusing its dominance by restricting access to the airport facilities (Vilnius Airport/RSS). 7 June 2007, e-Competitions Bulletin June 2007, Art N° 14177

Keserauskas S (2007e) The Lithuanian Competition Authority fines a professional association for recommending minimum fees to its members (Chamber of Auditors). 21 June 2007, e-Competitions Bulletin June 2007, Art N° 14070

Keserauskas S (2008a) The Lithuanian Supreme Administrative Court upholds the annulment of the NCA's Art 82 EC decision and sends the case back for re-investigation (Mažeikių nafta II). 8 December 2008, e-Competitions Bulletin December 2008, Art N° 23815

Keserauskas S (2008b) The Lithuanian NCA inflicts its highest fine ever on a professional association running confidential information exchange scheme on the raw milk procurement and dairy products markets (Dairies III). 28 February 2008, e-Competitions Bulletin February 2008, Art N° 17676

Keserauskas S (2008c) A Lithuanian administrative court upholds the NCA's findings of illegal information exchange among dairies (Dairies/Competition Council). 21 August 2008, e-Competitions Bulletin August 2008, Art N° 22374

Keserauskas S (2008d) The Lithuanian Competition Council ends Art 82 EC investigation with another fine being imposed on the State-controlled operator of the national airport for restricting access to the airport facilities (Vilnius Airport - Naftelf). 6 November 2008, e-Competitions Bulletin November 2008, Art N° 23816

Keserauskas S (2008e) The Vilnius District Administrative Court upholds the Lithuanian NCA's infringement decision on professional minimum fees (Chamber of Auditors). 14 February 2008, e-Competitions Bulletin February 2008, Art N° 17664

Keserauskas S (2009) The Lithuanian Supreme Administrative Court upholds the appeals against the NCA's decision and orders a reinvestigation of the role of two dairies in the non-pricing information exchange scheme (Dairies III). 11 June 2009, e-Competitions Bulletin June 2009, Art N° 27494

Keserauskas S (2010) The Lithuanian Competition Council issues fourth infringement decision against the State controlled airport for restricting access to the airport facilities (Vilnius Airport/RSS II). 21 January 2010, e-Competitions Bulletin January 2010, Art N° 30788

LTCC, The Competition Council finds AB Mažeikių nafta to have violated laws, Press Release of 22 December 2005., available at http://kt.gov.lt/en/index.php?show=news_view&pr_id=319. Accessed 23 Jan 2016

LTCC, Cartel in the paper market, Press Release of 26 October 2006., available at http://kt.gov.lt/en/index.php?show=news_view&pr_id=370. Accessed 23 Jan 2016

LTCC, For the infringement of Lithuanian and European competition rules – a fine imposed upon SE Vilniaus tarptautinis oro uostas, Press Release of 6 November 2008., available at http://kt.gov.lt/en/index.php?show=news_view&pr_id=574. Accessed 23 Jan 2016

LTCC (2009) The Lithuanian Supreme Administrative Court partly upholds the Competition Authority decision which fines members of paper cartel (Schneidersöhne Baltija). 16 October 2009 e-Competitions Bulletin October 2009, Art N° 33420

LTCC (2010a) The Lithuanian Supreme Administrative Court upholds Competition Authority's decision on abuse of dominance by an airport operator (Vilnius International Airport - Naftelf). 15 March 2010, e-Competitions Bulletin March 2010, Art N° 33462

LTCC, The additional investigation did not change the opinion of the Competition Council – the Mažeikiai company was abusing its dominant position, Press Release of 16 December 2010b., available at http://kt.gov.lt/en/index.php?show=news_view&pr_id=805. Accessed 23 Jan 2016

LTCC (2010c) The Lithuanian Competition Council imposes fines totalling €153,817 on two insurance companies for the conclusion of a prohibited agreement (Lietuvos draudimas, DK PZU Lietuva). 23 December 2010, e-Competitions Bulletin December 2010, Art N° 35716

LTCC, Competition Council imposes fines upon insurance companies, Press Release of 27 December 2010d., available at http://kt.gov.lt/en/index.php?show=news_view&pr_id=811. Accessed 23 Jan 2016

LTCC, Cartel agreement in the orthopedic articles production and trading market – sanctions upon the association, individual companies and the state patient fund, Press Release of 20 January 2011a. http://kt.gov.lt/en/index.php?show=news_view&pr_id=815. Accessed 23 Jan 2016

LTCC (2011b) The Lithuanian Competition Council imposes fines totalling €854 205 on producers of orthopaedic products and their association (Actualis, Idemus, Ortobatas). 20 January 2011, e-Competitions Bulletin January 2011, Art N° 35670

LTCC (2011c) The Lithuanian Court of first instance upholds Competition Authority's decision fining a company active in the petrol and diesel distribution for abusing its dominant position (Orlen Lietuva). 15 April 2011, e-Competitions Bulletin April 2011, Art N° 36588

LTCC (2011d) The Lithuanian Competition Council accepts commitments by distributors of TV channels (Viasat World and Viasat). 22 November 2011, e-Competitions Bulletin November 2011, Art N° 44199

LTCC, For price cartel fines imposed on 32 companies providing ship agency service and their association, Press Release of 8 December 2011e. http://kt.gov.lt/en/index.php?show=news_view&pr_id=945 Accessed 23 Jan 2016

LTCC (2011f) The Lithuanian Competition Council fines ship agency companies and the shipbrokers and agents association for concluding prohibited agreement in the market of ship agency services (Ship agency services). 8 December 2011, e-Competitions Bulletin December 2011, Art N° 44223

LTCC (2012a) The Lithuanian Supreme Administrative Court upholds the Competition Authority's decision on an agreement in the insurance sector (Lietuvos draudimas, DK PZU Lietuva). 20 April 2012, e-Competitions Bulletin April 2012, Art N° 46710

LTCC (2012b) The Lithuanian Supreme Administrative Court upholds NCA's decision on anticompetitive agreements in the orthopaedic products sector (Idemus, Ortopagalba, Ortopedijos centras). 17 May 2012, e-Competitions Bulletin May 2012, Art N° 48363

LTCC, A fine of more than five million litas for the prohibited agreement while selling tours online, Press Release of 7 June 2012c. http://kt.gov.lt/en/index.php?show=news_view&pr_id=1016 Accessed 23 Jan 2016

LTCC (2012d) The Lithuanian Competition Authority fines tours operators and travel agents for concerted practices relating to online sale of package tours (system Eturas). 7 June 2012, e-Competitions Bulletin June 2012, Art N° 48348

LTCC, Lithuanian Competition Council imposes fines on security services provider and three banks for restricting competition in cash handling and cash-in-transit services, Press Release of 20 December 2012e. http://kt.gov.lt/en/index.php?show=news_view&pr_id=1080 Accessed 23 Jan 2016

LTCC (2012f) The Lithuanian Competition Council imposes fines on cash handling services provider and three banks for restricting competition in cash handling and cash in transit services (G4S Lietuva, DNB bank, SEB bank and Swedbank). 20 December 2012, e-Competitions Bulletin December 2012, Art N° 51201

LTCC (2013a) The Lithuanian Supreme Court upholds Competition Council's decision finding abuse of dominant position in fuel sector (Orlen Lietuva). 21 January 2013, e-Competitions Bulletin January 2013, Art N° 51209

LTCC (2013b) The Lithuanian Competition Council closes an investigation on the suspected anti-competitive agreement between the members of the national guild of breweries. 23 December 2013, e-Competitions Bulletin December 2013, Art N° 63176

LTCC (2014a) The Supreme Administrative Court of Lithuania refers to the Court of Justice of the European Union for a preliminary ruling about concerted practices relating to online sale of package tours (Eturas). 17 January 2014, e-Competitions Bulletin January 2014, Art N° 67031

LTCC (2014b) The Lithuanian Competition Council establishes a restrictive agreement as regards limitation of beer production and finds an infringement of Article 5 of the Law on Competition and Article 101 TFEU (Guild of Breweries) 4 March 2014, e-Competitions Bulletin March 2014, Art N° 64467

LTCC (2014c) The Lithuanian Supreme Administrative Court annuls the fines imposed on the banks by the Competition Council, though confirms the restrictive character of the cash handling agreements (G4S). 8 April 2014, e-Competitions Bulletin April 2014, Art N° 65757

LTCC (2014d) The Supreme Administrative Court of Lithuania approves decision concluding that a national professional association and 32 association members entered into an anticompetitive agreement on the application of minimum tariffs for shipping agency services (LSAA). 8 April 2014, e-Competitions Bulletin April 2014, Art N° 65525

LTCC, UAB G4S Lietuva restricted competition within the markets of cash handling and cash-in-transit services, Press Release of 30 September 2014e. http://kt.gov.lt/en/index.php?show=news_view&pr_id=1498 Accessed 23 Jan 2016

LTCC (2014f) The Lithuanian Competition Council imposes fines on one bank for having implemented an anticompetitive agreement on the markets of cash handling and cash-in-transit services (G4S). 30 September 2014, e-Competitions Bulletin September 2014, Art N° 69362

LTCC, Anti-competitive agreement between Maxima LT and UAB Mantinga resulted in higher costs for consumers, Press Release of 8 December 2014g. http://kt.gov.lt/en/index.php?show=news_view&pr_id=1538 Accessed 23 Jan 2016

LTCC (2014h) The Lithuanian Competition Council imposes fines on a food retailer and a frozen bakery producer for having implemented an anticompetitive agreement (Maxima and Mantinga). 8 December 2014, e-Competitions Bulletin December 2014, Art N° 70666

Lurje D (2012) The Lithuanian Supreme Administrative Court confirms that a co-insurance pool agreement had the effect of restricting competition and upholds the decision of the NCA to impose fines (AB Lietuvos draudimas, UAB DK PZU Lietuva). 20 April 2012, e-Competitions Bulletin April 2012, Art N° 51470

Mataija M (2010) The European competition network and the shaping of the EU competition policy. Croat Yearb Eur Law Policy 6:75–101

Mencas P (2012a) The Lithuanian Competition Authority established agreements concluded through a common third party breaching Art 101 of the TFEU (Lietuvos konkurencijos taryba/Lithuanian Competition Council). 7 June 2012, e-Competitions Bulletin June 2012, Art N° 57285

Mencas P (2012b) The Lithuanian Competition Council fines security services provider and three banks for anticompetitive agreements concerning cash handling and cash-in-transit services (G4S Lietuva, DNB bank, SEB bank, Swedbank). 20 December 2012, e-Competitions Bulletin December 2012, Art N° 50879

Mencas P (2014) The Supreme Administrative Court of Lithuania confirms the presence of fault being an absolute precondition for competition law liability (G4S, DNB, SEB and Swedbank). 8 April 2014, e-Competitions Bulletin April 2014, Art N° 66152

Moisejevas R (2013) The Lithuanian Supreme Administrative Court declares that the Competition Council has to perform new evaluation of commitments since its decision lacked motives and was inconsistent (TEO/Viasat). 5 March 2013, e-Competitions Bulletin March 2013, Art N° 51788

Mykolaitis D (2012) The Lithuanian Competition Council adopts a broad interpretation of concerted practices under national rules and Art 101 TFEU (E-TURAS). 7 June 2012, e-Competitions Bulletin June 2012, Art N° 50540

Podgaiskyte V (2014) Waste management sector value changes in Lithuania along the last decade. Procedia Soc Behav Sci 110:512–519

Puksas A (2014a) The Lithuanian Competition Authority finds brewers guilty in breaching national competition rules and Article 101(1) TFEU (Lithuanian Association of Breweries). 4 Mar 2014, e-Competitions Bulletin March 2014, Art N° 64570

Puksas A (2014b) The Lithuanian Supreme Administrative Court returns a case to the Competition Authority for additional investigations (G4S). 8 April 2014, e-Competitions Bulletin April 2014, Art N° 65603

Puksas A (2014c) The Lithuanian Supreme Administrative Court reduced fines for undertakings involved in price fixing (Lithuanian Shipbrokers and Agents Association). 7 April 2014, e-Competitions Bulletin April 2014, Art N° 65602

Seikyte S (2006) The Lithuanian Competition Authority concludes that sharing of confidential information in the wholesale paper distribution markets violates both national competition provisions and Art 81 EC (Schneidersöhne Baltija). 26 October 2006, e-Competitions Bulletin October 2006, Art N° 12738

Stanikunas R, Burinskas A (2014) The impact of EU competition rules on Lithuanian competition law. Yearb Antitrust Regul Stud 7(9):87–108

Surblytė G (2009) The Competition Council of the Republic of Lithuania fines several undertakings for an agreement on a fixed tender fee (Advertising and Media Planning Agencies and their Association). 4 June 2009, e-Competitions Bulletin June 2009, Art N° 57276

Surblytė G (2010) The Competition Council of the Republic of Lithuania imposes a fine on an oil refinery for abuse of dominance after conducting an additional investigation (Orlen Lietuva). 16 December 2010, e-Competitions Bulletin December 2010, Art N° 57277

Surblytė G (2011) The Supreme Administrative Court of Lithuania issues a final judgement after several undertakings were found to have fixed a common tender fee (Association of Event Organizers). 27 May 2011, e-Competitions Bulletin May 2011, Art N° 57278

Surblytė G (2014) The Competition Council of the Republic of Lithuania terminates an investigation on compliance of actions with Article 7 of the Law on Competition and Article 102 TFEU (Viasat). 19 June 2014, e-Competitions Bulletin June 2014, Art N° 67857

Svetlicinii A (2014) Enforcement of the EU Competition Rules in Romania: application of the 'effect on trade' concept in the enforcement practice of the Romanian Competition Council. Rom Competition J 1:11–23, available at http://ssrn.com/abstract=2560680. Accessed 23 Jan 2016

Viederyte R (2014) Lithuanian maritime sector's economic impact to the whole Lithuanian economy. Procedia Soc Behav Sci 143:892–896

Virtanen D (2000) The new competition act in Lithuania. Eur Competition Law Rev 21(1):30–36

Wilks S (2005) Agency escape: decentralization or dominance of the European Commission in the modernization of competition policy? Governance 18(3):431–452

# Part II
# Challenges of Public Enforcement of EU Competition Rules Before the Commission

# The Role of the Settlement Procedure and Leniency Programme in the European Commission's Fight Against Cartels

Marc Barennes

**Abstract** In its fight against cartels, the European Commission relies on two distinct but complementary instruments. The first one is its Leniency Programme. The second one is the settlement procedure. This article examines the interplay between these instruments and draws some conclusions about their effects on the Commission's sanction policy over a 5-year period from 2010 until 2014. Most importantly, this article finds that the settlement procedure has become the norm. It has enabled the Commission to significantly reduce the duration of its proceedings and has dramatically reduced the number of appeals brought against Commission decisions while proving critical in allowing the Commission to adopt a greater number of decisions. The reason for the success of the settlement procedure is that it offers benefits to undertakings that go well beyond the 10% reduction in the fine provided for in the Settlement Notice. This article also shows that almost all the cases that led to a prohibition decision during this period started with an immunity application and that in the vast majority of cases the Commission received at least one application for a reduction in the fine, while at the same time half the undertakings that participated in the settlement procedure did not apply for or benefit from a reduction in the fine under the Leniency Programme. Finally, this article briefly addresses some of the questions that remain open for debate regarding these two instruments.

## 1 Introduction

The eradication of the cartels affecting the European Union has been a priority for the European Commission (hereinafter Commission) since the mid-1990s.[1] As one of the former EU Commissioners for Competition famously put it, cartels are

All opinions in this article are personal and may not be construed as reflecting the opinions of the General Court. All data in this article were publicly available at the time of writing this article on 8 April 2015.

[1] Almunia (2014).

M. Barennes (✉)
General Court of the European Union, Luxembourg, Luxembourg
e-mail: Marc.Barennes@curia.europa.eu

© Springer-Verlag Berlin Heidelberg 2017
V. Tomljenović et al. (eds.), *EU Competition and State Aid Rules*,
Europeanization and Globalization 3, https://doi.org/10.1007/978-3-662-47962-9_6

113

'cancers on the open market economy'.[2] For this reason, it is widely agreed that they should be considered and treated as 'the most egregious violations of competition law'.[3]

In its fight against cartels, the Commission relies on two key instruments. The first is its Leniency Programme, which was first adopted in 1996,[4] later transformed in 2002[5] and was last revised[6] in 2006 (hereinafter 2006 Leniency Notice).[7] In essence, the Leniency Programme is an investigatory instrument. It assists the Commission in uncovering cartels (which are secret by nature) by creating a prisoner's dilemma[8] and in gathering evidence of the infringement. It encourages undertakings to acknowledge their involvement in a cartel and to provide the Commission with as much evidence of that infringement as possible with a view to being rewarded with a total or partial reduction in their fine.

The second instrument, which was adopted in 2008,[9] is the settlement procedure. This procedure, which may not be assimilated into plea bargaining or negotiations[10] and which should not be mistaken for the commitments procedure,[11] is a decision-

---

[2]Monti (2000).

[3]See, for instance, 1998 OECD Council Recommendation Concerning Effective Action against Hard Core Cartels, adopted by the Council at its 921st Session on 25 March 1998 [C/M(98)7/PROV]. Available via http://www.oecd.org/competition/cartels/2752129.pdf. Accessed 30 Apr 2015. See also ICN Working Group on Cartels, Defining Hard Core Cartel Conduct, report prepared for the ICN 4th Annual Conference in Bonn, Germany, June 2005. Available via http://www.internationalcompetitionnetwork.org/media/library/conference_4th_bonn_2005/Effective_AntiCartel_Regimes_Building_Blocks.pdf. Accessed 30 Apr 2015.

[4]Commission Notice on the Non-Imposition of Fines or Reduction of Fines in Cartel Cases [1996] OJ C 207/4.

[5]Commission Notice on Immunity from Fines and Reduction of Fines in Cartel Cases [2002] OJ C 45/3.

[6]Commission Press Release, IP/06/1705, Competition: Commission adopts revised Leniency Notice to reward companies that report cartels, Brussels, 7 December 2006. Available via http://europa.eu/rapid/press-release_IP-06-1705_en.htm?locale=en. Accessed 30 Apr 2015.

[7]Commission Notice on Immunity from Fines and Reduction of Fines in Cartel Cases [2006] OJ C 298/17.

[8]See for instance in this regard Leslie (2006).

[9]Commission Regulation (EC) No 622/2008 of 30 June 2008 amending Regulation (EC) No 773/2004, as regards the Conduct of Settlement Procedures in Cartel Cases [2008] OJ L 171/3 and Commission Notice on the Conduct of Settlement Procedures in view of the Adoption of Decisions pursuant to Article 7 and Article 23 of Council Regulation (EC) No 1/2003 in Cartel Cases [2008] OJ C 167/1.

[10]See Point 2 of the Settlement Notice. See also Commission Press Release IP/08/1056, Antitrust: Commission Introduces Settlement Procedure for Cartels – Frequently Asked Questions, Brussels, 30 June 2008. Available via http://europa.eu/rapid/press-release_MEMO-08-458_en.htm. Accessed 30 Apr 2015.

[11]The settlement procedure, which only applies to cartels, should not be confused with the commitments procedure, which does not apply to cartels, and which provides for the adoption of decisions pursuant to Article 9 of Regulation No 1/2003, and whereby the Commission does not find an infringement in the past but only addresses future behaviour.

making tool. It allows the Commission to 'speed up the adoption of a [cartel] Decision' and the undertaking to obtain a reduction in its fine.[12] In essence, undertakings that engage in this procedure must, after getting the opportunity to discuss the matter with the Commission, acknowledge their participation in the cartel infringement as defined by the Commission and their willingness to pay the amount of the fine as previously determined by the Commission.[13]

This article examines the role of the settlement procedure and Leniency Programme in the Commission's fight against cartels. Section 2 of this article analyses the interplay between the procedure and the Programme. Section 3 draws some conclusions regarding the effects of this procedure and the Programme on the results obtained by the Commission over the past 5 years from 1 January 2010 until 31 December 2014.

## 2   The Interplay Between the Settlement Procedure and Leniency Programme

The settlement procedure and Leniency Programme are enshrined in different legal instruments, but they share a common legal basis and a common goal (see Sect. 2.1). They are also independent procedures that offer complementary benefits (see Sect. 2.2).

### 2.1   The Goals and Legal Basis of the Settlement Procedure and Leniency Programme

Firstly, the Leniency Programme and settlement procedure both reflect, in essence, the right that the Commission has to take into consideration the cooperation it receives from undertakings during an administrative procedure when fixing a fine. On the one hand, Commission Regulation No 622/2008[14] and the Settlement Notice[15] provide the rules that apply to the settlement procedure. They explicitly refer to the Commission's right to adopt a decision ordering, on the basis of Article 7 of Regulation (EC) No 1/2003, that a competition infringement be brought to an end and, on the basis of Article 23 of Regulation (EC) No 1/2003, that a fine be imposed on a competition infringer. On the other hand, the Leniency Notice does

---

[12]Commission Press Release IP/08/1056, cited at footnote 10 above.

[13]See Point 2 of the Settlement Notice.

[14]See footnote 9 above.

[15]Ibid.

not refer to any specific legal basis.[16] However, the General Court found in *Mamoli Robineterria v Commission*[17] that the Commission's right to totally or partially reduce a fine was at least implicitly enshrined in Article 23 of Regulation (EC) No 1/2003 on the ground that, according to the established case law, the Commission may take into consideration the cooperation provided by undertakings during an administrative procedure in determining a fine. The settlement procedure and Leniency Programme therefore share a common legal basis despite the fact they are both enshrined in two distinct legal instruments.

Secondly, even if they are distinct cooperation instruments, the settlement procedure, being a decision-making tool, and the Leniency Programme, being an investigatory tool, both share a common goal.[18] This goal is to allow the Commission to avail itself of 'free resources to deal with [additional] cases, [and] increase the detection rate and overall efficiency of the Commission's antitrust enforcement'.[19] To achieve this goal,[20] it is worthwhile highlighting that the Commission also relies on the 2006 Fining Guidelines[21] and the Cartels Directorate that it has put in place within DG Competition.

The 2006 Fining Guidelines that the Commission adopted in the same year as the currently applicable Leniency Programme significantly increased the amount of the fines imposed on competition law infringers in general[22] and on cartel participants in particular,[23] especially those that only manufacture one line of products. They were adopted on the premise that high fines combined with an effective Leniency Programme provide 'powerful "carrot and stick" inducements to be the first to reveal a cartel'.[24]

---

[16]It is worthwhile mentioning that, in the context of the transposition of the Private Damages Directive, the Commission launched a public consultation which ended on 25 March 2015 regarding, inter alia, a proposal to amend Regulation (EC) No 773/2004 relating to the conduct of proceedings by the Commission pursuant to Articles 81 and 82 EC. Available via http://ec. europa.eu/competition/consultations/2014_regulation_773_2004/regulation_773_2004_en.pdf. Accessed 30 Apr 2015. One of the proposed amendments consists in inserting an Article 4a in Regulation No 1/2003. This article explicitly provides for the Commission's right to reward cooperating undertakings with a total or partial reduction in fines 'which would have otherwise been imposed under Article 23(2) of Regulation No 1/2003'.

[17]Case T-376/10 *Mamoli Robineterria v Commission* ECLI:EU:T:2013:442, para 55 (Case C-679/13 P currently under appeal before the Court of Justice).

[18]See also Laina and Laurinen (2013). As rightly put by these authors, the settlement procedure and Leniency Programme work towards the same goal even if they are serving different purposes.

[19]Ibid. These authors, however, use this definition only regarding the settlement procedure.

[20]Kroes (2006).

[21]Guidelines on the Method of Setting Fines Imposed Pursuant to Article 23(2)(a) of Regulation No 1/2003 [2006] OJ C 210/2.

[22]Commission Press Release IP/06/857, Competition: Commission Revises Guidelines for Setting Fines in Antitrust Cases, Brussels, 28 June 2006. Available via http://europa.eu/rapid/press-release_IP-06-857_en.htm?locale=en. Accessed 30 Apr 2015.

[23]DG Competition website, information relating to Leniency. Available via http://ec.europa.eu/competition/cartels/leniency/leniency.html. Accessed 30 Apr 2015.

[24]OECD, Using Leniency to Fight Hard Core Cartels, Policy Brief, September 2001. Available via http://www.oecd.org/daf/competition/1890449.pdf. Accessed 30 Apr 2015.

The Cartels Directorate was created in 2005 and since then has been entrusted with the prime responsibility for handling cartels on the premise that 'a certain degree of specialization [was] needed for effective action against cartels'.[25] Given the specific and complex investigatory, procedural, legal and factual issues raised by cartels, concentrating specialised case handlers in one directorate allows the Commission to build on the experience it acquires in each case and adapt efficiently to the evolving challenges that their prosecution and sanctions raise. The efficiency of the settlement procedure and Leniency Programme depends therefore largely on the Commission's capacity to convince undertakings that the Cartels Directorate will eventually uncover the cartel infringement and that the Commission will then impose high fines on the undertakings that participated in it.

## 2.2 The Procedure and Benefits of the Settlement Procedure and Leniency Programme

Firstly, even if the settlement procedure and Leniency Notice are independent procedures, they are nonetheless connected at an early stage of the Commission proceedings. Explaining the precise functioning of the settlement procedure goes beyond the scope of this article.[26] However, it is worthwhile mentioning that after completing its investigation of the facts and after adopting a formal decision to initiate proceedings, the Commission retains a broad margin of discretion as to whether it will offer undertakings the opportunity to engage in the settlement procedure.[27] The Commission's discretion is without prejudice to the fact that parties may flag their interest in engaging in such a procedure.[28] The Commission has also put in place a screening test that helps it determine whether the settlement procedure should be adapted to deal with the case at hand.[29] The settlement procedure may be divided into four stages.[30]

---

[25]Saarela and Malric-Smith (2005), p. 53.

[26]For a detailed explanation of the functioning of the settlement procedure, see Laina and Laurinen (2013).

[27]Point 5 of the Settlement Notice.

[28]Laina and Laurinen (2013).

[29]Laina and Bogdanov (2014), p. 2. According to these authors, the 'screening' test that the Commission carries out includes taking into consideration the number of parties involved (the fewer parties, the easier a settlement may be reached), the number and proportion of leniency applicants (the more leniency applicants, the easier it is to reach a settlement), the degree of cooperation of the parties (the more opposition from the parties, the less chance there is of reaching a settlement), the agreement to the fine (the more aggravating the circumstances, the less willing the parties might be to accept the fine), the possibility of setting a precedent (the more novel the legal issues, the less the settlement decision is), and the existence of parallel enforcement procedures (which contribute to the complexity of the case) and private enforcement claims (which reduce the incentive of undertakings to admit their involvement in a cartel).

[30]Point 9 of the Settlement Notice.

The first stage of the settlement procedure is the initiation stage. The Commission may explore the undertakings' willingness to engage in the settlement procedure[31] by giving them a time limit within which they must declare in writing their interest in the procedure.[32] In parallel, whereas undertakings may normally make an application under the Leniency Programme at any stage of a standard procedure, the time limit fixed by the Commission for undertakings to manifest their interest in the settlement procedure becomes the deadline for them to apply for a reduction in the fine under the Leniency Programme. This is the only procedural connection that exists between the Leniency Programme and the settlement procedure. The other three stages of the settlement procedure are carried out independently of the Leniency Programme.

The second stage of the settlement procedure is the discussion stage. In practice, this stage is divided into three rounds of discussion.[33] According to Laina and Laurinen (2013), 'it is commonly accepted that the 10% reduction in fines for settling companies, which is cumulative with the reduction under leniency, is not the only reason for companies to settle'. During the first round, the Commission presents undertakings with its case and the key evidence it relies on. Undertakings may then present their arguments and evidence. During the second round of discussions, the Commission presents its conclusions regarding the arguments and evidence submitted by the parties with a view to reaching a common understanding. During the third round of discussions, the Commission indicates the maximum fine it will impose on a take-it-or-leave-it basis.

The third stage is the submission stage. During this stage, undertakings must first make an irrevocable settlement submission in which they acknowledge in clear and unequivocal terms their involvement in the infringement. They must also indicate that they will accept paying the fine as previously determined by the Commission.[34] Second, the Commission adopts a short Statement of Objections.[35] Third, the undertakings confirm in writing that this Statement of Objections reflects their submission.[36]

The fourth and last stage is the adoption phase. After the Advisory Committee on Restrictive Practices and Dominant Positions issues its opinion, the Commission adopts a decision ordering that the infringement be brought to an end and that a fine be imposed on the undertaking.[37] This decision is 20 to 40 pages long in practice, whereas a standard decision normally contains several hundred pages. In its decision, the Commission may grant a reduction in the fine under the settlement

---

[31]Points 11 and 13 of the Settlement Notice.

[32]Ibid.

[33]Laina and Laurinen (2013), pp. 3–4.

[34]Points 20(a) and (b) of the Settlement Notice. See also the two other requirements provided for in Points 20(c) and (d) of the Settlement Notice.

[35]Point 23 of the Settlement Notice.

[36]Point 26 of the Settlement Notice.

[37]Point 30 of the Settlement Notice.

procedure and Leniency Programme after applying the 10% cap, which sets the maximum amount of the fine that the Commission is allowed to impose.[38] The final decision may be challenged before the General Court, as would be the case for any other prohibition decision imposing a fine adopted on the basis of Articles 7 and 23 of Regulation No 1/2003.[39] It is worthwhile pointing out in this regard that EU courts have not yet had the opportunity to take a position as to whether undertakings that have benefited from a 10% reduction for cooperation with the Commission in the settlement procedure ought to lose the benefit of this reduction as a consequence of the fact that they eventually appealed the decision.[40]

Secondly, the settlement procedure and Leniency Programme offer complementary benefits to both the Commission and undertakings.[41]

On the one hand, the Leniency Programme offers, as a first benefit, a total or partial reduction in the fine to undertakings that fulfil, in essence, two requirements. The first requirement is that the undertaking must acknowledge its involvement in a cartel infringement and provide the Commission with information that allows it to carry out a targeted inspection or to establish the infringement.[42] In such cases, it may benefit from immunity from fines. If immunity is not available, the undertaking must bring evidence that has significant added value for the Commission in establishing the infringement.[43] It may then benefit from a reduction in the fine of 30 to 50% if it is the first undertaking to meet this requirement, 20 to 30% if it is the second or up to 20% if it meets this condition after the first two undertakings.[44] The second requirement is that the undertaking, whether it is an applicant for immunity[45] or a reduction in its fine,[46] must cooperate with the Commission, must have ended its involvement in the cartel and must not have destroyed, falsified or concealed evidence when contemplating making its application or have disclosed the fact or any of the content of its prospective application. As a second benefit, pursuant to Article 11(4) of the Private Damages Directive, undertakings that have benefited from immunity will not, unlike their co-participants in the cartel, be jointly and severally liable vis-à-vis all cartel victims. According to this article, they will only be liable vis-à-vis their own direct and indirect purchasers and providers, unless the cartel victims cannot obtain full compensation from the co-participants in the cartel.

On the other hand, the settlement procedure offers a 10% reduction in the fine to undertakings as a reward for their 'cooperation in the expeditious handling of the case'.[47] The essential requirement for this 10% reduction is that the undertaking

---

[38]Point 32 of the Settlement Notice.

[39]See, for instance, Laina and Laurinen (2013), p. 10.

[40]Laina and Laurinen (2013), p. 6.

[41]Point 33 of the Settlement Notice.

[42]Points 8(a) and (b) of the Leniency Notice.

[43]Point 24 of the 2006 Leniency Notice.

[44]Point 26 of the 2006 Leniency Notice.

[45]Points 12(a)-(c) of the Leniency Notice.

[46]Point 24 of the Leniency Notice.

[47]Points 2 and 21 of the Settlement Notice.

acknowledges its involvement in the cartel in the terms determined at the end of the discussions that it has had with the Commission and accepts the maximum fine that the Commission informed it that it would have to pay.[48] All parties in the settlement procedure are under a duty of confidentiality regarding the information they have access to during the procedure.[49]

It is widely agreed,[50] however, that the settlement procedure offers additional benefits to the 10% reduction in the fine, which on its own would be 'widely seen as not much of a carrot'.[51]

The first additional benefit is that the settlement procedure is considered by undertakings as allowing 'a more meaningful discussion with the Commission than what would [have been] possible in a standard procedure'.[52] The consequence of this 'more meaningful discussion' is that fines imposed at the end of the settlement procedure may well be lower than those that would have been imposed in the context of a standard procedure.[53] This is because the dialogue during the settlement procedure may influence the determination of the scope and duration of the infringement,[54] as well as the value of the affected turnover to be taken into consideration when calculating the fine. It may also influence the aggravating and mitigating circumstances that the Commission will take into consideration in determining the amount of the fine.[55] In essence, the Commission may want to 'focus more on the core infringement'[56] since it has a strong incentive to reach a settlement once it has decided to engage in the settlement procedure. This procedure is also beneficial to undertakings in so far as their incentive to appeal the final decision, and therefore incur additional legal costs and suffer from prolonged management distraction due to the proceedings, is reduced.[57]

The second additional benefit is that the 'decision adopted at the end of the procedure does not contain a full assessment of the facts as it would be in a contested case [and ...] this reduces the amount of publicly available information that could be used by potential damage claimants'.[58] In this last regard, it should be noted that the Private Damages Directive[59] provides that a national judge may not, in principle, order the disclosure of either the corporate statements made in the

---

[48]Points 20(a) and (b) of the Settlement Notice.

[49]Point 7 of the Leniency Notice.

[50]See Laina and Laurinen (2013), p. 7. See also Hansen et al. (2014).

[51]Hansen et al. (2014).

[52]Ibid.

[53]Ibid.

[54]Ibid.

[55]Snelders (2015).

[56]Ibid. See also Hansen et al. (2014).

[57]Ibid.

[58]Ibid.

[59]Directive 2014/104/EU of the European Parliament and of the Council on certain rules governing actions for damages under national law for infringements of the competition law provisions of the Member States and of the European Union, [2014] OJ L 349/1.

context of the Leniency Programme or the submissions made in the context of the settlement procedure.[60] All these benefits therefore add up as 'sweeteners' in addition to those resulting from the total or partial reductions in the fine that may be obtained under the Leniency Programme.

By way of conclusion on the interplay between the settlement procedure and Leniency Programme, it may be considered that the procedure and Programme are both designed to assist the Commission in efficiently pursuing its objective to deter, uncover and prohibit cartel behaviour, by offering distinct and complementary incentives to undertakings to turn their backs on their past illegal behaviour in the quickest and least financially damaging way for them.

# 3    The Effects of the Settlement Procedure and Leniency Programme on the Commission's Sanction Practice over the Past Five Years

The Commission's cartel decision practice over the past 5 years is analysed in the three tables that appear at the end of this article. Table 1 describes full settlement decisions, whereby a final prohibition decision was adopted against all parties by means of a settlement procedure. Table 2 describes hybrid decisions, whereby at least one of the parties opted out of the settlement procedure that it had started taking part in. Table 3 describes non-settlement decisions that were adopted pursuant to the standard procedure. Each one of these tables also indicates the number of undertakings that obtained (but not that applied for) a total or a partial reduction in the fine under the Leniency Programme. These three tables enable a series of conclusions to be drawn regarding the effects of the settlement procedure and Leniency Programme on the results that the Commission has obtained in its fight against cartels over the past 5 years.

## 3.1    The Effects of the Settlement Procedure on the Commission's Fight Against Cartels

As far as the settlement procedure is concerned, the first conclusion that may be drawn from Tables 1 to 3 is that use of the settlement procedure has taken precedence over the standard procedure to become the norm. Over the past 5 years, the settlement procedure has been used in 60% of the decisions that the Commission has adopted. Out of 27 decisions, 16 decisions were either full settlement or hybrid decisions, while 11 were non-settlement decisions. Even more representatively, for the year 2014 alone, 80% of the Commission's decisions

---

[60]Article 6(6) of the Private Damages Directive cited in footnote 59 above.

**Table 1** Full settlement cartel decisions

Full settlement cartel decisions

| Decisions | Duration of procedure[a] | Total fine (circa) | No of suspected undertakings | No of settling parties | No of non-settling parties | Immunity beneficiary | Reduction of fine beneficiaries | Appeals before the GC |
|---|---|---|---|---|---|---|---|---|
| 2014 | | | | | | | | |
| 39780 – *Paper Envelopes* (12/2014) | 4 years | €19m | 5 | 5 | 0 | 0 | 1 (50%) 1 (25%) 1 (10%) | 1 (brought in 2015) |
| 39924 – *Swiss Franc Interest Rate Derivatives (CHF Libor)* 21/10/2014 | 3 years | €61m | 2 | 2 | 0 | 1 | 1 (40%) | 0 |
| 39924 – *Swiss Franc Interest Rate Derivatives (Bid Asked Spreads)* (10/2014) | 3 years | €32m | 4 | 4 | 0 | 1 | 1 (30%) 1 (25%) | 0 |
| 39922 – *Car and Truck Bearings* (03/2014) | 3½ years | €953m | 6 | 6 | 0 | 1 | 1 (40%) 1 (30%) 2 (20%) | 0 |
| 39952 – *Power Exchanges* (03/2014) | 2 years | €6m | 2 | 2 | 0 | 0 | 0 | 0 |
| 39801 – *Polyurethane Foam* (01/2014) | 4 years | €114m | 4 | 4 | 0 | 1 | 3 (50%) | 0 |

| 2013 | | | | | | | | | |
|---|---|---|---|---|---|---|---|---|---|
| 39748 – Automotive Wire Harnesses (07/2013) | 3½ years | €141m | 5 | 5 | 0 | 1 | 1st and 2nd infringement 1 (40%) 1 (30%) 3rd infringement 1 (50%) 4th infringement 1 (45%) 5th infringement 1 (40%) 2 (30%) | 0 |
| **2012** | | | | | | | | | |
| 39611 – Water Management Products (6/2012) | 3½ years | €13m | 3 | 3 | 0 | 1 | 0 | 0 |
| **2011** | | | | | | | | | |
| 39600 – Refrigeration Compressors (12/2011) | 3 years | €161m | 5 | 5 | 0 | 1 | 1 (45%) 1 (25%) 1 (20%) 1 (15%) | 0 |
| 39605 – CRT Glass Bulbs (10/2011) | 2½ years | €128m | 4 | 4 | 0 | 1 | 1 (50%) | 0 |
| 39579 – Consumer Detergents (4/2011) | 3 years | €315m | 3 | 3 | 0 | 1 | 1 (50%) 1 (25%) | 0 |

(continued)

**Table 1** (continued)

Full settlement cartel decisions

| Decisions | Duration of procedure[a] | Total fine (circa) | No of suspected undertakings | No of settling parties | No of non-settling parties | Immunity beneficiary | Reduction of fine beneficiaries | Appeals before the GC |
|---|---|---|---|---|---|---|---|---|
| 2010 | | | | | | | | |
| 38511 – *DRAM* (05/2010) | 8 years (but 1½ after proposing to initiate settlement proceedings) | €331m | 10 | 10 | 0 | 1 | 1 (45%) 1 (27%) 3 (18%) | 0 |

Information extracted from DG Competition official press releases available on the DG Competition website

[a]The approximate duration taken into consideration from the immunity request or inspection date (whichever is earliest). In cases where the date of the application is not official, 3 months were added to the duration of the investigation

**Table 2** Hybrid cartel decisions

| Hybrid cartel decisions (2010–2014) | | | | | | | | |
|---|---|---|---|---|---|---|---|---|
| Decisions | Duration of procedure[a] | Total fine (circa) | No of suspected undertakings | No of settling parties | No of non-settling parties | Immunity beneficiary | Reduction of fine beneficiaries | Appeals before the GC |
| **2014** | | | | | | | | |
| 39792 – Steel Abrasives (04/14) | 4 years | €30m | 5 | 4 | 1 (SO sent within 6 months) | 1 | 0 | not known yet for non-settling party |
| 39965 – Canned Mushrooms (06/2014) | 2 years | €32m | 4 | 3 | 1 (SO not yet adopted) | 1 | 1 (30%) | not known yet for non-settling party |
| **2013** | | | | | | | | |
| 39914 – Euro Interest Rate Derivatives (EIRD) (12/2013) | 2 years | €1.3bn | 7 | 4 | 3 (SO sent within 6 months) | 1 | 1 (50%) 1 (30%) 1 (5%) | 1 by a settling party and not yet known for non-settling parties |
| 39861 – Yen Interest Rate Derivatives (YIRD) (12/2013) | 2 years | €470m | 7 | 6 | 1 (final decision adopted on 02/2015) | 1 | 1 (25%) 1 (35%, 30%) 1(35%, 30%, 100%, 40%) 1 (25%) | not known yet for non-settling party |
| **2011–2012** | | | | | | | | |
| No hybrid decisions | | | | | | | | |
| **2010** | | | | | | | | |
| 38866 – Animal Feed Phosphates (10/2010) | 7 years | €175m | 6 | 5 | 1 (sanctioned at the same time as settlement parties) | 1 | 1 (50%) 1 (25%) 1 (5%) | 1 |

Information extracted from DG Competition official press releases available on the DG Competition website

[a] The approximate duration taken into consideration from the immunity request or inspection date (whichever is earliest). In cases where the date of the application is not official, 3 months were added to the duration of the investigation

**Table 3** Non-settlement cartel decisions

NON-settlement cartel decisions (2010–2014)

| Decisions | Duration (circa)[a] | Total fine (circa) | No of suspected undertakings | No of settling parties | No of non-settling parties | Immunity beneficiary | Reduction of fine beneficiaries | Appeals before the GC (at least) |
|---|---|---|---|---|---|---|---|---|
| **2014** | | | | | | | | |
| 39610 – *Power Cables* (04/14) | 5 years | €301m | 11 | 0 | 11 | 1 | 1 (45% + some de facto immunity) | 13 |
| 39574 – *Smart Card Chips* (09/14) | 6 years | €138m | 4 | (discontinued settlement procedure in 2012) | 2 | 1 | 1 (30%) | 2 |
| **2013** | | | | | | | | |
| 39633 – *Shrimps* (11/2013) | 5 years | €28m | 4 | 0 | 4 | 1 | 1 (outside the scope of the Notice as a mitigating circumstance) | 2 |
| **2012** | | | | | | | | |
| 39437 – *TV and Computer Monitor Tubes* (11/2012) | 5 years | €1.47bn | 7 | 0 | 7 | 1 | 1 (40%) 1 (30%) 1 (10%) | 4 |
| 39462 – *Freight Forwarding* (3/2012) | 5 years | €169m | 14 | 0 | 14 | 1 | 1st infringement 1 (35%) 2nd infringement 1 (30%) 1 (25%) 3rd infringement 1 (50%) 1 (20%) 1 (5%) 4th infringement 1 (50%) 1 (25%) | 10 |

| | | | | | | | | |
|---|---|---|---|---|---|---|---|---|
| 39452 – Mountings for Window and Window-Doors (3/2012) | 5 years | €86m | 9 | 0 | 1 | 0 | 1 (45%) 2 (25%) | 1 |
| 2011 | | | | | | | | |
| 39482 – Exotic Fruit (10/2011) | 4 years at least (6 years at most) | €9m | 2 | 0 | 1 | 0 | 0 | 0 |
| 2010 | | | | | | | | |
| 39309 – LCD (12/2010) | 4 years | €648m | 6 | 0 | 1 | 0 | 1 (50%) 1 (20%) 1 (5%) | 1 |
| 39258 – Airfreight (11/2010) | 5 years | €799m | 11 | 0 | 1 | 0 | 1 (50%) 1 (25%) 4 (20%) 2 (15%) 1 (10%) | 9 |
| 38344 – Prestressing Steel (06/2010) | 8 years | €269m | 17 | 0 | 1 | 0 | 1 (50%) 1 (25%) 1 (20%) 2 (5%) | 28 |
| 39092 – Bathroom Fittings and Fixtures (06/2010) | 6 years | €622m | 17 | 0 | 1 | 0 | 2 (30%) | 17 |

Information extracted from DG Competition official press releases available on the DG Competition website

[a]The approximate duration taken into consideration from the immunity request or inspection date (whichever is earliest). In cases where the date of the application is not official, 3 months were added to the duration of the investigation

were full settlement or hybrid decisions. In particular, out of the ten decisions adopted in 2014, eight were either full settlement or hybrid decisions, while two were non-settlement decisions. This shows that only a few years after the adoption of the settlement procedure, the Commission managed to convince undertakings of its benefits over the standard procedure. Notably, these percentages exceed the prediction made in 2013 by the former Commissioner for Competition that 'around half of [Commission] cartel cases may be concluded with settlements in the coming years'.[61]

The second conclusion is that the settlement procedure has enabled the Commission to significantly reduce the duration of its proceedings. On average, over the past 5 years, it has taken the Commission approximately 4.8 years to adopt a non-settlement decision in comparison to approximately 2.7 years to adopt a settlement decision. In a small number of cases adopted in 2013 and 2014, the Commission even managed to adopt a settlement decision in as little as 2 years.[62] This highlights all the procedural efficiency gains that the settlement procedure offers in contrast to decisions adopted by way of the standard procedure of approximately 5 to 6 years in 2014.[63]

The third conclusion is that, over the past 5 years, the Commission's decision to initiate a settlement procedure has eventually led to the adoption of a full settlement decision in 70% of cases. In only one case[64] did the Commission discontinue the settlement procedure vis-à-vis all undertakings because of a lack of progress in the settlement talks and revert to a standard procedure. In four of the five cases where a hybrid decision was adopted, only one undertaking opted out of the procedure. The fact that as many as 30% of the settlement cases were hybrid cases may be interpreted in several ways. First, it may indicate that undertakings that are not satisfied with the Commission's legal or factual appraisal, or with the calculation of the fine, do not hesitate to walk away from the settlement procedure. Second, this percentage tends to show that the Commission might be more selective in future as to the cases in which it will offer the opportunity to engage in a settlement procedure.[65] Third, it must nonetheless be highlighted that even in hybrid decisions, which by definition constitute a partial failure of the settlement process,[66] there were procedural gains in so far as the Commission was still able, as shown in Table 2, to adopt a statement of objections concerning the non-settling undertakings within 6 months of the adoption of the settlement decision concerning the settling parties.[67]

---

[61] Almunia (2013).

[62] See Case COMP/39914 *EIRD* [2013]; Case COMP/39861 *YIRD* [2013]; Case COMP/39952 *Power Exchange* [2014]; Case COMP/39965 *Canned Mushrooms* [2014].

[63] See Case COMP/39610 *Power Cables* [2014]; Case COMP/39574 *Smart Card Chips* [2014] (in which the settlement procedure was discontinued).

[64] See Case COMP/39574 *Smart Card Chips* [2014].

[65] See Laina and Bogdanov (2014), p. 6, cited in footnote 29 above.

[66] De Coninck (2015).

[67] For a contrary opinion, see De Coninck (2015).

The fourth conclusion is that the settlement procedure has dramatically reduced the number of appeals brought against Commission decisions. Over the past 5 years, only three appeals[68] (out of the 17 full settlement and hybrid cases adopted) were lodged before the General Court. By way of comparison, all the 15 undertakings involved in the two non-settlement decisions[69] adopted in 2014 appealed.

The fifth conclusion is that in 2014 alone, the settlement procedure proved critical in allowing the Commission to adopt a greater number of decisions. On the one hand, it must be noted that the overall number of decisions adopted during the 2005–2009 period and the 2010–2014 period remained more or less equivalent despite the introduction of the settlement procedure in 2008. More specifically, according to DG Competition statistics, during the 2005–2009 period, 33 decisions were adopted and 205 undertakings were condemned, while during the 2010–2014 period 30 decisions were adopted and 192 undertakings were condemned.[70] On the other hand, in the year 2014, the Commission adopted approximately twice as many decisions as in each of the previous 3 years, namely ten decisions were adopted in 2014, while four or five decisions were adopted between 2011 and 2013. Furthermore, 80% of the decisions adopted in 2014 were not decisions adopted pursuant to the standard procedure.[71] The experience that the Commission has gained using this instrument over the past 5 years should prove useful in the coming years in allowing it to adopt a steady stream of cartel decisions.[72]

## 3.2   The Effects of the Leniency Programme on the Commission's Fight Against Cartels

As far as the enforcement by the Commission of the Leniency Programme is concerned, three main conclusions may be drawn from the three tables below.

The first is that almost all the cases that have led to a prohibition decision during the past 5 years started with an immunity application. Two percentages are particularly telling in this regard. First, 90% of all the prohibition decisions were adopted after an immunity application was lodged. Second, 100% of the cases that ended in a non-settlement decision started with an immunity application. These figures clearly show the critical role that the Leniency Programme plays in the Commission's capacity to trigger an investigation and to adopt a final prohibition decision.

---

[68]See Case COMP/3886 *Animal Feed Phosphates* [2010]; Case COMP/39914 *EIRD* [2013]; Case COMP/39780 *Paper Envelopes* [2014].

[69]See Case COMP/39610 *Power Cables* [2014]; Case COMP/39574 *Smart Card Chips* [2013].

[70]Statistics available via http://ec.europa.eu/competition/cartels/statistics/statistics.pdf. Accessed 30 Apr 2015.

[71]See the first paragraph of Sect. 3.1.

[72]See Laina and Laurinen (2013), p. 2.

The second conclusion is that, in addition to immunity applications, the Commission received applications for a reduction in the fine in a large majority of cases. In 80% of cases, it received one application for a reduction in the fine. In 60% of cases, it received two applications for a reduction in the fine and in 50% three. These percentages highlight the importance that applications for a reduction in the fine play in the Commission's capacity to establish the facts of a case.

The third conclusion is that, surprisingly enough, as many as 50% of undertakings that participated in the settlement procedure did not apply or benefit from a reduction in the fine under the Leniency Programme. Such a high percentage may seem counterintuitive in so far as it might be assumed that an undertaking willing to acknowledge its involvement in a cartel would also be wanting to obtain the highest reduction in its fine by applying under the Leniency Programme. In the absence of publicly available information regarding the reasons that lead these undertakings to settle without applying for a reduction under the Leniency Programme, this high percentage remains difficult to interpret.

# 4   Conclusion

The settlement procedure and Leniency Programme interplayed efficiently from 2010 to 2014 to offer considerable immediate benefits to both the Commission and undertakings. From the Commission's perspective, the procedure and Programme have enabled it to adopt decisions in a more expeditious way and with fewer appeals to defend before the General Court, or in the words of the recently appointed Commissioner for Competition, Vestager (2014): 'the record shows that [the Commission] is still getting better at catching the cartelists'.[73] From the undertakings' perspective, the settlement procedure and Leniency Programme have enabled them to turn the page on their cartel behaviour more swiftly and at a lower cost.

These immediate benefits ought to be balanced with the effects that the settlement procedure and Leniency Programme may have on the Commission's fight against cartels in the longer term.[74] Such a balancing exercise would require, in our view, examining two questions in particular. The first one is whether the quasi-systematic use of the settlement procedure and Leniency Programme could have a negative impact on cartel deterrence and on private enforcement. The second question is whether the Commission is able to develop new legal theories within the framework of the settlement procedure.

Finally, it still remains to be seen whether the General Court will apply the same standards of review when controlling decisions adopted pursuant to the settlement

---

[73]See Statement 14/2600 by Commissioner Vestager on the *Envelopes* cartel settlement decision, Brussels, 11 December 2014. Available via http://europa.eu/rapid/press-release_STATEMENT-14-2600_fr.htm. Accessed 30 Apr 2015.

[74]See in particular in this regard Waelbroek (2008). See also Ascione and Motta (2009).

procedure and those pursuant to the standard procedure, in particular regarding the amount of the fine.[75]

# References

Almunia J (2013) Remedies, commitments and settlements in antitrust. Speech 13/210 SV KartelRecht Brussels. Available via http://europa.eu/rapid/press-release_SPEECH-13-210_ en.htm. Accessed 30 Apr 2015

Almunia J (2014) Fighting against cartels: a priority for the present and for the future. Speech 14/281 SV Kartellrecht Brussels. Available via http://europa.eu/rapid/press-release_SPEECH- 14-281_en.htm. Accessed 30 Apr 2015

Ascione A, Motta M (2009) Settlement in cartel cases. In: Ehlerman CD, Marquis M (eds) European competition law annual 2008: antitrust settlements under EC competition law. Hart, Oxford

De Coninck R (2015) Settlements: an economic perspective. Concurrences law & economics workshop, 14 January 2015, Brussels. Available via http://www.concurrences.com/Photos/ Use-and-Abuse-of-Settlements-in-1692/. Accessed 30 Apr 2015

Hansen M, Van Gerven G, Laina F (2014) EU cartel settlements: are they working? Interview of Commission officials by Vascott D. Glob Competition Rev 16(5)

Kroes N (2006) Delivering on the crackdown: recent developments in the European Commission's campaign against cartels. 10th annual competition conference at the European Institute, Fiesole, Italy, 13 October 2006, Speech/06/595. Available via http://europa.eu/rapid/press- release_SPEECH-06-595_en.htm?locale=en. Accessed 30 Apr 2015

Laina F, Bogdanov A (2014) The EU cartel settlement procedure: latest developments. J Eur Competition Law Pract 5(10):717–727

Laina F, Laurinen E (2013) The EU cartel settlement procedure: current status and challenges. J Eur Competition Law Pract 4(4):302–311

Leslie CR (2006) Antitrust amnesty, game theory and cartel stability. J Corp Law, Winter 2006. Available at http://lesliecaton.com/wordpress/wp-content/uploads/2012/01/10-LESLIE- FINAL.pdf. Accessed 30 Apr 2015

Monti M (2000) Fighting cartels: why and how? Why should we be concerned with cartels and collusive behaviour? Speech/00/295, 3rd Nordic competition policy conference, Stockholm. Available via http://europa.eu/rapid/press-release_SPEECH-00-295_en.htm. Accessed 30 Apr 2015

Saarela A, Malric-Smith P (2005) Reorganisation of cartel work in DG Competition. Competition Policy newsletter, Summer 2005, p 53. Available via http://ec.europa.eu/competition/publica tions/cpn/2005_2_43.pdf. Accessed 30 Apr 2015

Snelders R (2015) The EU cartel settlement program: key elements, practical considerations & scope for abuse. Concurrences law & economics workshop, 14 January 2015, Brussels. Available via http://www.concurrences.com/Photos/Use-and-Abuse-of-Settlements-in-1692/. Accessed 30 Apr 2015

Waelbroek D (2008) Le développement en droit européen de la concurrence des solutions négociées (engagements, clémence, non-contestation des faits et transactions): que va-t-il rester aux juges? In: Global Competition Law Centre Working Papers Series GCLC, Working Paper 01/08

---

[75]Pursuant to Article 261 TFEU and Article 31 Reg. No 1/2003, the General Court may use its unlimited jurisdiction to review the amount of the fine imposed by the Commission.

# Fines and Fundamental Rights: New Challenges

## Ludovic Bernardeau

**Abstract** The borderline between EU competition law and criminal law may seem blurred considering the issue of whether fines are of a criminal nature. Even though principles of criminal-law origin exist in the form of general principles of EU competition law, judges seem reluctant to recognise such *criminalisation*. Does one have to pay for one's crime in the scope of competition law? No definite answer exists yet as this issue has so far not been resolved.

## 1 Introduction

According to the European Union (EU) legislator, the European Commission's (Commission) decision imposing a fine for an infringement of competition law 'shall not be of a criminal nature'.[1] However, it seems that, in the field of EU competition law, the EU judge acts more like a criminal-law judge. And this involves respect of certain fundamental rights. The purpose of this contribution is to address this issue with regard to the implementation of fundamental rights in the criminal area in the case law of both the Court of Justice of the European Union (Court of Justice) and the General Court of the European Union (General Court) in the context of EU competition law.

The views expressed in this paper are solely those of the author and do not necessarily represent the views of the General Court of the European Union. The author thanks Martyna Jurkiewicz and Etienne Thomas for their helpful assistance in the final drafting of this paper.

[1] Article 23(5) of Council Regulation (EC) No 1/2003 of 16 December 2002 on the implementation of the rules on competition laid down in Articles [101 TFEU] and [102 TFEE] [2003] OJ L1, p 1; see identical provisions of Article 15(4) of Council Regulation No 17 of 6 February 1962, the first Implementing Regulation on Articles [101 TFEU] and 102 [TFEU] [1962] OJ 13, p 20.

L. Bernardeau (✉)
General Court of the European Union, Luxembourg, Luxembourg

University of Paris-Nanterre, Nanterre, France
e-mail: Ludovic.Bernardeau@curia.europa.eu

© Springer-Verlag Berlin Heidelberg 2017
V. Tomljenović et al. (eds.), *EU Competition and State Aid Rules*,
Europeanization and Globalization 3, https://doi.org/10.1007/978-3-662-47962-9_7

The issue of the *criminalisation* of EU competition law has already been visited in legal literature, with the most authoritative account[2] following the Opinion of Judge B Vesterdorf as Advocate General in the first big cartel case brought before the General Court.[3] This issue has also been raised in the context of the European Convention for the Protection of Human Rights and Fundamental Freedoms (ECHR).[4] It is to be stressed in this context that the European Court of Human Rights (ECtHR) has clearly affirmed, in the now famous *Menarini* case, that a fine for breach of competition law of a State Party to the ECHR, i.e. in a domestic context, might, 'with regard to its severity, fall within the scope of criminal law' for the purposes of the right to a fair trial.[5] The Court of Justice has replied by ruling that, in the area of EU competition law, the right to a fair trial—or, in other (EU) words, the respect of the principle of effective judicial protection—is guaranteed by the duality of the judicial review[6]: the judicial review of legality, as well as the full review of legality under unlimited jurisdiction.[7]

Nonetheless, until now, the Court of Justice has neither endorsed nor settled the issue of the possible *criminal* nature of a fine for breach of EU competition law, at least *expressis verbis*. Does this mean that what is left unsaid is behind what is said? This containment might soon (have to) be given up as it follows from EU case law that fines are in fact, at least, 'similar to criminal law' or are 'quasi-criminal' according to the General Court[8] and, to a greater extent, according to some

---

[2]See Lenaerts (2007), p. 475.

[3]Opinion of Judge B Vesterdorf, Advocate General in Case T-1/89 *Rhône-Poulenc* v. *Commission* ECLI:EU:T:1991:38, hereinafter 'Opinion Vesterdorf'.

[4]See, in particular, Bombois (2012), pp. 31–57 No 30–57.

[5]See ECHR judgment *Menarini Diagnostics/Italy* of 27 September 2011 (No 43509/08, para 42); on this judgment, see, in particular, Muguet-Poullenec and Domenicucci 2012; on the criminal nature of fines under the ECHR, see Bernardeau and Christienne (2013), pp. 500–502 No II-1095 to II-1097, and Vallindas (2014), p. 191.

[6]According the 2nd Chamber of the Court of Justice: 'The review provided for by the Treaties thus involves review by the Courts of the European Union of both the law and the facts, and means that they have the power to assess the evidence, to annul the contested decision and to alter the amount of a fine. The review of legality provided for under Article 263 TFEU, supplemented by the unlimited jurisdiction in respect of the amount of the fine, provided for under Article 31 of Regulation No 1/2003, is not therefore contrary to the requirements of the principle of effective judicial protection in Article 47 of the Charter': Case C-386/10 *Chalkor* v. *Commission* ECLI:EU:C:2011:815, para 67; and Case C-389/10 *KME Germany and Others* v. *Commission* ECLI:EU:C:2011:816, para 133; *adde* judgment of the 5th Chamber of the Court of 10 July 2014; Case C-295/12 P *Telefónica e Telefónica de España* v. *Commission* ECLI:EU:C:2014:2062, paras 39–60; and the judgment of the 1st Chamber in Case C-434/13P *Commission* v. *Parker Hannifin Manufacturing and Parker-Hannifin* ECLI:EU:C:2014:2456, paras 74 and 75.

[7]On appeals before an EU judge exercising unlimited jurisdiction in the case of fines, see Bernardeau and Christienne (2013), pp. 795–883, No II-1544 to II-1682. *Adde*: Bosco (2014), p. 235.

[8]Even though the 'quasi-criminal' nature of fines has been invoked in some cases, the General Court has not yet ruled on the matter: see Case T-334/94 *Sarrió* v. *Commission* ECLI:EU:T:1998:97, para 159; and Joined Cases T-305/94, T-306/94, T-307/94, T-313/94 to T-316/94, T-318/94, T-325/94, T-328/94, T-329/94 and T-335/94, *Limburgse Vinyl Maatschappij (LVM)* v. *Commission* ECLI:EU:T:1999:80, para 224; Case T-220/00 *Cheil Jedang* v. *Commission* ECLI:

Advocates General[9] of the Court of Justice. In any event, the pleas relying on fundamental rights of a 'criminal law colour' before EU judges are not, *per se*, dismissed as manifestly inadmissible or manifestly unfounded or inoperative.

In essence, EU judges seem willing to resist answering the question whether fines in competition law are of a criminal nature and decline to explicitly determine to which category they should definitely belong. It seems therefore most appropriate to address the issue of the judge-made *criminalisation* of fines in EU competition law, and, furthermore, to assess the impact of complying with certain substantive and procedural requirements in the context of criminal law. This invites us to make a summary of the current state of EU case law on this matter (Sect. 2) before starting to outline the required evolution to which EU justice might (need to) aspire (Sect. 3).

## 2   De Lege Lata

Judge Vesterdorf as Advocate General stated that 'Fines which can be imposed on undertakings' for breach of competition law 'are in fact (. . .) of a criminal nature' and, very often 'the pleadings of the parties are comprehensible and coherent but for the reference to criminal law and criminal procedure terminology and notions'.[10] As a result, according to Advocate General Kokott, 'in the settled case-law of the Courts of the EU, criminal-law principles are applied to European competition law'.[11] Could it therefore be said that EU competition law judges are, in fact, criminal-law judges? It is certainly very tempting to answer this question in the affirmative, especially in the light of the fundamental rights of EU law that feed the competition case law of both the Court of Justice and the General Court, which reflect Beccaria's heritage for substance and procedure.

In his opus *Dei delitti e delle pene*, published in 1764, the great enlightenment philosopher Cesare Beccaria established the foundations of the essential principles

---

EU:T:2003:193, para 30; Case T-279/02 *Degussa* v. *Commission* ECLI:EU:T:2006:103, para 37. Nonetheless, the General Court recently ruled that, even if 'not at the "heart" of criminal law . . . competition law is indeed similar to criminal law': General Court Case T-541/08 *Sasol and Others* v. *Commission* ECLI:EU:T:2014:628, para 206.

[9]See, in particular, the Opinion of Advocate General Trstenjak in the Case C 510/06 *Archer Daniels Midland* v. *Commission* ECLI:EU:C:2008:280, para 49, footnote 20; and the Opinion of Advocate General J Kokott in Case C-501/11 *Schindler Holding e.a.* v. *Commission* ECLI:EU: C:2013:248, paras 25, 35, 153. We will particularly highlight that Advocate General J Kokott considered that 'administrative penalties, including those in the field of competition law, do fall within the scope of the criminal-law procedural guarantees under Article 6 ECHR, they are not part of the "hard core" of criminal law—and might also be described as being merely *similar to criminal law*'. View of Advocate General J Kokott in the Opinion Procedure 2/13 ECLI:EU: C:2014:2475, para 149.

[10]See Opinion Vesterdorf (n 3) p II-885.

[11]View of Advocate General J Kokott (n 9) para 149, footnote 95.

that have underlain the general framework of criminal law up to now.[12] And yet is it possible to find some traces of EU competition law in one of the 47 subdivisions that form the contents of Beccaria's work? The question might seem provocative, although not necessarily rhetorical, when it comes to either crime or punishment.

In the context of EU competition law, a crime is an infringement, and, in particular, an infringement of the Treaty provisions applicable to 'undertakings'. It must be noted that EU judges have very quickly recognised, in the form of general principles of EU law, fundamental rights deriving from principles of a criminal-law origin applicable to criminal offences.

First and foremost, particular mention should be made with regard to the principle of legality.[13] As has been consistently held in the field of competition law, this fundamental rule of criminal law requires that all laws must clearly define offences and the penalties that they attract.[14] This requirement is fulfilled when the individual concerned is in a position to identify from the plain wording of the provision in question and, if necessary with the assistance of the interpretation provided by the courts, the positive acts or omissions that might render him criminally liable.[15] And yet EU judges have affirmed clearly and without any reserves that the principle of legality stems from the shared constitutional traditions of the Member States.[16] In fact, the latter principle can be found in all legal systems of the Member States, and it is enshrined in Article 7 of the ECHR, whose provisions have been subsequently incorporated in Article 49 of the Charter of Fundamental Rights of the European Union (Charter).[17]

---

[12]See Beccaria (2012).

[13]See, for an application of the principle in non-competition law cases, Case C-546/09 *Aurubis Balgaria* ECLI:EU:C:2011:199, paras 42–43; for the application of the principle in competition law, see Case T-198/03 *Bank Austria Creditanstal* v. *Commission* ECLI:EU:T:2006:136, para 68; Case C-3/06 *Groupe Danone* v. *Commission* ECLI:EU:C:2007:88, paras 87–91; and Case T-138/07 *Schindler Holding and Others* v. *Commission* ECLI:EU:T:2011:362, paras 95–96.

[14]See Case T-11/05 *Wieland-Werke AG* v. *Commission* ECLI:EU:T:2010:201, paras 58–70; Case C-352/09 *ThyssenKrupp Nirosta* v. *Commission* ECLI:EU:C:2011:191, paras 79–83 and 86–88; Case T-299/08 *Elf Aquitaine* v. *Commission* ECLI:EU:T:2011:217, paras 187–189; Case T-138/07 *Schindler Holding and Others* v. *Commission* ECLI:EU:T:2011:362, paras 95–99; Case T-372/10 *Bolloré* v. *Commission* ECLI:EU:T:2012:325, paras 33–37, 42; Case T-400/09 *Ecka Granulate and non ferrum Metallpulver* v. *Commission* ECLI:EU:T:2012:675, paras 23–27.

[15]Case T-299/08 *Elf Aquitaine* v. *Commission* ECLI:EU:T:2011:217, paras 187–189; Case T-240/07 *Heineken Nederland and Heineken* v. *Commission* ECLI:EU:T:2011:284, paras 383–386; Case T-167/08 *Microsoft* v. *Commission* ECLI:EU:T:2012:323, para 84.

[16]Case C-266/06 *Evonik Degussa* v. *Commission* ECLI:EU:C:2008:295, para 38; T-138/07 *Schindler Holding and Others* v. *Commission* ECLI:EU:T:2011:362, paras 98–100.

[17]Joined Cases C-189/02 P, C-202/02 P, C-205/02 P to C-208/02 P and C-213/02 P *Dansk Rørindustri and Others* v. *Commission* ECLI:EU:C:2005:408, paras 215–219; Case C-266/06 *Evonik Degussa* v. *Commission* ECLI:EU:C:2008:295, para 38, *supra*; Case C-3/06 *Groupe Danone* v. *Commission* ECLI:EU:C:2007:88, paras 87–91; Case T-43/02 *Jungbunzlauer* v. *Commission* ECLI:EU:T:2006:270, para 71 and *seq*; Case T-99/04 *AC-Treuhand* v. *Commission* ECLI:EU:T:2008:256, paras 137–146.

Special mention must also be made of the corollary of the principle of legality, i.e. the principle of the non-retroactivity of criminal law.[18] The Court of Justice and the General Court have consistently held that this principle forms part of the general principles of Community law underlying all legal orders of the Member States, which is also enshrined in Article 7 of the ECHR and forms part of the general principles of law whose observance is ensured by the EU judicature.[19] This principle has, though unsuccessfully, been relied on to challenge the immediate application of the Commission guidelines on the method of setting fines, both those of 1998[20] and those of 2006.[21]

Some attention is also deserved for the principle of *non bis idem*, which, according to EU judges, constitutes a 'fundamental principle of the European Union law',[22] which forbids the condemnation or prosecution of undertakings once more for anti-competitive behaviour on the grounds upon which the undertaking had been already sanctioned or for which the undertaking had been found not responsible by a prior decision against which there could be no further appeal. In the field of EU competition law, the principle of *non bis idem* has been relied on in various factual backgrounds, in particular in the context of the cumulative application of national, EU and third-country laws,[23] in the context of the application of EU competition rules to global cartels and, finally, more recently, in the context of

---

[18]Case C-63/83 *R* v. *Kirk* ECLI:EU:C:1984:255, para 22; Case C-295/12 *Telefónica e Telefónica de España* v. *Commission* ECLI:EU:C:2014:2062, paras 147–149; Case T-541/08 *Sasol and Others* v. *Commission* ECLI:EU:T:2014:628, paras 202–214.

[19]Case T-17/99 *KE KELIT Kunststoffwerk* v. *Commission* ECLI:EU:T:2002:73, para 110; Case T-23/99 LR *AF 1998* v. *Commission* ECLI:EU:T:2002:75, para 219; Case T-220/00 *Cheil Jedang Corp* v. *Commission* ECLI:EU:T:2003:193, para 43; Joined Cases C-189 C-189/02 P, C-202/02 P, C-205/02 P to C-208/02 P and C-213/02 P *Dansk Rørindustri and Others* v. *Commission* ECLI:EU:C:2005:408, para 205.

[20]Joined Cases C-189/02 P, C-202/02 P, C-205/02 P to C-208/02 P and C-213/02 P *Dansk Rørindustri and Others* v. *Commission* ECLI:EU:C:2005:408, paras 198–233; Case T-329/01 *Archer Daniels Midland* v. *Commission* ECLI:EU:T:2006:268, paras 38–46; Case T-138/07 *Schindler Holding and Others* v. *Commission* ECLI:EU:T:2011:362, paras 118–119, 123–128, 133.

[21]Joined Cases T-373/10, T-374/10, T-382/10 et T-402/10 *Villeroy & Boch and Others* v. *Commission* ECLI:EU:T:2013:455, paras 371–376; Case T-375/10 *Hansa Metallwerke and Others* v. *Commission* ECLI:EU:T:2013:475, paras 154–159; Case T-380/10 *Wabco Europe and Others* v. *Commission* ECLI:EU:T:2013:449, paras 173–179; Case T-544/08 *Hansen & Rosenthal and H & R Wax Company Vertrieb* v. *Commission* ECLI:EU:T:2014:1075, para 287.

[22]Joined Cases C-238/99 P, C-244/99 P, C-245/99 P, C-247/99 P, C-250/99 P to C-252/99 P and C-254/99 *Limburgse Vinyl Maatschappij e.a.* v. *Commission* ECLI:EU:C:2002:582, paras 59–62; Case C-308/04 *SGL Carbon* v. *Commission* ECLI:EU:C:2006:433, para 26; Joined Cases T-217/03 and T-245/03 *FNCBV e.a. and Others* v. *Commission* ECLI:EU:T:2006:391, paras 340–344; Case C-289/04 *Showa Denko* v. *Commission* ECLI:EU:C:2006:431, para 50; Case T-24/07 *ThyssenKrupp Stainless* v. *Commission* ECLI:EU:T:2009:236, paras 141, 178–179, 183-190; Case C-17/10 ECLI:EU:C:2012:72, para 94.

[23]Case T-223/00 *Kyowa Hakko Kogyo* v. *Commission* ECLI:EU:T:2003:194, paras 96–98, 100–101, 103, 110–111; Case T-43/02 *Jungbunzlauer* v. *Commission* ECLI:EU:T:2006:270; Case C-397-03 *Archer Daniels Midland and Archer Daniels Midland Ingredients* v. *Commission* ECLI:EU:C:2006:328; Case C-328/05 *SGL Carbon* v. *Commission* ECLI:EU:C:2007:277.

interaction between the Commission and national competition authorities[24] that are competent to apply their national legislation, as well as Articles 101 TFEU and 102 TFEU.

Within the framework of EU competition law, punishment is essentially a fine. A fine for an infringement of both substantive and procedural rules of EU law is applicable to undertakings. It must further be observed that the EU judge has also very distinctly recognised, in the form of general principles of EU law, the principles of criminal-law origin as far as the penalty is concerned.

Moreover, it is also appropriate to mention the principle of judicial certainty, which, according to EU judges, constitutes a corollary of the principle of legality and a general principle of EU law.[25] The latter requires that all laws of the EU imposing or allowing a sanction to be imposed be clear and precise so as to enable the individuals in question to understand without ambiguity their rights and obligations arising thereunder and to enable them to make all necessary arrangements in advance.[26] This principle is applicable both to criminal-law rules and to specific administrative legal instruments imposing or allowing administrative sanctions to be taken.[27] In the context of EU competition law, this principle has been relied on in vain—at least so far at this stage—to contest, by way of an exception, the legality of the fines provided for in Regulation No 17[28] and Regulation No 1/2003.[29]

---

[24]Joined Cases C-204/00, C-205/00, C-211/00, C-213/00, C-217/00 and C-219/00 *Aalborg Portland and Others* v. *Commission* ECLI:EU:C:2004:6, paras 338–340; Case C-17/10 *Toshiba and Others* ECLI:EU:C:2012:72.

[25]See, for an application of the principle in non-competition law cases, Case C-137/85 *Maizena GmbH & Others* v. *BALM* ECLI:EU:C:1987:493, para 15; See, also, for an application in competition law, Case T-43/02 *Jungbunzlauer* v. *Commission* ECLI:EU:T:2006:270, paras 71–74; Case T-69/04 *Schunk et Schunk Kohlenstoff-Technik* v. *Commission* ECLI:EU:T:2008:415, paras 28–29, 32–34; Case C-266/06 *Evonik Degussa* v. *Commission and Council* ECLI:EU:C:2008:295, paras 38–40, 44–46.

[26]Case T-43/02 *Jungbunzlauer* v. *Commission* ECLI:EU:T:2006:270, para 71; Joined Cases C-189/02 P, C-202/02 P, C-205/02 P to C-208/02 P and C-213/02 P *Dansk Rørindustri and Others* v. *Commission* ECLI:EU:C:2005:408, paras 215–223; Case T-167/08 *Microsoft* v. *Commission* ECLI:EU:T:2012:323, para 84; Case T-364/10 *Duravit and Others* v. *Commission* ECLI:EU: T:2013:477, paras 67–69; Joined Cases T-373/10, T-374/10, T-382/10 and T-402/10 *Villeroy & Boch and Others* v. *Commission* ECLI:EU:T:2013:455, para 157; Case T-375/10 *Hansa Metallwerke and Others* v. *Commission* ECLI:EU:T:2013:475, paras 49–52; Case T-386/10 *Dornbracht* v. *Commission* ECLI:EU:T:2013:450, paras 59–63.

[27]Case C-137/85 *Maizena GmbH & Others* v. *BALM* ECLI:EU:C:1987:493, paras 14–15.

[28]Case T-23/99 *LR AF 1998* v. *Commission* ECLI:EU:T:2002:75, para 235; Case T-43/02 *Jungbunzlauer* v. *Commission* ECLI:EU:T:2006:270, paras 37–68; Case C-3/06 P *Groupe Danone* v. *Commission* ECLI:EU:C:2007:88, paras 26–30; Case T-99/04 *AC-Treuhand AG* v. *Commission* ECLI:EU:T:2008:256, paras 139–150.

[29]Case C-352/09 P *ThyssenKrupp Nirosta GmbH* v. *Commission* ECLI:EU:C:2011:191, paras 87–91; Case T-375/10 *Hansa Metallwerke e.a.* v. *Commission* ECLI:EU:T:2013:475, paras 53–56, 60–70; Case T-386/10 *Dornbracht* v. *Commission* ECLI:EU:T:2013:450, paras 68–70, 78, 146; Case T-384/09 *SKW Stahl-Metallurgie Holding and SKW Stahl-Metallurgie* v. *Commission* ECLI: EU:T:2014:27, para 206; T-40/10 *Elf Aquitaine* v. *Commission* ECLI:EU:T:2014:61, paras 332–342.

Besides, given the significant importance of the fines imposed, the principle of personality of the punishment can be found both in the Court of Justice's and General Court's case law.[30] According to this principle, one is liable only for one's own acts. This raises particular difficulties in the context of EU competition, especially for the groups and the successions of companies. The premise that *the undertaking is the author of the infringement* appears highly debatable, especially for the cases of joint and several liability, which could be assimilated to vicarious (criminal) liability. Even if sometimes mistakenly confused with the principle of the personality of the punishment, the principle that the fine must fit the offender is becoming more and more relied on before EU competition judges.[31] This principle implies taking into account the circumstances that are proper to each person involved. And yet this principle raises different issues relating, in the context of corporate groups and the restructuring of undertakings, to mitigating and aggravating circumstances, leniency, the 10% ceiling and the limitation period.

As has already been stated by Judge Vesterdorf as Advocate General, the formal framework of competition cases is 'formed by an administrative procedure followed by a judicial review of legality'. However, their content 'is largely characterised by a criminal-law procedure'.[32] Is this Menarini before the *Menarini* case? And this holds true both for an administrative procedure before the Commission and, to an even greater extent, for a judicial review before EU judges.

Both before the Commission and before EU judges, the principle of respect of the right to defence and the right of access to the file[33] constitute fundamental rights of EU law. The well-established case law on the matter has, of course, particular implications on EU competition law, and especially with respect to the addressees of the statements of objections, and to the authors held liable for an

---

[30]Case T-45/98 *ThyssenKrupp Staineless* v. *Commission* ECLI:EU:T:2001:288, para 63; Case T-220/00 *Cheil Jedang* v. *Commission* ECLI:EU:T:2003:193, para 185; Case T-38/02 *Groupe Danone* v. *Commission* ECLI:EU:T:2005:367, para 278; Case T-190/06 *Total and Elf Aquitaine* v. *Commission* ECLI:EU:T:2011:378, para 200; Case T-174/05 *Elf Aquitaine* v. *Commission* ECLI: EU:T:2009:368, para 184; Case T-144/07 *ThyssenKrupp Lifeten Ascenseurs* v. *Commission* ECLI: EU:T:2011:364, para 106; Case C-247/11 P *Areva and others* v. *Commission* ECLI:EU:C:2014:257, para 127; Case C-231/11 P *Commission* v. *Siemens Österreich and Others* et *Siemens Transmission & Distribution and Others* v. *Commission* ECLI:EU:C:2014:256, para 56.

[31]Case C-76/06 P *Britannia Alloys & Chemicals Ltd* v. *Commission* ECLI:EU:C:2007:326, para 44; Case T- 372/10 *Bolloré* v. *Commission* ECLI:EU:T:2012:325, para 228; Case C-243/12 P *FLS Plast A/S* v. *Commission* ECLI:EU:C:2014:2006, para 107; Case C-408/12 P *YKK* ECLI:EU: C:2014:2153, para 66.

[32]Opinion Vesterdorf (n 3) p II-893.

[33]Case C-85/76 *Hoffmann-La Roche* v. *Commission* ECLI:EU:C:1979:36, paras 9 and 17; Case T-30/91 *Solvay* v. *Commission* ECLI:EU:T:1995:115 paras 68 and 83; Case T-36/91 *ICI* v. *Commission* ECLI:EU:T:2004:253, paras 78 and 93–95; Case C-51/92 P *Hercules Chemicals* v. *Commission* ECLI:EU:C:1999:357, paras 75–79; Case C-62/86 *AKZO* v. *Commission* ECLI: EU:C:1991:286, paras 16 and 24; Case C-360/09 *Pfleiderer* ECLI:EU:C:2011:389, paras 31–32; Case C-536/11 *Donau Chemie and Others* ECLI:EU:C:2013:366, paras 29–33; Case T-404/08 *Fluorsid and Minment* v. *Commission* ECLI:EU:T:2013:321, para 30.

infringement, upon whom the obligation to pay the fine, *jointly and severally* or otherwise, is imputed.

With regard to fundamental rights in criminal procedure that feed competition law, it is clear, especially in the light of the Strasbourg case law, that today attention is focused on the right to a fair trial, which, on one hand, implies 'a right to take action in the court', i.e. a right to effective judicial protection that constitutes another general principle of EU law that is highly present in EU competition law case law.[34] On the other hand, the right to a fair trial requires that everyone shall be entitled to a public hearing that is settled within a reasonable time.[35] This applies to the procedures before both the EU courts and the Commission. This is also another general principle of EU law, which has recently undergone some important changes in the context of the imposition of fines since it has been held that a reduction in fines does not constitute an appropriate remedy for the unreasonable length of proceedings, before either the General Court or the Court of Justice.[36]

To conclude at this stage, the question that subsequently arises is whether, in the absence of the formal accession of the EU to the ECHR,[37] the 'fundamentalisation' of certain general principles of law will—or perhaps should—affect EU competition law. This question arises not only *de lege lata* but also, and in particular, *de lege ferenda*.

## 3 De Lege Ferenda

We shall now proceed to analyse the elements that are of particular importance for making a prospective analysis. This issue has become particularly challenging following the Opinion of 18 December 2014,[38] where the Court of Justice stated that the EU should not adhere to the ECHR (at least *rebus sic stantibus*). However, the Charter is in place and will not be surrendered. In the field of EU competition

---

[34]Case C-272/09 P *KME Germany AG, KME France SAS and KME Italy SpA* v. *Commission* ECLI:EU:C:2011:810, paras 97–110; Case C-386/10 P *Chalkor AE Epexergasias Metallon* v. *Commission* ECLI:EU:C:2011:815, paras 52; Case C-199/11 *Commission v. Otis NV and others* ECLI:EU:C:2012:684, paras 46-63; Case C-501/11 P *Schindler and Others v. Commission* ECLI: EU:C:2013:522, paras 35–36.

[35]Joined Cases C 341/06 P and C 342/06 P *Chronopost SA and La Poste/Commission* v. *Commission* ECLI:EU:C:2008:375 para 44 (*State Aid Case*); Case C-385/07 P Der Grüne Punkt - Duales System Deutschland v. Commission ECLI:EU:C:2009:456, paras 177–181, 186.

[36]C-40/12 P *Gascone Sack Deutschland* v. *Commission* ECLI:EU:C:2013:768, paras 80–85; Case C-50/12 P *Kendrion* v. *Commission* ECLI:EU:C:2013:771, paras 81–89.

[37]See Opinion 2/13 of the Court (Full Court) of 18 December 2014, pursuant to Article 218 (11) TFEU, Draft on an international agreement—Accession of the European Union to the [ECHR]—Compatibility of the draft agreement with the EU and FEU Treaties ECLI:EU: C:2014:2454; see also the previous Opinion of the Court on the accession by the Community to the ECHR, Opinion 2/94 of the Court of 28 March 1996 ECLI:EU:C:1996:140.

[38]Ibid.

law, both administrative and judicial authorities of the Member States, as well as
the EU authorities, i.e. the Commission, the General Court and the Court of Justice,
are under an obligation to respect the fundamental rights within the framework of
the EU and 'in the scope of application of EU law'. In any event, the general
principle of law with a criminal law colour should not be overlooked. On the
contrary, it is conceivable that the 'fundamentalisation' of such principles will
actually increase their importance, as well as their impact on EU competition law.

Sound law is required not only from EU judges. In the first place, it applies to the
legislature of the EU, which needs to modify this area of law and, in our view,
formally criminalise it. It needs to be said plainly: the criteria laid down in
Regulation No 1/2003 for the determination of the amount of fine by the Commission in the exercise of its wide discretion, on one hand, and, on the other, by the
General Court in the exercise of its unlimited jurisdiction prove to be inadequate.
The *gravity* and the *duration* criteria become increasingly vague and imprecise
when confronted with the complexity and increasing variety of infringements. In
this respect, the EU legislator should introduce imperative guidelines. This has been
done elsewhere, even when balancing legal certainty and the principle that the fine
must fit the offender. In our view, there are two main challenges with regard to the
exercise of unlimited jurisdiction: refined criteria for the fixation of fines and full
judicial review at the time the judge is ruling.

The intervention of the EU legislator is also required as far as the notion of
*undertaking* is concerned. It is imposed by the complexity of companies' configu-
rations nowadays. In litigations before the EU courts, it is quite common for the
companies forming the said *undertaking* to have evolved, in the course or from the
moment of committing the infraction, before the date the Commission adopts the
decision and before the EU judges adjudicate.[39] As a result, the above-mentioned
notion is, in fact, no longer effective. Indeed, the notion of 'undertaking' could
maintain its legitimacy, as far as the delimitation of the scope of competition law is
concerned. Nonetheless, as far as the payment of the fine is concerned, particular
confusion arises with regard to the concept of 'undertaking, associated companies
and fines', whether it comes to the 10% threshold,[40] the time limitation period,[41]

---

[39]Case T-122/07 *Siemens Österreich and VA Tech Transmission & Distribution* v. *Commission*
ECLI:EU:T:2011:70, paras 122–126; Case C-231/11 P *Commission* v. *Siemens Österreich and
Others et Siemens Transmission & Distribution and Others* v. *Commission* ECLI:EU:C:2014:256,
paras 90–94, 100–112; Joined Cases C-247/11 P and C-253/11 P *Areva and Others* v. *Commission*
ECLI:EU:C:2014:257, paras 47–52; Case T-448/07 *YKK and Others* v. *Commission* ECLI:EU:
T:2012:322, paras 196–204; Case C-408/12 P *YKK and Others* v. *Commission* ECLI:EU:
C:2014:2153, paras 80–92; Case T-64/06 *FLS Plast* v. *Commission* ECLI:EU:T:2012:102, paras
170–179; Case C-234/12 P, *FLS Plast* v. *Commission* ECLI:EU:C:2014:2006, paras 151–157.

[40]Case T-448/07 *YKK and Others* v. *Commission* ECLI:EU:T:2012:322; Case C-408/12 P *YKK
and Others* v. *Commission* ECLI:EU:C:2014:2153; Joined Cases T-71/03, T-74/03, T-87/03 and
T-91/03 *Tokai Carbon* v. *Commission* ECLI:EU:T:2005:220, para 390; Case T-189/10 *GEA
Group* v. *Commission* ECLI:EU:T:2015:504, p. 44.

[41]See Case T-485/11 *Akzo Nobel and Akcros Chemicals* v. *Commission* ECLI:EU:T:2015:517, p 25.

joint and several liability[42] or the principle that fines must fit the offender[43] and, in particular, when the EU judge decides to reduce the amount of fine with regard to one of the companies involved while the latter had been found jointly and severally liable with another.[44] Where is therefore the 'undertaking'? Would Regulation No 1/2003 not actually gain value by having some modifications?

Above all these technical questions, if, at the level of the Council and of the Parliament, an actual political commitment existed in the field of free competition, then the means of deterrence, recalled over and over again by the Commission and the EU judges, could, in our opinion, alone justify that this area of law be formally penalised. It would be sufficient to follow the American model[45] and the models adopted by some Member States, in particular England,[46] France[47] and Germany.[48] However, this kind of action should not be based only on an economic analysis from which it constantly results that, in the field of competition law, 'crime pays'. The Commission and the Parliament undoubtedly discussed this problem in an economic context, although still outside the scope of competition law. Further reflexion should be given to competition law, provided that it still constitutes a *credo* in the European construction.

In any event, the provisions of Article 83(2) TFUE could be tested as a legal basis: it does indeed provide:

> If the approximation of criminal laws and regulations of the Member States proves essential to ensure the effective implementation of a Union policy in an area which has been subject to harmonisation measures, directives may establish minimum rules with regard to the definition of criminal offences and

---

[42]Case T-122/07 *Siemens Österreich and VA Tech Transmission & Distribution* v. *Commission* ECLI:EU:T:2011:70; Case C-231/11 P *Siemens Österreich and Others et Siemens Transmission & Distribution and Others* v. *Commission* ECLI:EU:C:2014:256.

[43]Case T-372/10 *Bolloré* v. *Commission* ECLI:EU:T:2012:325, para 228; Case C-243/12 P FLS Plast A/S v. Commission ECLI:EU:C:2014:2006, para 107; Case C-408/12 P YKK ECLI:EU:C:2014:2153, para 66.

[44]See, in particular, the Opinion of Advocate General Wahl in Case C-597/13 P ECLI:EU:C:2015:207, para 2; Case T-548/08, *Total* v. *Commission* ECLI:EU:T:2013:434; Case C-286/11 P *Commission* v. *Tomkins* ECLI:EU:C:2013:29; Case T-42/11, *Universal* v. *Commission* ECLI:EU:T:2012:122.

[45]15 U.S. Code § 1 and § 2 (*Sherman Act*) anti-competition practices are punished by a fine and/or imprisonment up to 10 years at the discretion of the court.

[46]Competition Act 1998 and Enterprise Act 2002 recently amended by the Enterprise & Regulatory Reform Act 2013; in particular 'cartel offence', see Section 188 of the Act, which may be sanctioned both by a fine and imprisonment for up to 5 years.

[47]Article L-420-6 of French Commercial Code (Code de commerce) under the terms of which anti-competitive practices are punishable by a fine and imprisonment for up to 5 years.

[48]§ 298 and § 263 of the Criminal Code (Strafgesetzbuch,StGB) applicable only to natural persons (legal entities are subject to administrative fines). Under § 298 of the StGB bid-rigging is punishable by a criminal fine or imprisonment for up to five years. Under § 263 of the StGB, fraud is punishable by imprisonment for up to 5 years.

sanctions in the area concerned. Such directives shall be adopted by the same ordinary or special legislative procedure as was followed for the adoption of the harmonisation measures in question.

This could only clarify matters for the EU judge.

# References

Beccaria C (2012 first published in 1764) Dei delitti e delle pene. Feltrinelli, Milan

Bernardeau L, Christienne J-P (2013) Les amendes en droit de la concurrence – Pratique décisionnelle et contrôle juridictionnel. Larcier, Brussels

Bombois T (2012) La protection des droits fondamentaux des entreprises en droit européen répressif de la concurrence. Larcier, Brussels, pp 31–57

Bosco D (2014) La compétence de pleine juridiction du juge de l'Union quant aux amendes prononcées par la Commission européenne en matière de concurrence. In: Mahieu S (ed) Contentieux de l'Union européenne – Questions choisies. Larcier, Brussels p 235

Lenaerts K (2007) Réflexions sur la preuve et sur la procédure en droit communautaire de la concurrence. In: Baudenbacher C, Gulmann C, Lenaerts K, Coulon E, Barbier de la Serre E (eds) Liber amicorum en l'honneur de Bo Vesterdorf. Bruylant, Brussels, p 475

Muguet-Poullenec Gw, Domenicucci D (2012) Amende infligée par une autorité de concurrence et droit à une protection juridictionnelle effective: les enseignements de l'arrêt Menarini de la CEDH. Revue Lamy de la concurrence 30, No 1988

Vallindas G (2014) Sanction, juges de l'Union, juges nationaux et CEDH: nouvelles perspectives du contentieux européen de la concurrence. In: Mahieu S (ed) Contentieux de l'Union européenne – Questions choisies. Larcier, Brussels p 191

# Part III
# Selected Issues of Private Enforcement
# of EU Competition Law

# The Disclosure of Evidence Under the 'Antitrust Damages' Directive 2014/104/EU

Anca D. Chirita

**Abstract** The aim of this contribution is to reflect on the principles underpinning the disclosure of evidence under Directive 2014/104/EU, namely the principles of proportionality, effectiveness, equivalence and consistency. It also aims to review the legislative techniques that the Directive has used in order to codify the previous case law of the European Union (EU) courts and to discuss several recent rulings, including *Carglass*, *Pilkington*, *Evonik Degussa* and others. Finally, the author draws conclusions on the adequacy of the achieved codification of the previous case law on the disclosure of evidence and access to such evidence, as well as on its potential implications for the Member States.

## 1 Introduction

The primary aim of this contribution is to reflect on the principles underpinning the disclosure of evidence under Directive 2014/104/EU[1] (hereinafter: the Directive), namely the principles of proportionality, effectiveness, equivalence and consistency. Its secondary aim is to review the legislative techniques that the Directive has used in order to codify the previous case law of the European Union (EU) courts and to discuss several recent rulings, including *Carglass*, *Pilkington*, *Evonik Degussa* and others.

The contribution seeks first to locate the scope of the disclosure of evidence by clarifying the meaning and the importance of such evidence and by examining the

---

This contribution is based on a presentation delivered at the 4th Petar Šarčević international conference on 'EU Competition and State Aid Rules: Interaction between Public and Private Enforcement' in Rovinj, Croatia. The author would like to thank the organisers of the wonderful conference, the editors and commentators, especially Vlatka Butorac Malnar, Judges Vesna Tomljenović, Marc Jaeger, Viktor Kreuschitz and Miro Prek, and also Marc Barennes and Nuria Bermejo Gutierrez.

[1]Directive 2014/104/EU of the European Parliament and of the Council of 26 November 2014 on certain rules governing actions for damages under national law for infringements of the competition law provisions of the Member States and of the European Union [2014] OJ L 349/1.

A.D. Chirita (✉)
Durham University, Durham, UK
e-mail: a.d.chirita@durham.ac.uk

© Springer-Verlag Berlin Heidelberg 2017
V. Tomljenović et al. (eds.), *EU Competition and State Aid Rules*,
Europeanization and Globalization 3, https://doi.org/10.1007/978-3-662-47962-9_8

147

categories of evidence. It goes on to examine the established rule on the disclosure of evidence in the light of the principle of transparency and its legal exceptions.

Finally, the author draws conclusions on the adequacy of the achieved codification of the previous case law on the disclosure of evidence and access to such evidence, as well as on its potential implications for the Member States.

## 1.1   The Scope of the Disclosure of Evidence

It is first necessary to shed light on the scope of the Directive. The Directive aims to harmonise existing national rules governing actions for damages for infringements of the competition law provisions of the Member States and of the EU. Neither the Official Journal of the EU[2] nor the preparatory work[3] undertaken before the enactment of the Directive refers to 'antitrust' damages. This latter designation (Antitrust Damages Directive) is a common occurrence in policy statements[4] and beyond.

The effectiveness of a *private* enforcement of competition law, including civil actions for damages, depends on its successful coordination with the tools available for the public enforcement of competition law. Under civil law, actions in pursuit of compensation for anticompetitive infringements of competition law complement the *public* enforcement of Articles 101 and 102 TFEU.

Recital 6 of the Directive considers that the existence of 'divergent' rules could practically 'jeopardise the proper functioning of the internal market'. This perceived shortcoming is the outcome of a lack of harmonisation of the substantive and procedural rules applicable to actions for damages. The victims of an infringement of competition rules have to seek access to the documents included in the competition file. The material right to access files often becomes indispensable for the lodging of actions for damages. This right is enshrined in Article 41 of the EU Charter of Fundamental Rights of the European Union. Accordingly, any individual should have access to his/her own file.

Nonetheless, the above right is exposed to certain procedural safeguards that limit the disclosure of evidence that is available on file. An underlying rationale for such limitations is to respect 'the legitimate interests of confidentiality and of professional and business secrecy', as mentioned in the EU Charter.[5] Therefore,

---

[2]See Directive 2014/104/EU (n 1).

[3]See the Amendments by the European Parliament to the Commission proposal: Directive of the European Parliament and of the Council on certain rules governing actions for damages under national law for infringements of the competition law provisions of the Member States and of the European Union of 9 April 2014. Available via http://ec.europa.eu/competition/antitrust/actionsdamages/directive_en.html. Accessed Jul 2016.

[4]See European Commission, press release IP/14/1580, 'Antitrust: Commission welcomes Council adoption of Directive on antitrust damages actions', Brussels, 10 November 2014.

[5]See Article 41 of the EU Charter of Fundamental Rights of the EU.

both the material right to access and the procedural rule governing the disclosure of evidence have to be revisited in order to establish the existence of any remaining divergence between them.

Furthermore, the overall objective of reaching substantive and procedural convergence is reflected by the principle of effectiveness. This principle requires coherence between the public and the private enforcement of competition law, i.e. between administrative and civil laws. In this context, the disclosure of evidence indeed remains instrumental in the administration of evidence. Allowing the disclosure of evidence in *civil* actions for damages becomes essential, as does clearly setting out the situations in which revealing such evidence could jeopardise other major public or private interests of the parties concerned. The present contribution seeks to challenge the existence of such interests from the perspective of the principle of transparency.

## 1.2   The Purpose of the Disclosure of Evidence

In actions for damages, so-called information asymmetries have often made it difficult for the victims to claim compensation. The procedure for the administration of evidence expects the victim to bring forward the necessary evidence. Unfortunately, such evidence is held exclusively by the infringer or by third parties. In particular, Recital 14 of the Directive recognises that this procedural hurdle could pose the risk of unduly impeding the principle of effectiveness, as is currently enshrined in Recital 11 of the Directive.

In practice, anyone wishing to recover damages for anticompetitive infringements can effectively exercise this right only where access to all the necessary evidence kept in the competition file is granted. Furthermore, in order to observe the principle of equality of arms, the defendant also has to be granted access to the same evidence.

The Directive empowers national courts to order the disclosure of all necessary evidence, especially where the latter is in the possession of third parties or competition authorities. The courts have to observe the principle of sincere cooperation, as enshrined in Article 4(3) TEU. Therefore, Recital 15 of the Directive recalls that the general principles of legal and administrative cooperation are applicable whenever the courts order public authorities to disclose administrative evidence.

## 1.3   The Meaning of Evidence

Article 2(13) of the Directive clarifies the meaning of evidence as referring to 'all types of means of proof' that could be declared as admissible before courts, i.e. 'documents and all other objects containing information', regardless of the medium in which the information is stored. Both Recital 28 and Article 2(17) of the

Directive refer to 'pre-existing information' that exists independently of the proceedings of a competition authority. In an action for damages, national courts can order the disclosure of such pre-existing information.

When it comes to prioritising who will have to furnish the necessary evidence, both Recital 29 and Article 6(10) of the Directive make competition authorities the last possible resort. The latter scenario can happen whenever such evidence cannot possibly be obtained from another party or from a third party.

## 1.4   The Object of Disclosure

According to Recital 16 and Article 5(2) of the Directive, national courts should be in a position to order the disclosure of 'specified items' of evidence or of relevant 'categories of evidence'. The latter have to be defined 'precisely and narrowly'.[6] According to Article 6(4)(a) of the Directive, a request for the disclosure of a category of evidence will first look at the nature, subject matter or content of the documents that need to be disclosed and will then look at the timing or other criteria.

The Directive does not cover the disclosure of the internal documents of competition authorities.[7] The same applies to the correspondence between them. Instead, Article 6(3) of the Directive acknowledges that it has to observe the EU and national rules and practices on the protection of the internal documents of competition authorities and of the correspondence between them.

## 1.5   The Use of Evidence

Both Recital 31 and Article 7(1) of the Directive clarify that evidence may be used by any natural or legal person that obtains access to the file of a competition authority, and by his/her own successors, including acquirers. Nonetheless, Recital 32 of the Directive reminds us that the effective use of evidence in private actions for damages should not 'unduly detract' from the overall effectiveness of competition law. Therefore, in order to maintain effectiveness, certain evidence will be inadmissible in private actions. Furthermore, the evidence obtained from a competition authority cannot be made the object of trade.

---

[6]See Directive 2014/104/EU (n 1) Recital 16.
[7]Ibid, Recital 21 and Article 6(3).

## 1.6   The Misuse of Evidence

Recital 33 of the Directive highlights several unfortunate situations where, as soon as an action for damages has been initiated, evidence is destroyed or concealed. National courts are called upon here to impose deterrent penalties. The same applies to situations where there is a failure to protect confidential information or where there is an abusive use of information following its disclosure. Article 8(1) of the Directive mandates national courts to impose penalties on the parties or third parties concerned for failure or refusal to comply with a disclosure order, for the destruction of evidence, for failure or refusal to protect confidential information and for breach of the limits on the use of evidence.

## 2   The Fundamental Principles Underpinning the Established Rule of Disclosure

### 2.1   The Principle of Consistency

When applying Articles 101 and 102, both the Commission and the national competition authorities have to adopt a 'common approach' to the disclosure of evidence.[8] The procedural rule on disclosure has to be applied in the spirit of the principle of consistency. In a similar vein, the approach to be undertaken by the judiciary to the issue of disclosure has to be coherent with the above framework; otherwise, dealing with divergent approaches adopted by the competition authorities and judiciary could in turn trigger the criticism of inconsistency. Therefore, Recital 34 of the Directive emphasises the need to avoid inconsistency in the application of Articles 101 and 102.

### 2.2   The Principles of Effectiveness and Equivalence

The principle of the effectiveness of public enforcement of competition law is enshrined in Article 4 of the Directive. This principle requires that Member States safeguard national rules and the procedure applicable to private claims for damages without making the exercise of a supranational right, namely the 'Union right to full compensation', 'practically impossible or excessively difficult'.

Under Article 4 of the Directive, the principle of equivalence requires that the rules and procedures regarding the recovery of compensation for infringements of Articles 101 and 102 be as favourable to claimants as the existing ones available for

---

[8]Ibid, Recital 21.

similar infringements of national competition law. Recital 24 of the Directive reaffirms the principle of effectiveness as standing above the disclosure of evidence by the courts. Therefore, the judiciary is expected to cautiously balance the principle of effectiveness against disclosure with the exception of leniency statements and settlement submissions. For instance, the disclosure of corporate statements made under the shield of leniency could be seen as undermining the detection and punishment of secret cartels and effective enforcement against them.

To a certain extent, the judicial review of the admissibility of disclosure will be limited by the principle of effectiveness. In other words, any rules on the disclosure of evidence have to work towards an 'effective' public enforcement of competition law.[9] This means that a difficult balance has to be struck between even more transparency being achieved through a disclosure of evidence and many other 'major' public or private interests of the parties concerned.

Furthermore, in the interests of the principle of effectiveness, not 'every single document' will have to be disclosed.[10] By way of a legislative codification, Recital 22 of the Directive posits that an action for damages could never be based on all of the evidence available on file with the competent competition authority. This codified requirement had previously been expressed by the Court of Justice in *EnBW Energie*[11] as follows:

In order to ensure the effective protection of the right to compensation enjoyed by a claimant, there is no need for every document relating to a proceeding under Article 101 TFEU to be disclosed to the claimant, as it is highly unlikely that the action for damages will need to be based on all the evidence in the file relating to that proceeding.[12]

In *Axa Versicherung*,[13] the General Court emphasised the major role played by the principle of the effectiveness of the public enforcement of competition law in the context of the expected efficacy and successful implementation of leniency programmes both at the national and supranational levels:

Leniency programmes are useful tools to uncover and bring an end to infringements of the competition rules, thereby contributing to the effective application of Articles 101 and 102 TFEU. Furthermore, the effectiveness of these programmes could be compromised if documents relating to leniency proceedings were disclosed to persons wishing to bring an action for damages. The view can reasonably be taken that the prospect of such disclosure would deter persons

---

[9]Ibid, Recital 23.

[10]Ibid, Recital 22.

[11]See Case C-365/12 P *European Commission v. EnBW Energie Baden-Württemberg AG* ECLI: EU:C:2014:112.

[12]Ibid, paras 106–108.

[13]Case T-677/13 *AXA Versicherung AG v. European Commission* ECLI:EU:T:2015:473.

involved in an infringement of the competition rules from having recourse to such programmes.[14]

However, the Court recognised the need for a case-by-case analysis of any disclosure that could negatively affect the above principle of effectiveness:

> Although such considerations may justify a refusal to grant access to certain documents included in the file of a proceeding pursuant to the competition rules, they do not necessarily mean that access may be systematically refused.[15]

## 2.3   The Principle of Proportionality

As a matter of principle, proportionality requires that disclosure should be ordered only where the victim makes a plausible assertion of the harm caused by the defendant.[16]

According to Article 5(1) of the Directive, there must be a 'reasoned justification containing reasonably available facts and evidence'. In essence, the principle of proportionality makes it possible for the national courts to 'limit the disclosure of evidence to that which is proportionate'.[17]

According to Article 5(3) of the Directive, national courts have to consider the following: the legitimate interests of all the parties and third parties concerned; whether the claim is supported by available facts and evidence justifying disclosure; the scope and cost of disclosure, especially for third parties; and whether an eventual disclosure concerns confidential information. In addition, Article 6(4) of the Directive refers to other 'proportionality' criteria. These are recommended where the evidence is in the file of a competition authority.

An order of disclosure will follow where a request has been formulated with regard to the nature, subject matter or contents of documents in the possession of a competition authority or where the evidence is related to an action for damages. The principle of proportionality has to be balanced, first, against the risk of uncovering the investigation strategy of a competition authority by revealing documents that are part of a file and, second, against the risk of having a negative effect on the way in which undertakings cooperate with the competition authorities.[18]

The party asking for disclosure has a duty to specify any items or categories of evidence 'as precisely and narrowly as possible'.[19] In this sense, the Directive

---

[14]Ibid, para 118.

[15]Ibid, para 119.

[16]See Directive 2014/104/EU (n 1) Article 5(1).

[17]Ibid, Article 5(3).

[18]Ibid, Recital 23.

[19]Ibid, Recital 23.

exposes the shortcomings of so-called fishing expeditions. The latter involve a 'non-specific' and 'overly broad' disclosure of evidence. For example, a generic disclosure of documents in the file of a competition authority or submitted by a party in the context of a particular case would run counter to the primary duty to define narrowly items or categories of evidence. In practice, the principle of proportionality entails an expectation that a potential disclosure of information does not go beyond what is necessary to protect the interests of the persons concerned.[20]

## 3 The Principle of Transparency

In line with the principle of transparency, which essentially favours a wider disclosure of evidence, Article 5(8) of the Directive does not rule out that Member States may maintain or introduce rules that allow for a wider disclosure of evidence. This is 'without prejudice' to those situations where confidential information needs to be disclosed or the evidence is in the file of a competition authority.

According to Article 5(7) of the Directive, before national courts will order any disclosure of evidence, those from whom the disclosure is sought have to be first offered the opportunity to be heard. As indicated in its Recital 20, the Directive aims to observe[21] the provisions of Transparency Regulation 1049/2001,[22] which sets out the rules governing public access to documents issued by the European Parliament, the Council and the Commission, as well as the relevant case law under the Regulation.[23]

However, the right to access documents is also subject to certain limitations dictated by public or private interests. Under Article 4 of the Transparency Regulation, a difficult balance has to be struck between the various interests favouring disclosure and those dismissing it. In the context of the right to access documents stemming from EU institutions, a conflict has emerged between the wider interpretation of the general Transparency Regulation and a narrower reading of the underpinning principle of transparency under the specialist Implementing Merger Regulation 802/2004.[24] Under Article 4(2) of the former Transparency Regulation, third parties have to be consulted before the application of potential exceptions to

---

[20]Case T-462/12 *Pilkington Group Ltd v. European Commission* ECLI:EU:T:2015:508, para 87.

[21]See the last sentence of Recital 20, which reads as follows: 'This Directive should be without prejudice to such rules and practices under Regulation (EC) No 1049/2001'.

[22]Regulation no 1049/2001 of the European Parliament and of the Council of 30 May 2001 regarding public access to European Parliament, Council and Commission documents [2001] OJ L 145/43.

[23]See Directive 2014/104/EU (n 1) Article 6(2).

[24]Regulation no 802/2004 of the European Commission of 7 April 2004 implementing Council Regulation (EC) no 139/2004 on the control of concentrations between undertakings [2001] OJ L 133/47.

the principle of transparency; otherwise, a potential disclosure could affect the commercial interests of the parties concerned. However, third parties do not have access to any documents included in the file, confidential information or internal documents of the Commission.

In *Carglass*,[25] the General Court clarified that reliance on the general presumption established by Article 4 of the Transparency Regulation cannot be used to deny the disclosure of information; otherwise, Regulation 1/2003[26] would be rendered meaningless, and the Commission would not be allowed to publish the content of its administrative decisions. It could even reverse the burden of proof by asking the Commission to demonstrate that the disclosure does not concern secret or confidential business information.

With regard to these procedural rules established by the Transparency Regulation and its subsequent case law, it becomes clear that certain limitations imposed on the disclosure of evidence under the Directive will prove challenging to the wider reading of the principle of transparency. Leaving aside leniency statements and settlement submissions to which, as third parties, the victims of infringements of competition law will have no access, the Directive establishes that for the preparation of actions for damages, it will suffice that such access to other relevant documents is nevertheless made available.[27]

In *Pfleiderer*,[28] national courts were offered some flexibility when ordering the disclosure of leniency documents, but the Directive moves in the opposite direction. This raises concerns over its effectiveness as a mechanism that is capable of assisting the victims of cartel activities.[29] In the light of *Pfleiderer*, national judges could still establish, on a case-by-case basis, whether they could disclose such evidence. They were empowered to perform a balancing exercise that could see judges favouring private or public enforcement. Before the enactment of the Directive, one representative of the European Parliament[30] favoured the approach adopted in *Pfleiderer* and suggested leaving it to national judges to have the final say on the disclosure of evidence.

In an action for damages, national judges will assist plaintiffs by reviewing whether the content that is being exempted from disclosure indeed falls under the scope of the deserved protection, i.e. statements made under leniency or settlement submissions. According to Article 6(7) of the Directive, following a 'reasoned request', a national court will examine such evidence in order to establish whether

---

[25]See Case T-465/12 *AGC Glass Europe SA, AGC Automotive Europe SA, AGC France SAS, AGC Flat Glass Italia Srl, AGC Glass UK Ltd, AGC Glass Germany GmbH* EGC ECLI:EU:T:2015:505.

[26]Council Regulation (EC) No 1/2003 of 16 December 2002 on the implementation of the rules on competition laid down in Articles 81 and 82 of the Treaty [2003] OJ L 1/1.

[27]See Directive 2014/104/EU (n 1) Recital 27.

[28]Case C-360/09 *Pfleiderer AG v. Bundeskartellamt* ECLI:EU:C:2011:389.

[29]Lundqvist and Andersson question why the Commission enacted a Damages Directive that will make it more difficult for cartel victims to gain access to incriminating documents. See Lundqvist and Andersson (2016), pp. 165–186.

[30]See Schwab (2014), p. 66.

it is part of a leniency application or a settlement. Under Article 6(8) of the Directive, partial disclosure is yet another possibility.

For the purpose of judicial scrutiny of such evidence, national courts may ask for the help of a competition authority. The competition authorities are then expected to submit written observations to the national courts as to whether the disclosure of evidence is proportionate.[31] In other words, the national courts of the European Union will gain access to documents to which the plaintiffs do not have access. The judiciary will verify and eventually disclose any content falling outside the scope of protection from disclosure. This extra layer of rigorous judicial scrutiny is ultimately intended to preserve the integrity of the process of the withholding of evidence. It is expected that the national courts, as ultimate and objective arbiters, will clarify this matter and, wherever possible, empower the plaintiffs in actions for damages by providing them with access to the necessary evidence.

However, this additional protection could very well remain ineffective. It sits rather awkwardly with Recital 30 of the Directive. The latter asks competition authorities to submit their observations to national courts in this particular regard. This demand is intended to revisit the principles of proportionality and transparency, in particular the impact that an eventual disclosure of evidence will have on the principle of effectiveness. Inherent tensions between these principles will actually see competition authorities trying to tip the balance in favour of an effective public enforcement and judges ultimately being reluctant to agree on a wider disclosure if this will interfere with the principle of effectiveness. For example, Member States are even required to set up a system whereby a competition authority is constantly informed of any requests for the disclosure of information.[32]

In a hypothetical scenario where the judiciary follows the written observations of a competition authority by not recommending disclosure, it is then the private enforcement of competition law that is doomed to fail. This author believes that the principle of effectiveness has to be applied cautiously. Such treading carefully is necessary for a successful implementation of the Directive; otherwise, by always placing the principle of effectiveness ahead of the principles of transparency and of proportionality, the legislative drafting of the Directive will simply curb the victims' appetite for compensation and ruin their chances of success. Why draft a 'Damages Directive' if it is not intended to benefit the victims of anticompetitive conduct? This question should have been asked from the very beginning. A reading of the Commission's welcoming of the Directive clarifies what the present directive is designed to achieve in the view of its legislative initiator, namely 'a more effective enforcement of the EU antitrust rules overall: it will fine-tune the interplay between private damages claims and public enforcement, in particular leniency and settlement programmes'.[33]

---

[31]See Directive 2014/104/EU (n 1) Recital 30 and Article 6(11).

[32]Ibid, Recital 30.

[33]See EU Commission, 'Antitrust: Commission welcomes Council adoption of Directive on antitrust damages actions', press release IP/14/1580, Brussels, 10 November 2014.

On a positive note, the most encouraging prospect being introduced by the Directive lies in the hands of the judiciary. National courts are now empowered to order companies to disclose the necessary evidence, as long as this exercise remains within the ambit of the principle of proportionality.

# 4   The Rule on Disclosure

Under Article 5(4) of the Directive, national courts have the power to order the disclosure of evidence. Where the evidence is relevant to an action for damages but contains confidential information, the courts have to protect this information. However, an interest in avoiding actions for damages cannot justify this protection.[34] The Directive goes on to require the courts to observe legal professional privilege under Article 5(6).

# 5   Limitations Imposed on Disclosure

The established rule on the disclosure of evidence is not without any limitations. Indeed, several limitations are now imposed on the disclosure of evidence. They are guided by both private and public interests. Following the model offered by Article 4 of Transparency Regulation 1049/2001, private interest primarily concerns business secrets or confidential information, while public interest lies in the decision-making process of a competition authority or the judiciary.

## 5.1   Private Interest in Business Secrets and Confidential Information

Recital 18 of the Directive has to be interpreted as a relative exception from the rule governing the disclosure of evidence. This exception requires that business secrets and other confidential information be adequately protected. It is also in line with the protection afforded to business secrets and other confidential information by Regulation 773/2004,[35] as amended by Regulation 2015/1348.[36]

---

[34]See Directive 2014/104/EU (n 1) Article 5(5).

[35]See Article 15(2) and Article 16(1) of Commission Regulation (EC) No 773/2004 of 7 April 2004 relating to the conduct of proceedings by the Commission pursuant to Articles 81 and 82 of the EC Treaty [2004] OJ L 123/22.

[36]See Commission Regulation (EU) 2015/1348 of 3 August 2015 amending Regulation (EC) no 773/2004 relating to the conduct of proceedings by the Commission pursuant to Articles 81 and 82 of the EC Treaty [2015] OJ L 208/3.

National courts are expected to identify suitable means in order to ensure the protection of any such sensitive data, for example by redacting sensitive passages in documents, conducting hearings in camera, restricting access to the evidence required or producing non-confidential summaries.[37] Nonetheless, such protective measures have to facilitate the exercise of the right to claim compensation.[38] This exception is therefore for the benefit of the party concerned.

The requirement to 'produce non-confidential summaries' could be seen as codifying in light of the General Court's ruling against the Commission's previous denial of partial access to non-confidential versions of requested documents in the *Heat Stabilisers*[39] case. While the Court rightfully acknowledged that Article 4 of the Transparency Regulation has to be interpreted and applied restrictively, it considered that, nevertheless, the Commission should have carried out an individual assessment of the content of such documents. In particular, the Court reproached the Commission for not having facilitated even partial access to a non-confidential version of the document concerned. The Court then reviewed the Commission's perceived failure to provide 'explanations as to how access to that document could specially and actually undermine' the interest protected by an exception to disclosure.

The Directorate-General for Competition has adopted helpful Guidance on the preparation of public versions of Commission Decisions.[40] It offers useful examples of confidential information that qualifies as business secrets, including technical and/or financial information relating to an undertaking's know-how, margin calculations and price structures, production secrets and processes, supply sources, quantities produced and sold, market shares, customer and distributor lists, marketing plans, costs and methods of assessing costs, and sales strategy.[41] Paragraph 13 of the Guidance also offers useful examples of information that can normally be disclosed. This category includes, for instance, the Commission's assessment of evidence and the results of its investigation, information that is publicly available or that has lost its commercial importance due to the passage of time, data from and about another undertaking and statistical or aggregate information.

In addition, the Directorate-General for Competition has adopted Best Practices on the disclosure of information in data rooms that applies to 'antitrust' proceedings under Articles 101 and 102.[42] Accordingly, Article 2(8) of the Best Practices recalls that, under Article 339 TFEU, the Commission has a general 'duty to protect

---

[37] See Directive 2014/104/EU (n 1) Recital 18.

[38] Ibid.

[39] See Case T-181/10 *Reagens SpA v. European Commission* ECLI:EU:T:2014:139.

[40] See paragraphs 9 and 10 of the Guidance on the preparation of public versions of Commission Decisions adopted under Articles 7 to 10, 23 and 24 of Regulation 1/2003, adopted on 4 June 2015. Available via http://ec.europa.eu/competition/antitrust/guidance_on_preparation_of_public_ver sions_antitrust_04062015.pdf. Accessed Oct 2015.

[41] Ibid, paragraph 10.

[42] Best Practices on the disclosure of information in data rooms in proceedings under Articles 101 and 102 TFEU and under the EU Merger Regulation, adopted on 2 June 2015.

confidential information that could seriously harm the undertaking if disclosed'. Exceptionally, such confidential information may be disclosed when the disclosure is necessary to prove antitrust infringements or to safeguard the rights of defence of the parties.[43] For example, the addressees of a Statement of Objections have the right to access the non-confidential electronic version of the Commission's file.[44] This does not apply to internal documents and confidential information, such as business secrets and other confidential information.[45]

According to Article 2(7) of the Best Practices, data collected from third parties, such as data referring to costs, prices, sales, bidding, margins etc., constitute confidential business secrets. It is often impossible to disclose in a timely manner a non-confidential version of quantitative data.[46] Qualitative information, such as the internal strategy of competitors, can only exceptionally be disclosed for an effective exercise of the rights of defence. In particular, Article 3(14) of the Best Practices raises another common concern over the exchange of sensitive, internal and strategic information that could facilitate collusion. Should the Directorate-General for Competition allow qualitative information to be disclosed, the information has first to be anonymised, for instance by translation into the same language, changing the currency, redacting territories or aggregating figures, etc.[47]

In any case, Article 2(8) of the Best Practices goes on to clarify that confidential information should never be disclosed where the parties have already gained access to non-confidential versions of the requested documents. When deciding on disclosure, the Directorate-General for Competition enjoys discretion over whether the disclosure is 'necessary and proportionate'.[48] Several other criteria are mentioned in Article 2(11) of the Best Practices. These criteria refer to the timing of the request for disclosure, the nature and sensitivity of the information, the progress of the case, the resources available in data rooms, the risk of information leaks, as well as the need for speed. All in all, the above Best Practices offer more concrete and helpful examples than the Damages Directive itself when it comes to particular categories of evidence.

A practical example of the various categories of protected information is offered by *Carglass*.[49] The first category includes customer names, product descriptions and any information that could enable an individual customer to be identified. The second includes the allocation of quotas, price agreements, pricing calculations and price changes, while the third one includes administrative information. The disclosure of customer relations represents 'inherently confidential' information that is unknown to specialist circles.

---

[43]Ibid, Article 2(8).

[44]Ibid, Article 2(5).

[45]Ibid, Article 2(6).

[46]Ibid.

[47]Ibid, Article 3(17).

[48]Ibid, Article 2(10).

[49]See *Carglass* (n 25).

However, the obligation of professional secrecy extends beyond business secrets to information meeting the requirements laid down in *Bank Austria Creditanstalt*.[50] Namely, information known to a limited number of persons, whose disclosure is liable to cause serious harm to the person who has provided it or to third parties, must be objectively worthy of protection. This obligation requires the Court to assess whether the Commission has observed the prohibition on its disclosure, as foreseen under Article 28(2) of Regulation 1/2003.[51] With regard to an organic peroxide cartel (*Pergan*),[52] the Court did not allow access to a non-confidential version of the Commission's decision in order to respect the reputation and dignity of the undertaking concerned. Similarly, the Commission denied access to non-confidential information concerning an Air Cargo cartel (*Schenker*)[53] as it would have harmed commercial interests. In the *Axa Versicherung* case,[54] granting access to roughly 90 per cent of the documents of the file could have harmed the same commercial interests of the undertaking concerned.

Disclosure of this information 'could undermine' the effectiveness of the leniency programme in the same way as disclosure of the 'leniency documents' in the strict sense, in so far as such disclosure may result in third parties becoming aware of commercially sensitive information or confidential information relating to the cooperation of the parties contained in the documents.

Under Article 8(2) of Decision 2011/695/EU,[55] the Hearing Officer can issue a reasoned decision to disclose information that does not constitute a 'business secret or other confidential information' or for whose disclosure there is an 'overriding interest'.

In *Pilkington*,[56] the confidential information in question covered business secrets, other information whose disclosure would have seriously harmed the commercial interests of an undertaking and personal data.[57] 'Inherently confidential' was considered to refer to information that was known only to a limited number of individuals and the disclosure of which was likely to cause harm. In this respect, the appellant argued that the Hearing Officer had failed to establish the inherently confidential character of the contested information. Pilkington argued that the publication of the *Carglass* decision could reveal its list of customers, including

---

[50]See Case T-198/03 *Bank Austria Creditanstalt v. European Commission* ECLI:EU:T:2006:136. On the earlier case law on disclosure of evidence, see Carlton et al. (2008); on recent developments, see Howard (2015), MacLennan (2016), Vandenborre et al. (2015), p. 747.

[51]See *Bank Austria Creditanstalt* (n 50) para 27; Case T-474/04 *Pergan Hilfsstoffe für industrielle Prozesse v. European Commission* ECLI:EU:T:2007:306.

[52]See *Pergan* (n 51).

[53]Case T-534/11 *Schenker AG v. European Commission* ECLI:EU:T:2014:854.

[54]See *AXA Versicherung* (n 13).

[55]Decision 2011/695 of the President of the European Commission of 13 October 2011 on the function and terms of reference of the hearing officer in certain competition proceedings [2011] OJ L 275/29.

[56]See *Pilkington* (n 20).

[57]Ibid, para 35.

car models or parts supplied at specific times. This information is classified as 'category I' protected information, in contrast to 'category II' information that is unknown even to specialist circles. Pilkington disputed the historical character of both categories, arguing that their disclosure could offer 'an extremely detailed insight' into its relations with customers.[58] In contrast, the Hearing Officer considered that 'category I' information regarding customer or product names, descriptions and any other information is 'by its very nature' known to third parties.[59]

The published decision contained no list of customers or distributors. Therefore, historical information describing the cartel infringement was no longer considered to be confidential.[60] The Hearing Officer followed the same reasoning for 'category II' information.[61] Ultimately, the Court endorsed the Hearing Officer's finding of historical information, namely that

> information which was secret and confidential but is five or more years old and must, accordingly, be regarded as historical, does not remain either secret or confidential unless, exceptionally, the party concerned demonstrates that, despite its age, that information continues to constitute an essential element of its commercial position or that of the third party concerned.[62]

By publishing a fuller version of its decision, the Commission was entitled to consider the interests of the victims seeking compensation for anticompetitive conduct.[63] Although the information on prices agreed with each customer and the quantities of car parts represented business secrets, the information had lost its confidential character. The members of the cartel had exchanged it with competitors.[64] The main producers had fixed car glass prices.[65] Ultimately, the Hearing Officer agreed to redact the references to the manufacturer, brand and models mentioned in the *Carglass* decision.[66]

## 5.2   Public Interest in the Decision-Making Process

Recital 25 of the Directive introduced another possible exception where a disclosure of evidence would inappropriately interfere with an ongoing investigation by a

---

[58]Ibid, para 37.
[59]Ibid, para 49.
[60]Ibid, para 50.
[61]Ibid, para 54.
[62]Ibid, para 58.
[63]Ibid, para 59.
[64]Ibid, para 60.
[65]Ibid, para 68.
[66]Ibid, para 68.

competition authority. For example, information that is the object of a Statement of Objections sent to the parties suspected of an anticompetitive infringement, and replies to such a statement or to further requests for information, should be disclosed only after the respective competition authority has closed its proceedings, with the exception of the adoption of interim measures.[67] This exception seeks to protect the integrity of competition investigations.

Similarly, the Guidance on the preparation of public versions of Commission Decisions[68] highlights several categories of information that, if published, could jeopardise the Commission's investigations. These categories include quotations from corporate statements under the shield of leniency, information that could help to identify a leniency applicant and voluntary, i.e. self-incriminating, admissions of participation in cartel activities.

Article 6 of the Directive mentions that the following categories of evidence should be disclosed only after the adoption of a decision by the competition authority: (a) information prepared for the proceedings of a competition authority, (b) information drawn up and sent in the course of such proceedings and (c) withdrawn settlement submissions.

According to Article 7(2) of the Directive, before a competition authority has closed its proceedings, this kind of evidence can either be declared inadmissible in an action for damages or be otherwise protected under national rules.

General exceptions to the disclosure of information are foreseen by the Amendments to the Commission Notice on the cooperation between the Commission and national courts of the Member States,[69] namely that

> the Commission may refuse to transmit information to national courts for overriding reasons relating to the need to safeguard the interests of the European Union or to avoid any interference with its functioning and independence, in particular by jeopardising the accomplishment of the task entrusted to it.[70]

In the view of this author, the above refusals by the Commission to cooperate with national judges are justifiable. They could be subsumed under the Directive's wider public interest category as this concerns the functioning and independence of the European Union. Specific exceptions to the rule on the disclosure of information to national courts are further justifiable where the disclosure would 'unduly affect the effectiveness of enforcement of the competition rules by the Commission'.[71] In

---

[67]See Directive 2014/104/EU (n 1) Article 6(5).

[68]See paragraph 22(c) of the Guidance on the preparation of public versions of Commission Decisions adopted under Articles 7 to 10, 23 and 24 of Regulation 1/2003 (n 40).

[69]See paragraph 26 of the Amendments to the Commission Notice on the cooperation between the Commission and courts of the EU Member States in the application of Articles 81 and 82 EC [2015] OJ C 256/04.

[70]Ibid, paragraph 26.

[71]Ibid.

particular, these exceptions seek to avoid interference with pending investigations on the one hand and with the functioning of leniency programmes and settlement procedures on the other.

Overall, the above exception from disclosure could be seen as codifying Article 4(3) of Transparency Regulation 1049/2001. Accordingly, access to a document that is used internally or received by an institution will be refused as long as that institution has not yet taken a decision. It is feared that its disclosure could seriously undermine the institution's decision-making process. The exception to this rule will be where there is 'an overriding public interest' in the disclosure of evidence. According to the second paragraph of Article 4(3), non-disclosure can be prolonged even after a decision has been taken where the document contains 'opinions for internal use as part of deliberations and preliminary consultations'. The same reason and exception applies as in the first paragraph of Article 4(3) of the Transparency Regulation. Article 27(2) of the special Regulation 1/2003 also excludes from disclosure internal documents of the Commission or other national competition authorities.

The Court of Justice has previously ruled on a potential undermining of the Commission's decision-making process in the appeal against *Gas Insulated Switchgear*.[72] In this case, the document contained opinions for internal use only by the Commission as part of its deliberation process and consultations. The Court considered that third parties should have no access to such internal documents on the basis of the specific rules governing access under Regulations 1/2003 and 773/2004 as a blind reliance on a wider reading of the Transparency Regulation, although favourable to third parties, would undermine the above public interest. The interpretation followed by the Court has to be seen as an endorsement of the limitations imposed on the principle of transparency under the special Regulations. The latter take precedence over the Transparency Regulation. Another tenor of the Court's ruling recognised the existence of a 'general presumption' against the disclosure of evidence that could undermine the protection of protected interests. The Court had previously recognised the existence of a general presumption.[73] However, this presumption does not rule out that, by proving the contrary, the disclosure of a specific document is not covered by the above presumption or that there is an overriding public interest in favour of its disclosure by virtue of Article 4 (3) of the Transparency Regulation.

Similarly, the General Court ruled on the Commission's denying the parties concerned access to an internal study of the costs and benefits to merchants accepting different methods of payment.[74] In the view of the Court, the

---

[72]See *EnBW Energie* (n 11).

[73]See C-239/07 P *European Commission v. Technische Glaswerke Ilmenau* ECLI:EU:C:2010:376 para 61 on access to the administrative file regarding state aid; Case C-404/10 P, *European Commission v. Éditions Odile Jacob* ECLI:EU:C:2012:393 para 123 on access to documents in mergers; Case C-477/10 P *European Commission v. Agrofert Holding* ECLI:EU:C:2012:394 para 64; *EnBW Energie* (n 11) para 81.

[74]See Case T-516/11 *MasterCard v. European Commission* ECLI:EU:T:2014:759.

Commission first had to assess the applicability of any of the exceptions to the principle of transparency under Regulation 1049/2001. For this purpose, the Commission should have explained how access could undermine its decision-making process. This reflected the Court's expectation that the Commission would also demonstrate how an eventual disclosure could 'specifically and actually' undermine any protected interests. In the words of the Court, the undermining of the Commission as an institution could have been proven by 'attempts to influence and exert external pressure or curtail its independence'.

Generally, the exceptions imposed on the disclosure of internal evidence held by a European institution have to be interpreted strictly. Furthermore, there must be a risk of a 'specific and actual adverse effect' on the protected interest.[75] In *Unión de Almacenistas de Hierros de España*,[76] the Commission denied access to the draft decisions of the Spanish Competition Authority, its file and the summaries of its conversations with the Spanish Competition Authority.

The Commission relied on Article 4(2) of the Transparency Regulation, including the undermining of its internal decision-making process. In this case, access had been denied even after the closing of the proceedings of the Spanish Competition Authority. The Commission relied on the general presumption that the disclosure of such sensitive information could undermine the undertakings' commercial interests and ongoing investigations.[77] The information sent to the Commission was received by the Spanish Competition Authority in the context of an investigation under Article 101.[78]

Irrespective of the investigation being conducted by a public authority of a Member State, the Court of Justice interpreted the wording of Article 4(2) of the Transparency Regulation to include 'inspections, investigations and audits' that are not limited to those of the EU institutions.[79] While Article 4(3) of the Transparency Regulation seeks to protect 'the institution's decision-making process', the Court had required that these exceptions

> be interpreted as seeking to protect not only the activities of the institutions of the European Union, but also interests specific to a Member State, such as the protection of inspections, investigations and audits conducted by the services of the authority of that Member State.[80]

---

[75]See Case C-615/13 P *Client Earth, Pesticide Action Network Europe v. European Food Safety Authority* ECLI:EU:C:2015:489.

[76]Case T-623/13 *Unión de Almacenistas de Hierros de España v. European Commission* ECLI:EU:T:2015:268.

[77]Ibid, para 15.

[78]Ibid, para 43.

[79]Ibid, para 44.

[80]Ibid, para 44, citing Case C-64/05 P, *Sweden v. European Commission* ECLI:EU:C:2007:802 para 83.

Article 11(4) of Regulation 1/2003 governs access to documents sent to the Commission by a national competition authority. Recitals 15 and 32 of this regulation demand that the confidentiality of the information exchanges and consultations among the Commission and its national competition authorities be safeguarded.[81] Since parties to the proceedings do not have access to such documents, the Court of Justice ruled that, *a fortiori*, the specialist regulation[82] prevents the disclosure of such documents to anyone else. A potential disclosure could harm the undertakings' commercial interests, irrespective of the pending status of proceedings.[83] It runs the risk of 'adversely affecting the willingness of undertakings to cooperate when such a procedure is pending'.[84] Furthermore, exceptions relating to sensitive documents may apply for 30 years or more.[85]

In its recent Opinion,[86] the Commission reiterated that, during pending proceedings, a disclosure of information obtained through access to a file 'could seriously undermine a pending investigation'.[87]

## 5.3   Public Interest in the Effectiveness of Leniency and Settlements

Recital 24 of the Directive states that the Directive itself does not 'affect the right of the courts to consider the interests of an effective public enforcement'. It is argued that this aspect could be inherently problematic as the same courts have to defend the interests of an effective private enforcement of competition law. The success of the latter relies on the courts' willingness to order disclosures. Yet Recital 24 of the Directive appears to expect exactly the contrary. In particular, Recital 26 of the Directive details an important limitation on disclosure benefitting directly those undertakings that cooperate under leniency or engage with settlement procedures. Such cooperation and/or engagement contribute to the efficacy of the detection and fining of cartels. In fact, both are indispensable tools used to achieve an effective enforcement of competition law. This is because the majority of cartels come to light following the successful implementation of the leniency policy.

---

[81] Ibid, para 57.

[82] Ibid, para 58.

[83] Ibid, para 71.

[84] Ibid, para 71.

[85] See Transparency Regulation (n 22) Article 4(7).

[86] Commission Opinion of 29 October 2015, Opinion of the European Commission in application of Article 15(1) of Council Regulation (EC) No 1/2003 of 16 December 2002 on the implementation of the rules on competition laid down in Articles 81 and 82 of the Treaty, CT.00928 – Interchange fee litigation before the High Court of Justice, Chancery Division: Sainsbury's Supermarkets Ltd v. MasterCard Incorporated and Others, C (2015) 7682 final.

[87] Ibid, para 8.

An eventual disclosure of self-incriminating, corporate statements made under the shield of either leniency or settlement submissions could generate distrust in such cooperation or engagement. In this regard, Regulation 2015/1348 has already noted that 'undertakings may be dissuaded from cooperating with the Commission if doing so might have negative consequences for their position in civil proceedings'.[88] According to Article 15(1)(b) of this Regulation, access to voluntary corporate statements made under leniency or to a settlement submission can only exceptionally be granted at the premises of the Commission. Access to such corporate statements made under leniency will be granted solely for the purpose of exercising the parties' rights of defence.[89] Similarly, the Amendments both to the Commission Notice on the rules for access to the Commission file[90] and to the Commission Notice on Immunity from fines and reduction of fines in cartel cases[91] grant access to the file only conditionally, that is, for the purposes of judicial or administrative proceedings. In the same vein, Recital 33 of the Commission Notice on Immunity from fines and the reduction of fines in cartel cases[92] acknowledges that access to corporate statements will be granted solely to the addressees of a statement of objections provided that these parties, including their legal counsels, undertake a commitment not to make any hard or electronic copy of any information to which such access is granted.

Therefore, it does not come as a great surprise when Article 6(6) of the Directive requires that leniency statements and settlement submissions included in the file of a competition authority must never be disclosed by national courts. This could be interpreted as an *absolute* exception from the disclosure of evidence.[93] Article 7 (1) of the Directive goes further in that it requires that such evidence be declared as inadmissible in an action for damages or be otherwise protected under national rules.

In its recent Opinion,[94] the Commission recognised that the Court has to balance the interests of the victims of antitrust violations against those of an effective enforcement of competition law.[95] It went on to suggest that

> although the rules of the Damages Directive are not, in the context of the present proceedings, a bar to the Court ordering (...) disclosure (...), in the

---

[88]See Commission Regulation (EU) 2015/1348 (n 36) Recital 4.

[89]Ibid, Article 16a(2).

[90]See paragraph 48 of the Amendments to the Commission Notice on the rules for access to the Commission file in cases pursuant to Articles 81 and 82 of the EC Treaty, Articles 53, 54 and 57 of the EEA Agreement and Council Regulation (EC) No 139/2004 [2015] OJ C 256/03.

[91]See Recital 34 of the Amendments to the Commission Notice on Immunity from fines and reduction of fines in cartel cases [2015] OJ C 256/1.

[92]See Recital 33 of the Commission Notice on Immunity from fines and reduction of fines in cartel cases [2006] OJ C 298/21, as amended by Amendments to the Commission Notice (n 91).

[93]For a similar opinion, see Dunne (2015), p. 9.

[94]Commission Opinion (n 86).

[95]Ibid, para 15.

Commission's view, the principle of sincere cooperation as laid down in Article 4(3) TEU requires the Court to give considerable weight to the considerations reflected in those legislative provisions when carrying out its balancing test.[96]

The above suggests that the principle of sincere cooperation will triumph where an effective public enforcement could be challenged through a request for disclosure.

In *Axa Versicherung*,[97] the General Court recognised the 'importance of actions for damages brought before national courts in ensuring the maintenance of effective competition'.[98] In light of *Donau Chemie*,[99] the Court went on to suggest that

> the mere argument that there is a risk that access to evidence contained in a file in competition proceedings which is necessary as a basis for those actions may undermine the effectiveness of the leniency programme in which those documents were disclosed to the competent competition authority cannot justify a refusal to grant access to that evidence.[100]

On the contrary, the Court rightfully recognised that

> the fact that such a refusal is liable to prevent those actions from being brought, by giving the undertakings concerned, who may have already benefited from immunity, at the very least partial, from pecuniary penalties, an opportunity also to circumvent their obligation to compensate for the harm resulting from the infringement of Article 101 TFEU, to the detriment of the injured parties, requires that refusal to be based on overriding reasons relating to the protection of the interest relied on and applicable to each document to which access is refused.[101]

This means that the competent competition authorities may justify a refusal to disclose evidence 'only if there is a risk that a given document may actually undermine the public interest relating to the effectiveness of the leniency programme in question'.[102] Therefore, the recommendation of the Court to the Commission and national courts is very welcome in the sense that when they are

---

[96]Ibid, para 16.

[97]See *AXA Versicherung* (n 13).

[98]Ibid, para 120.

[99]Case C-536/11 *Bundeswettbewerbsbehörde v. Donau Chemie AG and Others* ECLI:EU: C:2013:366 para 46.

[100]Ibid.

[101]Ibid, para 121.

[102]Ibid, para 122.

called upon to take a decision, in legal and procedural frameworks that are admittedly different, on whether to grant access to documents collected in the context of the implementation of a leniency programme which are included in the file of a proceeding pursuant to the competition rules, they must refrain from taking an inflexible and absolute stance liable to undermine either the effective application of the competition rules by the public authorities entrusted with ensuring their observance or the effective exercise of individuals' rights flowing from these rules.[103]

In the end, it all comes down to a comprehensive balancing exercise. This will consider the special interests of the party asking for disclosure, i.e. in securing access to the documents necessary to support an action for damages, as well as any other available alternatives for the same purpose, against 'the actual harmful consequences'[104] that could emerge from such disclosure.[105]

In any event, the protection offered to an undertaking that chooses to cooperate goes beyond the administrative to civil liability. Recital 26 of the Directive also refers to 'criminal' liability that exists solely at the level of Member States. This is not the case under EU competition law: fines never exceed a maximum of 10 per cent of the annual turnover of the accused undertaking, and there is no European public prosecutor to send corporate managers and directors to prison for alleged cartel activity. While it is, indeed, true that undertakings could simply choose not to cooperate[106] if they were exposed to an administrative fine or, even more so, to having their managers criminally prosecuted, this author disagrees with the contentment of civil impunity. A further discharge of civil liability could practically undermine the effectiveness of the private enforcement of competition law that the present directive aims to enhance. It is difficult not to see how by not disclosing the evidence that is necessary for damage claims one could ever strengthen private, civil enforcement.

In light of all of the above considerations, it is argued that the present leniency shield made up of three layers, namely administrative, criminal and civil, is overly protective. A two-layer protection against administrative liability coupled with the inexistence of criminal liability would suffice to maintain the attractiveness of the leniency policy, and it should also incentivise the competition authorities to rely on it less than on their own detection efforts.[107] In other words, the excuse founded in the inability to detect cartels by one's own efforts comes at the expense of

---

[103]Ibid, para 123.

[104]Ibid.

[105]Kirst and van den Bergh (2016) are rather fearful that such a balancing exercise will proceed in the absence of 'clear guidance from EU courts'.

[106]See European Commission (2015), p. 4.

[107]For a similar opinion, see Guttuso (2015), p. 395; on the risk of relying too much on leniency, see Wils (2016), p. 26; for contrary views that it is essential not to weaken the effectiveness of the leniency programmes, see Wils (2009), p. 3; Wagner-von Papp (2016), p. 54.

diminishing further the effectiveness of the private enforcement of competition law. Certainly, there are many means to detect cartels other than whistle-blowing, for example by becoming an employee of the company suspected of cartel activity, by visiting their business premises, etc. Of course, the latter alternatives cannot be adopted easily without the shield of criminalisation itself. However, neither prison nor pecuniary damages for the victims of cartels mean that whistle-blowers will never have their business reputation tarnished as cheaters and rogue traders. It follows that whoever is ahead of the others in this multilateral dilemma of whether to blow or not to blow the whistle gets everything. It also places the Commission in the back corner as it becomes more of an Office for Hearing such whistle-blowers, while everyone else expects the Commission to do more. So far, the Commission has never quantified the overall financial loss to the EU budget stemming from these offerings of administrative impunity.

Comparatively, under the US Corporate Leniency Policy (1993),[108] a first applicant will qualify for full immunity from criminal prosecution and fines. Under the Antitrust Criminal Penalty Enforcement Enhancement and Reform Act (2004), the same applicant could see a significant reduction when it comes to civil liability, namely the 'actual' damage caused by a secret cartel. As has already been suggested,[109] this is a 'sweetening of the carrot' instead of liability for treble, i.e., triple, damages caused by the entire cartel. In contrast, under the EU Damages Directive, an entire discharge of civil liability is the sweetest carrot ever seen by rogue businesses. This comparative analysis is aggravated by the fact that EU competition law does not pursue criminal prosecutions against cartelists, and nor does EU civil law apply similar treble damages as in the US.

Looking forward to achieving an absolute sweetening of the civil liability regime, towards the end of Recital 26 of the Directive, it is concluded that 'voluntary and self-incriminating' statements and settlement submissions, including 'verbatim quotations' from them, are exempted from disclosure. This represents an absolute exception from disclosure. It is firmly believed by the legislative initiators and commentators alike that by limiting the above exceptions to statements made under leniency, the private enforcement of competition law, namely the award of damages, will not be affected. Only time will tell whether the implementation of the Directive will improve victims' chances of succeeding in damage claims.

However, the above limitations on disclosure could remain inapplicable when it comes to publishing the administrative decision itself. This means that at least a slight tarnishing of the reputation of cartel members can be anticipated and welcomed by the victims of cartels. A recent example is Evonik Degussa's opposition to the publication by the Commission of a non-confidential version of its decision.[110]

---

[108]Available via http://www.justice.gov/atr/corporate-leniency-policy. Accessed Jan 2016.

[109]See Harrison and Bell (2006), p. 226; Hewitt (2005), p. 173; Gilbert and Romanenko (2012), p. 385.

[110]See Case T-341/12 *Evonik Degussa GmbH v. European Commission* ECLI:EU:T:2015:51.

Degussa argued that this version would contain confidential information that the company had made available to the Commission under leniency, including the names of customers and indications of Degussa's commercial relationships. The disclosure of such confidential information could expose Degussa to civil actions for damages before national courts. In contrast, the Commission argued that references to documents included in the administrative file could not be considered as business secrets or other confidential information. In accordance with Article 8 of the mandate of the Hearing Officer,[111] Degussa had been informed in writing of the Commission's intention to disclose information that might constitute a 'business secret or other confidential information'. It was for the Hearing Officer to establish whether that information may be disclosed 'because it does not constitute a business secret or other confidential information or because there is an overriding interest in its disclosure'.[112] *Mutatis mutandis*, the Hearing Officer decides on the disclosure of information by publication in the Official Journal.

The Commission had already notified Degussa of its decision to publish a more detailed, non-confidential version of the administrative decision against the company, as required by the principle of transparency. Degussa disputed the confidential character of the information required to be disclosed since the company had made certain statements under leniency and had voluntarily submitted documents during the Commission's investigation. The company argued that such information was legally privileged on the basis of Article 339 TFEU and Article 30(2) of Regulation 1/2003 and that it met the requirements established in *Bank Austria Creditanstalt*,[113] namely (1) the information was known only to a small number of persons, (2) the disclosure of information could cause a serious prejudice and (3) the non-disclosure of such information was objectively necessary, irrespective of the existence of contrary interests favouring its disclosure. Furthermore, the publication of the decision in question could cause Degussa a 'serious prejudice' and expose it to a 'higher risk', namely being required to pay compensation in actions for damages before national courts.

However, according to a well-established line of case law, historical information, i.e. older than five years or more, can no longer be classified as secret or confidential information.[114] Contrary to Degussa's argument that the publication of a non-confidential version of the administrative decision could harm its reputation, the publication of the decision itself was intended to shed light on the important role played by Degussa in the infringement of Article 101 TFEU, as well as on the continuation of this infringement for almost seven years. This was rightfully so

---

[111]See Decision 2011/695/EU (n 55).

[112]Ibid, Article 8(2).

[113]See *Bank Austria Creditanstalt* (n 50) para 33.

[114]See Case T-1/89-T-4/89 and T-6/89-T-15/89 *Rhône-Poulenc v. European Commission* ECLI: EU:T:1990:69 para 23; Case T-383/03 *Hynix Semiconductor v. Council of the European Union* ECLI:EU:T:2005:57 para 60; Case T-108/07 *Diamanthandel A. Spira v. European Commission* ECLI:EU:T:2013:367 para 65.

since there is no special protection afforded to undertakings infringing Article 101 in the sense of having the details of their illegal behaviour protected from disclosure to the wider public. Furthermore, it is in the interest of economic operators to know about any such infringements that could expose them to economic sanctions.[115]

The General Court agreed that Degussa's opposition to the publication by the Commission of information that described in detail Degussa's participation in the said infringement could not be justified on the grounds that this could affect its reputation and commercial interests. Degussa was interested in protecting itself from potential claims for damages, which was not worthy of any special protection on the part of the Commission. In this context, the Court recalled the right of victims to claim compensation as established by EU case law.[116]

As the same Court had rightly acknowledged in its *Carglass* ruling:

> the exposure to legal proceedings seeking damages is, to the extent that it were to materialise, no more than the indirect consequence of the applicants' participation in an infringement of Article 101 and cannot therefore be worthy of protection.[117]

In particular, there is a public interest in being informed of the reasons behind the administrative decision and of the kind of anticompetitive conduct liable to expose undertakings to penalties.[118] Furthermore, if it so chooses, the Commission may publish a fuller version of its decision than 'the minimum necessary'.[119] The only requirement is that the information being disclosed observe the protection of professional secrecy. The Court ruled out that the identity of the appellants' customers could still be included in the *Carglass* decision. However, the Court recognised that the efficacy of the Commission's leniency programmes could be affected by the disclosure of leniency documents to those victims planning to initiate actions for damages.[120] This would happen irrespective of a total or partial impunity from fines applied by the Commission or national competition authorities.[121] The publication of the documents in question could make it easier for third parties to establish prejudice in claims for damages. Nevertheless, where the Commission considers it appropriate, it can publish a full or detailed version of

---

[115]See *Pergan* (n 51) para 33.

[116]See Case C-453/99 *Courage and Crehan* ECLI:EU:C:2001:465 paras 24 and 26; Joined Cases C-295/04-C-298/04 *Manfredi and Others* ECLI:EU:C:2006:461; Case C-199/11 *Europese Gemeenschap v. Otis NV and Others* ECLI:EU:C:2012:684 para 41.

[117]*Carglass* (n 25) para 43.

[118]Ibid, para 43.

[119]Ibid, para 52.

[120]See *Pfleiderer* (n 28) para 26.

[121]Ibid, para 26.

its administrative decision insofar as the required publication safeguards business secrets and other confidential information.[122]

# 6 Concluding Reflections on the Legislative Drafting of the Directive

One apparent conflict of interest between the public and private enforcement of competition law originates in the legislative proposal of the Directive, as put forward by one of its beneficiaries, which include the Commission's Directorate-General for Competition. These critical aspects have already been detailed in the previous sections of this contribution.

The overall drafting of the Directive is not overly inspiring. This remains so, as both the substantive and procedural rules governing actions for damages are again to be found at greater length in the various recitals of the Directive itself rather than being detailed in the text of its articles. The Directive is faithful to a previous Proposal.[123] It is the result of political compromise. In essence, the Directive has derived useful inspiration from the Transparency Regulation and the preceding case law of the EU courts. This is to be welcomed as a favourable development for third-party victims. However, the reiteration of the various exceptions aimed at enhancing the public enforcement of competition law can be feared ultimately to limit the real chances of the success of such actions for damages. This is the case with self-incriminating statements that have been included on the 'black list' of exceptions to the disclosure of evidence.

However, when reviewing the proposal for the Directive, the Committee of Permanent Representatives (COREPER) agreed that all of the other documents accompanying such statements would remain 'disclosable'.[124] This represents fairly the greatest achievement of the Directive when it comes to facilitating access to evidence for the victims of cartels. Anything else, by which this author means 98 per cent of the contents of the famous 'Damages Directive', is in the detail about how and what not to disclose to the victims in actions for damages. This is not bad news at all. One has to remind readers that the majority of cartel fines are industrial.[125] The victims of cartel activity are intermediate consumers, i.e. other

---

[122]See *Bank Austria Creditanstalt* (n 50) para 33.

[123]See Amendments by the European Parliament to the Commission proposal, including Amendment 2 (A 7-0089/2) by Sharon Bowles on behalf of the Committee on Economic and Monetary Affairs and Report (A 7-0089/2014) by Andreas Schwab. Available via http://www.europarl. europa.eu/sides/getDoc.do?pubRef=-//EP//NONSGML+AMD+A7-2014-0089+002-002+DOC +PDF+V0//EN. Accessed 14 Nov 2015.

[124]See Council of the European Union, 'New rules to facilitate damage claims for antitrust violations', Brussels, 26 March 2014, 8136/14. Available via http://www.consilium.europa.eu/ uedocs/cms_data/docs/pressdata/en/intm/141926.pdf. Accessed 14 Nov 2015.

[125]Chirita (2015), pp. 407–441.

businesses, rather than humble citizens. These citizens have neither the time nor the money to litigate successfully. Is this then not 'Much Ado about Nothing'?

# References

ABA Section of Antitrust Law (2006) 2005 Annual review of antitrust developments. In: Hewitt PB (ed) American Bar Association, 2006, p 137

Carlton R, Lawrence J, McElwee M (2008) Confidentiality and disclosure in European Commission antitrust proceedings: the case for clarity. Eur Competition J 4:401

Chirita AD (2015) The judicial review of the European Union industrial cartels. Zeitschrift für europarechtliche Studien 18:407–441

Dunne N (2015) Courage and compromise: the Directive on Antitrust Damages. Eur Law Rev 4:9

European Commission (2015) The Damages Directive: towards more effective enforcement of the EU competition rules. Competition Policy Brief 1:4

Gilbert P, Romanenko V (2012) Proposals for reform. In: Foer AA, Stutz RM (eds) Private enforcement of antitrust law in the United States: a handbook. Edward Elgar, Cheltenham, p 385

Guttuso L (2015) From 'mono' to 'stereo': fine-tuning leniency and settlement policies. World Competition 38:395

Harrison G, Bell M (2006) Recent enhancements in antitrust criminal enforcement: Bigger sticks and sweeter carrots. Houst Bus Tax J 6:226

Howard A (2015) Disclosure of infringement decisions in competition damages proceedings: how the UK courts are leading the way ahead of the Damages Directive. J Eur Competition Law Pract 6:256

Kirst P, van den Bergh R (2016) The European Directive on Damages Actions: a missed opportunity to reconcile compensation of victims and leniency incentives. J Competition Law Econ 12:1

Lundqvist B, Andersson H (2016) Access to documents for cartel victims and cartel members: is the system coherent? In: Bergström M, Iacovides M, Strand M (eds) Harmonising EU competition litigation: the new directive and beyond. Hart, Oxford, pp 165–186

MacLennan J (2016) Fundamental rights: Pilkington and the right to confidentiality in published decisions. J Eur Competition Law Pract 7:194

Schwab A (2014) Finding the right balance: the deliberations of the European Parliament on the draft legislation regarding damage claims. J Eur Competition Law Pract 5:66

Vandenborre I, Goetz T, Kafetzopoulos A (2015) Access to file under European competition law. J Eur Competition Law Pract 6:747

Wagner-von Papp F (2016) Access to evidence and leniency materials. Social Science Research Network, p 54. Available via http://papers.ssrn.com/sol3/Papers.cfm?abstract_id=2733973. Accessed Mar 2016

Wils WPJ (2009) The relationship between public antitrust enforcement and private actions for damages. World Competition 32:3

Wils WPJ (2016) The use of leniency in EU cartel enforcement: an assessment after twenty years. World Competition 39:327–388

# The *Kone* Case: A Missed Opportunity to Put the Standard of Causation Under the Umbrella of the EU

Vlatka Butorac Malnar

**Abstract** In 2014, the CJEU rendered a very interesting judgment in the *Kone* case, for the first time addressing the issue of the admissibility of claims for damages caused by umbrella pricing. This paper focuses on the most intriguing issues surrounding umbrella claims, in particular the issue of causation.

## 1 Introduction

It is well established in the case law of the CJEU that any person who has suffered damage as a result of violation of EU competition rules is entitled to claim compensation for the loss suffered.[1] The EU's determination to make private enforcement of competition rules more effective has been demonstrated by the enactment of Directive 2014/104/EU of the European Parliament and of the Council of 26 November 2014 on certain rules governing actions for damages under national law for infringements of the competition law provisions of the Member States and of the European Union (hereinafter: the Antitrust Damages Directive)[2] that was due to be implemented into the national legislation of the Member States by the end of 2016. While awaiting the legal changes at the national level, the number of claims for such damages has already been gradually increasing, particularly in the Netherlands, the UK and Austria. Claims of both direct and indirect customers of the infringers are becoming progressively more successful in court proceedings. This trend goes to show that the legal climate of antitrust damage procedures in Europe is gaining momentum. The extent of this favourable inclination towards antitrust litigation was demonstrated by the CJEU judgment in *Kone* involving, for the first time, the issue of the admissibility of claims for the compensation of loss resulting from umbrella pricing.

---

[1] Case C-453/99 *Courage and Crehan* ECLI:EU:C:2001:465; Joined Cases C-C-295/04 to C-298/04 *Manfredi and Others* ECLI:EU:C:2006:461.

[2] [2014] OJ L 349.

V. Butorac Malnar (✉)
Faculty of Law, University of Rijeka, Rijeka, Croatia
e-mail: vlatka@pravri.hr

© Springer-Verlag Berlin Heidelberg 2017
V. Tomljenović et al. (eds.), *EU Competition and State Aid Rules*,
Europeanization and Globalization 3, https://doi.org/10.1007/978-3-662-47962-9_9

Umbrella pricing occurs when an undertaking not party to a cartel raises prices for its products more than it would have done without the cartel, benefiting 'from a larger price setting freedom due to the fact that its competitors form a cartel'.[3] Because such undertakings are 'under the umbrella of the cartel',[4] this effect of the cartel is called the 'umbrella effect'. From an economic perspective, umbrella effects arise when cartelists reduce output and increase prices. The decreased volume of cartelised products and their increased price lead to a change in demand for substitute products produced by competing undertakings not party to the cartel. This increase in demand, in turn, leads to higher prices of such products.[5] Consequently, rather than being caused by a cartel, damage in such a case is caused due to a cartel.

It is commonly understood in competition law that umbrella pricing is legitimate conduct because undertakings on the market have 'the right to adapt themselves intelligently to the existing and anticipated conduct of their competitors'.[6] Accordingly, by adopting such pricing policy, undertakings not party to a cartel do not violate EU competition rules and thus may not be held liable for compensation for the loss resulting therefrom. In such a case, compensation may only be required from cartel members because it is the cartel activity that enables third undertakings to impose higher prices. However, from a legal perspective, a very delicate question arises—whether cartel members should be held liable for independent pricing decisions made by third parties and, if so, under what conditions.

In *Kone*, the CJEU essentially concluded that national legislation, which categorically excludes any civil liability of cartel members for losses resulting from umbrella pricing, is incompatible with EU law. The judgment was remarkably brief and somewhat blurry as it failed to give precise criteria for establishing causation. Rather than providing definite answers, the judgment raised new questions in relation to the umbrella effect, and only time will tell how national courts will approach such cases in practice.

Building upon the findings of the CJEU in *Kone* and the respective opinion of Advocate General Kokott, this paper aims to discuss the most interesting legal and policy issues of umbrella claims and, in particular, the issue of causation. A growing area of research[7] identifies the concept of causation as a central factor in

---

[3]Franck (2015), p. 135.

[4]Ibid, citing Areeda et al. (2007), para 347, p. 198.

[5]For detailed economic analyses of 'umbrella effects', see Inderst et al. (2013), Blair and Maurer (1982). 'Umbrella effects tend to positively depend on the degree of substitutability between products (closer substitutes will trigger a larger response in demand) and the size of a cartel (a cartel with small coverage is likely to lead only to a moderate price increase and therefore less diversion'. Friederiszick and Rauber (2015), p. 8.

[6]Joined Cases 40 to 48, 50, 54 to 56, 111, 113 and 114-73 *Coöperatieve Vereniging 'Suiker Unie' UA and others v. Commission* ECLI:EU:C:1975:174.

[7]See, for example, Havu (2015), Dunne (2014), Inderst et al. (2013), Israel et al. (2014), Gamble (2014), Franck (2015), Schreiber and Savov (2014), Mataranga (2015), Pace (2015), Lianos (2015), Havu (2015), Hansberry et al. (2014).

the success of antitrust litigation. The author puts forward the proposition that in deciding, in *Kone*, the CJEU had the legitimacy to establish a clear standard of causation and, in the interest of legal certainty and efficiency of EU law, should have followed the opinion of AG Kokott.

This paper is further divided into five parts. After presenting the background of the *Kone* case and a summary of the CJEU findings, the author engages in comparative analyses of the standing of umbrella claimants and in ascertaining the intrinsic link to causation. She proceeds by exploring whether causation is a matter of EU rather than national law in order to substantiate her view supporting the construction of a unified EU standard of causation for the purposes of antitrust damage claims. The author then evaluates the standard of causation advanced by AG Kokott. Finally, she explains the implications of the judgment in *Kone* for Croatian rules on causality, discusses the remaining ambiguities and puts forward a possible approach to establishing causation under Croatian law.

## 2 The Judgment in *Kone*

### 2.1 Background

In 2007, the European Commission imposed fines totalling EUR 992 million on Kone, Otis, Schindler and ThyssenKrupp for their involvement in anticompetitive practices in breach of Article 101(1) TFEU,[8] which consisted of operating a bid-rigging cartel on the Belgian, German, Dutch and Luxembourg markets for the installation and maintenance of elevators and escalators. This agreement became known as the 'elevator cartel'.

On October 2008, the Oberster Gerichtshof, the Austrian appellate court in matters involving law on cartels, upheld the order of the Kartellgericht (Antitrust Court) by which the members of the 'elevator cartel' were fined for distorting the Austrian market, although Thyssenkrupp was excluded from being fined due to its successful application for leniency.[9] According to the findings of the court, from the 1980s to early 2004, the members of the cartel coordinated their activities in respect of over half of the commercial volume of machinery sold in Austria, divided markets and allocated customers, affecting the price development that would have otherwise occurred.

ÖBB-Infrastruktur, a subsidiary of Österreichische Bundesbahnen (Austrian Federal Railways), brought a follow-on action for damages to the overall amount of EUR eight million before the Austrian civil courts against Kone, Otis, Schindler and Thyssenkrupp. ÖBB argued that it incurred losses as a direct and indirect customer of the various cartel members. In addition, it claimed to have suffered a

---

[8]Treaty on the Functioning of the European Union (hereinafter: TFEU) [2008] OJ L 115.
[9]Oberster Gerichtshof, 17.10.2012, 7 Ob 48/12b, *Kone AG and others v. ÖBB- Infrasktur AG*.

substantial portion of the overall loss, EUR 1.8 million, as a customer of a third undertaking not party to the cartel that had charged higher prices for its products due to the cartel (umbrella pricing). Arguing that such pricing is attributable to the cartel, ÖBB claimed compensation for the resulting loss from the cartel members.

The Austrian first-instance court dismissed as unfounded the part of ÖBB's claim related to umbrella-induced losses, while Oberlandesgericht Wien, the Austrian appellate court, set aside the judgment. Ultimately, proceedings were brought before Oberster Gerichtshof, the Austrian Supreme Court, sitting as a court of appeal on points of law. The latter took the view that, according to Austrian law, the loss resulting from umbrella effects cannot be attributed to cartel members as an adequate causal link required by Article 1295 of the Allegemeines Bürgerliches Gesetzbuch (ABGB)[10] could not be established. Oberster Gerichtshof argued that, according to the established case law on Article 1295 ABGB, an adequate causal link is established when consequences of a particular conduct could have been 'foreseen *in abstracto* by the infringers, including accidental losses, but not atypical ones'.[11] The court considered the loss caused by umbrella pricing as too remote and largely determined by factors unrelated to the cartel.[12] In addition, the court found that the loss was not covered by the protective purpose of the competition law provisions—a specific requirement of Austrian law related to the establishment of the link of unlawfulness.[13] It found that the provision infringed by cartel members did not have as its object the protection of umbrella pricing victims and that consequently umbrella pricing misses the link of unlawfulness.[14] As described, the application of Austrian law practically excludes *a priori* any liability of cartel members for the losses resulting from umbrella effects. This outcome raised doubts in the Oberster Gerichtshof as to whether Austrian law was compatible with the principle of the effectiveness of EU law.

## 2.2 Findings of the CJEU

The CJEU held that Article 101 TFEU precludes the interpretation and application of domestic legislation such as the Austrian one, which categorically excludes the liability of cartel members for umbrella effects. The CJEU built its arguments on

---

[10]Article 1295 ABGB reads as follows: 'Any person shall be entitled to seek compensation for injury caused by another person who caused that injury through his fault, whether the injury was caused by breach of a contractual obligation or was unrelated to a contract'. Case C-557/12 *Kone AG and others v. ÖBB- Infrastruktur AG* ECLI:EU:C:2014:1317, para 3.

[11]*Kone* (n 1) para 14.

[12]Ibid, paras 12–14.

[13]The protective provision is contained in the second sentence of Art 1311 ABGB according to which 'the person responsible for injury caused is the person who has infringed a provision aimed at preventing accidental injuries'. Ibid, para 4.

[14]Ibid, para 15.

the basic principles of EU law developed by previous case law. Most notably, the CJEU recalled the judgments in *Courage*,[15] *Manfredi*,[16] *Otis*[17] and *Donau Chemie*[18] to reiterate the obligation of national courts to safeguard the rights of individuals derived from the direct effect of Articles 101 and 102 TFEU.[19] As on many previous occasions, it expressed the view that the full effectiveness of Article 101 TFEU would be put at risk if it were not open for any individual to claim damages for loss suffered, umbrella claimants included.[20] The CJEU recognised that compensation is conditional upon the finding of a causal relationship between that harm and a violation of Article 101 TFEU,[21] a problem directly pertinent to umbrella claims and regulated by national laws. According to the principle of state procedural autonomy in the absence of EU rules governing the matter, it is up to the national legislation to lay down detailed rules governing the right to claim compensation, including those related to the establishment of causation, provided that the principles of effectiveness and equivalence are observed.[22] However, according to the CJEU, an upfront dismissal of umbrella claims based on national legal standards runs against the principle of effectiveness of EU law.

In order to substantiate its view, the CJEU went on to consider, as a matter of principle, whether losses resulting from umbrella pricing may be attributable to the members of a cartel. It held that market price is one of the main factors taken into consideration by competing undertakings in establishing their own prices. In a situation of a cartel maintaining artificially high prices, competing undertakings not party to the cartel will also choose to set prices at a higher level than they would have done in the absence of a cartel.[23] It follows that 'a loss being suffered by the customer of an undertaking not party to a cartel, but benefiting from the economic conditions of umbrella pricing [. . .] is one of the possible effects of the cartel that the members thereof cannot disregard'.[24] By accepting such a view, the CJEU essentially found that the umbrella effect of a cartel may be foreseeable for its members and thus the loss resulting therefrom may be attributable to them. Rightly, this conclusion is limited to the particular circumstances of the case and the conditions on the relevant market. In the light of the foregoing, the CJEU found that claimants who suffer losses due to umbrella pricing, even in situations where they do not have contractual links with the cartelists, may *obtain* compensation from the members of a cartel under two conditions:

---

[15]*Courage and Crehan* (n 2) para 26.

[16]*Manfredi* (n 2) para 60.

[17]Case C-199/11 *Otis and Others* ECLI: EU:C:2012:684, para 41.

[18]Case C-536/11 *Donau Chemie and Others* ECLI: EU:C:2013:366, para 21.

[19]Case C-557/12 *Kone AG and others v. ÖBB- Infrastruktur AG* ECLI:EU:C:2014:1317, para 20.

[20]Ibid, para 21.

[21]Ibid, para 21.

[22]Ibid, para 24.

[23]Ibid, para 29.

[24]Ibid, para 30.

(a) if, under the specific circumstances of a case, it is established that the cartel is liable for the effect of umbrella pricing on the market; and
(b) if those circumstances could not be ignored by the cartelists.[25]


# 3   Standing of Umbrella Claimants

When it comes to the standing of umbrella claimants, the findings in *Kone* come as no surprise. After all, already in *Courage*[26] and all the cases that followed, the CJEU ruled that *any* person injured by antitrust practices is entitled to claim compensation for the loss suffered. Upholding umbrella claims is thus a natural development of the CJEU case law on antitrust damages.

The Antitrust Damages Directive has also addressed the issue of standing. Article 3 of the Directive essentially codifies the CJEU case law on antitrust standing by stipulating that Member States must ensure that '*any natural or legal person* who has suffered harm caused by an infringement of competition law is able to claim and obtain full compensation of that harm'. While this approach to standing is very broad so as to cover any person who has suffered damage caused by anticompetitive practices, it addresses in more detail only legal issues pertinent to direct and indirect customers of the infringers. In other words, it clarifies and facilitates the legal position of customers vertically linked to the infringers. Because umbrella claimants are not vertically linked to the infringers, as there is no direct or indirect contractual relationship with the infringers, rules on standing, passing on overcharges and evidentiary burden related to indirect customers will not apply. This legal lacuna, however, does not rule out the standing of umbrella claimants as the principled position that any person who suffered damage may claim and obtain compensation still applies. Furthermore, Article 11(4) of the Directive explicitly refers to 'other injured parties' besides direct and indirect purchasers, a term that may very well cover umbrella claimants. Viewed from this perspective, the judgment in *Kone* only reinforced the extensive rule on standing and made it clear that no person may be ruled out from the outset as a possible antitrust claimant.

While EU law is increasingly more favourable to upholding standing for all private claimants, on the other side of the Atlantic the situation is not as clear when it comes to umbrella plaintiffs. While noting that the US Supreme Court has not yet addressed the issue, it must also be remarked that, in most cases, the US courts have been reluctant to grant standing to umbrella claimants, 'finding their claims to be inadmissibly contingent, speculative, and complex'.[27]

---

[25]Ibid, para 34.

[26]*Courage and Crehan* (n 2) para 26.

[27]Mahr et al. (2014). See *Antoine Garabet, MD, Inc. v. Autonomous Techs. Corp.*, 116 F. Supp. 2d 1159 (C.D. Cal. 2000); *Mid-West Paper Products Co. v. Continental Group, Inc.*, 596 F.2d 573 (3d Cir. 1979); *In re Coordinated Pretrial Proceedings in Petroleum Products, Antitrust*

In order to understand better the position of American courts, it is necessary to briefly point to the rules on antitrust standing.[28] Antitrust standing is 'a doctrine that embodies the notion, [...] that a plaintiff may not bring suit unless the alleged injury she has suffered was proximately caused by the defendant's alleged anti-competitive conduct'.[29] The antitrust standing doctrine was developed by the US Supreme Court case law interpreting the very broad language of Section 4 of the Clayton Act,[30] according to which 'any person [...] injured in his business or property by reason of anything forbidden in the antitrust laws may sue [...] and recover threefold the damages by him sustained [...]'. While the wording of Section 4 of the Clayton Act resembles very much the wording of Article 3 of the Antitrust Damages Directive, in as much as it confers the right to sue to all injured parties, the 'lower federal courts have been virtually unanimous in concluding that Congress did not intend the antitrust laws to provide a remedy in damages for all injuries that might conceivably be traced to an antitrust violation'.[31]

The criteria for establishing antitrust standing were refined by the US Supreme Court in the case *Associated General Contractors*,[32] known as the AGC test. According to the AGC test, in order to establish antitrust standing, the following criteria must be cumulatively fulfilled:

> (1) the nature of the plaintiff's alleged injury; that is, whether it was the type the antitrust laws were intended to forestall; (2) the directness of the injury; (3) the

---

*Litigation*, 691 F.2d 1335 (9th Cir.1982); *Mylan*, 62 F.Supp.2d 39; *Gross v. New Balance Athletic Shoe, Inc.*, 955 F.Supp. 242, 246–247 (S.D.N.Y.1997). Some other District courts have allowed plaintiffs to proceed under an umbrella theory. See, for example, *In re Bristol Bay, Alaska, Salmon Fishery Antitrust Litigation*, 530 F.Supp. 36 (W.D.Wash.1981); *In re Beef Industry Antitrust Litigation*, 600 F.2d 1148, 1166 n. 24 (5th Cir.1979); *In re Arizona Dairy Products Litigation*, 627 F.Supp. 233, 235–236 (D.Ariz.1985).

[28]In order to maintain an antitrust action, antitrust plaintiffs in the USA have to establish antitrust standing. See *Associated General Contractors of California, Inc. v. California State Council of Carpenters*, 459 U.S. 519 (1983).

[29]Law 360 (2009).

[30]§ 4 of the Clayton Act. 15 U. S. C. § 15.

[31]*Hawaii v. Standard Oil Co.*, 405 U.S. 251, 263, n. 14 (1972). Based on this understanding of the legislative history of the Clayton Act, from as early as 1977, in the well-known case of *Illinois Brick*, the US Supreme Court ruled out the antitrust standing of indirect purchasers. *Illinois Brick v. Illinois*, 431 U.S. 720, 97 S.Ct. 2061, 52 L.Ed.2d 707 (1977). The Illinois Brick doctrine has since been criticised and proposals were put forward in favour of rejecting the doctrine and recognising antitrust standing for indirect purchasers. See Antitrust Modernization Commission (2007). The Antitrust Modernization Commission was created pursuant to the Antitrust Modernization Commission Act of 2002, Pub. L. No. 107-273, §§ 11051-60, 116 Stat. 1856. The Antitrust Modernization Commission terminated on 31 May 2007.

[32]*Associated General Contractors of California, Inc. v. California State Council of Carpenters*, 459 U.S. 519(1983).

speculative measure of the harm; (4) the risk of duplicative recovery; and (5) the complexity in apportioning damages.[33]

In the *Garabet* case[34] involving umbrella effect, the District Court, C.D. California, found none of the criteria to be fulfilled, pointing particularly to the fact that umbrella injury is not the type of injury protected by antitrust laws and to the complexity and the remoteness of the claim. As to the latter, the District Court, C.D. California, argued that 'umbrella liability necessarily involves unacceptable processes of speculation and complexity in the award or calculation of damages'. Further, the Court cited the US Court of Appeals, Third Circuit, decision in *Mid-West Paper Products*:[35]

> The outcome of any attempt to ascertain what price the defendants' competitors would have charged had there not been a conspiracy would at the very least be highly conjectural. As noted in *Hanover Shoe*, '[a] wide range of factors influence a company's pricing policies. Normally the impact of a single change in the relevant conditions cannot be measured after the fact; indeed a businessman may be unable to state whether, had one fact been different ..., he would have chosen a different price'.[36]

If one compares the legal reasoning of the Austrian Court in *Kone* and the US District Court in the *Garabet* case, the similarity of arguments is inescapable. Under Austrian law, the loss caused by the umbrella effect is not covered by the protective purpose of competition rules, and an adequate causal link is missing due to the independent pricing decisions of non-members of the cartel, whereby the causality chain is broken. As a result, under Austrian law, just as under the US Clayton Act, umbrella claimants do not enjoy standing to sue.

The CJEU opted for a different approach. As long as there is antitrust injury, no matter how remote, there is a possibility to sue the infringers. However, such a standpoint does little for distant claimants such as umbrella claimants. In order to actually *obtain* compensation, umbrella claimants must be able to demonstrate, *inter alia*, the existence of a causal link between the anticompetitive practice and their loss. It thus appears that the issue of the standing of umbrella claimants is intrinsically linked to the issue of causation. Although the CJEU tried to connect the two issues in *Kone*, it did so ineffectively. In fact, the CJEU was addressed with the

---

[33]*Am. Ad Mgmt., Inc. v. Gen. Tel. Co.*, 190 F.3d 1051, 1054–1055 (9th Cir. 1999) (citing AGC, 459 U.S. p 535).

[34]*Antoine Garabet, M.D., Inc. v. Autonomous Techs. Corp.*, 116 F. Supp. 2d 1159, (C.D. Cal. 2000).

[35]*Mid-West Paper Products Co. v. Continental Croup*, 596 F.2d 573, 585–586 (3d Cir. 1979).

[36]Ibid, p. 1168.

issue of standing,[37] and yet its ruling refers to the requirements for obtaining compensation. The two may not be used interchangeably as the admission of a claim does not necessarily lead to a successful outcome, which in cases involving claims for damages is the compensation of the loss suffered. However, given the consistency in translation into other official languages of the EU,[38] the choice of words does not seem to be accidental, but instead it 'would appear to emphasise that it is the right of reparation rather than the mere availability of a cause of action that is guaranteed by the EU law'.[39] This view taken by the CJEU is more a question related to private enforcement as admitting claims that are never likely to succeed would render such claims obsolete. Yet by failing to regulate the most critical issue in obtaining compensation—the EU standard of causation[40]—the deliberation of the CJEU is of theoretical rather than practical value.

The facts in *Kone* presented a very good opportunity for the CJEU to express its views on causation and establish a coherent and precise EU standard of causation. Instead of taking this opportunity, the CJEU merely introduced the element of foreseeability in defining causation, leaving open the issue of directness of the causal nexus. According to the CJEU in *Kone*, so long as an umbrella effect may be attributable to the cartel, and foreseeable to cartelists, they *may* be held liable for the resulting loss. While this, essentially economic, issue is very important for deciding on foreseeability, it does not help to overcome the problem of the directness of the umbrella claims. Consequently, with such a vague ruling, the CJEU left national courts and potential umbrella claimants wondering what standards of causation should be applied to the facts of the case.

## 4 Causation: A Matter of EU or National Law?

While the CJEU invites Member States to regulate causation on the ground of the principle of state procedural autonomy, it nevertheless gives indefinite guidance on its substance. Therefore, a legitimate and important question arises as to whether

---

[37]The exact question read: 'Is Article 101 TFEU (Article 81 EC, Article 85 of the EC Treaty) to be interpreted as meaning that any person *may claim* [emphasis added] from members of a cartel damages also for the loss which he has been caused by a person not party to the cartel who, benefiting from the protection of the increased market prices, raises his own prices for his products more than he would have done without the cartel (umbrella pricing), so that the principle of effectiveness laid down by the Court requires *the grant of a claim* [emphasis added] under national law?' Ibid, para 17.

[38]When compared linguistically, the judgment wording is consistent: 'dobiti naknadu' in Croatian, 'ottenere il risarcimento' in Italian, 'obtenir la reparation' in French.

[39]Dunne (2014), p. 1822. On the same point, see Havu (2015), p. 138.

[40]Lianos points to economic research to substantiate its claim that 'an approach focusing on compensation and corrective justice requires that causation be proven and this will inevitably become a central issue in action for damages for competition law infringements, eventually regulating the extent of competition damages litigation in Europe'. Lianos (2015), p. 172, with accompanying footnote 7.

causality is a matter of EU or national law. This is important from the positions of both the umbrella claimants and the national courts, which need to know what law to apply to this issue, i.e. how to draw the line between national and EU laws on the matter.

In its early case law, the CJEU made the finding of the non-contractual liability of the infringers for the losses caused by their anticompetitive conduct conditional upon establishing causation.[41] The CJEU never reasoned this issue. It appears that it only recognised the requirement of causality as an essential legal prerequisite for obtaining compensation derived from non-contractual liability common to all legal systems of the EU Member States. While the requirement itself thus became a matter of EU law, the standard for establishing causation remained fully a matter of national laws as an exercise of the principle of state procedural autonomy, conditional upon the principles of equivalence and efficiency of EU law. In *Manfredi*, the CJEU stated:

> In the absence of Community rules governing the matter, it is for the domestic legal system of each Member State to designate the courts and tribunals having jurisdiction and to lay down the detailed procedural rules governing actions for safeguarding rights which individuals derive directly from Community law [. . .].[42]

The CJEU continued that the rules governing the exercise of those rights include '[. . .] those on the application of the concept of causal relationship, provided that the principles of equivalence and effectiveness are observed'.[43] Up until the judgment in *Kone*, neither of the two principles was used by the CJEU in the context of competition law to limit the Member States' procedural autonomy in regulating the content of causality. This initial straightforward divide between EU and national law made it clear that national standards of proving causation are to be applied to the facts of the case. Given the importance of causality and the diversity of national standards for establishing causation, this might not have been the best solution. This is particularly so because the prospect for obtaining damages might be quite different across Member States, with the potential of leading to forum shopping, the facts in *Kone* being a good example thereof.[44]

It is beyond the scope of this paper to analyse the complex intricacies of the CJEU developed standard of procedural autonomy in general terms. Many have voiced their opinion on this issue,[45] and what may be observed as common ground

---

[41]*Courage and Crehan* (n 2) para 26; *Manfredi* (n 2) para 60; *Otis and Others* (n 18) para 41.

[42]*Manfredi* (n 2) para 62.

[43]Ibid, paragraph 64.

[44]On this point, see the opinion of Advocate General in Case C-557/12 *Kone AG and others v ÖBB- Infrastruktur AG* ECLI:EU:C:2014:45, para 29.

[45]On this point see Bobek (2011), Bobek (2010), Tridimas (2006), Havu (2016), Arnull (2011). Van Cleynenbreugel (2012), Prechal and Widdershoven (2011). According to some, the vigour of

is that the argumentation used by the CJEU raises serious concerns of ambiguity and inconsistency. Unfortunately, the same may be said in the aftermath of the judgment in *Kone* as it only blurred the dividing lines between EU and national laws on causation. Given its modest contribution in unifying the standard of causation, the question remains: what is the core content of procedural state autonomy in regulating this issue?

Historically, the CJEU has demonstrated its tendency to extend the limits of its intervention in matters previously recognised as being under the legislative jurisdiction of the Member States, relying on the principles of equivalence and efficiency of EU law.[46] After all, it is the task of the CJEU to interpret EU law and make sure that rights derived therefrom are being observed at the national level. The harmonising trend is particularly observable in areas where the Member States have failed to agree on the EU standards unifying national substantive rules by means of EU legislation. Causation is certainly one such example. From as early as 2008, in the preparatory studies of the Antitrust Damages Directive, the Commission stressed the principles of equivalence and, in particular, of efficiency, expressing the opinion that they 'can influence the notions of causation as existing in national civil law'.[47] Yet, in *Kone*, the CJEU employed the principle of full effectiveness of Article 101 TFEU, along with the principles of equivalence and efficiency for the most part, only to form a 'negative harmonization framework by identifying the limits of legality of the national legislation related to antitrust law private enforcement'.[48] In other words, any interpretation of a national law that undermines the full effectiveness of Article 101 TFEU 'would lead to its illegality and consequently its non-applicability'.[49] At the same time, by including the element of foreseeability into the standard of causation, the CJEU went beyond the mere defining of the negative harmonisation framework. The result was a very modest twist in favour of unification of the national standards of causation. Viewed from this perspective, the ruling in *Kone* is, or rather could have been, very important and should be observed as a matter of principle. What is puzzling

---

the CJEU in applying the principle of effectiveness completely eliminated the principle of procedural autonomy of the Member States and, as a consequence, the latter should be reconsidered. See Bobek (2011).

[46]See, for example, Case C-128/93 *Fisscher* ECLI:EU:C:1994:353; Case C-394/93 *Alonso-Pérez* ECLI:EU:C:1995:400; Joined Cases C-46/93 and C-48/93 *Brasserie du Pêcheur SA* ECLI:EU:C:1996:79; Case C-246/96 *Magorrian and Cunningham* ECLI:EU:C:1997:605; Case C-78/98 *Preston* ECLI:EU:C:2000:247; Joined Cases C-52/99 and C-53/99 *Camarotto and others* ECLI:EU:C:2001:112; Case C-432/05 *Unibet (London) Ltd and Unibet (International) Ltd* ECLI:EU:C:2007; Case C-40/08 *Asturcom Telecomunicaciones SL* ECLI:EU:C:2009:615.

[47]Commission staff working paper accompanying the White Paper on damages actions for breach of the EC antitrust rules {COM(2008) 165 final} {SEC (2008) 405} {SEC (2008) 406} /SEC/2008/0404 final, p. 77.

[48]Pace (2015), pp. 136–137.

[49]Ibid, p. 138.

about the CJEU judgment in *Kone* is why, despite having decided to touch upon the issue of causality, it failed to go the distance in clarifying its precise content.

The recently adopted Antitrust Damages Directive is of no relevance in this regard either as it says very little on causation. It is only in the context of quantification of harm that the Directive mentions the rebuttable presumption that cartel infringements cause harm.[50] However, the Directive is silent on the standard of causation to be used in finding liability. This silence goes back to the Green Paper[51] and White Paper[52] on damages caused by antitrust infringements, deliberately avoiding regulating the standard of causation.[53] This is evidenced by the fact that preparatory studies identified causation as one of the main hurdles for claimants in obtaining compensation for loss suffered.[54] Irrespective of these findings, from the outset of the legislative procedure, causation has been ignored by the EU legislator.[55] Most probably, such distancing from defining causation relates to a much broader problem of unifying tort law in general. There is no doubt that tort law plays an important part in maintaining the full effectiveness of EU rules of law. The rights guaranteed by EU law are to be afforded protection before national courts also in terms of making efficient remedies available to injured parties. Yet, regardless of its recognised importance,[56] no EU legislative act attempts to regulate this matter comprehensively.

The CJEU would have done better had it followed the opinion of Advocate General (AG) Kokott in *Kone* and raised the issue of the standard of causation at the EU level. AG Kokott presented very detailed argumentation supporting the proposition that causation should be a matter of EU rather than national law. AG Kokott advanced the following opinion on the issue:

---

[50]Art 17(2) of the Antitrust Damages Directive.

[51]Green Paper – Damages actions for breach of the EC antitrust rules {SEC(2005) 1732} COM/2005/0672 final.

[52]White Paper on damages actions for breach of the EC antitrust rules {SEC(2008) 404} {SEC (2008) 405} {SEC(2008) 406} /COM/2008/0165 final.

[53]Green Paper – Damages actions for breach of the EC antitrust rules {SEC(2005) 1732} COM/2005/0672 final.

[54]See Ashurst (2004). On the same point, see Commission staff working paper accompanying the White Paper on damages actions for breach of the EC antitrust rules {COM(2008) 165 final} {SEC (2008) 405} {SEC (2008) 406} /SEC/2008/0404 final, p. 77. The latter stressed the complexity of proving causation, and expressed the view that it is arguable that the differences in the application of differing legal notions of causation will not lead to widely diverging results.

[55]The Practical Guide on quantifying harm mentions explicitly that standards of causation are essentially a matter of national law. Practical Guide quantifying harm in actions for damages based on breaches of Article 101 or 102 of the treaty on the functioning of the European union {C(2013) 3440}. See also Art 4 of the Antitrust Damages Directive.

[56]The importance of tort law is evidenced by the effort made by the European Group on Tort Law that aims to contribute to the enhancement and harmonisation of tort law in Europe through the framework provided by its Principles of European Tort Law (PETL). The results of this ongoing research however, have not yet resulted in any EU legislative act. For more on PETL, see the official website http://civil.udg.edu/php//index.php?id=128. Accessed 8 Apr 2016.

A closer examination of the judgment in *Manfredi* and also of a number of other more recent judgments of the Court of Justice shows, [...] that, as things currently stand, it is not so much the existence of claims to compensation (i.e. the question of whether compensation is to be granted) that is dictated by national law as, rather, the details of application of such claims and the rules for their actual enforcement (i.e. the question of how compensation is to be granted), that is to say, in particular, jurisdiction, procedure, time-limits and the furnishing of proof.[57]

Furthermore, AG Kokott noted that the right to claim compensation is directly derived from Article 101 TFEU and thus it may not be dependent on the requirements of national laws.[58] In addition, she reiterated that it is clear from the *Manfredi* case that the persons entitled to claim compensation and the types of losses covered are both predetermined by EU law.[59] Referring to umbrella claims, AG Kokott continued:

The focus of interest of such an assessment will, rather, be the much more fundamental question of whether cartel members can be held civilly liable at all for this kind of loss and whether they can be sued by persons who are not their direct or indirect customers (that is to say, the 'whether' of compensation). That question cannot be left to the legal orders of the Member States alone.[60]

Undeniably, in the opinion of AG Kokott, the Member States are not autonomous in establishing the criteria of liability in antitrust damage cases as this is fully a matter of EU law. National laws are autonomous only in establishing procedural details of application and enforcement of EU rules.

This standpoint of AG Kokott has been criticised by some, in this way also upholding the CJEU's reluctance to define the content of causation.[61] Most of the arguments revolved around the fear that EU-introduced standards of liability would 'clash with the core working of national systems' tort law'.[62] This argument, however, is not necessarily true. Competition-law-related actions for damages have been singled out from the general tort rules by the very enactment of the Antitrust Damages Directive. We are witnessing the introduction of quite novel concepts and procedures for the purpose of facilitating antitrust private actions for damages—rules previously unknown to national legal systems (such as the pass-on requirement) or potentially different from general tort rules (such as rules on limitation periods, the definition of damage or the calculation of damage). This

---

[57]Ibid, para 23.

[58]Ibid, para 24.

[59]Ibid, para 27.

[60]Ibid, para 28.

[61]Mataranga (2015), Franck (2015).

[62]Mataranga (2015), p. 364.

*lex specialis* could very well apply to other tort law concepts, such as causation, without necessarily distorting the general notions and application of tort law. After all, specific EU tort law requirements already exist in the ambit of state liability for violation of EU law, and their application before national courts does not seem to distort the working of national systems' tort laws in general.

Some have directed even stronger criticism at the CJEU when arguing that its basic finding on the preclusion of national legislation, such as the Austrian one, was in itself a far-fetched decision. According to Franck,[63] the question of harmonisation of national laws should be left to the legislative institutions rather than the CJEU as the former have the legal authority,[64] democratic legitimacy and political responsibility in this regard.[65] Furthermore, Franck continues that the preservation of the division of powers in the EU and institutional balance demand that CJEU refrains from overstretching the principle of effectiveness of the EU law as a mechanism for harmonising liability requirements. This is so because CJEU findings, having the power of primary EU law, bind the EU legislature, thereby limiting its competence.[66] As much as Franck's arguments might be persuasive and legalistically correct, they appear to be overly formalistic and missing the point of private antitrust enforcement in general.

Private antitrust litigation is meant to serve a double purpose. On one hand, it is meant to complement public enforcement in as much as litigants themselves become enforcers of EU competition rules.[67] On the other, it is meant to safeguard the rights of individuals who have suffered harm as a result of the violation of competition rules. The two roles of the private enforcement of competition rules are equally important, and both require the introduction of an efficient and uniform private enforcement mechanism across Member States. In *VEBIC*[68] and *Donau Chemie*,[69] the CJEU already suggested that 'national solutions in the sphere of procedural autonomy must in competition cases be evaluated from the point of view of the practical effects or goals of competition law'.[70] If we were to advance the restrictive judicial review of the CJEU in applying the principles of the full effectiveness and efficiency of EU law, the achievement of EU antitrust policy objectives would be jeopardised.

---

[63]Franck (2015).

[64]Pursuant to Art 103 TFEU. See Franck (2015), p. 166.

[65]Ibid, p. 156.

[66]Ibid, pp. 158–159.

[67]Public and private enforcement are considered the 'two pillars of enforcement of EC antitrust rules'. Staff working paper, para 3.

[68]Case C-439/08 *VEBIC* ECLI:EU:C:2010:739.

[69]Case C-536/11 *Bundeswettbewerbsbehörde v. Donau Chemie AG and Others* ECLI:EU:C:2013:366.

[70]Havu (2015), p. 141.

In other areas of law,[71] the principles of efficiency and effectiveness have been used extensively by the CJEU to form positive harmonisation frameworks, bringing about the interpretative unification of EU rules necessary for the achievement of a particular EU policy goal. It thus remains unclear why the CJEU refrained from doing the same in *Kone*, particularly having been invited to do so and supported by AG Kokott's arguments. The final word in safeguarding the achievement of EU policy objectives rests with the CJEU. The Antitrust Damages Directive itself expressly states that 'all national rules governing the exercise of the right to compensation [...] including those concerning aspects not dealt with in the directive such as the notion of causal relationship [...] must observe the principles of effectiveness and equivalence'. The CJEU is the only EU institution entrusted with the role of safeguarding those principles. Finally, if one accepts the finding that action for damages is a right directly derived from Article 101 TFEU, then there is no impediment for the CJEU to interpret the wording and the intent of Article 101 TFEU with a view to harmonising the content of such a right in detail. From the viewpoint of the full effectiveness of EU competition rules, the parties to the proceedings and national judges, it would be much more efficient and predictable to have the standard of causation in antitrust litigation defined at the EU level.

The need for guidance in establishing causation is demonstrated by the facts and complexities of the *Kone* case itself. By ruling out the outcome of the application of Austrian *adequation* theory, the CJEU essentially demands Austrian courts to give a different meaning to a nationally recognised standard of causation in order to give full effect to the EU right to claim and obtain compensation for the loss suffered by the infringement of EU competition rules. If, following the judgment in *Kone*, the Austrian theory of causation must lead to an opposite result (supporting the standing of umbrella claimants), this theory needs to be essentially reinterpreted by the Austrian national courts, at least for the purposes of establishing the standing of umbrella claimants, and yet Austrian judges are left without any guidance on how to do so. Simply put, if this were a game of tennis between the litigants in *Kone*, the CJEU's judgment has left intact the court boundaries but decided that a ball out of play is to be considered a ball in play, leaving the umpire—the Austrian court—with no guidance as to how to make such a decision. In this situation, the one changing the outcome should offer a new criterion for decision-making. If the existent rule, such as the well-established Austrian legal standard on adequate causal link, has to bend to achieve previously unacceptable results, an EU standard replacing the national one would be in place. In addition, a question also arises as to whether Austrian courts may approach differently the issue of causation when establishing standing and when establishing liability. Having in mind the hurdle placed before Austrian courts, as well as all other national courts in establishing

---

[71]For example, in the area of state liability for breach of EU law, consumer protection, public procurement, environmental protection.

causation, it would have been more efficient if the CJEU had offered guidance on ways to achieve the goals presented before them.

# 5 Standard of Causation Proposed by AG Kokott

Once AG Kokott had presented arguments for legitimising the intervention of EU law into the question of causality, she went on to establish a standard of causation to be applicable by all Member States. AG Kokott proposes the introduction of a *'sufficiently direct causal nexus* between the harmful conduct and the damage alleged'. This standard already exists in EU law in the context of non-contractual liability of the EU pursuant to Article 340 TFEU. AG Kokott argues that, for the sake of consistency, the same standard should apply to all civil liability cases.[72] Furthermore, she points out that the term 'sufficiently direct causal link' should be understood not as a single causal link but rather as a 'contributory cause'.[73] This qualification is very important since the perceived non-culpability of cartel members for umbrella pricing rests on the assumption that the causal chain is broken due to the independent pricing decision made by cartel non-members. The latter view implies that the causal link may be established only if a particular infringement is the only cause of the damage suffered. According to AG Kokott, however, in cases involving umbrella damages, the causal chain is traceable back to the cartel if a person not party to a cartel in determining his prices 'is (also) guided by the relevant trading conditions and accordingly – and in an entirely foreseeable manner – follows the price initiative taken by a cartel'.[74] To support her view, AG Kokott uses, for the purpose of comparison, indirect damages caused within the vertical chain. Rightly, she stresses that passing on overcharges down the vertical chain is also influenced by an independent third party pricing decision. It is up to any injured party to decide whether to increase their prices on a downstream market as a result of a cartel-created price increase in the upstream market. Yet the Antitrust Damages Directive expressly acknowledges that this kind of passing on is traceable back to cartel members and thus they may be held liable for the losses thereby incurred.[75] The same kind of reasoning should apply to umbrella-induced losses.

As to the requirement of foreseeability, AG Kokott advances the view that events that are foreseeable are those that 'the cartel members ought reasonably to take into consideration on the basis of practical experience [. . .] unlike loss which results from an entirely extraordinary train of events and, therefore, ensues via an atypical causal chain'.[76] Relying on economic arguments, AG Kokott concludes

---

[72]AG opinion, para 34.

[73]Ibid, para 36.

[74]Ibid, para 37.

[75]Ibid, para 38.

[76]Ibid, para 42.

that umbrella effects may be foreseeable to cartel members under the particular circumstances of the case.

In general, the opinion of AG Kokott is very well argued, and it offers a balanced approach to a unified standard of causation. Although AG Kokott's advance of a unified criterion of causation for all claims to compensation for infringement of EU law is perhaps far-fetched, this standard of causation is certainly acceptable for antitrust damages. This way, general tort rules would remain intact in the majority of situations, while national judges would receive guidance in the particular field, where establishing causation under national standards may prove to be too difficult or even impossible.[77] Therefore, her solution could have been of high practical value for national judges who would thus retain the appreciable margin of discretion in evaluating actual cases. The proposed standard of causation would not automatically lead to liability of cartel members for umbrella effects but would instead shift the 'umbrella pricing decision from the level of pure theory to that of production of evidence'.[78] This observation is very much to do with creating an efficient private enforcement regime across the EU, and AG Kokott's criterion of causation should have been upheld by the CJEU in its judgment in *Kone*.

# 6  Implications of the *Kone* Judgment for Croatian Rules on Causality

Considering that at the time of writing this paper, the Antitrust Damages Directive was not yet implemented into Croatian legislation, the analysis takes into consideration general tort rules. According to Croatian general tort rules, every person is obliged to refrain from taking any action that may cause damage to others.[79] In addition, any person who causes damage to another is obliged to make compensation.[80] Standing to sue is given to any person who has suffered legally recognisable harm, the latter being defined as a loss of a person's assets (actual loss), the halting of an increase in assets (loss of profit) and violation of privacy rights (non-material damage).[81]

In order to obtain compensation, similarly to other legal systems of the EU, the plaintiff has to prove causation,[82] one of the legal requirements for the finding of non-contractual liability for damage. Under general Croatian tort law, there is no presumption of causality, and the burden of proof rests with the claimant. However, unlike in Austrian law, the issue of causality in Croatian law is not linked to the

---

[77]See Bukovac Puvača et al. (2015), p. 85.

[78]Ibid, para 82.

[79]Art 8 of the Obligations Act Official journal, Narodne novine, 35/2005, 41/2008, 125/2011, 78/2015 (hereinafter: OA).

[80]Arts 1045 et seq. OA.

[81]Art 1046 OA.

[82]Croatian legal theory defines causality as a link between the harmful act (as a cause) and the damage (as a result). Gorenc et al. (2014), p. 1704.

issue of standing, or rather the admissibility of a claim, because in condemnatory claims, such as claims for damages, the legal interest of a claimant is presumed.[83] Therefore, Croatian national legislation would not lead to results precluded by EU law on the same grounds as in *Kone*. While umbrella claims would be admissible before national courts, establishing causation *ad meritum* would be a rather difficult task for the claimants.

In Croatian law, the generally accepted causation theory is the *adequation* theory, which resembles the Austrian legal standard on adequate causal link. Under this theory, what is relevant is the 'typical' cause of damage, that is, the one that *regularly causes* the given harmful consequences.[84] If applied narrowly, this approach to defining causality may cause problems to umbrella claimants. Although economic evidence may point to the creation of umbrella effects on the market in a particular case, a national judge may decide not to consider the damages resulting therefrom as a type of damage regularly caused by a cartel. If such an understanding of a 'typical' cause of damage were accepted, umbrella-induced losses would be considered an atypical cause of damage not fulfilling the causation criteria. In addition, under Croatian law, the causal link has to be unbroken as the tortfeasor will not be liable for the damage that occurred after the link is broken by either an event or human act.[85] Accordingly, the closer the harmful act and the damage are, the easier it is for the claimant to establish causation. Direct purchasers of the infringer are thus in a much more favourable position than indirect purchasers, and even more so in comparison with umbrella claimants. In the latter case, national judges are likely to consider the causation chain broken due to independent pricing decisions made by cartel non-members.

On the positive side, in Croatia, national judges have very wide discretion in deciding when the requirement of causation has been satisfied as there are no specific legal *rules* regulating this issue. Because causation is decided on a case-by-case basis, the same kind of event may be considered to have caused particular damage in one case and not to have caused damage in another.[86] For that reason, national judges may decide to apply the *adequation* theory more extensively in order to capture umbrella claimants in cases where a cartel indeed caused umbrella effects on the market. However, due to the specific nature of antitrust losses, it would be very beneficial if national judges had some guidance in that regard. Undeniably, the issue of causation in competition-related claims has to be approached in a particularly vigilant manner, taking account of the fact that losses incurred on the market will always have more than one cause. The criterion proposed by AG Kokott might have been very helpful in this situation. However, not having been accepted by the CJEU, the national courts will have to resort to

---

[83]See Gž-2082/32 of 24/03/1992 Okružni sud Zagreb. See also Triva et al. (1986), p. 248; Opatić (2002), pp. 7–8.

[84]See Vs, Rev-2552/82 of 5/05/1983, PSP 23/101.

[85]Ibid, p. 84; Gorenc et al. (2014), p. 1705.

[86]See more Bukovac Puvača et al. (2015), p. 81.

some other means of achieving the EU policy goals in antitrust private enforcement. In an earlier paper co-authored with Bukovac Puvača,[87] we forwarded a possible solution in interpreting the *adequation* theory, very much applicable to umbrella claims as well. The starting point should be the understanding that, in competition cases, causal link should connect three elements: (1) the harmful act, (2) distortion of the market and (3) harm to the given victim. With that in mind, in each particular case, the courts should insist on finding a direct causal link between the harmful act and the market distortion, as well as a link between the market distortion and the damage suffered by a specific victim. By doing so, the courts would bridge the requirement of a direct causal link between the infringement and the loss suffered. In the next step, national judges should establish whether the induced damage was foreseeable to the infringers. The answer to that question should again depend on the particular circumstances of the case. The legal evaluation of those circumstances should depend on the economic findings. With such an approach, causation would be more easily traceable back to cartel infringers, rendering the establishment of the EU right to full compensation more effective.

# 7  Conclusion

*Kone* is undeniably a very important case in as much as it has raised issues previously not contemplated by the CJEU or the EU legislators. The facts of the case highlighted the importance of defining the standard of causation for the purposes of antitrust litigation. Research also recognises its central role, and yet the considerations of procedural autonomy of the Member States seem to have outweighed the concerns of full effectiveness of the EU right to obtain antitrust damages. Drawing upon these two standpoints, in the present analyses we have attempted to identify arguments in favour of the unification of the standard of causation for the purposes of antitrust litigation, believing this to be an imperative tool in achieving the pursued EU policy goal of an efficient system of private enforcement of EU competition rules. It has been argued that the issue of causation is a matter of EU law, and thus there is no obstacle in defining its content at the EU level. Being well balanced and practical, the proposal made by AG Kokott should have been followed by the CJEU. Since the CJEU failed to take this opportunity to unify the standard of causation, the respective national rules remain of primary relevance. Hence, the paper has analysed the implications of the *Kone* judgment for the Croatian rules on causality and identified difficulties that are likely to be encountered by claimants and judges alike. A broad interpretation of the Croatian *adequation* theory of causation is needed if any of the claimants and, in particular, indirect and umbrella claimants are to be successful in claiming umbrella damages. In order to bridge the gap between the infringement and the loss, national judges

---

[87]Bukovac Puvača and Butorac Malnar (2008), p. 264.

could approach causation by first linking the infringement to the distortion of the market and then linking the damage to the market distortion. The described approach would facilitate establishing a direct link between the injury and the loss suffered. The assessment of foreseeability should rest fully on economic evidence pertinent to the particular circumstances of the case.

**Acknowledgement** This paper was supported by the Croatian Science Foundation project no 9366 'Legal Aspects of Corporate Acquisitions and Knowledge Driven Companies' Restructuring'.

# References

Antitrust Modernization Commission (2007) Report and recommendations. http://govinfo.library. unt.edu/amc/report_recommendation/amc_final_report.pdf. Accessed 23 May 2016

Areeda PE, Hovenkamp RD et al (2007) Antitrust law, vol II, 3rd edn. Woulters Kluwer, New York

Arnull A (2011) The principle of effective judicial protection in EU law: an unruly horse? Eur Law Rev 36(1):51–70

Ashurst (2004) Study on the conditions of claims for damages in case of infringement of EC competition rules, Analysis of economic models for the calculation of damages. http://ec. europa.eu/competition/antitrust/actionsdamages/comparative_report_clean_en.pdf. Accessed 8 Apr 2016

Blair RD, Maurer VG (1982) Umbrella pricing and antitrust standing: an economic analysis. Utah Law Rev 763:779–785

Bobek M (2010) The new European judges and the limits of the possible. In: Łazowski A (ed) Source the application of EU law in the new member states: 'Brave New World'. TMC Asser Press, The Hague, pp 127–153.

Bobek M (2011) Why there is no principle of 'procedural autonomy' of the member states. In: de Witte B, Micklitz H (eds) The European Court of Justice and the autonomy of the member states. Intersentia, Antwerp, pp 305–324

Bukovac Puvača M, Butorac Malnar V (2008) Izvanugovorna odgovornost za štetu prouzročenu povredom pravila tržišnog natjecanja. Hrvatska pravna revija 8(12):32–54

Bukovac Puvača M et al (2015) Obvezno pravo - posebni dio II - izvanugovorni obvezni odnosi. Novi Informator, Zagreb

Dunne N (2014) It never rains but it pours? Liability for 'umbrella effects' under EU competition law in *Kone*. Common Mark Law Rev 51:1813–1828

Franck J-U (2015) Umbrella pricing and cartel damages under EU competition law. Eur Competition J 11(1):135–167

Friederiszick HW, Rauber M (2015) A fleet without a captain? Taking stock of European antitrust litigation post EU Directive. CPI Antitrust Chronicle, January 2015(1)

Gamble R (2014) The European embrace of private enforcement: this time with feeling. Eur Competition Law Rev 35(10):469–479

Gorenc V et al (2014) Komentar Zakona o obveznim odnosima. Narodne novine, Zagreb

Hansberry D et al (2014) Umbrella effect: damages claimed by customers of non-cartelist competitors. J Eur Competition Law Pract 5(4):196–205

Havu K (2016) EU law in member states' courts: adequate judicial protection and effective application: ambiguities and nonsequiturs in guidance by the Court of Justice. Contemp Read Law Soc Just 8(1):158–187

Havu K (2015) Competition restrictions, 'umbrellas' and damages claims – comment on *Kone*. Glob Competition Litig Rev 8(3):134–142

Inderst R, Maier-Rigaud F, Schwalbe U (2013) Umbrella effects. Working paper series, 2013-ECO-17, IESEG School of Management. http://www.ieseg.fr/wp-content/uploads/2013-ECO-17_Maier-Rigaud.pdf. Accessed 26 May 2016

Israel M et al (2014) A lift for claimants. AG Kokott hands down her opinion on umbrella pricing. Competition Law Insight 13:12–13

Law 360 (2009) Indirect purchaser standing in federal court: take 2. https://www.omm.com/files/upload/indirectpurchaserstanding.pdf. Accessed 26 May 2016

Lianos I (2015) Causal uncertainty and damages claims for the infringement of competition law in Europe. Yearb Eur Law 34(1):170–231

Mahr E et al (2014) Letter of the editors. Int Civil Redress Bull 2:1

Mataranga C (2015) Kone AG v OBB-Infrasktur AG. Eur Competition Law Rev 36(8):362–365

Opatić N (2002) Pravni interes u građanskom parničnom postupku. http://www.pravnadatoteka.hr/pdf/Pravni%20interes%20u%20gradjanskom%20parnicnom%20postupku.pdf. Accessed 28 Apr 2016.

Pace LP (2015) The ECJ's judgement in *Kone* and private enforcement's 'negative harmonization framework': another brick in the wall. Rivista Italiana di Antitrust 1:133–143

Prechal S, Widdershoven R (2011) Redefining the relationship between 'Rewe-effectiveness' and effective judicial protection. Rev Eur Adm Law 4(2):31–50

Schreiber T, Savov V (2014) Kone v Commission: umbrella damages claims. J Eur Law Pract 5(8):548–550

Tridimas T (2006) General principles of EU law, 2nd edn. OUP, Oxford

Triva S et al (1986) Građansko parnično procesno pravo. Narodne novine, Zagreb

Van Cleynenbreugel P (2012) The confusing constitutional status of positive procedural obligations in EU law: observations on effective judicial protection and national procedural autonomy in the wake of *Boxus*. Rev Eur Adm Law 5(1):81–100

# Cross-Border Aspects of EU Competition Law Enforcement: Comprehensive Reform Needed?

**Mihail Danov**

**Abstract** Private international law has an important role to play in cross-border EU competition law actions because businesses and consumers in several countries may suffer harm caused by infringements of Articles 101 and 102 TFEU. On 21 May 2015, the CJEU rendered its judgment in the first case in which the judges were asked to opine on the way the Brussels I regime applies in private antitrust damage claims with an international element. The case exposes some of the problems of the EU model of administration of justice in cross-border competition law disputes. The aim of this paper is to engage with some competition law cases with a view to identifying the main weaknesses of the current institutional framework. It shows that, due to the specific nature of the EU competition law infringements, a level of delay appears to be common under the current institutional architecture, and as a result there are no effective remedies for many of the injured parties. It is submitted that the inability of the current regime to adequately deal with the cross-border implications of the EU competition law infringements could hamper the effectiveness of any national legislation in implementing the Directive on antitrust damage actions and the Commission Recommendation setting out common principles for collective redress proceedings. A case is made for research studies which consider how to improve the effectiveness of the current enforcement regime whilst factoring in the cross-border nature of the majority of the EU competition law infringements.

## 1 Introduction

European integration has incentivised cross-border trade, encouraging pan-European business activities. There are a significant number of multinational groups of companies doing business in several jurisdictions. If such groups of companies engage in anti-competitive practices, then businesses and consumers in several countries may be adversely affected. The increasing number of

M. Danov (✉)
University of Exeter, Exeter, UK
e-mail: M.Danov@exeter.ac.uk

© Springer-Verlag Berlin Heidelberg 2017
V. Tomljenović et al. (eds.), *EU Competition and State Aid Rules*,
Europeanization and Globalization 3, https://doi.org/10.1007/978-3-662-47962-9_10

pan-European business strategies poses new challenges for the EU legislator, who may need, among other things, to devise an effective competition law enforcement regime. The aim of this paper is to outline the difficulties that injured parties face when trying to obtain an effective remedy for the harm caused to them by EU competition law infringements in a cross-border context.

The paper will consider the enforcement pattern displayed in the case law, along with some important legislative developments in order to demonstrate how complicated (time-consuming and costly) it is for injured parties to access an effective remedy in cross-border cases. An analysis of some of the reported cases will be undertaken with a view to identifying the problems that arise in the European context under the current institutional framework. Before doing this, some preliminary remarks will be made, setting out the policy-makers' enforcement objectives in the light of some relevant research studies.

## 2 Preliminary Remarks: Competition Enforcement Objectives

The goals of the competition law enforcement policy may be summarised as follows: (1) to detect competition law infringements,[1] (2) to bring those infringements to an end, (3) to impose sanctions on the infringing undertakings with a view to deterring anti-competitive behaviour, (4) to provide redress to those who have suffered harm.[2] The last objective is significant in the light of the Charter of Fundamental Rights of the European Union,[3] which guarantees 'the right to an effective remedy'[4] for everyone whose Treaty rights have been violated.[5] The importance of the right to an effective remedy was reiterated in the Strasbourg Programme, which sets out the EU Justice Agenda for 2020,[6] as well as in the Brussels I Regulation (recast),[7] which allocates jurisdiction in cross-border EU competition law cases. Under the current enforcement regime, the EU competition law provisions may be enforced in private proceedings before national courts, as well as in public-administrative proceedings where a public authority may adopt a decision establishing that there has been an infringement of EU competition law.

---

[1] See more in Huschelrath (2014), p. 9.

[2] See more in Wils (2005), pp. 116–118; Komninos (2008), pp. 7–8.

[3] Charter of Fundamental Rights of the European Union [2000] OJ C 364/1.

[4] Article 47(1) of the Charter of Fundamental Rights of the European Union.

[5] Directive 2014/104/EU on Antitrust Damages Actions; Case C-453/99 *Courage* v. *Crehan*, ECLI:EU:C:2001:465; Joined Cases C-295/04 to C-298/04 *Vincenzo Manfredi* v. *Lloyd Adriatico Assicuriazioni* ECLI:EU:C:2006:461.

[6] Commission, 'The EU Justice Agenda for 2020 – Strengthening Trust, Mobility and Growth within the European Union' (Communication) COM (2014) 144 final, para 4.1(ii).

[7] Recital 38 of Regulation (EU) No 1215/2012 of 12 December 2012 on jurisdiction and the recognition and enforcement of judgments in civil and commercial matters ('Brussels I recast').

The public enforcement pillar is very important under the current institutional framework. The 2013 Report on Competition Policy[8] does suggest that '[s]ince May 2004, the Commission has ... [adopted] over 120 decisions. NCAs, on their part, have investigated over 1600 cases in the same period, giving rise to more than 600 enforcement decisions.'[9] An economic analysis of the important role of public enforcement has been made by Huschelrath,[10] who addressed the question whether the current fine levels are deterrent-optimal. His data set includes information on the case (i.e., cartel type, cartel duration, number of cartel members, affected industry, relevant geographic market, duration of cartel investigation, the role of leniency, the overall level of fines), as well as on the infringing undertaking (i.e., individual length of cartel participation, the level of individual fines imposed, the undertaking's leniency application, the value of the fine reduction). The data were derived from all cartel cases decided by the European Commission from 2000 to 2011.[11] On this basis, Huschelrath concludes that

empirical studies mostly suggest that current fine levels are too low to reach optimal deterrence. However, as these studies mostly fail to take further components of the entire fine package into account – individual punishments, private damage claims, effects on stock prices, effects on firm reputation – the question whether price-fixing in the EU is really under-deterred continues to remain open.[12]

Therefore, the private antitrust damage actions appear to be important, with a view to creating an effective enforcement regime, in the light of Huschelrath's findings. The European Commission has noted that private antitrust enforcement is less effective than is desirable in the EU.[13] It has been submitted that there is a 'concentration of antitrust damages actions in three EU jurisdictions: the UK, Germany and the Netherlands'.[14] Moreover, in spite of the fact that the UK appears to be among the most attractive jurisdictions in Europe, the existence of an enforcement gap there had been noted by the UK Government.[15] It was concluded

---

[8]Report from the Commission to the European Parliament, the Council, the European Economic and Social Committee and the Committee of the Regions COM (2014) 249 final.

[9]Report from the Commission to the European Parliament, the Council, the European Economic and Social Committee and the Committee of the Regions COM (2014) 249 final, p. 5.

[10]Huschelrath (2014).

[11]Huschelrath (2014), p. 25.

[12]Huschelrath (2014), pp. 36–37.

[13]Commission Staff Working Document, 'Executive Summary of the Impact Assessment' SWD (2013) 204 final.

[14]Commission Staff Working Document, 'Executive Summary of the Impact Assessment' SWD (2013) 204 final [7] (emphasis in the original). See also: Danov and Dnes (2013), Kammin and Becker (2013).

[15]Department for Business Innovation & Skills, 'Private actions in competition law: a consultation on options for reform – government response' (January 2013) [3.6]. https://www.gov.uk/government/uploads/system/uploads/attachment_data/file/70185/13-501-private-actions-in-competition-law-a-consultation-on-options-for-reform-government-response1.pdf. Accessed 2 June 2015.

that 'the strong sense from the [UK] consultation was that [competition law] cases are almost exclusively between large companies, and that smaller companies and consumers still have no realistic way of challenging breaches of competition law or gaining redress'.[16] The case for the ineffectiveness of the current private international law regime may be strengthened by the results of the comparative study on private enforcement across Europe, which was undertaken by Rodger.[17] Although Peyer's report[18] indicates that there are more private antitrust damage cases brought before national courts in Germany, he acknowledges that 'if private litigation is narrowed down to cases against hard-core violations such as cartels, fewer cases would appear in the dataset'.[19] In his analysis, Rodger[20] concludes that 'competition litigation culture in the UK [. . .] is in a state of infancy'.[21]

In view of the foregoing, the following questions will be addressed: What are the difficulties that injured parties face in a cross-border context? What are the issues that may need to be addressed by the policymakers, with a view to devising a competition law enforcement system that functions effectively (in terms of achieving the set of enforcement objectives) across Europe?

## 3   Cross-Border Aspects: Difficulties as Highlighted by the Case Law

In this section, the author demonstrates that, due to the cross-border nature of the EU competition law infringements, there are some important issues that may adversely affect the injured parties' effective access to remedies which might in turn impact on their litigiousness under the current regime. The issues are deduced from the enforcement pattern that was displayed in three recent cases: *CDC Cartel Damage Claims Hydrogen Peroxide SA*,[22] *Deutsche Bahn*[23] and *National Grid*.[24]

*CDC*[25] was the first case in which the Court of Justice of the European Union was asked to provide interpretation and opine on the way the Brussels I Regulation

---

[16]ibid [3.5].

[17]Rodger (2012).

[18]Peyer (2012). See more in Rodger (2014).

[19]Peyer (2012), p. 23.

[20]Rodger (2012). See also Rodger (2014).

[21]Rodger (2012), p. 43.

[22]Case C-352/13 *Cartel Damage Claims (CDC) Hydrogen Peroxide SA* v. *Akzo Nobel NV, Solvay SA/NV, Kemira Oyj, FMC Foret SA* ECLI:EU:C:2015:335.

[23]*Deutsche Bahn AG & Ors v. Morgan Advanced Materials Plc (formerly Morgan Crucible Co Plc)* [2013] EWCA Civ 1484. See also: *Deutsche Bahn AG & Ors v. Morgan Advanced Materials Plc (formerly Morgan Crucible Co Plc) (European Commission intervening)* [2014] UKSC 24.

[24]*Secretary of State for Health and others v. Servier Laboratories Ltd and others; National Grid Electricity Transmission plc v. ABB Ltd and others* [2013] EWCA Civ 1234.

[25]*Cartel Damage Claims* (n 22). See also Reher (2013).

applies in private antitrust damage claims with an international element. In this case, the private damage claim was preceded by a decision of the European Commission establishing a competition law infringement, which lasted from 31 January 1994 to 31 December 2000.[26] The Commission's investigation, which commenced with a surprise inspection of the undertakings' premises, was prompted by a leniency application dated 13 December 2002.[27] In May 2006, the Commission decided that a number of *undertakings* that were engaged in business activities across Europe[28] had infringed Article 101 TFEU.[29] Since the term 'undertaking' denotes a broader concept for the purposes of Article 101,[30] the Commission noted that it must 'define the undertaking that is to be held accountable for the infringement of Article [101 TFEU] by identifying one or more legal persons to represent the undertaking'.[31] That said, the Commission stated that '[t]he fact that it has been shown that a parent company is responsible for the conduct of its subsidiary does not in any way exonerate the subsidiary of its own responsibility'.[32] On 16 March 2009, CDC commenced a damage action against Evonik Degussa, which has its registered office in Germany, as well as against six other companies domiciled in the Netherlands, Belgium, Finland, France and Spain. The claimant company, which was domiciled in Belgium, purchased damage claims from 71 companies established in 13 different Member States. The competition law damage claim was brought before the *Landgericht*, Dortmund. However, the claim against the only defendant domiciled in Germany was settled in September 2009. All the remaining defendants challenged the jurisdiction of the German court, relying on the fact that the claimant against the 'anchor defendant' (i.e., the only German-domiciled defendant) was withdrawn. In addition, the defendants invoked the jurisdiction and arbitration clauses incorporated in their supply contracts with various injured parties. The German court made a preliminary reference to the Court of Justice. The request was received in June 2013. In its judgment, rendered on 21 May 2015 (i.e., nearly 2 year later), the CJEU held:

> Article 6(1) of Regulation No 44/2001 must be interpreted as meaning that the rule on centralisation of jurisdiction in the case of several defendants, as established in that provision, can apply in the case of an action for damages, and for disclosure in that regard, brought jointly against *undertakings* which

---

[26]Case COMP/F/38.620 – *Hydrogen Peroxide and perborate*, Commission Decision of 03.05.2006 relating to a proceeding pursuant to Article 81 of the EC Treaty and Article 53 of the EEA Agreement C(2006) 1766 final [351–360].

[27]ibid [63] and [367].

[28]ibid [88].

[29]See the Commission decision. Available via Eur-Lex. http://eur-lex.europa.eu/legal-content/EN/TXT/PDF/?uri=CELEX:32006D0903&from=EN. Accessed 18 June 2015.

[30]See the judgment in Case C-41/90 *Klaus Höfner and Fritz Elser* v. *Macrotron GmbH* ECLI:EU:C:1991:161. See also: *Hydrogen Peroxide and perborate* (n 26) [371].

[31]ibid [372].

[32]ibid [375].

have participated in different places and at different times in a single and continuous infringement, which has been established by a decision of the Commission, of the prohibition of anti-competitive agreements, decisions and concerted practices provided for under EU law, even where the applicant has withdrawn its action against the sole co-defendant domiciled in the same State as the court seised.[33]

It is beyond doubt that it is important for litigation to be centralised in cross-border EU competition actions against multiple defendants in order to avoid the risk of (potentially) irreconcilable judgments, as well as to minimise the litigation (or enforcement) costs if different actions are brought in different Member States. As noted elsewhere,[34] there is a need for a jurisdiction rule that allows a claimant (or multiple claimants) to centralise litigation against a group of companies before the courts in his (or their) preferred jurisdiction. Such a rule would allow a claimant (or rather multiple claimants) to effectively pursue his (or their) legitimate right to an effective remedy (which may be an important development for the effective enforcement of competition law in a diverse Union).

However, the wording of the judgment poses questions. One may wonder why the CJEU decided to use the concept of undertaking when interpreting the scope of jurisdiction rules under the Brussels I Regulation, which allocates jurisdiction in claims against 'persons domiciled in a Member State'.[35] It is well established that the EU competition law concept of 'undertaking', as opposed to that of 'person' used in the Brussels I recast, 'can embrace a number of legal entities, as long as they act as a single economic unit, and no legal entity acts independently for any relevant purpose'.[36] Indeed, a specific feature of most EU competition law cases is that infringing undertakings often use a network of subsidiaries to implement cartel agreements.[37] In this light, it is even more dificult to explain why the CJEU went further to use the registered office of an undertaking[38] as a connective factor when interpreting the Brussels I regime. The following questions are bound to arise in private competition law proceedings: Where is the registered office of an undertaking within the meaning of Articles 101 and 102 TFEU? Or rather, does the court refer to the registered office of the company that is the addressee of the Commission decision? Does the court refer to the registered office of any subsidiary (which

---

[33]*Cartel Damage Claims* (n 22) para 33 (emphasis added).

[34]Danov (2013).

[35]See Article 4 of the Brussels I Regulation (recast).

[36]*Roche Products Limited, Roche Vitamine Europe AG (Switzerland), F. Hoffmann-La Roche AG (Switzerland) v. Provimi Limited* [2003] EWHC 961 (Comm) [30]. See *Cooper Tire & Rubber Company Europe Limited & Others* [2010] EWCA Civ 864 [47].

[37]*Hydrogen Peroxide and perborate* (n 26) [88].

[38]Compare *Cartel Damage Claims* (n 22) para 53.

may not even be an addressee of the Commission decision finding the infringement) as long as it forms part of an infringing undertaking?[39] Does the court interpretation mean that it would be open for a claimant to establish jurisdiction against one of the subsidiaries to centralise litigation against the whole group of companies, as well as against the other group/s of companies party to the same anti-competitive agreement? It is far from certain what the answers to these questions are. There are very complex issues arising in a cross-border context. Some of the difficult issues were considered by Mr Justice Teare in *Cooper Tire*, where it was held:

> An undertaking in European competition law is an economic unit. That unit is engaged in an economic activity. The prohibition in Article [101] is on agreements by such undertakings or economic units but Article [101] is infringed not only by making an agreement contrary to Article [101] but also by the implementation of such agreements. An undertaking may act by or through those legal entities which constitute the undertaking. Whilst the infringement of Article [101] is that of the undertaking, liability for the resulting fine or damages must be attached to a legal person. Where a subsidiary is personally involved in the infringement by implementing the offending agreement there is no need to enquire into whether or not the subsidiary is involved by having decisive influence over another legal entity. Since the legal entity which makes the offending agreement plainly has knowledge of it, a rational consequence of the concept of an undertaking as a single economic entity, made up of its constituent legal entities, is that the undertaking has knowledge of the offending agreement. There is therefore no need, before attaching liability to a legal entity which is part of that undertaking and has implemented the offending agreement, to allege and prove that that legal entity had knowledge of the offending agreement. It is sufficient that the undertaking had such knowledge.[40]

However, the decision of the Court of Appeal in the same case[41] does suggest that the issue of the parent company's liability 'for what its subsidiary has done'[42] could be subject to heated debates between parties in proceedings before national courts. The existing uncertainty would inevitably impact on the litigation costs as well as on the parties' expectations about the outcome of the case. Furthermore,

---

[39]*Toshiba Carrier UK Ltd and Other v. KME Yorkshire Limited & Others* [2012] EWCA Civ 169. See also: Danov (2016), pp. 110–131.

[40]*Cooper Tire & Rubber Company v. Shell Chemicals UK Limited* [2009] EWHC 2609 (Comm) [50].

[41]*Cooper Tire & Rubber Company Europe Limited & Others* [2010] EWCA Civ 864.

[42]Ibid [45].

complex issues may arise in cases where the private damage actions are initiated against a subsidiary forming part of a corporate group that consists of numerous subsidiaries all of which form a single infringing 'undertaking' for the purposes of Article 101 and 102 TFEU. The problems were exposed in the *Emerson* case.[43] In this case, the defendant, despite being part of an infringing undertaking, was not named in the operative part of the Commission infringement decision (i.e., *dispositif*).[44] The court noted that even if a local subsidiary, which is not an addressee of a Commission decision, is part of an infringing undertaking within the meaning of Article 101 TFEU, the local subsidiary in question is not to be identified 'as an infringing party so as to render it liable, as a separate entity, to [an injured party] for infringement of competition law'.[45] As a result, in *Emerson*, the claim against the English subsidiary was struck out because there was no evidence that the subsidiary had infringed EU competition law, so that no follow-on action (under the legislative framework which was in force at the time) could be initiated before the Competition Appeal Tribunal against the subsidiary that was not an addressee of the Commission decision. The English Court of Appeal stated that the principle of legal certainty 'would be undermined if an entity which was not an addressee of a decision of the Commission could be made liable to proceedings in national courts based on it'.[46]

Therefore, the use by the CJEU of the EU competition law concept of under-taking in a case where the court was asked to interpret the scope of jurisdiction rules for the purposes of the Brussels I Regulation (recast) could generate some ambiguity because an infringing undertaking is often a corporate group with numerous subsidiaries (all of which form a single infringing undertaking). On the one hand, the legal entities forming part of an infringing undertaking could argue that the CJEU ruling in the *CDC* case means that a claim could only be brought against the companies that are addressees of the Commission decision. On the other hand, the injured parties could interpret the ruling broadly submitting that the claims could be brought against any legal entity, even one that is not an addressee of the Commission decision finding the infringement, as long as it forms part of an infringing undertaking for the purposes of Articles 101 and 102 TFEU. This means that, following the CJEU judgment in *CDC*, a level of ambiguity will remain in the area. Indeed, it is highly likely that the existing level of ambiguity would be exploited by strategic litigants, inflating the injured parties' litigation costs. Even more worrying is that 15 years after the end of the infringement, the CJEU rendered

---

[43]*Emerson Electric Co & Ors v. Mersen UK Portslade Ltd (sued as and formerly Le Carbone (Great Britain) Ltd* [2012] EWCA Civ 1559.

[44]See *Emerson Electric Co v. Morgan Crucible Company PLC and Ors* [2011] CAT 4 [11 and 38].

[45]*Emerson Electric Co & Ors v. Mersen UK Portslade Ltd (sued as and formerly Le Carbone (Great Britain) Ltd)* [2012] EWCA Civ 1559 [81].

[46]*Emerson Electric Co & Ors v. Mersen UK Portslade Ltd (sued as and formerly Le Carbone (Great Britain) Ltd)* [2012] EWCA Civ 1559 [83].

a judgment dealing only with the issue of jurisdiction, and the compensation for the injured parties in this cross-border case was yet to be provided.

The fact that only several jurisdictions appear to be attracting cross-border EU completion law actions for damages strongly suggests that the issue of jurisdiction is significant for claimants. The point may be well illustrated by making reference to the *Deutsche Bahn* case.[47] In this case, Deutsche Bahn (and 29 other claimants) brought antitrust damage claims against Morgan (and five other defendants). The claim was preceded by a decision of the European Commission finding an infringement of Article 101 TFEU.[48] The price-fixing cartel engaged in a single and continuous EU competition law infringement, which lasted from October 1988 to 1999. The cross-border nature of the infringement can be easily demonstrated by the Commission's findings that the 'cartel covered all of the Contracting Parties of the EEA where demand existed [...]. It also covered a number of countries in Eastern Europe and the Middle East.'[49] The UK-based defendant, Morgan, being the first leniency applicant, was granted full immunity from the fines. All the addressees of the Commission's decision, but Morgan, appealed against the Commission's decision. The General Court dismissed the infringers' appeals in judgments rendered on 8 October 2009.[50]

The private damage EU competition law action was brought in the UK on 15 December 2010. On the claimant's side, there were originally 12 claimants established in Germany, six claimants from the UK,[51] five claimants from the Netherlands, two claimants from Portugal, two claimants from Italy, two from Sweden, one from Spain and one from Norway; on the defendant's side, there were three defendants from Germany, one from the UK, one from Austria and one from France.[52] Hence, in this case, as in *CDC*, the claimants wanted to sue multiple defendants under Article 8(1) (ex-Article 6(1)) of the Brussels I recast. However, to rely on Article 8(1), the claimants had to establish a 'good arguable case'[53] that the

---

[47]*Deutsche Bahn AG and others v. Morgan Advance* [2013] CAT 18, 15 August 2013. See more: Danov and Becker (2014).

[48]Case C.38.359 – *Electrical and Mechanical Carbon and Graphite Products,* Commission Decision of 3 December 2003 relating to a proceeding under Article 81 and Article 53 of the EEA Agreement against C Conradty Nürnberg GmbH, Hoffmann & Co. Elektrokohle AG, Le Carbone Lorraine SA, Morgan Crucible Company plc, Schunk GmbH and Schunk Kohlenstofftechnik GmbH, jointly and severally, and SGL Carbon AG [2004] OJ L 125/45.

[49]Case C.38.359 – *Electrical and Mechanical Carbon and Graphite Products* [50]. http://ec.europa.eu/competition/antitrust/cases/dec_docs/38359/38359_36_1.pdf. Accessed 2 June 2015.

[50]Case T-68/04 *SGL Carbon* v. *Commission* ECLI:EU:T:2008:414; Case T-69/04 *Schunk and Schunk Kohlenstoff-Technik* v. *Commission* ECLI:EU:T:2008:415; Case T-74/04 *Carbone-Lorraine* v. *Commission* ECLI:EU:T:2006:60.

[51]Subsequently, by an order dated 19 April 2011, the CAT gave permission to one of the UK claimants to withdraw its claim.

[52]Case 1173/5/7/10 *Notice of a Claim for Damages under Section 47A of the Competition Act 1998.*

[53]*Bob Distilleries BV (trading as Bols Royal Distilleries) and another v. Superior Yacht Services* [2006] UKPC 45 [28].

English court had jurisdiction and that the requirements of Article 8(1) of the Brussels I recast had been satisfied.[54] To this end, it must be shown that 'there is a real issue between the Claimants and one of the Anchor Defendants, that is, an issue which cannot be struck out'.[55] Morgan was the only UK defendant that was the 'anchor defendant' for the purpose of Article 6(1) of Brussels I (now Article 8 (1) of the Brussels I recast). Therefore, with a view to defeating the claimants' strategy[56] to bring their cross-border action in the UK, the defendants made a strike-out application on the ground that the claim against Morgan had been brought after the 2-year limitation period had elapsed.[57] The application, to have the claim against Morgan struck out on the ground that the claim had been out of time,[58] succeeded before the Competition Appeal Tribunal.[59] Although the English Court of Appeal[60] rejected the application, the UK Supreme Court[61] reversed the decision of the Court of Appeal.

The developments clearly show that, due to the level of uncertainty (or ambiguity) in cross-border cases,[62] the parties spent a considerable amount of time and money arguing about preliminary issues.[63] Indeed, the appellate history in the *Deutsche Bahn* case shows that the English court has rendered six judgments[64] and many orders[65] on various aspects of dispute. In view of these difficulties, the UK claimants had to change their tactics by requesting the Competition Appeal Tribunal to lift the stay to their claims against the other five defendants.[66] In particular, the UK claimants—aiming to establish jurisdiction in England—had to base their damage claims on Article 5(3) of Brussels I (now

---

[54]*Cooper Tire & Rubber Company v. Shell Chemicals UK Limited* [2009] EWHC 2609 (Comm) [36]. See also *Roche Products Limited, Roche Vitamine Europe AG (Switzerland), F Hoffmann-La Roche AG (Switzerland) v. Provimi Limited* [2003] EWHC 961 (Comm) [46–49].

[55]*Cooper Tire & Rubber Company v. Shell Chemicals UK Limited* [2009] EWHC 2609 (Comm) [37]. See also *FKI Engineering v. Dewind Holdings* [2007] EWHC (Comm) [32].

[56]Lawrence and Morfey (2013).

[57]*Deutsche Bahn AG v. Morgan* [2011] CAT 16 [12].

[58]*Deutsche Bahn AG v. Morgan* [2011] CAT 16 [12].

[59]*Deutsche Bahn AG v. Morgan* [2011] CAT 16 [68].

[60]*Deutsche Bahn AG v. Morgan* [2012] EWCA Civ. 1055 [121]. See more: Danov and Becker (2014).

[61]*Deutsche Bahn AG v. Morgan* [2014] UKSC 24.

[62]Danov and Dnes (2013).

[63]See more in Lawrence and Morfey (2013).

[64]*Deutsche Bahn AG v. Morgan* [2011] CAT 16; *Deutsche Bahn AG v. Morgan* [2011] CAT 18; *Deutsche Bahn AG v. Morgan* [2011] CAT 22; *Deutsche Bahn AG v. Morgan* [2012] EWCA Civ 1055; *Deutsche Bahn AG v. Morgan* [2013] EWCA Civ 1484; *Deutsche Bahn AG v. Morgan* [2014] UKSC 24.

[65]See more in Case 1173/5/7/10 *Deutsche Bahn AG & Others v. Morgan Crucible Company PLC & Others.* http://www.catribunal.org.uk/237-6896/1173-5-7-10-Deutsche-Bahn-AG--Others. html. Accessed 17 June 2015.

[66]*Deutsche Bahn AG v. Morgan* [2013] CAT 18, 15 August 2013 [10].

Article 7(2) of the Brussels I recast) rather than Article 6(1) of Brussels I (now Article 8(1) of the Brussels I recast).[67] This was done despite the fact that, under Article 7(2), the English court would have jurisdiction to compensate the claimants 'in respect of the damage which occurred in England',[68] which may be an insignificant proportion of the whole harm caused by the cartelists. The claimants' tactics strongly suggest that the injured parties perceived that there were some advantages for them to sue in England rather than somewhere else. The fact that the claimants insisted on suing in England despite the fact the jurisdiction of Article 7 (2) is limited to local harm[69] clearly shows how important the issue of jurisdiction is for the claimants. That said, it should be noted that, following the UK Supreme Court decision, the parties reached an agreement to settle their claims.[70] Nonetheless, it should be pointed out that the proceedings in one of the leading (and most attractive) European jurisdictions (at the time) appeared to be terminated approximately 10 years after the end of the cartel arrangements and more than 20 years after the infringement started, which questions the effectiveness of the current enforcement regime. The issues might be excerbated post-*Brexit* in so far as the English and Welsh courts might no longer form part of the EU civil justice system.

The level of complexity and the importance of cross-border aspects in EU competition law cases for establishing liability were also displayed in the *National Grid* case.[71] This case shows an enforcement pattern that is similar to the one demonstrated in *CDC* and *Deutsche Bahn*. The follow-on damage claim was preceded by a decision of the European Commission establishing an infringement.[72] A leniency application was made by one of the infringers, ABB. The cartel was worldwide, so the infringing undertakings were engaging in cross-border anticompetitive practices, which covered the period from 15 April 1988 to 11 May 2004. The EU competition law damage actions commenced in November 2007. Mr Justice Roth specified some of the difficulties by making the following observation:

There [were] 22 defendants to the claim. Some were addressees of the Decision; others [were] subsidiaries of addressees of the Decision. The relationship of the defendants [was] complicated by various transfers of companies and businesses, often with changes of name since both the period of the cartel and the Decision.[73]

---

[67]Case 1173/5/7/10, *Deutsche Bahn AG & Others v. Morgan Crucible Company PLC & Others* [96].

[68]*Cooper Tire & Rubber Company Europe Limited & Others* [2010] EWCA Civ 864 [65]. See also *Cartel Damage Claims* (n 22) para 55.

[69]See more: *Cartel Damage Claims* (n 22) para 55.

[70]See Case 1173/5/7/10 *Deutsche Bahn AG & Others* – Order of the Chairmen (Adjournment) – 29 September 2014 CAT; Order of the Chairmen (Withdrawal of claims) – 12 November 2014.

[71]*National Grid Electricity Transmission Plc v. ABB Ltd and others* [2009] EWHC 1326 (Ch).

[72]Case COMP/F/38.899 – *Gas Insulated Switchgear*, Commission Decision of 24.01.2007 relating to a proceeding pursuant to Article 81 of the EC Treaty and Article 53 of the EEA Agreement C (2006) 6762 final.

[73]*National Grid Electricity Transmission Plc v. ABB Ltd and others* [2014] EWHC 1555 (Ch).

The proceedings in the UK were stayed[74] since there was an appeal against the Commission's decision before the General Court.[75] In November 2012, the claimant made an application for specific disclosure against the French Alstom defendants and Areva.[76] The English High Court granted the disclosure order. The defendants appealed against the High Court's judgment. In the Court of Appeal, the defendants argued that compliance with the order for a disclosure would expose them to a risk of prosecution under the French blocking statute. They also submitted that EC Regulation 1206/2001 should be used instead. The English Court of Appeal held:

> [t]he orders in question were, respectively, for the provision of further information and disclosure. They were orders of a procedural nature in the pending claims and their making was, therefore, governed by the *lex fori,* namely the law of England and Wales. The domestic authorities to which we were referred show that the fact that such orders might, if complied with, expose the parties subject to them to the risk of prosecution under a foreign law provides no defence to their making. The English court still retains a jurisdiction under the *lex fori* to make them, although it has a discretion as to whether to do so in the particular circumstances. In the present cases, both Henderson and Roth JJ correctly recognised that, and they exercised their discretion to make the orders now under challenge.[77]

The English Court of Appeal dismissed the defendant's appeal. The judgment clearly demonstrates that, due to the cross-border nature of EU competition law infringements, evidence may often be out of the jurisdiction in which the proceedings are taking place. Procedural history also shows that there were six interim judgments in *National Grid*.[78] The trial was scheduled to commence on 9 June 2014,[79] but the case was subsequently settled.[80] Although the English claim form was issued on 17 November 2008, compensation was obtained by the claimant

---

[74]*National Grid Electricity Transmission Plc v. ABB Ltd and others* [2009] EWHC 1326 (Ch) [48].

[75]Joined Cases T-122/07 to T-124/07 *Siemens Osterreich and Others* v. *Commission* ECLI:EU:T:2011:70. See also Joined Cases C-231/11 P to C-233/11 P *Commission* v. *Siemens AG Osterreich and others* ECLI:EU:C:2014:256.

[76]*National Grid Electricity Transmission Plc v. ABB Ltd and others* [2013] EWHC 822 (Ch).

[77]*National Grid Electricity Transmission Plc v. ABB Ltd and others* [2013] EWCA Civ 1234.

[78]*National Grid* (n 74); *National Grid Electricity Transmission Plc v. ABB Ltd and others* [2011] EWHC 1717 (Ch); *National Grid Electricity Transmission Plc v. ABB Ltd and others* [2012] EWHC 869 (Ch); *National Grid Electricity Transmission Plc v. ABB Ltd and others* [2013] EWHC 822 (Ch); *National Grid Electricity Transmission Plc v. ABB Ltd and others* [2013] EWCA Civ 1234; *National Grid Electricity Transmission Plc v. ABB Ltd and others* [2014] EWHC 1555 (Ch).

[79]*National Grid Electricity Transmission Plc v. ABB Ltd and others* [2014] EWHC 1555 (Ch).

[80]Berwin et al. (2014). One of England's largest cartel damages claim. http://www.blplaw.com/media/download/National_Grid_case_study_BLP.pdf. Accessed 18 June 2015.

approximately 10 years after the end of the cartel arrangements and more than 25 years after the infringement had started. It should be noted that, in a follow-on action in relation to the *Gas Insulated Switchgear* cartel, a Dutch court rendered the first cartel damage judgment in Holland.[81] However, no follow-on actions were brought in the majority of the Member States. In the circumstances, it could well be argued that there was no full compensation for the great majority of injured parties across Europe.

A closer look at the way the above mentioned cases developed demonstrates that the cross-border aspects of EU competition law cases (and the issue of jurisdiction) are not the only issues that may need to be carefully considered by policymakers with a view to facilitating private parties' access to effective remedies in cross-border cases. The point was captured well by Mr Justice Roth, who noted that '[o]ne reason why these proceedings have made such slow progress is that no trial can take place in any event until all the relevant appeals before the EU courts are determined'.[82] Indeed, the length of the proceedings in these cases appears to be an important issue, which does question the effectiveness and efficiency of the remedies available for injured parties in cross-border cases. The settlements were reached about 10 to 15 years after the end of the competition law infringements. Moreover, in spite of the fact that the infringements caused harm to businesses and consumers across Europe, it seems that remedies were available only for the injured parties that were prepared to devote a significant amount of time and money to cover the costs of cross-border litigation. More importantly, the claims in *CDC*, *Deutsche Bahn* and *National Grid* were preceded by public enforcement actions initiated by the Commission.[83] This poses the question how effectively the enforcement objectives may be pursued if injured parties would normally have to wait for a public authority to adopt a decision finding a competition law infringement[84] before they could bring follow-on competition law damage actions across Europe. How effective is the current institutional architecture in a cross-border context?

## 4    Instructional Architecture: Difficulties as Highlighted by the Case Law

The aim of this section is to analyse some cases, demonstrating how the current institutional architecture influences the litigants' strategies and the suing decision of the injured parties. In the UK, the problems regarding the institutional architecture

---

[81]See more in Linklaters (15 February 2013). Linklaters briefing: First cartel damages judgment in the Netherlands. http://www.linklaters.com/News/LatestNews/2013/Pages/Linklaters-briefing-First-cartel-damages-judgment-Netherlands.aspx. Accessed 17 June 2015.

[82]*National Grid Electricity Transmission Plc v. ABB Ltd and others* [2012] EWHC 869 (Ch) [75].

[83]Wils (2009), pp. 12–14.

[84]Section 33 of the Commission Recommendation on Collective Redress.

were exposed—in a domestic context—in *Enron Coal Services Ltd (In Liquidation) v. English Welsh & Scottish Ltd*.[85] In this case, Lord Justice Jacob noted that 'the "split" jurisdiction of regulator for infringement, tribunal for causation and assessment of damages also needs some reconsideration'.[86] An important aspect of the UK enforcement regime was outlined by Lasok QC, who made the following observation:

> *Enron* [2011] EWCA Civ 2 is an example of a follow-on action in which the defendant's opportunity, to re-run before a court evidence considered by the competition authority, undermined the court's confidence in the relevance and/or strength of passages in the competition authority's decision. A rather different problem arises where, in the infringement decision, the competition authority is using the facts found by it to drive a particular theory, which may cause difficulties in a follow-on action if it becomes necessary to link the infringement to the facts of the case and, more particularly, the facts relating to causation and loss.[87]

The issues may be even more complex in a cross-border context where private proceedings are preceded by a decision of the Commission establishing a competition law infringement committed by undertakings, which often consist of numerous subsidiaries doing business across Europe. Moreover, as already noted, in *Deustche Bahn*,[88] an important preliminary issue may be when the limitation period for a non-appealing defendant (which, on this occasion, was a leniency applicant) begins.[89] In this case, the English courts had to consider what the nature of a Commission decision was and how an appeal from some of the addressees of the decision affected the position of non-appealing defendants. The UK Supreme Court held:

> A Commission Decision establishing infringement of article 81 (now article 101) constitutes in law a series of individual decisions addressed to its individual addressees. The only relevant decision establishing infringement in relation to an addressee who does not appeal is the original Commission Decision. Any appeal against the finding of infringement by any other addressee is irrelevant to a non-appealing addressee. Under section 47A(5) [of the Competition Act 1998], the relevant decision establishing that article 81 had been infringed is thus in the present case the Commission Decision dated 3 December 2003, and, once the time for the appellant to appeal against that Decision had expired on 13 February

---

[85]*Enron Coal Services Ltd (In Liquidation) v. English Welsh & Scottish Ltd* [2011] EWCA Civ 2.

[86]*Enron Coal Services Ltd (In Liquidation) v. English Welsh & Scottish Ltd* [2011] EWCA Civ 2 [149].

[87]Lasok (2013), p. 209.

[88]*Deutsche Bahn AG v. Morgan Advanced Materials plc* [2014] UKSC 24.

[89]See more in Akman (2013).

2004, the respondents had under section 47A(8) [of the Competition Act 1998] two years within which to bring a follow-on claim.[90]

With this in mind, one may argue that the current institutional framework poses practical difficulties for litigants in EU competition law cases. The following questions are bound to arise: What if only some addressees of a Commission decision appeal against the decision finding the infringement? If the appellants are unsuccessful and they remain jointly and severally liable for the whole harm, can they bring a claim for contribution against the leniency applicant in a case where the primary claim against him would be time barred? If the appellants are successful and the Commission decision is annulled against them, how will such an annulment affect the outcome of private damage proceedings against non-appealing addressees of the Commission decision?[91] Referring to the last question, the UK Supreme Court took the following view:

> a non-appealing addressee of a Commission Decision may, at least theoretically, find itself carrying full civil liability (without any fellow cartel members from which it may seek contribution) in respect of a cartel, the existence of which has been negatived on appeal by its alleged fellow cartel members. All that can be said is that, if there was really no cartel (or a more limited cartel than found by the Commission Decision), it might be difficult for a claimant to prove that it had suffered any loss caused thereby. Further, in the case of a whistle-blower like the present appellant, a hypothesis of no cartel is self-evidently unreal.[92]

Although the questions are considered to be academic at present, the issue might be very complex in cases where a whistle-blower had submitted a tactical leniency application (with a view to damaging his competitors' reputation) and the General Court subsequently annulled the Commission decision.

Indeed, liability may be a very contentious issue in cases where the internal relationships ascertaining the shares of those held jointly and severally liable are disputed. The Court of Justice[93] ruling, following an appeal from the European Commission's decision in *Gas Insulated Switchgear*,[94] exposes the problems under the current enforcement regime. One of the issues in this case was: who should determine the internal relationships ascertaining the shares of those held jointly and severally liable for the payment of fines? The CJEU held:

> neither Regulation No 1/2003 nor EU law in general contain rules for the resolution of such a dispute, which concerns the internal allocation of the debt

---

[90]*Deutsche Bahn AG v. Morgan Advanced Materials plc* [2014] UKSC 24 [28].

[91]*Deutsche Bahn AG v. Morgan Advanced Materials plc* [2014] UKSC 24 [27].

[92]*Deutsche Bahn AG v. Morgan Advanced Materials plc* [2014] UKSC 24 [27].

[93]*Commission v. Siemens AG Osterreich and others* ECLI:EU:C:2014:256 (n 75).

[94]Case COMP/F/38.899 (n 72).

for the payment of which the companies concerned are held jointly and severally liable. [...] In those circumstances, where there is no contractual agreement as to the shares to be paid by those held jointly and severally liable for payment of the fine, it is for the national courts to determine those shares, in a manner consistent with EU law, by applying the national law applicable to the dispute.[95]

Therefore, EU private international law has certainly an important role to play in such cases. More importantly, it is beyond doubt that the issue of the liability of a corporate group that is considered as one undertaking may be even more contentious in private actions because, as previously noted,[96] it may be far from clear 'which legal entities within a corporate group are liable for an infringement of Article 101(1) TFEU and to what extent'.[97]

Hence, one could argue that the current institutional framework (which is characterised by several sets of proceedings: a set of proceedings before a regulator with a view to establishing an infringement, and a number of sets of proceedings before various national courts for the injured parties to claim compensation) may be far from effectively and efficiently functioning in cross-border cases. Indeed, *CDC* and *National Grid* do suggest that, due to the fact that a substantial amount of time elapses from the start, as well as from the end of the competition law infringement, the private damage claimants may often try to get access to the Commission file that was compiled in the course of the preceding public-administrative proceedings. To this end, two different approaches were demonstrated by the claimants.

In *CDC*, an application was made on the basis of Article 11(1) and (2) of Regulation (EC) No 1049/2001. The claimant requested 'full access to the statement of contents of the case-file in the hydrogen peroxide decision (the "statement of contents")'.[98] The Commission dismissed the claimant's request on the ground that any disclosure could adversely affect the commercial interests of the cartelists and undermine the decision-making process and effectiveness of the leniency programme.[99] The claimants made an appeal against the Commission decision. The General Court allowed the appeal by holding:

> even if the fact that actions for damages were brought against a company could undoubtedly cause high costs to be incurred, even if only in terms of legal costs, and even if the actions were subsequently dismissed as unfounded, the fact remains that the interest of a company which took part in a cartel in avoiding such actions cannot be regarded as a commercial interest and, in any event, does

---

[95]*Commission* v. *Siemens AG Osterreich and others* ECLI:EU:C:2014:256 (n 75), paras 61–62.

[96]Danov (2013).

[97]See the reference request by Mr Rabinowitz in *Cooper Tire & Rubber Company Europe Limited & Others* [2010] EWCA Civ 864 [47].

[98]Case T-437/08 *Cartel Damage Claims Hydrogen Peroxide SA* v. *European Commission* ECLI:EU:T:2011:752, para 3.

[99]See Article 4(2) of Regulation (EC) No 1049/2001.

not constitute an interest deserving of protection, having regard, in particular, to the fact that any individual has the right to claim damages for loss caused to him by conduct which is liable to restrict or distort competition.[100]

The General Court went further to acknowledge the important role that the damage actions would play by stating that 'the leniency and co-operation programmes whose effectiveness the Commission is seeking to protect are not the only means of ensuring compliance with EU competition law'.[101]

In *National Grid*, the claimant sought disclosure from the defendant of the confidential version of the decision and of the responses to the Commission's Statement of Objection, as well as to the various requests for information.[102] After carefully considering the various policy considerations and benefiting from the first Commission intervention under Article 15(3) of Regulation 1/2003, the English court considered the full version of the Commission decision and ordered that some of the passages be disclosed.[103] In the light of these developments, it was not surprising that the Commission Work Programme 2012[104] identified that interrelation between private enforcement and public enforcement was an important area where a legislative measure would be needed.

The Directive on certain rules governing actions for damages under national law for infringements of the competition law provisions of the Member States and of the European Union was adopted. It is intended to approximate the national rules governing actions for damages[105] by dealing with such issues as disclosure of evidence, the effect of decisions of national competition authorities in other Member States, limitation periods, joint and several liability, passing-on defence and quantification of harm. The Directive aims '[t]o ensure undertakings' continued willingness to approach competition authorities voluntarily with leniency statements or settlement submissions, such documents should be exempted from the disclosure of evidence'.[106] But how effective is the current model, which presupposes several sets of proceedings (i.e., proceedings before a regulator and follow-on proceedings before a national court (or rather before national courts across the EU, perhaps))? How effective is the cooperation between the regulator/s and various national courts? Most recently, in *Emerald Supplies*, Mr Justice Smith expressed an interesting view:

---

[100]*Cartel Damage Claims Hydrogen Peroxide SA* v. *European Commission* (n 98) para 49.

[101]ibid para 77.

[102]*National Grid Electricity Transmission Plc v. ABB Ltd and others* [2012] EWHC 869 (Ch) [16].

[103]ibid [58].

[104]Commission Work Programme 2012, p. 3. http://ec.europa.eu/atwork/pdf/cwp2012_annex_en. pdf. Accessed 15 June 2015.

[105]Recital 9 of Directive 2014/104/EU on Antitrust Damages Actions.

[106]Recital 26 of Directive 2014/104/EU on Antitrust Damages Actions.

Although the letter was sent in the '*spirit of co-operation*' between the national courts and the EC there does not with respect to the Commission seem to be much co-operation from it. Despite the fact that it must be self-evident that 4 years even just to consider working out the non confidential part of the Decision is completely unacceptable no steps are being made to speed up that process and no indication is given as to when the whole process will be finalised.[107]

As already noted elsewhere,[108] if an injured party has to wait for a public authority to adopt a decision establishing a competition law infringement, then there will be a significant delay in providing redress for private parties. This means that there would be several sets of proceedings: public proceedings establishing an infringement and imposing fines and private proceedings, seeking to compensate the various injured parties across Europe. It is a real issue that such proceedings might often run in parallel in a number of Member States. Therefore, the effective coordination of the various sets of related proceedings and their length in particular are important issues, which must be addressed with a view to providing effective remedies for private parties in EU competition law cases. An institutional reform must be considered not least because it is well established that '[d]elays can render the judicial protection of the rights ineffectual, reduce the value of the rights, adversely affect economic activity and lead to economic distortions'.[109] The issues would be significant because, due to the cross-border nature of EU competition law infringements, harm would be often caused to injured parties in several jurisdictions. Indeed, there is a strong case that an ineffective and inefficient institutional architecture may adversely affect the injured parties' access to effective remedies, leaving an enforcement gap.[110]

## 5   Some Conclusions to Be Drawn

The case law strongly suggests that the weaknesses of the Brussels I regime, which is not suited (and was perhaps not even indented to be suited) to dealing with the specific aspects of cross-border EU competition law actions,[111] would hamper the effectiveness of the current enforcement regime. The lack of an appropriate legislative framework to address the cross-border implications of EU competition law infringements strongly suggests that any national legislation in the implementation of the Directive on antitrust damages and common principles for collective redress

---

[107] *Emerald Supplies v. British Airways* [2014] EWHC 3513 (Ch) [27].

[108] See more in Danov (2015).

[109] Zuckerman (1999), p. 12.

[110] See more in Danov (2015).

[111] See more in Danov et al. (2013).

proceedings would be less effective than is desirable in a cross-border context. Indeed, in the *CDC* case,[112] the shortcomings of Brussels I were explicitly put forward by AG Jääskinen, who stated:

8. First of all, I must point out that it appears to me that the Brussels I Regulation, the aim of which is to create a system of rules of jurisdiction for the Union in respect of cross-border disputes in civil and commercial matters, is not fully geared towards ensuring effective private implementation of the Union's competition law (or 'private enforcement', as it is usually called in this field) in circumstances such as those in this case.

9. The application of certain provisions of that regulation is likely to lead to a territorial division of jurisdiction between the courts of the Member States which might, on the one hand, be inadequate from the point of view of the geographical scope of EU competition law or, on the other hand, make it more difficult for persons adversely affected by unlawful restrictions of competition to seek and obtain full reparation for the damage that they have suffered. It seems to me, therefore, possible that the authors of such restrictions could use those provisions of international private law to bring about a situation in which the civil-law consequences of a single, serious infringement of Union competition rules are to be determined in the context of a series of actions scattered across the various Member States.[113]

The case for reforming the Brussels I regime is compelling.[114] However, as already noted,[115] the way the Brussels I Regulation is shaping the litigants' strategies in cross-border cases is not a competition law specific concern and needs to be examined in a wider context in Europe.[116] There is a case for significant institutional reform, aiming to improve the effectiveness of the current EU private international law framework. The need for such reform was first signalled by a Report by the Working Party on the Future of the European Communities' Court System.[117] The EUPILLAR research project has put forward detailed proposals for reform in this area on the basis of an empirical study conducted between 2014 and 2016.[118]

---

[112]*Cartel Damage Claims* (n 22).

[113]Opinion of AG Jääskinen in *Cartel Damage Claims (CDC) Hydrogen Peroxide SA* v. *Akzo Nobel NV, Solvay SA/NV, Kemira Oyj, FMC Foret SA* ECLI:EU:C:2014:2443, paras 8–9.

[114]Danov (2013), Danov (2012).

[115]Danov (2013).

[116]See Hess (2012), p. 1112.

[117]'Report by the Working Party on the Future of the European Communities' Court System' (Working Party for the European Commission, January 2000) pp. 34–35. http://ec.europa.eu/dgs/legal_service/pdf/due_en.pdf. Accessed 17 June 2015.

[118]See research project JUST/2013/JCIV/AG/4635 on 'Cross-Border Litigation in Europe: Private International Law Legislative Framework, National Courts and the Court of Justice of the

As part of an even wider reform, there is a strong case that the questions—whether there is an effective remedy for injured parties suffering harm in cross-border EU competition law cases and how effective/efficient the current competition law enforcement regime is—must be carefully considered by researchers and policymakers in the European context. It may be far from effective and indeed far from efficient to have one set of proceedings before a national competition authority (NCA) in order to establish a breach of competition law and several sets of proceedings (often running in parallel) before the various Member State courts in order for the different injured parties to obtain redress.[119] The current institutional enforcement architecture,[120] in which a regulator is regarded as being better placed to detect and establish an infringement and, subsequently, a national court is better placed to award damages, appears to be ineffective in providing effective remedies for injured parties in cross-border EU competition law cases. Moreover, it is not only that such an institutional enforcement architecture is inefficient in so far as proceedings raising the same issues of fact and law are not being consolidated at present, but also it is questionable whether or not the process in public-administrative proceedings before competition authorities is fair.[121] Whilst a national court would apply civil procedure rules that presuppose respect of due process, an NCA would apply administrative procedure rules that could potentially raise concerns as to the undertaking's right to a fair trial and hearing.[122]

Therefore, there is a strong case that the current institutional framework may need to be revised with a view to ensuring that there are effective remedies for injured parties (in line with the objectives of the Strasbourg programme). The need for research may be further justified by a research study undertaken by Hodges,[123] who has raised three important questions:

> First, is current policy, and in particular the 2013 proposal, still reliably well-founded? [...] Second, should policy be re-assessed, especially on the basis of issuing a revised impact assessment, so that we know whether and how significant the residual problem is? Third, the method of making major policy decisions based on reliance on a single study can be seriously questioned: should the whole methodology be reviewed? In my view, the answer to these questions is: no, yes, and yes.[124]

---

European Union'. See more: P. Beaumont, M. Danov, K. Trimmings and B. Yuksel (eds), Cross-Border Litigation in Europe (Hart Publishing, Oxford 2017).

[119]See more in Danov et al. (2013).

[120]Wils (2009).

[121]Lidgard (2012), pp. 403, 421.

[122]Forrester (2009), Nazzini (2012).

[123]Hodges (2014).

[124]Hodges (2014), p. 258.

Therefore, appropriately conducted comparative studies must be undertaken in a European context. Such studies should gather empirical data and take a view on how effective the current enforcement regime is and how it should be reformed. The question how private and public enforcement should best interrelate in order to devise an effective enforcement regime in Europe must be addressed head-on. This deduction could be strengthened even further by the UK decision to leave the EU which means that the EU civil justice system might no longer rely on the English judges to dispense justice in cross-border EU competition law disputes between private parties.

# References

Akman P (2013) Period of limitations in follow-on competition cases: the elephant in the room? ESRC CCP Working Paper Series

Danov M (2012) EU competition law enforcement: is Brussels I suited to dealing with all the challenges? Int Comp Law Q 61(1):27–54

Danov M (2013) Jurisdiction in cross-border EU competition law cases: some specific issues requiring specific solutions. In: Danov M, Becker F, Beaumont P (eds) Cross-border EU competition law actions. Hart, Oxford, pp 167–196

Danov M (2015) Collective redress and competition law claims: some specific issues. In: Lein E, Faigrieve D, Crespo M, Smith V (eds) Collective redress in Europe – why and how? British Institute of International and Comparative Law, London, pp 337–357

Danov M (2016) Private antitrust enforcement and private international law: recent developments. In: Nagy CI (ed) The procedural aspects of the application of competition law: European Framework – Central European Perspectives. Europa Publishing, Groningen, pp 110–131

Danov M, Becker F (2014) Governance aspects of cross-border EU competition law actions: theoretical and practical challenges. J Priv Int Law 10:359–401

Danov M, Dnes S (2013) Cross-border EU competition litigation: new evidence from England and Wales. In: Danov M, Becker F, Beaumont P (eds) Cross-border EU competition law actions. Hart, Oxford, pp 33–59

Danov M, Becker F, Beaumont P (eds) (2013) Cross-border EU competition law actions. Hart, Oxford

Forrester IS (2009) Due process in EC competition cases: a distinguished institution with flawed procedures. Eur Law Rev 34:817–847

Hess B (2012) The Brussels I regulation: recent case law of the Court of Justice and the Commission's proposed recast. Common Mark Law Rev 49:1075–1112

Hodges C (2014) Fast, effective and low cost redress: how do public and private enforcement and ADR compare? In: Rodger B (ed) Competition law: comparative private enforcement and consumer redress in the EU. Kluwer, The Hague, pp 255–289

Huschelrath K (2014) Public enforcement of anti-cartel laws – theory and empirical evidence. In: Huschelrath K, Scheitzer H (eds) Public and private enforcement of competition law in Europe. Springer, Berlin, pp 9–37

Kammin J, Becker F (2013) Cross-border EU competition litigation: qualitative interviews from Germany. In: Danov M, Becker F, Beaumont P (eds) Cross-border EU competition law actions. Hart, Oxford, pp 61–79

Komninos AP (2008) EC private antitrust enforcement: decentralised application of EC competition law by national courts. Hart, Oxford

Lasok KPE (2013) Some procedural aspects and how they could/should be reformed. In: Danov M, Becker F, Beaumont P (eds) Cross-border EU competition law actions. Hart, Oxford, pp 207–214

Lawrence J, Morfey A (2013) Tactical manoeuvres in UK cartel damages litigation. In: Danov M, Becker F, Beaumont P (eds) Cross-border EU competition law actions. Hart, Oxford, pp 149–158

Lidgard HH (2012) Due process in European competition procedure: a fundamental concept or a mere formality? In: Cardonnel P, Rosas A, Wahl N (eds) Constitutionalising the EU judicial system: essays in honour of Pernilla Lindh. Hart, Oxford, pp 403–421

Nazzini R (2012) Administrative enforcement, judicial review and fundamental rights in EU competition law: a comparative contextual-functionalist perspective. Common Mark Law Rev 49:971–1006

Peyer S (2012) Germany – comparative private enforcement and collective redress in the EU. Available via Competition law. Comparative private enforcement & consumer redress in the EU. http://www.clcpecreu.co.uk/pdf/final/Germany%20report.pdf. Accessed 17 June 2015

Reher T (2013) Specific issues in cross-border EU competition law actions brought by multiple claimants in a German context. In: Danov M, Becker F, Beaumont P (eds) Cross-border EU competition law actions. Hart, Oxford, pp 159–165

Rodger B (2012) Competition law: comparative private enforcement & consumer redress in the EU – UK Report. Available via Competition law. Comparative private enforcement & consumer redress in the EU. http://www.clcpecreu.co.uk/pdf/final/UK%20report.pdf. Accessed 17 June 2015

Rodger B (ed) (2014) Competition law: comparative private enforcement and consumer redress in the EU. Kluwer, The Hague

Wils WPJ (2005) Principles of European antitrust enforcement. Hart, Oxford

Wils WPJ (2009) The relationship between public antitrust enforcement and private actions for damages. World Competition 32:3–26

Zuckerman A (1999) Justice in crisis: comparative dimensions of civil procedure. In: Zuckerman A (ed) Civil justice in crisis: comparative perspectives of civil procedure. Oxford University Press, Oxford, pp 3–52

# Part IV
# Contemporary Topics of State Aid Law Enforcement

# The Role of National Courts in the Enforcement of the European State Aid Rules

**Viktor Kreuschitz and Nuria Bermejo**

**Abstract** After the judgment *Deutsche Lufthansa*, the role of national courts in the enforcement of the European State aid rules seems to be difficult to understand. Nevertheless, these difficulties are more theoretical than real. The role of national courts is linked to the direct effect of the standstill clause and to the activity of the Commission. On the basis of this clause, national courts protect individual rights against the premature enforcement of a measure of aid. In doing so, they are bound by the Commission's decision to open the formal investigation procedure showing its doubts concerning the compatibility of the measure that was prematurely enforced. However, when the Commission has adopted no decision, they have to decide on its character of State aid. In addition, national courts have to decide in every case which are the appropriate remedies to offset the negative consequences of unauthorised granting of State aid. As will be seen, these are not limited to the recovery. A proper understanding of the role of national courts in the enforcement of State aid rules helps to answer the strong criticism raised by that judgment, which, in the light of the considerations made in this article, does not seem founded.

## 1 Introductory Remarks

The prior control of State aid is a matter of two actors that develop complementary but separate roles.[1] The first actor is the Commission, which, according to Article 108(1) and (2) TFEU, as interpreted and applied by a well-established case law, has

---

The opinions expressed by the authors are strictly personal.

[1]See Case C-284/12 *Deutsche Lufthansa AG v. Flughafen Frankfurt-Hahn GmbH* ECLI:EU: C:2013:755, para 27, see also Case C-27/13 *Flughafen Lübeck GmbH v Air Berlin plc & Co Luftverkehrs-KG* ECLI:EU:2014:240, para 24.

V. Kreuschitz (✉)
General Court of the European Union, Luxembourg, Luxembourg
e-mail: Viktor.Kreuschitz@curia.europa.eu

N. Bermejo
Faculty of Law, Autonomous University of Madrid, Madrid, Spain
e-mail: nuria.bermejo@uam.es

© Springer-Verlag Berlin Heidelberg 2017
V. Tomljenović et al. (eds.), *EU Competition and State Aid Rules*,
Europeanization and Globalization 3, https://doi.org/10.1007/978-3-662-47962-9_11

exclusive competence in the assessment of the compatibility of the aid.[2] The second actor is the Member State's national judge. Neither the Treaty nor Regulation 659/1999 expressly mentioned the latter, until the amendment introduced by Regulation 734/2013, of 22 July 2013 (see in that regard the new Article 23 (a), entitled 'Cooperation with national courts').[3] Certainly, the role of national courts in the enforcement of State aid was recognised by the ECJ relatively early. However, understanding it clearly does not seem to be easy, especially after the concerns raised by practitioners following the EU court decisions in the cases *Deutsche Lufthansa AG* and *Flughafen Lübeck GmbH*. Concerning the judgment in *Deutsche Lufthansa*, one commentator said:

> Until yesterday's judgment, courts were not bound by Commission decisions opening proceedings and had to make their own assessment. The judgment is surprising as previously, it was understood that such preliminary decisions did not produce legal effects on parties and so, they could not be challenged by parties. In view of the legal effects of opening decisions recognised by yesterday's judgement, we question whether parties should now be able to challenge such decisions.[4]

This article aims to clarify the role of national courts in the enforcement of the European State aid rules in the light of case law in order to address the concerns expressed by practitioners after that judgment. To this end, our contribution will deal with the following questions. First, we focus on the standstill clause as set out in the last sentence of Article 108(3) TFUE, restated in Article 3 of Regulation 1589/2015, which seems to be the basis for the intervention of national courts in the enforcement of European State aid rules. Second, we examine the role played by national courts in the enforcement of the State aid rules and show that this role is closely linked, on the one hand, to the direct effect of the standstill clause and the protection of individual rights and, on the other hand, to the activity of the Commission. As will be shown, on the basis of the direct effect of the standstill clause, national courts protect individual rights against the illegal or unauthorised granting of aid. In doing so, they are bound by the Commission's decision opening the formal investigation procedure. However, when the Commission has adopted no decision, they have to decide whether the measure at issue constitutes State aid (see *infra* Sect. 2). It is in this latter case and when deciding in an examination *ex post* whether a measure is covered by a Block Exemption Regulation (see *infra* Sect. 4) that the role of national courts in the enforcement of the State aid rules is more significant. Third, we examine the remedies that national courts may adopt in order to offset the negative consequences of the unauthorised granting of aid. As we will

---

[2]Ibid, para 28.

[3]Regulation 659/1999 has been replaced by Council Regulation (EU) 2015/1589 laying down detailed rules for the application of Article 108 of the Treaty on the Functioning of the European Union (TFEU) [2015] OJ L 248/9. Cooperation with national courts is now foreseen in Article 29 of that Regulation.

[4]Rivas (2013).

see, they are 'full' remedies—and not simply interim measures—and they can take different forms, not being limited to the recovery of the aid (see *infra* Sect. 3). Fourth, all these considerations provide good arguments to answer the criticism raised by practitioners to the judgment in *Deutsche Lufthansa* (see *infra* Sect. 5).

# 2 National Courts and State Aid Rules

## 2.1 The Starting Point: The Standstill Clause

As is widely known, Article 107(1) TFEU considers any aid granted by a Member State or through State resources that distorts or threatens to distort competition, in so far as it affects trade between Members States, incompatible with the internal market. According to the Treaty, aid considered incompatible with the internal market must be suppressed or modified by the Member States (Article 108 (2), first paragraph, TFEU).

As it may not be wise to leave to Member States the control of their own activities, save as otherwise provided, the Commission is essentially charged with the enforcement of the system, particularly concerning the compatibility of the aid with the internal market (Article 108(1) and (2) TFEU). The reason for this is that Article 107(3) TFEU exclusively allows the approval of State aid in the public interest and the Commission is the body independent of the Member States called upon to be the guardian of the common interests.[5] Hence, pursuant to Article 108 TFEU, the Commission shall monitor all systems of aid existing in the Member States. According to the consistent case law of the ECJ, the finding that aid may be incompatible with the internal market is to be arrived at, subject to review by the Court, by means of an appropriate procedure, which it is the Commission's responsibility to set in motion. Therefore, Articles 107 and 108 TFEU confer on the Commission a principal and exclusive role in regard to establishing the eventual incompatibility of State aid.[6]

At this point, it is useful to recall that, according to this procedure, the Commission has to be informed by the Member States in sufficient time to submit its comments on any plan tending to grant or to alter a measure of aid so as to decide, in a preliminary examination, whether the measure at issue constitutes State aid and, in the case of an affirmative answer, whether it is compatible with the internal market and to authorise it (Article 108(3), first sentence, TFEU, and Article 4(2)–

---

[5]Di Bucci (2008), p. 44. See also in that regard the so-called *Spaak Report*, Comité intergouvernemental créé par la Conférence de Messine, Rapport des Chefs de Délégation aux Ministres des Affaires Etrangères, Bruxelles, 21 avril 1956.

[6]See Case C-354/90 *Fédération nationale du commerce extérieur des produits alimentaires and Syndicat national des négociants et transformateurs de saumon (FNCE) v. French Republic* ECLI: EU:C:1991:440, paras 9 and 14. See also Case C-110/02 *Commission v. Council* ECLI:EU: C:2004:395, para 29; and Case C-234/99 *Niels Nygård* v. *Svineafgiftsfonden* ECLI:EU: C:2002:244, para 62.

(3) of Regulation 2015/1589). Nevertheless, if the Commission has doubts concerning the compatibility of the aid, it has to open the formal investigation procedure provided for in Article 108(2) TFEU, with the purpose of clarifying them (Article 108(3), second sentence, TFEU, and Article 4(4) of Regulation 2015/1589).[7] In order to ensure the effectiveness of these provisions, Article 108(3), last sentence, TFEU, lays down a prohibition to implement any measure of aid before a final decision assessing its compatibility has been adopted. This prohibition, restated in Article 3 of Regulation 2015/1589, is known as the standstill clause and grants the Commission a period free of interference to examine the measure and to decide, without any doubt, on its compatibility with the internal market. In the words of the ECJ, '[. . .] in order to achieve this purpose, the implementation of planned aid is to be deferred until the doubt as to its compatibility is resolved by the Commission's final decision'.[8] In this context, the standstill clause is explained by the ECJ as a mechanism tending '. . .to ensure that a system of aid cannot become operational before the Commission has had a reasonable period in which to study the proposed measures in detail and, if necessary, to initiate the procedure provided for in Article [108(2) TFEU]'.[9]

It follows from Article 108(3), last sentence, TFEU, that the prohibition set out in that provision persists until the procedure 'has resulted in a final decision'. In the light of the rationality of the standstill clause, a 'final decision' is the Commission's decision putting an end to the administrative procedure in any of its possible forms authorising the measure of aid. Therefore, a 'final decision' may be the Commission's decision closing both the preliminary examination and the formal investigation, finding that the measure at issue is not an aid (no aid decision; see Article 4(2) and Article 9(2) of Regulation 2015/1589) or that it is an aid but compatible with the internal market (positive decision) (Article 4(3) and Article 9(3) of Regulation 2015/1589). But a 'final decision' may also be the Commission's decision closing the formal investigation procedure and finding that the aid is not compatible with the internal market (negative decision) (Article 9(5) of Regulation 2015/1589). An interesting question arises when an aid is implemented after a positive decision only to be annulled by the European Union courts at a later date. In this regard, the ECJ has ruled that 'the aid in question is deemed, in accordance with the first paragraph of Article [264 TFUE], not to have been declared compatible by the annulled decision, with the result that its implementation must be regarded as unlawful' and that the annulment of a positive decision '. . .puts a stop, retroactively, to the application of the presumption of lawfulness to the Commission's decision'.[10] Moreover, the ECJ has pointed out that

---

[7]Case C-400/99 *Italy v. Commission* ECLI:EU:C:2005:275, para 47; Case C-47/10 P *Austria v. Commission* ECLI:EU:C:2011:698, para 70; and Case C-131/15 P *Club Hotel Loutraki AE et al v. Commission* ECLI:EU:C:2016:989, paras 30, 32 and 33.

[8]Case C-199/06 *CELF and Ministre de la Culture et de la Communication v. Société internationale de diffusion et d'édition* ('*CELF I*') ECLI:EU:C:2008:79, para 48.

[9]Ibid, para 36; and *Deutsche Lufthansa AG* (n 1) para 40.

[10]*CELF I* (n 8) paras 63–64.

so long as the Commission has not taken a decision approving aid, and so long as the period for bringing an action against such a decision has not expired, the recipient cannot be sure as to the lawfulness of the proposed aid which alone is capable of giving rise to a legitimate expectation on his part.[11]

Consequently, according to the above-mentioned case law, the Commission's decision cannot be considered 'final', within the meaning of Article 108(3), last sentence, TFEU, either until the period for bringing an action against the aforementioned decision has expired or until the European Union courts have completed a review of its legality. In these circumstances, implementing measures adopted having regard to a positive decision cannot stay out of reach of national courts. As the ECJ ruled:

[a]fter the annulment of a positive decision of the Commission, a recipient of unlawfully implemented aid is not precluded from relying on exceptional circumstances on the basis of which it had legitimately assumed the aid to be lawful and thus from declining to refund that [...]. However, [...] in respect of circumstances where the Commission had initially decided not to raise any objections to the aid in issue, [...] such fact could not be regarded as capable of having caused the recipient undertaking to entertain any legitimate expectation since that decision had been challenged in due time before the Court, which annulled it.[12]

As Article 108(3), last sentence, TFEU prohibits the implementation of any measure by Member States until the procedure 'has resulted in a final decision', it makes the approval of the measure of aid by the Commission a decisive element. Thus, according to this clause, aid can only be granted with the prior authorisation or approval of the Commission declaring the measure compatible.[13] A measure enforced in violation of this clause has been considered by the EU courts as invalid,[14] unlawful[15] or illegal,[16] all these adjectives denoting an infringement of the aforementioned clause. The decisive element being the approval of the measure by the Commission, the prohibition included in the standstill clause can be infringed either because the aid was granted without being notified to the Commission[17] or because, despite the notification, it was granted before a final decision approving the aid was adopted and, where appropriate, confirmed by the EU

---

[11]Ibid, para 67.

[12]Ibid, paras 65–66.

[13]Ibid, para 48.

[14]*FNCE* (n 6) para 11; and Joined Cases C-261/01 and C-262/01 *Belgische Staat v. van Calster and Others* ECLI:EU:C:2003:571, para 63.

[15]Case C-39/94 *SFEI and Others v. La Poste and Others* ECLI:EU:C:1996:285, para 67; and Case C-672/13 *OTP Bank Nyrt v. Magyar Állam y Magyar Államkincstár* ECLI:EU:C:2015:185, para 66.

[16]See *van Calster and Others* (n 14) paras 62 and 73.

[17]See Case C-120/73 *Gebrüder Lorenz GmbH v. Federal Republic of Germany and Land Rheinland-Pfalz* ECLI:EU:C:1973:152, para 8. See also *FNCE* (n 8) para 11; and *SFEI* (n 15) para 39. By contrast, Article 107 TFEU is not directly applicable. See Case C-74/76 *Ianelli & Volpi S.p.A. v. Ditta Paolo Meroni* ECLI:EU:C:1977:51, paras 10–12.

courts.[18] Hence, the notification of the measure as such cannot be regarded as an adequate precondition for lawfully granting the aid.

It follows that the unlawful or illegal nature of a measure depends exclusively on facts: if the aid was granted without or prior to approval, it is illegal or unlawful and remains illegal or unlawful forever since these factual elements cannot be changed retroactively. In this regard, it is important to underline that the unlawfulness of the aid, resulting from the infringement of the standstill clause, is independent of the compatibility of the aid. Aid that the Commission cannot approve after a substantial examination pursuant to Article 107(3) TFEU or any other act of secondary legislation or a soft-law instrument is considered to be incompatible aid. As already stated, factual elements underlying the infringement of the standstill clause cannot be changed retrospectively. Thus, as laid down by the case law, the illegality of a measure cannot be affected 'by the fact that the measure has been held to be compatible with the [internal] market by a final decision of the Commission'.[19] More specifically, the ECJ has already held that

> the Commission's final decision does not have the effect of regularizing *ex post facto* implementing measures which were illegal or unlawful because they had been taken in breach of the prohibition laid down in the last sentence of Article [108(3) TFEU], since otherwise the direct effect of that prohibition would be impaired and the interests of individuals, which are to be protected by national courts, would be disregarded.

According to this case law, '[a]ny other interpretation would have the effect of according a favourable outcome to the non-observance of that provision by the Member State concerned and would deprive it of its effectiveness'.[20] For that reason, the consequences of the unlawfulness cannot be linked to the outcome of the examination of the compatibility of the aid. National courts will have to draw all the appropriate conclusions of the infringement of the standstill clause, even when the Commission's final decision considers the unlawful or illegal aid compatible with the internal market. The question is to decide which are the appropriate conclusions in every case (see *infra* Sect. 3.2).

## 2.2 The Direct Effect of the Standstill Clause

The ECJ recognised a direct effect to the standstill clause in its very early case law. Thus, the ECJ ruled in *Costa*, when interpreting the former Article 93 TCEE (now Article 108 TFEU):

---

[18]See the case law cited in nn 10–12.

[19]See *van Calster and Others* (n 14) para 62.

[20]See *FNCE* (n 6) para 16; Case C-368/04 *Transalpine Ölleitung in Österreich* ECLI:EU: C:2006:644 paras 41, 42 and 54; *CELF I* (n 8) para 40; *van Calster and Others* (n 14) para 63; and Case C-667/13 *Estado português v. Banco Privado Português SA and Massa Insolvente do Banco Privado Português SA* ECLI:EU:C:2015:151, para 60.

By so expressly undertaking to inform the Commission 'in sufficient time' of any plans for aid, and by accepting the procedures laid down in Article [108 TFEU], the States have entered into an obligation with the Community, which binds them as States but creates no individual rights except in the case of the final provision of Article [108(3) TFEU], which is not in question in the present case.[21]

This statement was the basis for the recognition of a direct effect to the standstill clause. This direct effect was further developed and concretised in *Lorenz*:

The prohibition on implementation referred to in the last sentence of Article [108](3) has a direct effect and gives rise to rights in favour of individuals, which national courts are bound to safeguard. [. . .]

Thus the direct effect of the prohibition extends to all aid which has been implemented without being notified and, in the event of notification, operates during the preliminary period, and when the Commission sets in motion the contentious procedure, up to the final decision.[22]

This reasoning was based on the idea that the last sentence of former Article 93 (3) TCEE (now Article 108(3) TFEU) establishes procedural criteria that, according to the case law,[23] national courts can appraise.[24] As a result, national courts are called upon to come into play on the enforcement of the European State aid rules. This means that individuals can go before national courts, asking them to enforce the prohibition of implementation of any measure of aid when the State infringes it, granting an aid that could be considered as a State aid. More precisely, at the request of individuals, i.e. competitors being harmed by the unauthorised granting of the aid, national courts must adopt any necessary measure to stop the infringement of the clause and to repair its negative consequences. The extent of this role will be examined in more detail in the following sections.

## 2.3   One Legal Regime, Two Authorities

The direct effect of the standstill clause is the first milestone in the analysis of the role of national courts in the enforcement of State aid rules. As follows from the previous section, the role played by national courts is closely linked to the direct effect of the standstill clause and to the protection of individuals' rights benefiting

---

[21]See Case C-6/64 *Costa v. ENEL* ECLI:EU:C:1964:66.

[22]Case C-120/73 *Lorenz* ECLI:EU:C:1973:152, para 8. This definition is also expressed, among others, in *FNCE* (n 6) para 11; *SFEI* (n 15) para 39; *Deutsche Lufthansa* (n 1) para 29; and Case C-69/13 *Mediaset* ECLI:EU:C:2014:71, para 19.

[23]See Case 77/72 *Carmine Capolongo v. Azienda Agricole Maya* ECLI:EU:C:1973:65, para 6.

[24]Keppenne and Gross (2008), p. 395.

from this direct effect. The involvement of national courts is the result of the direct effect of the prohibition on the implementation of planned measures of aid as laid down in the last sentence of Article 108(3) TFEU. Consequently, the system of control of State aid can be seen as a matter of two actors, that is, the Commission and national courts. As the ECJ has acknowledged, they develop complementary but separate roles.[25] This results in a sort of decentralised enforcement of State aid rules. The Commission is the principal actor and, as mentioned above, according to Article 108(1) and (2) TFEU, has exclusive competence in the assessment of the compatibility of the aid measures with the internal market.[26] By contrast, it is for the national courts to ensure that the rights of individuals are safeguarded where the obligation to give prior notification of State aids to the Commission pursuant to Article 108(3) TFEU is infringed.[27] In this respect, the ECJ has denied the Commission's power to declare aid illegal solely on the ground that the obligation to notify had not been complied with and without having to investigate whether the aid was compatible with the internal market.[28]

It follows from the above that individuals cannot challenge, on the basis of Article 107 TFEU alone, the compatibility of a measure with the internal market before national courts or ask them to decide on the compatibility of the measure, which has to be qualified as State aid. As laid down by the case law, in proceedings before national courts, individuals can merely propose, under certain circumstances, that a request for a preliminary ruling be addressed to the ECJ aimed at establishing whether a Commission decision concerning State aid is valid and whether the measure constitutes State aid.[29] As the General Court ruled:

> [s]ince the power to hold a [EU] measure invalid, if it is raised before a national court, is reserved for the Court of Justice, a national court which considers the decision invalid is required to refer a question to the Court of Justice for a preliminary ruling under Article [267] of the Treaty.[30]

---

[25]See *FNCE* (n 6) para 8; *SFEI* (n 15) para 41; *Deutsche Lufthansa* (n 1) paras 27 and 28; Case C-590/14 P *Dimosia Epicheirisi Ilektrismou AE (DEI) v. Alouminion tus Elladis VEAE and Commission* ECLI:EU:C:2016:797, paras 95 and 96; and Case C-574/14 *PGE Górnictwo i Energetyka Konwencjonalna SA and Prezes Urzędu Regulacji Energetyki* ECLI:EU:C:2016:686, paras 30–31.

[26]Case C-119/05 *Lucchini* ECLI:EU:C:2007:434, paras 51–52; *Deutsche Lufthansa* (n 1) para 28; *DEI* (n 25) para 96; and *PGE Górnictwo* (n 25) para 31.

[27]See, to that effect, Joined Cases *van Calster and Others* (n 14) para 75; Case C-295/97 *Piaggio* ECLI:EU:C:1999:313, para 31; and *Transalpine Ölleitung in Österreich* (n 20) para 38.

[28]*FNCE* (n 6) para 13, referring to Case C-301/87 *France v. Commission* ECLI:EU:C:1990:67; and Case C-142/87 *Belgium v. Commission* ECLI:EU:C:1990:125.

[29]Case C-188/92 *TWD Textilwerke Deggendorf v. Germany* ECLI:EU:C:1994:90, paras 17, 18 and 24. The time-limit laid down to challenge the decision must not have expired.

[30]Case T-188/95 *Waterleiding Maatschappij 'Noord-West Brabant' NV v. Commission* ECLI:EU: T:1998:217, para 147, citing Case C-314/85 *Foto-Frost v Hauptzollamt Lübeck-Ost* ECLI:EU: C:1987:452, paras 14–17.

At first sight, it may seem that national courts develop a kind of secondary or ancillary role.[31] However, this role is only apparently secondary. On the one hand, in quantitative terms, there has been a remarkably large increase in the number of State aid cases examined by national courts, the largest number of them in France, Italy and Germany, followed by the Netherlands, Spain, Sweden and Austria.[32] On the other hand, in qualitative terms, despite the preponderant role played by the Commission in assessing the compatibility of the aid, national courts may have to decide, under certain circumstances, whether a measure can be considered an aid, according to Article 107(1) TFEU. It might be considered that, at least in these specific circumstances, they carry out a task similar to that of the Commission, applying the provisions of this article to the measure at issue. In particular, this is the case when an individual—i.e., a competitor—brings before them an action asking for relief against an unlawful measure, on which the Commission has not taken a position on the basis of Article 107(1) TFEU. In contrast, where the Commission has adopted a decision to open the formal investigation procedure, national courts will be bound by this decision, which enumerates the Commission's doubts concerning the character of State aid of the measure at issue, i.e. the nature of aid and its compatibility with the internal market.[33]

In the light of the above, national courts can face two different situations when they examine a measure of aid illegally granted: first, when the Commission has adopted a decision to open the formal investigation procedure, in which case they are bound by that decision, and, second, when the Commission has not yet adopted this decision, in which case they have to make an assessment of whether the measures constitute aid themselves. These two situations, which are examined below, must be taken into account for a clear understanding of the role of national courts in the enforcement of European State aid rules.

**The Commission Has Adopted a Decision to Open the Formal Investigation Procedure** According to the case law, the Commission's decision to open the formal investigation, adopted on the basis of Article 4(4) of Regulation 2015/1589, has binding effect on national courts. More precisely, the ECJ has ruled that once the Commission has adopted a position about the measure of aid in its decision to open the formal investigation procedure, national courts have merely to consider the measures to be taken and adopt all those necessary with a view to drawing the appropriate consequences of the infringement of the notification obligation. The ECJ considered that even if in its final decision the Commission were to conclude

---

[31]Keppenne and Gross (2008), pp. 394–396.

[32]'The 2006 Study on the Enforcement of State Aid Rules at National Level' (update 2009) p 2 http://ec.europa.eu/competition/state_aid/studies_reports/enforcement_study_2009.pdf.

[33]With regard to the Commission's doubts concerning the character of State aid and the decision to open the formal investigation procedure, see *Italy v. Commission* (n 7) para 47; *Austria v. Commission* (n 7) para 70; and *Club Hotel Loutraki AE et alt v. Commission* (n 7) paras 30, 32 and 33.

that there were no aid elements, the preventive aim of the State aid control system established by the TFEU requires that

> following the doubt raised in the decision to initiate the formal examination procedure as to the character of that aid measure and its compatibility with the internal market, its implementation should be deferred until that doubt is resolved by the Commission's final decision.[34]

Thus, as the ECJ pointed out, the fact that the assessments carried out in this decision are preliminary in nature does not deprive the decision of legal effects.[35]

In this context, national courts examining this measure of aid and having the Commission's decision to open the formal investigation procedure in their hands do not need to answer the question of whether the measure constitutes State aid. The Commission has already provisionally answered this question in its decision, by making a preliminary assessment of the character of aid of the measure and demonstrating its doubts about the compatibility of this measure with the internal market. Certainly, the Commission's preliminary assessment is not definitive, and it is open to further clarification in cooperation with the Member State concerned and eventually with interested parties. However, it 'fills' the first part of national courts' reasoning in the enforcement of the standstill clause, as long as it shows the Commission's doubts about the measure. Therefore, the adoption of this decision is sufficient to consider the aid unlawful or illegal because the aid should not have been enforced until the Commission adopted a final decision clarifying all doubts and authorising the aid.

The approach followed by the ECJ in *Deutsche Lufthansa* is reasonable. In this regard, it is important to note, as laid down by the judgment, that

> the application of the EU rules on State aid is based on an obligation of sincere cooperation, set out in Article 4(3) TEU, between the Member States and their national courts, on the one hand, and the Commission and the Courts of the European Union on the other, in the context of which each acts on the basis of the role assigned to it by the Treaty.[36]

It must also be recalled that the Commission has exclusive competence to decide about the compatibility of a measure of aid with the internal market. Since the Commission, by adopting the decision to open the formal investigation procedure, has already made a preliminary assessment of the character of State aid, national courts must refrain from adopting any conflicting decision, which limits their capacity of judgement.[37] This is tantamount to saying that national courts are bound by the Commission's decision to open the formal investigation procedure

---

[34]*Deutsche Lufthansa* (n 1) para 40.

[35]Ibid, paras 36, 37, 40 and 42; and Case C-27/13 *Flughafen Lübeck GmbH v. Air Berlin plc & Co. Luftverkehrs-KG* ECLI:EU:C:2014:240, paras 20–23.

[36]*Deutsche Lufthansa* (n 1) para 41. Article 4(3) TEU sets out the principle of sincere cooperation: 'Pursuant to the principle of sincere cooperation, the Union and the Member States shall, in full mutual respect, assist each other in carrying out tasks which flow from the Treaties'. More recently, see also *PGE Górnictwo* (n 25) para 33.

[37]Keppenne and Gross (2008), pp. 397–398.

and they cannot conclude that, despite the Commission's doubts, the measure at issue is not an aid. As the ECJ ruled, 'in the context of that cooperation, national courts must take all the necessary measures, whether general or specific, to ensure fulfilment of the obligations under EU law and refrain from those which may jeopardize the attainment of the objectives of the Treaty'. In particular, 'they must refrain from taking decisions which conflict with a Commission decision, even if it is provisional'.[38] In any case, when national courts disagree with the Commission's assessment in the decision to open the formal investigation procedure, they can refer a preliminary question to the Court of Justice for a preliminary ruling in order to determine the validity of the decision.[39]

As national courts are bound by the Commission's decision to open the formal investigation procedure and they cannot develop an autonomous analysis of the nature of the measure, their role in the enforcement of the State aid rules in these cases can be rightly considered secondary or ancillary. This consideration must also be extended to their role in recovering the aid considered incompatible with the internal market.

**The Commission Has Not Adopted a Decision Concerning the Aid** When the measure at issue has not been notified to the Commission or, if notified, the Commission has not yet adopted a decision to open the formal investigation procedure— i.e., because the investigation is in a preliminary phase—there is no 'filling' element for the courts attempting to enforce the standstill clause. Thus, it falls to the national courts to anticipate the analysis in order to decide whether the standstill clause was infringed. This means that national courts have to decide whether the measure at issue constitutes State aid within the meaning of Article 107(1) TFEU in order to determine whether it has been implemented without the approval of the Commission.[40] Here, national courts are in unchartered territory,[41] where they will have to appreciate facts and law, even if they cannot take a definitive decision either on the character of aid or on the compatibility of the measure. In effect, national courts, in order to be able to use the powers conferred on them, will have to fulfil complex tasks that may sometimes involve economic considerations (i.e., the application of the market investor test or the *Altmark* criteria).[42] According to the case law, they 'may have cause to interpret the concept of aid contained in Article 107 (1) TFEU in order to determine whether a measure has been introduced in disregard of Article 108(3) TFEU'.[43] Thus, as the ECJ ruled that

---

[38] *Deutsche Lufthansa* (n 1) para 41; *Flughafen Lübeck GmbH* (n 35) para 24; *DEI* (n 25) para 100; and *PGE Górnictwo* (n 25) para 33.

[39] *Deutsche Lufthansa* (n 1) para 44. See also Case C-222/04 *Cassa di Risparmio di Firenze et al* ECLI:EU:C:2006:8, paras 72–74.

[40] See *FNCE* (n 6) para 10; *Lucchini* (n 26) para 50; and *Deutsche Lufthansa* (n 1) paras 34–35.

[41] Keppenne and Gross (2008), p. 398.

[42] 'The 2006 Study on the Enforcement of State Aid Rules at National Level' (n 32) pp. 3–4.

[43] Case 78/76 *Steinike & Weinlig v. Federal Republic of Germany* ECLI:EU:C:1977:52, para 14; *SFEI* (n 15) para 49; Case C-345/02 *Pearle and Others* ECLI:EU:C:2004:448, para 31; and *Transalpine Ölleitung in Österreich* (n 20) para 39. See also *FNCE* (n 6) para 10.

it is for these courts to verify, *inter alia*, whether the measure at issue constitutes an advantage and whether it is selective, that is to say whether it favours certain undertakings or certain producers within the meaning of Article 107(1) TFEU.[44]

After having decided that the measure constitutes aid within the meaning of Article 107(1) TFEU, national courts have also to determine the exact time of the granting of the aid in order to be able to decide whether it was granted in breach of Article 108(3) TFEU. In this regard, it must be noted that the decisive moment is not that of payment or transfer of the advantage but the granting in terms of taking a definitive decision that binds the Member State and assumes an unconditional commitment.[45] A further important decision to be taken by the court is on the categorisation of whether the measure is a new aid or an existing aid.[46] Finally, national courts have to examine whether the aid is covered by a block exemption regulation, in which case there is no infringement of the last sentence of Article 108(3) TFEU, since the purpose of such a regulation is to authorize aid in general terms.[47]

The fulfilment of these tasks by national courts may raise some difficulties. On the one hand, national courts lack experience in the application of Article 107 (1) TFEU—or, at least, they have much less experience than the Commission—which makes the complex task of interpreting Article 107(1) TFEU difficult. In particular, national courts often lack the appropriate means to establish the factual information necessary for their decision, which, as was already mentioned, may involve complex economic considerations.[48] On the other hand, the application of these provisions by different courts, in different countries, can lead to inconsistency at Union level. In order to minimise these problems, two mechanisms have come into force; the first is foreseen in Article 29 of Regulation 2015/1589, and the second is the well-established preliminary reference procedure set out in Article 267 TFEU. However, recently a third mechanism came into play when the Commission adopted the Notice on the Notion of State Aid as referred to in Article 107 (1) TFUE, aiming to facilitate the application of this rule.[49]

*Article 29 of Regulation 2015/1598* This provision formalises the Commission's willingness to assist national courts in applying the definition of State aid and requires them to cooperate with the Commission in the investigation of the case.[50]

---

[44]*Transalpine Ölleitung in Österreich* (n 20) para 39; and *Deutsche Lufthansa* (n 1) paras 34–35.

[45]Case C-426/15 P *Diputación Foral de Bizkaia* ECLI:EU:C:2016:757, para 37; and Case C-76/15 *Vervloet et al* ECLI:EU:C:2016:975, paras 122–125.

[46]See in this regard Case C-312/90 *Spain v. Commission* ECLI:EU:C:1992:282, paras 15–17; Case C-47/91 *Italy v. Commission* ECLI:EU:C:1994:358, paras 24–26; Case C-44/93 *Namur-Les Assurances du Crédit SA* ECLI:EU:C:1994:311, paras 30–33; and Case C-6/12 *P Oy* ECLI:EU: C:2013:525, paras 41–43.

[47]Keppenne and Gross (2008), pp. 398–399.

[48]'The 2006 Study on the Enforcement of State Aid Rules at National Level' (n 32) p. 4.

[49]Commission Notice on the Notion of State Aid as Referred to in Article 107(1) of the Treaty on the Functioning of the European Union [2016] OJ C262/1.

[50]Concerning this 'willingness', in the previous regime, see Meij (2007), p. 7.

This article sets a mechanism of cooperation concerning both the appreciation of facts and the application of law, namely Article 107(1) TFEU.[51] According to this article, national courts can ask the Commission to send the relevant information in its possession or give its opinion on the case (Article 29(1) of Regulation 2015/1589).[52] The Commission, in turn, can ask to intervene before national courts as *amicus curiae*, submitting written or oral observations to the national courts (Article 29(2) of Regulation 2015/1589).[53] It can also ask the court dealing with the case to transmit all relevant documents for the investigation at its disposal (Article 29(2), final paragraph, of Regulation 2015/1589).[54]

*Preliminary Reference*  When the interpretation of EU law and, more precisely, of Articles 107(1) and 108(3) TFEU seems problematic, national courts have at their disposal the preliminary reference procedure.[55] Under the conditions of Article 267 TFEU, national courts can refer a preliminary reference to the ECJ in order to clarify the interpretation of EU law provisions concerning a relevant question to the case at issue.[56] The practice shows that national courts may request a preliminary reference from the ECJ even after having asked for the Commission's opinion on the case, with which they disagreed.[57] This makes sense, as long as, according to the case law, even if they are not bound by the Commission's position, they must take them into account 'as a factor of assessment' when adopting their decision.[58]

**The Notice on the Notion of State Aid**  In addition to the aforementioned instruments, the Commission has recently adopted the Notice on the Notion of State Aid as referred to in Article 107(1) TFEU, with the purpose of contributing to 'an easier, more transparent and more consistent application of the notion of State aid as referred to in Article 107(1) TFEU', which both the Commission and national courts have to apply across the Union.[59] For sure, this Notice will help national courts to deal with the notion of 'State aid' when enforcing the standstill clause. Even if this notice does not provide answers to all the different issues raised by the application of Article 107(1) TFUE, it still appears valuable and useful.

---

[51]See *SFEI* (n 15) paras 50 and 53, based on the Commission Notice on Cooperation between National Courts and the Commission in the State Aid Field [1995] OJ C312/8, replaced by the Commission Notice on the Enforcement of State Aid Law by National Courts [2009] OJ C85/01.

[52]See also Section 3 of Commission Notice on the Enforcement of State Aid Law by National Courts (n 51), recitals 77–98.

[53]However, until 2009, cases where the Commission intervened as *amicus curiae* in national proceedings were still rare. 'The 2006 Study on the Enforcement of State Aid Rules at National Level' (n 32) p. 3.

[54]Nehl (2014), p. 248.

[55]Meij (2007), p. 7.

[56]*Deutsche Lufthansa* (n 1) para 44; and *PGE Górnictwo* (n 25) para 40.

[57]Nehl (2014), p. 248.

[58]*Mediaset* (n 22) paras 28–31.

[59]Commission Notice on the Notion of State Aid as Referred to in Article 107(1) of the Treaty on the Functioning of the European Union [2016] OJ C262/1, recitals 1 and 2.

As national courts have to interpret and apply Article 107(1) TFEU when deciding on the aid character of the measure, their role in the enforcement of the State aid rules cannot be considered secondary or ancillary, but substantial and significant. Moreover, access to national courts can be seen by individuals—i.e., mainly competitors—as an instrument to react directly and immediately against the implementation of measures that have to be considered as State aid granted without prior approval. In these cases, the competitor does not need to complain to the Commission and wait until it decides to open the procedure under Article 108(2) TFEU and adopt a negative decision. The complainant can submit an application to national courts invoking the aid character of the measure and asking them to adopt all the necessary measures to remedy the breach of the standstill clause. In fact, available data show that there has been an increasing number of cases where competitors have claimed the recovery of unlawfully granted State aid or the adoption of injunctive measures to prevent or suspend the granting of unlawful aid.[60] However, it must be pointed out that national courts' decisions are adopted with the specific purpose of applying the standstill clause and putting an end to the breach of procedural rules. Therefore, they cannot bind the Commission in its wider analysis of the compatibility of the aid.[61]

Finally, it must be pointed out that, according to the case law, Article 108 (3) TFEU

> may be relied upon by individuals only if the national measures in question constitute State aid within the meaning of article 107(1) TFEU and if the procedure for review provided for in Article 108(3) TFEU has not been complied with.[62] Where it is apparent from the facts of the case that the procedural rules provided for in Article 108(3) were followed, it is in any event unnecessary to inquire into the nature of the national measure concerned.[63]

# 3   Remedies Against the Infringement

## 3.1   Obligation to Remedy the Consequences of the Infringement

National courts do not comply with their tasks by simply declaring that the enforcement of the measure breached the standstill clause. They must ensure that all the appropriate conclusions will be drawn from the infringement.[64] In this context, it

---

[60]'The 2006 Study on the Enforcement of State Aid Rules at National Level' (n 32) p. 4.

[61]*Deutsche Lufthansa* (n 1) paras 14–16.

[62]*Steinike and Weinlig v Federal Republic of Germany* (n 43) para 14.

[63]Joined Cases C-91/83 and C-127/83 *Heineken Brouwerijen* ECLI:EU:C:1984:307, para 11.

[64]*CELF I* (n 8) para 41; *SFEI* (n 15) para 40; *Deutsche Lufthansa* (n 1) para 42; *Flughafen Lübeck* (n 35) para 25; and *DEI* (n 25) para 100. The ECJ ruled that such an obligation exists when 'there is no doubt regarding the classification as State aid'. See Case C-1/09 *Centre d'exportation du livre*

should be recalled that the Commission's final decision does not have the effect of regularising, retrospectively, State measures that were invalid or unlawful because they had been taken in disregard of the standstill clause.[65] As the ECJ ruled, due to the unlawfulness of granting aid, operators other than the recipient of such aid—i.e., competitors—suffer earlier than they would have had to from the effects of compatible aid.[66] Thus, as the ECJ has repeatedly stated, national courts have to remedy the consequences of the infringement in order to avoid the unlawful aid remaining at the free disposal of the beneficiary before the Commission has adopted a final decision.[67] Moreover, as the ECJ stressed, national courts have to grant relief to the individuals suffering the consequences of the breach of the first sentence of Article 108(1) TFEU. Therefore, national courts are not allowed to merely stay the proceedings until the final decision is adopted.[68]

In view of the above, national courts have to develop concrete activity to remedy the consequences of the illegal granting of aid. On this point, the ECJ ruled that national courts must adjudicate both on the validity of the measures giving effect to the aid and on the recovery of the aid granted.[69] These remedies are the most intense, from the point of view of their effects, because they tend to remove the unlawful measure of aid from the market from both legal and factual points of view. For this reason, the ECJ ruled that having regard to the importance of the proper functioning of the internal market of compliance with the procedure for prior review of planned State aid, national courts must, in principle, order the recovery in accordance with the procedural rules of domestic law.[70] However, this consideration has to be immediately nuanced. Firstly, as the ECJ has acknowledged, there may be exceptional circumstances in which it would be inappropriate to recover the aid.

The reference to 'exceptional circumstances' was introduced in the case law, starting with *Commission v. Germany*[71] and *SFEI and Others*[72] and further developed in *CELF I*. In this case, the ECJ ruled that a recipient of illegally granted aid is not precluded from relying on exceptional circumstances on the basis of which it had legitimately assumed the aid to be lawful and thus declined to refund that aid.[73]

---

*français and Ministre de la Culture et de la Communication v. Société internationale de diffusion et d'édition (SIDE)* ('*CELF II*') ECLI:EU:C:2010:136, para 36.

[65] See n 22.

[66] *CELF I* (n 8) para 50.

[67] *CELF II* (n 64) para 30; and *Deutsche Lufthansa* (n 1) para 31.

[68] See *SFEI* (n 15) para 40; and *CELF II* (n 64) para 32.

[69] *FNCE* (n 6) para 12; *CELF I* (n 8) para 45; C-390/98 *HJ Banks & Co Ltd v. The Coal Authority and Secretary of State for Trade and Industry* ECLI:EU:C:2001:456, paras 73–74; and *Deutsche Lufthansa* (n 1) para 30. With respect to the validity, see also Case C-275/10 *Residex Capital IV CV and Gemeente Rotterdam* ECLI:EU:C:2011:814, paras 31, 33, 34 and 44–48.

[70] *SFEI* (n 15) paras 68 and 70; Case C-71/04 *Administración del Estado v. Xunta de Galicia* ECLI:EU:C:2005:493, para 49; and *Transalpine Ölleitung in Österreich* (n 20) para 45.

[71] Case C-5/89 *Commission v. Germany* ECLI:EU:C:1990:320, para 16.

[72] *SFEI* (n 15) para 70. These 'exceptional circumstances' were also examined by Advocate General Jacbos in his opinion in *SFEI* (n 15) paras 74–76.

[73] *CELF I* (n 8) paras 42 and 43. See also *Residex Capital IV* (n 69) para 35; and *OTP Bank Nyrt* (n 15) para 72.

The ECJ also recalled that 'if such a case is brought before a national court, it is for that court to assess the circumstances of the case, if necessary after obtaining a preliminary ruling on interpretation from the ECJ'.[74] Then the ECJ pointed out one specific case in which recovery is not required, since 1999 foreseen in the Procedural Regulation—see, in that regard, Article 14(1) of Regulation 659/1999 and Article 16(1) of Regulation 2015/1589—according to which '[t]he Commission shall not require recovery of the aid if this would be contrary to a general principle of Community law'.[75] However, the Court noted as well that the circumstances, where the Commission had initially decided not to raise any objections to the aid at issue, 'could not be regarded as capable of having caused the recipient undertaking to entertain any legitimate expectation, if that decision had been challenged in due time before a European Union Court'.[76] In *CELF II*, the ECJ underlined, when considering the conditions to adopt safeguard measures against illegally granted aid and order its recovery, '...that no exceptional circumstances have been found which would make recovery inappropriate'.[77] To date, the case law does not provide examples illustrating the meaning of 'exceptional circumstances'. Only in *HJ Banks & Co Ltd* did the ECJ decide differently due to the particular circumstances of the case.[78]

Secondly, the recovery of aid is not the only means of guaranteeing the effectiveness of the standstill clause. National courts may suspend the implementation of the measure.[79] They may also order the aid recipient to pay interest in respect of the period of unlawfulness, i.e., from the date of granting until the date of the positive decision of the Commission. As an alternative to the recovery, national courts may order the placement of funds on a blocked account.[80] Moreover, national courts may—independently of any obligation to recover the aid—order the State to compensate for damages if such applications are brought in the national courts by competitors that incur a loss or damage as a result of the unlawful granting of aid.[81] For the purposes of calculating the sums to be paid by the recipient, the obligation to remedy the consequences of the unlawful granting of aid extends also, save for exceptional circumstances, to the period between a Commission decision declaring the aid to be compatible with the internal market and the annulment of that decision by EU courts. Consequently, national courts have at their disposal a large range of remedies—according to the case law, all the possible remedies

---

[74]*CELF I* (n 8) para 43.

[75]Ibid, para 44.

[76]Ibid, para 66.

[77]*CELF II* (n 64) para 36.

[78]*HJ Banks & Co Ltd* (n 69) paras 77–79.

[79]*SFEI* (n 15) para 69; *Deutsche Lufthansa* (n 1) para 43; and *Flughafen Lübeck* (n 35) para 26.

[80]*CELF II* (n 64) para 36.

[81]*CELF I* (n 8) para 52–53; *SFEI* (n 15) para 75; and *Transalpine Ölleitung in Österreich* (n 20) para 56.

foreseen by national procedural rules—to remove the consequences of the illegality and to repair the damages occurred.

However, in contrast to the aforementioned case law, in three recent cases, the ECJ seems to exclude such alternative remedies and orders recovery as the only method of guaranteeing the effectiveness of the standstill clause of Article 108 (3) TFEU, probably due to some specificities of these cases.[82] Therefore, these judgments should not be read as limiting the range of remedies that national courts have at their disposal to redress the consequences of illegal aid.

In order to see how these remedies can interplay, it is useful to distinguish between the cases in which the aid has not been fully implemented and the cases in which the aid was fully implemented.

*Not Fully Implemented State Aid Measures* In these cases, national courts may suspend any new payment and recover the payments already made to the beneficiary.[83] According to the case law:

> a finding that aid has been granted in breach of the last sentence of Article 108(3) TFEU must in principle lead to its repayment in accordance with the procedural rules of domestic law. Any other interpretation would encourage Member States to disregard the prohibition laid down in [the aforementioned Article].[84]

In fact, as the ECJ pointed out, 'if national courts could only order suspension of any new payment, aid already granted would subsist until the Commission's final decision finding the aid incompatible with the common market and ordering its repayment'.[85] According to Article 16(2) of Regulation 2015/1589, the part of the aid recovered will include interests from the date on which it was at the disposal of the beneficiary until the date of recovery. Alternative remedies to the recovery— i.e., the placement of the funds on a blocked account—seem possible. However, as already mentioned, there may be exceptional circumstances in which it would be inappropriate to order repayment of the aid.[86] That said, the recovery of the part of the aid already granted is independent of the right of the State to reinstate the aid once the Commission declares it compatible with the internal market. After the approval of the aid by the Commission, which declares the aid compatible with the internal market, there is no reason to uphold the measures resulting from the infringement of the standstill clause.

The fact that the aid has not been fully implemented does not exclude the State from being subject to the payment of compensation for the damages or losses incurred as a result of the unlawful implementation of the aid. Moreover, as will

---

[82]These cases are *OTP Bank Nyrt* (n 15) paras 69–72; Case C-690/13 *Trapeza Eurobank Ergasias AE v. Agrotiki Trapeza tis Ellados AE (ATE) and Pavlos Sidiropoulos* ECLI:EU:C:2015:235, paras 51–53; and *DEI* (n 25) para 100.

[83]*Deutsche Lufthansa* (n 1) para 43; and *Flughafen Lübeck* (n 35) para 26.

[84]*SFEI* (n 15) paras 68 and 69; and *OTP Bank Nyrt* (n 15) para 76. In this sense, see also *FNCE* (n 6) paras 12 and 16.

[85]*SFEI* (n 15) para 69.

[86]Ibid, para 70.

be seen, national courts can adopt *interim measures*—i.e., suspend the implementation of the measure or recover the sums granted as an aid and consign them—until the judgment is delivered (see *infra* Sect. 3.2).

*Fully Implemented Measures* In all circumstances, national courts must order the payment of interest by the beneficiary for the period of unlawfulness.[87] This is the minimum and necessary remedy that national courts must apply to redress the negative consequences of unlawful aid. In particular, recovery from the beneficiary may be unnecessary when the Commission's final decision considers an unlawful aid compatible with the internal market. In this case, even in the absence of exceptional circumstances, EU law does not impose on the Member State the full recovery of the aid. The payment of interests, equivalent to the interest of sums borrowed on the market for the period of the illegal possession of aid, can offset the negative consequences for competitors of the unauthorised granting of aid.[88]

Likewise, national courts may order the recovery of the sums granted to the beneficiary as an aid.[89] According to Article 16(2) of Regulation 2015/1589, the aid recovered will include interests from the date on which it was at the disposal of the beneficiary until the date of recovery. The recovery of the aid with interests is considered particularly justified when the aid may be afterwards considered incompatible with the internal market in a negative decision. In this case:

> [i]t is in no way established that an undertaking which has unlawfully received State aid could, were it not for that aid, have obtained an equivalent amount by way of loan from a financial institution under normal market conditions and thus have that amount at its disposal prior to the Commission decision.[90]

In this context, the ECJ also ruled that within the framework of domestic law, it may seem appropriate to order the recovery of the unlawful aid, plus interest, when after the Commission has declared the aid compatible with the internal market, the Member State intends to grant that aid again subsequently.[91] According to the ECJ:

> a measure which consisted only in an obligation of recovery without interest would not be appropriate, as a rule, to remedy the consequences of the unlawfulness if the Member State were to re-implement that aid after the Commission's final positive decision. Since the period between the recovery and the reimplementation would be shorter than that between the initial implementation and the final decision, the aid recipient, would bear, if it had to borrow the amount repaid, less interest than it would have paid if, from the outset, it had to borrow the equivalent of the unlawfully granted aid.[92]

---

[87]*CELF I* (n 8) paras 50–53 and 55.

[88]Ibid, paras 46, 52 and 55.

[89]*SFEI* (n 15) paras 68 and 70; and *CELF II* (n 64) para 37.

[90]*CELF II* (n 64) paras 37 and 38.

[91]*CELF I* (n 8) paras 54 and 55.

[92]*CELF I* (n 8) para 54. However, critics, Keppenne and Gross (2008), pp. 404–407.

Nevertheless, as already mentioned, the recovery of the aid shall not be required 'if it would be contrary to a general principle of [Union] law'.[93] As an alternative, the ECJ ruled that national courts may

> order the placement of the funds on a blocked account so that they do not remain at the disposal of the recipient, without prejudice to the payment of interest for the period between the expected implementation of the aid and its placement on that blocked account.[94]

In any case, the recovery and the interest to be paid by the beneficiary do not have a punitive character.

In addition, national courts may order compensation for damages to be paid for the period of unlawfulness.[95] As will be seen, in these cases, they can also adopt *interim measures* (see *infra* Sect. 3.2).

## 3.2 Remedies and Interim Measures

It must be stressed that remedies are not interim measures. For a clear understanding of the role of national courts in the enforcement of State aid rules, both categories have to be distinguished. The remedies to be adopted by national courts do not aim to prevent any harm, but they have a permanent, not simply provisional, character and represent a definitive reaction against an infringement. Once the standstill clause has been breached, national courts must prefer definitive remedies as compared to provisional or interim measures and choose among the definitive remedies the most appropriate in the particular circumstances of the case, in terms of the reasons developed in point 3.1 above. National courts may even adopt them once the Commission has decided that the unlawful measure is compatible with the internal market. This was confirmed by the ECJ, which ruled that the role of national courts set out in the last sentence of Article 108(3) TFEU 'goes beyond that of a judge ruling on an application for interim relief' and corresponds to the duty imposed on national courts to provide protection in such a case against the consequences of the unlawful granting of aid.[96]

As remedies are not interim measures, there is no need to fulfil the criteria of Article 13(2) of Regulation 2015/1589, for provisional recovery, or the criteria for interim measures set by the national procedural rules. Taking the contrary view would make it more difficult for national courts to adopt effective remedies against the infringement of the standstill clause and, consequently, to protect individuals against the distortion of competition caused by an illegally granted aid.

---

[93]*CELF I* (n 8) para 44.

[94]*CELF II* (n 64) para 37, which was inspired by recitals 61 and 62 of the Commission Notice on the Enforcement of State Aid Law by National Courts (n 51).

[95]*CELF I* (n 8) para 55; and *Transalpine Ölleitung in Österreich* (n 20) para 56.

[96]*SFEI* (n 15) para 67.

However, these considerations do not mean that national courts cannot adopt interim measures. When national courts are examining an illegally granted aid, they may order provisional or interim measures if they consider this necessary.[97] According to the ECJ, this will be the case when it is likely that some time will elapse before the national court gives its final judgment on the unlawful grant of State aid. Under these circumstances, it is for the national court to decide whether it is necessary to order interim relief such as the suspension of the measures at issue in order to safeguard the interest of the parties.[98] In particular, national courts may provisionally suspend the granting of aid after having consulted the Commission or refer a case to the ECJ for a preliminary ruling concerning the nature of the measure.[99] Recently, the ECJ ruled that national courts may adopt interim measures in order to respect the principle of *res judicata* and avoid ruling on the validity of contracts already decided by civil law courts until the Commission adopts a final decision closing the examination of measures granting aid by way of civil law contracts. At the same time the ECJ underlined that, when a breach of the third sentence of Article 108(3) TFEU is claimed, the force of res judicata extends only to the legal claims on which the national court has ruled and therefore does not preclude a court from ruling, in a later dispute, on points of law on which there is no ruling in that definitive decision.[100]

Nevertheless, when national proceedings run in parallel to a Commission investigation, certain national courts are most likely to adopt interim remedies on the basis of the Commission Notice on the Enforcement of State Aid Law by National Courts.[101] In this way, national courts can link their decisions drawing the consequences from the infringement of the standstill clause to the Commission's final decision, imposing interim measures in the meantime. From a formal point of view, this solution seems appropriate, but from a substantive point of view, it raises doubts. Once the standstill clause has been infringed, national courts, at the request of individuals, must react against the infringement, preferring 'final remedies' to 'interim remedies' to address the consequences of illegality. When adopting their decisions, national courts can benefit from the mechanism of cooperation set in Article 29 of Regulation 2015/1589, concerning both the appreciation of facts and the interpretation of Article 107(1) TFEU.

> Interim measures that national courts can adopt should not be confused with the injunctions
> foreseen in Article 13 of Regulation 2015/1589. The latter enable the Commission to adopt
> interim measures (injunctions) during the administrative procedure under Article 108

---

[97]*FNCE* (n 6) para 12; and *SFEI* (n 15) paras 52–53. More recently, see also *Deutsche Lufthansa* (n 1) para 43; *Flughafen Lübeck* (n 35) para 26; and *DEI* (n 27) para 101.

[98]*SFEI* (n 15) para 52; and *Transalpine Ölleitung in Österreich* (n 20) para 46.

[99]*SFEI* (n 15) para 53; and *DEI* (n 25) para 101. Concerning the adoption of interim measures by national courts in other areas, see Joined Cases C-143/88 and C-92/89 *Zuckerfabrik Süderdithmarschen AG v. Hauptzollamt Itzehoe and Zuckerfabrik Soest GmbH v. Hauptzollamt Paderborn* ECLI:EU:C:1991:65, paras 28–29. See also Commission Notice on the Enforcement of State Aid Law by National Courts (n 51) recital 60.

[100]Case C-505/14 *Klausner Holz Niedersachsen* ECLI:EU:C:2015:742, para 35 and 36.

[101]Commission Notice on the Enforcement of State Aid Law by National Courts (n 51) recital 62.

(2) TFEU.[102] Pursuant to Article 13(1) of the aforementioned Procedural Regulation, the Commission may, after giving the Member State concerned the opportunity to submit its comments, adopt a decision requiring the Member State to suspend any unlawful aid until the Commission has taken a decision on the compatibility of the aid with the common market (hereinafter referred to as a 'suspension injunction'). In addition, the Commission may, after giving the Member State concerned the opportunity to submit its comments, adopt a decision requiring the Member State provisionally to recover any unlawful aid until the Commission has taken a decision on the compatibility of the aid with the internal market (hereinafter referred to as a 'recovery injunction'), if the three criteria set out in Article 13(2) of the Procedural Regulation are fulfilled (i.e., aid character of the measure at issue, urgency to act and serious risk of substantial and irreparable damage to a competitor). Such injunctions may be adopted at the same time as the decision to initiate the procedure under Article 108(2) TFEU or may be subsequent thereto. It follows from the binding nature of such injunctions that national courts are bound and that, if they are seized by an individual who relies on the standstill clause, they are not allowed to take a position different from that of the Commission.[103] They are also not allowed to stay the recovery procedure at the request of beneficiaries but have to guarantee the full execution of the injunction.

Certainly, granting the Commission the possibility to adopt injunctions during the administrative procedure under Article 108 TFEU allows it to prudentially react against illegally granted aid, which may render nugatory the system established in this article.[104] However, remedies to be adopted by national courts against unlawful measures and injunctions pursuant to Article 13 of Regulation 2015/1589 can overlap. This explains the sound criticism of some authors pointing out that granting the Commission the possibility to adopt the aforementioned injunctions violates the exclusive competence of national courts in the enforcement of Article 108(3), last sentence.[105] Respecting the distribution of competences between the Commission and national courts requires the Commission to make reasonable use of these injunctions, avoiding any interference in national courts' activity when they have been asked to enforce the standstill clause in a particular case. By contrast, when no application has been brought before national courts, there is no reason to impede the Commission from adopting any of the injunctions pursuant to Article 13 of Regulation 2015/1589 in order to prevent any negative consequences of the illegally granted aid—for instance, when a positive decision has been contested before the General Court or the Court of Justice, until the decision is confirmed by these courts.

---

[102]See to that effect *SFEI* (n 15) para 43.

[103]Keppenne and Gross (2008), p. 401.

[104]Case C-301/87 *France v. Commission (Boussac)* ECLI:EU:C:1990:67, paras 18 and 19; and *Italy v. Commission* (n 46) para 26.

[105]Keppenne and Gross (2008), p. 401, fn 37.

## 3.3 Are Alternative Measures Instead of Ordering Recovery Allowed?

In certain situations, national courts might be tempted to abolish the State aid character of measures by eliminating elements, which seem to make them covered by Article 107(1) TFEU, for instance their selective nature, rather than ordering the suspension of the implementation or the provisional recovery of unlawful aid. This will particularly be the case where the national court has the power of annulment of legislative acts or administrative decisions. In the light of the difficulties that the fulfilment of their tasks may raise (see *supra* Sect. 2.3), national courts may see this possibility as an inviting easy way.

The ECJ has held that national courts must preserve the interests of individuals. However, in so doing, it must also take full account of the interests of the EU.[106] With regard to the partial rebate of tax constituting an unlawful aid measure because it was granted in breach of the obligation of notification, it would not be compatible with the interest of the Union to order that such a rebate be applied to other undertakings if such a decision would have the effect of extending the circle of beneficiaries of State aid, thus leading to an increase in the aid granted, instead of its elimination.[107] In particular, care must be taken by the national courts to ensure that whatever remedies they grant are such that they eliminate the effects of the aid granted in breach of Article 108(3) TFEU and not merely extend it to a further group of beneficiaries without abolishing the State aid character. With regard to the envisaged cancellation of a State guarantee considered to be an unlawful State aid, the ECJ held that EU law does not impose any specific conclusion that the national courts must necessarily draw with regard to the validity of the acts relating to implementation of the aid. However, as follows from the consistent case law of the ECJ, given that the objective of the measures that the national courts are bound to take in the event of infringement of Article 108(3) TFEU is, essentially, to restore the competitive situation existing prior to the payment of the aid in question, those courts must ensure that the measures they take with regard to the validity of the above-mentioned acts make it possible for such an objective to be achieved. Accordingly, it is for the national court to determine whether cancellation of a guarantee may, given the circumstances specific to the dispute before it, be a more effective means of achieving that restoration than other measures.[108]

---

[106]See, by analogy, Case C-5/89 *Commission* v. *Germany* ECLI:EU:C:1990:320, para 19.

[107]See, to that effect, Joined Cases C-393/04 and C-41/05 *Air Liquide Industries Belgium* ECLI: EU:C:2006:403, para 45.

[108]*Residex Capital IV* (n 69) paras 44–46.

## 3.4   Procedures to Be Applied

In the absence of EU law governing the matter, it is for the domestic legal system of each Member State to designate the courts and tribunals having jurisdiction and to lay down the detailed procedural rules governing actions for safeguarding rights that individuals derive from the direct effects of EU law, provided that such rules are not less favourable than those governing similar domestic actions (*principle of equivalence*) and that they do not render practically impossible or excessively difficult the exercise of rights conferred by Union law (*principle of effectiveness*).[109] As regards the national rules relating to the determination of an individual's standing and legal interest in bringing proceedings, the ECJ has held that EU law requires that such rules do not undermine the right to effective judicial protection when exercising the rights conferred by that legal system.[110] Even if this seems to be evident, it should be mentioned that this requirement has been fulfilled in Germany only since a judgment of the *Bundesgerichtshof*, which overturned its old jurisprudence.[111] Furthermore, national rules governing the requirement of proof must not affect the scope or effectiveness of EU law. Any requirement of proof, which has the effect of making it virtually impossible or excessively difficult to demonstrate the character of a State aid of the character of a measure or the incompatibility of those measures with EU law, is contrary to that principle of effectiveness.[112]

## 4   National Courts and Block Exemption Regulations

Council Regulation (EC) 994/98, amended by Council Regulation 733/2013, enables the Commission to adopt so-called Block Exemption Regulations for State aid. With these Regulations, the Commission can declare specific categories of aid compatible with the internal market if they fulfil certain conditions, thus exempting them from the requirement of prior notification and Commission approval. Consequently, they do not need to be approved individually for each case by the Commission.

---

[109]See Case C-276/01 *Steffensen* ECLI:EU:C:2006:403, para 60 and the case law cited therein; and Case C-526/04 *Laboratoires Boiron SA* v. *Union de recouvrement des cotisations de sécurité sociale et d'allocations familiales (Urssaf) de Lyon* ECLI:EU:C:2006:528, para 51.

[110]See Joined Cases C-87/90 to C-89/90 *Verholen and Others* ECLI:EU:C:1991:314, para 24; Case C-13/01 *Safalero* ECLI:EU:C:2003:447, para 50; and Case C-174/02 *Streekgeweest Westelijk Noord-Brabant* v. *Staatssecretaris van Financiën* ECLI:EU:C:2005:10, para 18.

[111]Judgment of 10 February 2011, I ZR 136/09. The *locus standi* of the competitor is derived from the last sentence of Article 108(3) TFEU, which is directly applicable. The previous jurisprudence disregarded that provision and was based exclusively on national legislation.

[112]Quigley (2009), p. 459.

According to Article 1(2) and (3) of the Authorizing Council Regulation (EC) 994/98, for Block Exemption Regulations to have the intended effects, they must stipulate the purpose of the aid, the categories of beneficiaries, the aid intensity (or maximum State aid amounts), the conditions for cumulating State aid and the conditions of monitoring rules.

Based on this authorization, the Commission adopted the following block exemption Regulations:

– Commission Regulation (EC) 68/2001 of 12 January 2001 on the application of Articles 87 and 88 of the EC Treaty to training aid[113];

– Commission Regulation (EC) 70/2001 of 12 January 2001 on the application of Articles 87 and 88 of the EC Treaty to State aid to small and medium-sized enterprises[114];

– Commission Regulation (EC) 2204/2002 of 12 December 2002 on the application of Articles 87 and 88 of the EC Treaty to State aid for employment[115];

– Commission Regulation (EC) 1628/2006 of 24 October 2006 on the application of Articles 87 and 88 of the Treaty to national regional investment aid granted by Member States.[116]

These regulations were replaced by the General Block Exemption Regulation [Commission Regulation (EC) 800/2008 of 6 August 2008 declaring certain categories of aid compatible with the common market in application of Articles 87 and 88 of the EC Treaty][117] and subsequently by Commission Regulation (EU) 651/2014 declaring certain categories of aid compatible with the internal market in application of Articles 107 and 108 TFEU.[118]

Commission Regulation (EC) 69/2001 on the application of Articles 87 and 88 of the Treaty on the '*de minimis*' aid exempted from the notification requirement minor grants considering that they do not fall within the definition of State aid in Article 107 (1) TFEU.[119] This Regulation was replaced by Commission Regulation (EC) 1998/2006 on the application of Articles 87 and 88 of the Treaty on the '*de minimis*' aid,[120] which was subsequently replaced by Commission Regulation (EC) 1407/2013 on the application of Articles 107 and 108 TFEU to *de minimis* aid.[121]

---

[113]OJ L 10 dated 13 January 2001, p. 20. Regulation last amended by Commission Regulation (EC) 1976/2006.

[114]OJ L 10 dated 13 January 2001, p. 33. Regulation last amended by Commission Regulation (EC) 1976/2006 (OJ L 368 dated 23 December 2006, p. 85), extending the scope of application of the regulation to research and development State aid.

[115]OJ L 337 dated 13 December 2002, p. 3. Commission Regulation last amended by Regulation (EC) 1976/2006.

[116]OJ L 302 dated 1 November 2006, p. 29.

[117]OJ L 214 dated 9 August 2008, p. 3. Further details in Deiberova and Nyssens (2009), p. 27.

[118]OJ L 187 dated 29 June 2014, p. 1.

[119]OJ L 10 dated 13 January 2001, p. 30.

[120]OJ L 379 dated 28 December 2006, p. 5.

[121]OJ L 352 dated 24 December 2013, p. 1. See Berghofer (2007), p. 11.

The General Block Exemption Regulation has—as have the guidelines and the framework—a binding effect on the Commission: it cannot grant approval in a particular case derogating from this regulation. If this is necessary due to special circumstances, the General Block Exemption Regulation must also be changed or adjusted with the 'deviant' decision. Moreover, this Regulation has direct effect in the Member States. National authorities, including national courts, are bound by the General Block Exemption Regulation without requiring any special implementation at national level.

As with the General Block Exemption Regulation, certain categories of aid are declared compatible with the internal market, provided the conditions set out in the aforementioned Regulation are met, the usual pre-inspection by the Commission is omitted or is replaced by an *ex post* control by national courts and the national law provides the procedural condition, such as a claim of legitimacy against competitors. Thus, the block exemption regulations are a rare form of decentralisation of State aid control that, nevertheless, strengthen the role of national courts in the enforcement of State aid rules.[122] Inasmuch as national courts do not limit their activity to enforcing a Commission decision concerning a specific measure, but develop an autonomous examination, these cases constitute another example where the role of national courts in the enforcement of State aid rules cannot be considered merely secondary or ancillary.

## 5  Answering Criticism of the Judgment in *Deutsche Lufthansa*

### 5.1  Good Reasons for Such a Criticism?

The judgment in *Deutsche Lufthansa*, which was considered the 'leading case' on the binding effects of the Commission's decision to open the formal investigation procedure, has led to strong criticism mainly among German practitioners and judges. Criticism is mostly based on the following arguments. First, the Commission's decision to open the formal investigation procedure contains only a provisional and superficial assessment of the character of State aid of the measure at issue. Only in its final decision may the Commission conclude that this measure is not an aid or, despite being an aid, that it is compatible with the internal market. Nevertheless, according to the judgment in *Deutsche Lufthansa*, as the Commission decides to open the formal investigation procedure, national courts will have to order the recovery of the illegally granted aid, which seems excessive.[123] Second,

---

[122]Sinnaeve (2001), p. 69.

[123]Ghazarian (2014), pp. 113–114; Giesberts and Kleve (2014), p. 645; Nicolaides (2014), pp. 411–413; Soltész (2013a), p. 3774; Soltész (2013b), pp. 643–644; von Bonin and Wittenberg (2014), p. 69.

the binding effects of the Commission's decision preclude national courts from appreciating autonomously the character of aid of the measure at issue, which affects the independence of the judiciary.[124] Third, these effects may impair the rights of the defence of the beneficiaries, who can be affected by the decision to open the formal investigation procedure without any opportunity to express their points of view in front of the Commission.[125] And, fourth, the recovery of aids affected by this decision would increase the risk of insolvency of undertakings.[126]

In this regard, it is important to point out that the ECJ has, in at least two cases, already ruled the binding effect of the Commission's decision to open the formal investigation procedure.[127] Moreover, this effect was also recognised by authorised voices.[128] Thus, it is not easy to understand why the judgment in *Deutsche Lufthansa* has given rise to such a reaction among practitioners. Furthermore, it is difficult to sympathise with the criticism put forward by practitioners as it is not founded. First, it must be noted that the provisional character of the decision to open the formal investigation procedure is not relevant in this context. This decision shows the Commission's doubts concerning the character of State aid of the measure at issue. It is, thus, sufficient to consider that the measure of aid was executed without prior authorisation and to conclude that the standstill clause was infringed (see *supra* Sect. 2.3). In addition, as already explained, the unlawfulness of an aid is different from the incompatibility of the aid with the internal market (see *supra* Sect. 2.1). Moreover, as shown above, recovery is not the sole remedy at the disposal of national courts. They have a large range of remedies available— according to the case law, all the possible remedies foreseen by the national procedural rules—to remove the consequences of the illegality and to repair the damages occasioned (see *supra* Sect. 3). Thus, the judgment in *Deutsche Lufthansa* cannot be read as forcing national courts to order the recovery of the unlawful aid in every case. Indeed, a national court may not order recovery if there are exceptional circumstances in which it would be inappropriate to order repayment of the aid or if it is contrary to EU law principles (see *supra* Sect. 3.1). Moreover, as it follows from that judgment, when the measure has not been fully implemented, 'national courts **may** decide to suspend the implementation of the measure in question and order the recovery of payments already made' (emphasis added). Alternative remedies to the recovery—i.e., the placement of the funds on a blocked account—seem possible. Furthermore, according to the decision, national courts '[...] **may also** decide to order provisional measures in order to safeguard both the

---

[124]Koenig (2014), p. 2.

[125]Berrisch (2014), pp. 254–255; Ghazarian (2014), p. 112; Giesberts and Kleve (2014), p. 646; Koenig (2014), p. 2; Soltész (2013a), p. 3774; Soltész (2013b), p. 644.

[126]Soltész (2013b), p. 644; von Bonin and Wittenberg (2014), p. 69.

[127]*Spain v. Commission* (n 46) para 23; and *Italy v. Commission* (n 7) para 59. According to the last judgment 'Such a decision might also be invoked before a national court called upon to draw all the consequences arising from infringement of the last sentence of Article 88(3) EC'.

[128]Keppenne and Gross (2008), p. 400.

interests of the parties concerned and the effectiveness of the Commission's decision to initiate the formal examination procedure' (see *supra* Sect. 3.2) (emphasis added).[129] When the measure has been fully implemented and the Commission considers in its final decision that it is compatible with the internal market, the payment of interest is the minimum and necessary remedy that national courts must apply to redress the negative consequences of an unlawful aid (see *supra* Sect. 3.2). Second, the independence of the judiciary cannot be affected by the sole fact that national courts are bound by the Commission's decision to open a formal investigation. As pointed out above, the content of the Commission's decision only fills the first part of national courts' reasoning in the enforcement of the standstill clause (see *supra* Sect. 2.2). Once the infringement of the standstill clause has been proven, national courts are independent in deciding how to deal with it and to choose the appropriate remedies. Moreover, if national courts disagree with the Commission's decision, they may refer a question to the ECJ for a preliminary ruling on its own motion.[130] Third, it is true that the beneficiary of the aid has no rights guaranteed by EU law. From a procedural point of view, the beneficiary is just the recipient of an aid, whose enforcement is in principle prohibited until the Commission adopts a decision approving it in the public interest. In fact, the recipient of the decision is the Member State.[131] Nevertheless, the beneficiary can protect himself against the decision to open a formal investigation and its eventual consequences. He can—if directly and individually concerned—challenge the opening of the formal investigation procedure pursuant to Article 263(4) TFEU before the General Court because, under certain circumstances, it is an attackable act.[132] However, according to the case law, not every decision to open the formal investigation procedure can be challenged before the European courts (see *infra* Sect. 5.2). But, as will be seen, if the beneficiary of the aid has no *locus standi* for direct action and cannot challenge this decision before the General Court, he can always cast doubt on the validity of the Commission's decision before the national courts with the purpose of making the court submit a question for a preliminary ruling to the Court of Justice (see *infra* Sect. 5.2). Finally, and fourth, concerning the increased risk of insolvency, it is enough to note that insolvency cannot be invoked as a reason not to recover an unlawful aid.[133]

---

[129]*Deutsche Lufthansa* (n 1) para 43. Clearer in *Flughafen Lübeck* (n 35) para 26.

[130]*Deutsche Lufthansa* (n 1) para 44. However, critical of this possibility, Sánchez Graells (2013).

[131]Martin-Ehlers (2014), p. 251.

[132]Flynn (2004), p. 289; Martin-Ehlers (2014), p. 251.

[133]Idot (2010), p. 84.

## 5.2 Challenging the Decision to Open the Formal Investigation Procedure

Despite the above considerations, it must be noted that an important issue lies behind all this criticism. As observed, one of the pieces of criticism underlines the fact that recognising the binding effects of the Commission's decision to open the formal investigation procedure may have negative consequences on the rights of the beneficiaries.[134] This criticism opens the debate on the legal effects of the decision to open the formal investigation procedure and, subsequently, the attackable character of this decision before EU courts.

In this respect, it is necessary to begin by noting that the beneficiary of an aid does not participate in the preliminary examination procedure, previous to the decision to initiate the formal investigation procedure. Regulation 2015/1589 does not provide that interested parties can submit comments until this decision is adopted and the formal investigation procedure is opened (Article 6). Nevertheless, the fact that the beneficiary cannot submit any comment during the preliminary examination procedure does not mean that he does not have any possibility to react. As will be seen, the beneficiary of an aid can contest, under certain conditions, the decision to open the formal investigation procedure before the General Court and the Court of Justice. Thus, he has a way to protect his interests before national courts impose on him, according to the case law, all the necessary consequences of the unlawful character of the aid.

It is clear to everyone that the decision to open the formal investigation procedure is an intermediate act. As is widely known, an intermediate measure

> is not [...] capable of forming the subject-matter of an action if it is established that the illegality attaching to that measure can be relied on in support of an action against the final decision for which it represents a preparatory step. In such circumstances, the action brought against the decision terminating the procedure will provide sufficient judicial protection.[135]

To be the subject matter of an action brought before EU courts, an intermediate act has to produce independent legal effects. In such circumstances, the action brought against the decision terminating the procedure will not provide sufficient judicial protection.[136] In regard to the Commission's decision to open the formal investigation procedure, the General Court noted that the decision has to produce an effect 'which is immediate, certain and sufficiently binding in relation to the Member State to which it is addressed and the beneficiary or beneficiaries of the measure under examination'.[137]

---

[134]Soltész (2013b), pp. 644–645; Ghazarian (2014), pp. 111–113; Koenig (2014), p. 2.

[135]Case C-463/10 *Deutsche Post AG and Federal Republic of Germany v. Commission* ECLI:EU:C:2011:656, para 53, and the case law mentioned.

[136]*Deutsche Post AG* (n 135) para 54, and the case law mentioned.

[137]Case T-251/13 *Gemeente Nijmegen v. Commission* ECLI:EU:T:2015:142, para 29.

In two important judgments, the General Court ruled that, when a measure of aid has not been fully implemented, the decision to open the formal investigation procedure is an attackable act. The arguments invoked to support this conclusion are the following:

> A decision to initiate the formal investigation procedure in relation to a measure in the course of implementation and classified by the Commission as new aid necessarily alters the legal implications of the measure under consideration and the legal position of the recipient firms, particularly as regards the continued implementation of the measure. Until the adoption of such a decision, the Member State, the recipient firms and other economic operators may think that the measure is being lawfully implemented as a general measure not falling within the scope of Article 87(1) EC or as existing aid. On the other hand, after its adoption there is at the very least a significant element of doubt as to the legality of the measure which, without prejudice to the possibility of seeking interim relief from the court, must lead the Member State to suspend its application, since the initiation of the formal investigation procedure excludes the possibility of an immediate decision that the measure is compatible with the common market, which would enable it to continue to be lawfully implemented. Such a decision might also be invoked before a national court called upon to draw all the consequences arising from infringement of the last sentence of Article 88 (3) EC. Finally, it is capable of leading the firms which are beneficiaries of the measure to refuse in any event new payments or new advantages or to hold the necessary sums as provision for possible subsequent financial compensations. Businesses will also take account, in their relations with those beneficiaries, of the uncertainty cast on the legal and financial situation of the latter.[138]

Nevertheless, the solution changes when the aid has been fully granted. In three decisions, the General Court ruled that, in such a situation, the decision to open the formal investigation procedure is not an attackable act.[139] According to the General Court, the effect produced by the decision to open the formal investigation procedure may be the recovery of the sums paid to the beneficiary. However, according to them, this effect will not be immediate because, on the one hand, it may only be adopted if the conditions set out in Article 13 of Regulation 2015/1589 are fulfilled and, on the other hand, because, according to the judgment in *Deutsche Lufthansa*, where national courts entertain doubts as to whether the measure at issue constitutes State aid within the meaning of Article 107(1) TFEU or as to the validity or interpretation of the decision to initiate the formal examination procedure, national courts may seek clarification from the Commission and, in accordance with the second and third paragraphs of Article 267 TFEU, as interpreted by the Court, they may or must refer a question to the Court for a preliminary ruling.[140] Moreover, it follows from the case law that the recovery of the aid can be excluded when it is not compatible with EU principles or under exceptional circumstances.[141]

---

[138]See Joined Cases T-346/99, T-347/99 and T-348/99 *Diputación Foral de Álava and Others v. Commission* ECLI:EU:T:2002:259, para 34; and Case T-332/06 *Alcoa Transformazioni Srl v. Commission* ECLI:EU:T:2009:79, para 36.

[139]See *Gemeente Nijmegen* (n 137) paras 37–48; Case T-517/12 *Alro SA v. Commission* ECLI:EU:T:2014:890, para 42; and Case T-129/13 *Alpiq RomIndustries Srl and Alpiq RomEnergie Srl v. Commission* ECLI:EU:T:2014:895, para 42.

[140]*Deutsche Lufthansa* (n 1) para 44.

[141]*Alro* (n 139) paras 40–41; and *Alpiq* (n 139) paras 38–39.

If the decision to open the formal investigation procedure can be considered as an attackable act, the fact that the beneficiary of the aid cannot actively take part in the administrative procedure before the Commission will not be objectionable. The beneficiary will have the chance to contest the decision before the General Court and the Court of Justice. In the light of case law, this is the case when the aid has not been fully enforced.[142] However, as explained, when the aid has been fully enforced, this possibility seems to be excluded by the General Court. In any event, this does not mean that the beneficiary of an aid does not have any chance to defend his interests since he will always have the possibility to cast doubt on the validity of the Commission's decision before the national courts—i.e., when a competitor goes before these courts asking for the enforcement of the standstill clause—with the purpose of making the court submit a question for a preliminary ruling to the Court of Justice.[143] Yet this will not be admissible if he lacks standing because he failed to challenge the decision within the time limits set in the Treaty.[144] It follows that at least the beneficiary has indirectly the chance to defend his interests. Thus, there is no justification, not even in this point, for the strong criticism raised against the judgment in *Deutsche Lufthansa*.

# 6 Conclusion

It has been shown that the difficulties raised by the judgment in *Deutsche Lufthansa* for the proper understanding of the role of national courts in the enforcement of EU State aid rules are more theoretical than real. Even though—according to this judgment—national courts are bound by the Commission's decision to open the formal investigation procedure, their role has not changed substantially. They continue to enforce the standstill clause in the last sentence of Article 108(3) TFEU. When the Commission has not adopted any decision concerning the measure of aid, national courts develop a significant role, deciding the character of aid of the measure at issue in order to enforce this clause in the interest of individuals—i.e., the competitors of the beneficiaries of the aid, asking for relief against an illegally granted aid. This role is of particular interest to the competitors because they will have the chance to ask national courts for immediate relief against the unlawful implementation of an aid, even when the Commission has not (yet) adopted a position concerning the character of State aid of the measure at issue. However, due to the complex nature of the tasks that they are called upon to carry out, cooperation with

---

[142]See, also, Flynn (2004), p. 289.

[143]Ibid, p. 293. Bermejo (2016), pp. 12–15 has expressed a particular view regarding the possibility to contest before the EU courts the decision to open the formal investigation procedure when the aid has been fully enforced.

[144]*TWD Textilwerke Deggendorf* (n 29) paras 17, 18 and 24. See also ibid, p 293; Nehl and Kreuschitz (2017).

the Commission seems absolutely necessary. In any event, the ECJ will ensure the harmonious interpretation of Article 107 TFEU through the preliminary reference. Only if national courts are fully aware of their important role and establish constructive dialogue with the Commission will they be in a position to produce a consistent output that contributes to the non-distorted functioning of the internal market.

By contrast, when the Commission has adopted a decision opening the formal investigation procedure, national courts will be bound by this decision, and their role is 'limited' to draw all the necessary consequences of the infringement resulting from the unauthorised granting of aid in the interest of individuals. However, this cannot be seen as an attack on the independence of national courts. It is just the necessary consequence of the distribution of roles between the Commission and national courts, which also follows from the obligation of sincere cooperation as set out in Article 4(3) TEU. It reflects the necessity to grant the Commission a period free from interference to adopt a decision concerning the compatibility of the aid. Despite its provisional character, the decision to open the formal investigation procedure shows the Commission's doubts concerning the compatibility of the State aid and, therefore, the need to examine it within a sound administrative procedure.

As unlawfulness and incompatibility are different categories, the conclusions to be drawn by national courts from the breach of the standstill clause cannot be affected by a subsequent analysis of the compatibility of the aid carried out by the Commission. The binding effect of the decision to open the formal investigation procedure does not impair the rights of defence of the beneficiaries. Even if the beneficiaries of the aid are not parties to the administrative procedure, they can contest this decision to open the formal investigation procedure before the European courts when the aid has not been fully granted. In this case, according to the case law, the decision can be considered an attackable act. However, this possibility was rejected by the General Court when the decision has been fully enforced. In these cases, the preliminary reference can offer an (indirect) way to take into consideration the beneficiary's interest to contest the Commission's decision to open the formal investigation procedure.

# References

Berghofer M (2007) The new de minimis regulation: enlarging the sword of Damocles? Eur State Aid Law 6(1):13–16

Bermejo N (2016) El juez nacional y las ayudas de Estado ilegales. Actualidad Administrativa 1:1–22

Berrisch GM (2014) Mehr Fragen als Antworten – Keine Klärung der 'Bindungswirkung' von beihilferechtlichen Eröffnungsentscheidungen der Kommission. EuZW 7:253–256

Deiberova K, Nyssens H (2009) The new General Block Exemption Regulation (GBER): what changed? EStAL 8(1):27

Di Bucci V (2008) Quelques aspects institutionnels du droit des aides d'Etat. In: EC State aid law. Le Droit des Aides d'Etat dans la CE. Liber Amicorum F. Santaolalla, Wolters Kluwer, The Netherlands, pp 43–64

Flynn L (2004) Remedies in European courts. In: Biondi A, Eeckhout P, Flynn J (eds) The law of State aid in the European Union. OUP, Oxford, pp 283–301

Ghazarian L (2014) Binding effect of opening decisions – Lufthansa AG v FFH. EStAL 13(1): 106–114

Giesberts L, Kleve G (2014) EuGH stärkt Vollzugsverbot bei staatlichen Beihilfen. NVwZ:643–646

Idot L (2010) Regards sur les mutations du droit des aides d'État. Concurrences 1:79–86

Keppenne JP, Gross K (2008) Quelques considérations sur le role du juge national dans le contrôle des aides d'Etat. In: EC State Aid Law. Le Droit des Aides d'Etat dans la CE. Liber Amicorum F. Santaolalla, Wolters Kluwer, The Netherlands, pp 391-408

Koenig C (2014) Bindung nationaler Gerichte an Kommissionsbeschlüsse zur Eröffnung des förmlichen Prüfverfahrens. EWS 1:1–3

Martin-Ehlers A (2014) Die Bindungswirkung einer Eröffnungsentscheidungen der Kommission im Beihilenrecht. EuZW:247–252

Meij AWH (2007) Balancing substance and procedure in state aid practice – an update on recent developments in EC case law. In: Bartosch A (ed) 5th Experts' Forum on new developments in European State aid law. European State Aid Law Quarterly, Brussels, pp 7–19

Nehl HP (2014) 2013 Reform of EU State aid procedures: how to exacerbate the imbalance between efficiency and individual protection. EStAL 13(2):235–249

Nehl HP, Kreuschitz V (2017) EU State aid litigation in a quasi-federal system. In: Hoffmann HCH, Micheau C (eds) State aid law for European Union. OUP, Oxford (in press)

Nicolaides P (2014) Are national courts becoming an extension of the Commission? EStAL 13(3): 409–413

Quigley C (2009) European State aid law and policy, 2nd edn. Hart, Oxford, p 459

Rivas J (2013) National courts are now bound by Commission decisions on State aid opening proceedings. Bird&Bird News Center. Available at http://www.twobirds.com/en/news/articles/2013/global/eu-national-courts-are-now-bound-by-commission-decisions-on-state-aid-opening-proceedings. Accessed Mar and Sept 2015

Sánchez Graells A (2013) CJEU toys with one stop shop approach and muddies the waters of State aid analysis (C-284/12). Available at http://howtocrackanut.blogspot.com/2013/11/cjeu-toys-with-one-stop-shop-approach.html. Accessed Mar and Sept 2015

Sinnaeve A (2001) Die ersten Gruppenfreistellungen: Dezentralisierung der Beihilfenkontrolle? EuZW 12(3):69–76

Soltész U (2013a) Bindungswirkung der Eröffnung beihilferechtlicher Prüfverfahren. NJW 52: 3771–3774

Soltész U (2013b) Effet utile taken to extremes: does an opening decision already trigger the 'stand-still obligation'? EStAL 2013:643–645

von Bonin A, Wittenberg T (2014) Beihilfenrecht: Bindungswirkung von Eröffnungsentscheidungen der Kommission für nationale Gerichte. EuZW:65–69

# Tax Incentives as State Aid

Nicola Chesaites

**Abstract** In the European Union, direct taxation is generally a matter of national law that falls within the exclusive competence of the Member States. While Member States are free to design their own tax systems as they see fit, they must comply with Union law, including the rules on State aid. In recent years, the Commission has embarked on an ambitious path of using the State aid rules to address Member States' tax treatment of some of the world's largest multinationals. In doing so, it has had to grapple with some of the most challenging questions in EU State aid law and its interface with national fiscal regimes, namely in relation to determining when a tax measure is 'selective' by favouring certain undertakings or the production of certain goods. The appropriateness and legitimacy of the use of State aid rules as a tool to achieve these goals aside, the Commission's recent enforcement efforts have raised some important questions concerning the interpretation of the selectivity criterion under EU State aid law. This criterion will be tested before the EU courts in pending cases in the near future, and this could have far-reaching consequences for the reach of EU State aid law enforcement and, ultimately, the scope of Member States' sovereignty in the field of taxation.

## 1 Introduction

In the European Union (EU), direct taxation is generally a matter of national law that falls within the exclusive competence of the Member States. There are some notable exceptions. These include value added tax and excise duties on alcohol, tobacco and energy. However, as a rule, Member States are free to design their own tax systems, making their own policy choices as to where to allocate the tax burden and to spread that burden as they see fit across different factors of production.

The views expressed in this paper are those of the author alone, and should not be attributed directly or indirectly to Quinn Emanuel Urquhart & Sullivan UK LLP.

N. Chesaites (✉)
Quinn Emanuel Urquhart & Sullivan UK LLP, London, UK
e-mail: nicolachesaites@quinnemanuel.com

© Springer-Verlag Berlin Heidelberg 2017                                  253
V. Tomljenović et al. (eds.), *EU Competition and State Aid Rules,*
Europeanization and Globalization 3, https://doi.org/10.1007/978-3-662-47962-9_12

If Member States so choose, they are also free to adopt harmonised EU rules on taxation, by unanimous agreement of all 28 Member States, insofar as it is deemed necessary to ensure the establishment and functioning of the internal market and avoid the distortion of competition.[1]

However, the freedom of Member States to design their own tax systems is not unfettered. Member States' national tax rules must be compatible with Union law;[2] harmful tax competition between Member States should, in principle, be avoided; and, importantly, Member States must comply with EU State aid rules.

In practice, tax measures represent a substantial proportion of State aid, in the EU.[3] And while it was only in the late 1990s that the European Commission appeared to focus on the enforcement of State aid rules in the field of taxation, this increasing focus has recently taken centre stage as the Commission has embarked on an ambitious path of using the State aid rules to address Member States' tax treatment of some of the world's largest multinationals. In doing so, the Commission has had to defend its actions against rare, direct criticism from the United States Treasury.[4] More importantly, it has had to grapple with some of the most challenging questions in EU State aid law and its interface with national fiscal regimes—questions that will soon come before the EU courts in pending legal challenges.

This paper will begin by addressing the relationship between the rules on harmful tax competition and fiscal State aid. Next, it will provide an overview of the State aid rules as they apply to fiscal measures before assessing some of the key challenges inherent in determining whether certain tax incentives can be regarded as State aid.

## 2 Harmful Tax Competition Measures and Fiscal State Aid Enforcement Distinguished. Or Not?

Harmful tax competition can arise where a Member State sets substantially lower rates of corporation tax, relative to other Member States in the internal market. In the context of free movement within the internal market, this can skew the conditions of competition in that Member State's favour. By contrast, in broad terms, State aid arises where the State confers a fiscal advantage on certain undertakings or the production of certain goods. In a speech in 2002, Mario Monti, then Director General of Competition at the European Commission, stated that rules on harmful tax

---

[1] Article 113 of the Treaty on the Functioning of the European Union (TFEU).

[2] Case C-446/03 *Marks & Spencer* ECLI:EU:C:2005:763, para 29.

[3] The European Commission's latest scoreboard figures up until 2014 show that, in the last decade, tax exemptions have accounted for at least 30% of all Member State aid measures, save in 2006 when the figure dipped to 28.5%: European Commission State Aid Scoreboard 2015.

[4] Financial Times, 'Vestager denies Brussels is targeting US companies in tax probes', 29 February 2016.

competition relate to *"measures that may affect the location of mobile capital within the Union"*, while State aid provisions apply when a tax system is discriminatory and favours only certain enterprises or certain activities. He went on to signal that State aid rules *"cannot be used as an alternative tool to achieve harmonisation in the field of taxation, which concerns the alignment of the general fiscal systems in Member States"*.

However, despite their differences, there is an overlap between measures resulting in harmful tax competition and those that constitute State aid. Where, for example, a Member State sets substantially lower rates of corporation tax relative to other Member States, which is specifically targeted at non-resident companies, this could potentially be regarded as both a harmful tax measure and State aid. More significantly, a symbiotic relationship has developed between initiatives to address harmful tax competition and enforcement of State aid rules in the field of taxation, with increased political consensus to tackle harmful tax competition often providing the impetus for greater enforcement against fiscal State aid.[5]

There are various tools to address harmful tax competition. Harmful tax competition in the EU can be addressed through Articles 116 and 117 of the Treaty on the Functioning of the European Union (TFEU).[6] Under Article 116 TFEU, the Council can adopt directives by qualified majority to eliminate national measures that distort competition in the internal market, although this provision has not been used to address fiscal measures despite a number of complaints regarding low taxation rates in Ireland and Luxembourg.[7] Under Article 117 TFEU, Member States must notify the Commission of provisions that it intends to introduce or amend that may cause distortions of competition.

Instead, harmful tax competition has been addressed at EU level by political cooperation between the Member States. In December 1997, following an informal meeting in Verona of EU economic affairs and finance ministers, the Council adopted a non-binding Code of Conduct for business taxation (Code).[8] The purpose of the Code was to detect measures that affect the location of business activity in the Union by targeting non-residents and providing them with more favourable tax treatment than that which is generally available in the Member State concerned. To identify those measures, the Code set out five guiding criteria, key among which would seem to be whether tax advantages are granted without any real economic activity and substantial economic presence in the Member States and whether the rules for profit determination in respect of activities within a multinational group departs from internationally accepted principles, notably those of the Organisation

---

[5]See Luja (2003) at 484.

[6]See the Opinion of Advocate General Geelhoed in Case C-308/01 *GIL Insurance and Others* ECLI:EU:C:2004:252, paras 74–77.

[7]Quigley (2015), p. 150.

[8]Conclusions of the ECOFIN Council Meeting on 1 December 1997 concerning taxation policy (98/C 2/01), Annex 1, Resolution of the Council and the Representatives of the Governments of the Member States, meeting within the Council of 1 December 1997 on a code of conduct for business taxation [1998] OJ C 2/1.

for Economic Cooperation and Development (OECD). Member States committed to a standstill, undertaking to refrain from introducing harmful tax measures in future, and a rollback of such measures and practices, as soon as possible.

The work of identifying harmful tax measures and monitoring the application of the Code was assigned to the Code of Conduct Group under the chairmanship of UK Paymaster General Dawn Primarolo (also referred to as the Primarolo Group). In a report of November 1999,[9] the Primarolo Group identified 66 harmful tax measures, including 40 in the EU, 3 in Gibraltar and 23 in dependent or associated territories, which Member States had committed to dismantle under the Code.

The Code also recognised that harmful tax competition measures could potentially fall within the scope of EU State aid rules and noted the Commission's commitment to publish guidelines on the application of State aid rules to measures relating to direct business taxation. Following up on this commitment, in 1998, the Commission adopted a notice on the application of State aid rules to measures relating to direct business taxation[10] (1998 Notice) as part of the *"wider objective of clarifying and reinforcing the application of the State aid rules in order to reduce distortions of competition in the single market"*.[11] In the 1998 Notice, the Commission announced its intention 'to examine or re-examine case by case [. . .] the tax arrangements in force in the Member States'.[12] This was a turning point in the application of State aid rules to fiscal measures in that it marks the point from which the Commission began to seriously tackle fiscal aid granted by EU Member States by adopting a raft of decisions condemning national tax measures relating to company coordination centres,[13] logistic centres,[14] finance companies[15] and corporate treasuries.[16]

A second wave of increased enforcement of State aid rules in the field of taxation in the EU coincided with the joint initiative of the G20 and the OECD in 2013 to address base erosion and profit shifting (BEPS), referred to as the G20-OECD BEPS

---

[9]Report of the Code of Conduct (Business Taxation) of 23 November 1999, SN 4901/99, to the ECOFIN Council on 29 November 1999.

[10]Commission Notice on the application of State aid rules to measures relating to direct business taxation [1998] OJ C 384/3. The repeal of the 1998 Notice is provided for in the 2016 Commission Notice on the notion of State aid pursuant to Article 107(1) TFEU [2016] OJ C 262/01, para 229.

[11]Commission 1998 Notice (n 10), para 2.

[12]Commission 1998 Notice (n 10), para 4.

[13]Commission Decision 2003/512/EC of 5 September 2002 on State Aid C 47/01, German Coordination Centres, [2003] OJ L 177/17; Commission Decision 2003/501/EC of 16 October 2002 on State Aid C 49/2001, Luxembourg Coordination Centres [2003] OJ L 153/40; Commission Decision 2003/755/EC of 17 February 2003 on State Aid C 15/02, Belgian coordination centres [2003] OJ L 282/25.

[14]Commission Decision 2004/76/EC of 13 May 2003 on State Aid C 45/2001, French Headquarters and Logistic Centres [2004] OJ L 23/1.

[15]Commission Decision 2003/438/EC of 16 October 2002 on State Aid C 50/2001, Luxembourg Finance Companies, [2003] OJ L 153/40.

[16]Commission Decision 2003/883/EC of 11 December 2002 on State Aid C 46/2001, Central Corporate Treasuries [2003] OJ L 330/23.

project. The purpose of the project was to address exploitation by large multinationals of gaps and mismatches in tax rules in different countries to artificially shift profits to jurisdictions with low or no taxation, resulting in little or no overall corporate tax liability. On 19 July 2013, the OECD published its Action Plan on BEPS[17] at the invitation of the G20. Point 5 of the Action Plan called for a revamp in the work on harmful tax practices 'with a priority on improving transparency, including compulsory spontaneous exchange on rulings related to preferential regimes, and on requiring substantial activity for any preferential regime'. It was timely, therefore, that in July 2013, the Commission's Directorate-General for Competition set up within the State aid directorate, the 'Task Force Tax Planning Practices' (Task Force).[18] Since then, the Commission has opened formal, high-profile investigations into tax rulings by Ireland (in relation to Apple), the Netherlands (in relation to Starbucks), Luxembourg (in relation to Fiat Finance and Trade Ltd, or FFT),[19] Amazon,[20] McDonald's;[21] and Belgium.[22] It has concluded five of those investigations with negative decisions requiring the recovery of taxes by Luxembourg, the Netherlands, Ireland and Belgium. The Commission has also extended its investigation of tax rulings to all Member States and opened informal investigations into patent-box tax regimes in ten Member States (these investigations are discussed further below).

Ultimately, these developments suggest that measures to combat harmful tax competition and enforcement of State aid rules in the field of taxation appear are closely interlinked.

# 3 Overview of the Requirement for National Tax Measures to Comply with EU State Aid Rules

## 3.1 Tax Measures as a Form of State Aid

It is remarkable that the Commission's enforcement against fiscal State aid measures only got seriously underway less than two decades ago given that the requirement that Member States' national tax rules must be compatible with EU State aid rules could be inferred from the broad terms of the relevant Treaty provisions from the outset.

Article 107(1) TFEU stipulates that:

---

[17]OECD (2013).

[18]See Desai (2014), p. 575.

[19]European Commission Press Release 2014b IP/14/663.

[20]European Commission Press Release 2015b IP/14/1105.

[21]European Commission Press Release 2015c IP/15/6221.

[22]European Commission Press Release 2015d IP/15/4080.

*[. . .] any aid granted by a Member State or through State resources in any form whatsoever which distorts or threatens to distort competition by favouring certain undertakings or the production of certain goods shall, in so far as it affects trade between Member States, be incompatible with the internal market.*

This provision, which has remained essentially unchanged since the original Treaty of Rome 1957,[23] and specifically the terms *"through State resources in any form whatsoever"*, makes clear that the form through which aid is granted, fiscal or otherwise, is irrelevant. Also, although the term 'aid' suggests that positive intervention by the State is required in the form of a subsidy, thereby apparently excluding tax exemptions, the early case law established that the State aid rules extend more broadly to

*interventions which in various forms, mitigate the charges which are normally included in the budget of an undertaking and which, without therefore being subsidies in the strict meaning of the word, are similar in character and have the same effect.*[24]

In 1974, the Court put the matter beyond doubt in *Italy v. Commission*,[25] when it held that the aim of the Treaty rules concerning State aid

is to prevent trade between Member States from being affected by benefits granted by the public authorities which, in various forms, distort or threaten to distort competition by favouring certain undertakings or the production of certain goods.

It added that the causes or aims of the national measures were not determinative and what mattered was their effects; *"[c]onsequently, the alleged fiscal nature or social aim of the measure in issue cannot suffice to shield it from the application of Article 92 [now Article 107 TFEU]"*.[26]

---

[23]The terms of Article 92(1) of the Treaty of Rome 1957 are essentially mirrored in Article 107 (1) TFEU.

[24]Cases 30/59 *De Gezamenlijke Steenkolenmijnen in Limburg v. High Authority* ECLI:EU:C:1961:2, p 19; confirmed in Case C-387/92 *Banco Exterior de España v. Ayuntamiento de Valencia* ECLI:EU:C:1994:100, para 13.

[25]Case C-173/73 *Italy v. Commission* ECLI:EU:C:1974:71.

[26]Case 173/73 (n 25), para 13; Case C-241/94 *France v. Commission* CLI:EU:C:1996:353, paras 19 and 20.

## 3.2 Determining the Existence of State Aid

Four cumulative conditions must be met for a measure to be found to constitute illegal State aid: (1) the measure must confer an advantage, (2) it must be granted through State resources, (3) it must distort competition and affect trade between Member States and (4) it must be selective in that it favours certain undertakings or the production of certain goods. The 1998 Notice describes how these criteria apply in respect of measures relating to direct business taxation. The 2016 Notice on the notion of State aid pursuant to Article 107(1) TFEU (2016 Notice), which superseded the 1998 Notice, also provides guidance on 'Specific issues concerning tax measures' and describes in detail how State aid rules apply to cooperative societies, undertakings for collective investment, tax amnesties, tax settlements and rulings, depreciation/amortisation rules, flat-rate tax regime for specific activities, anti-abuse rules and excise duties.[27]

**Conferral of an Advantage**  A measure will fulfil the first criterion if it confers an advantage by relieving the beneficiary of charges that are normally borne from its budget. Fiscal measures can confer an advantage in a number of ways. While this can be done through positive means, such as a tax credit, fiscal State aid is generally granted through negative measures, such as a special tax rate, a deferral of the date on which tax becomes payable, special rules enabling the offset of losses against profits, tax deductions and (accelerated) depreciations, amortisations, exemptions, an amnesty or write-off of tax liability. Aid can also be granted indirectly by deductions from taxable income for investments made by third parties in beneficiary industries or companies.[28]

**State Resources**  Where a State foregoes tax revenue that it would normally have received, this is regarded as equivalent to the consumption of State resources,[29] and the second criterion is thereby satisfied, as confirmed by the Court in its early case law set out above.

**Threat of Distortion of Competition and Effects on Trade Between Member States**  According to the terms of Article 107(1) TFEU, aid need only threaten to distort competition. When State aid strengthens the position of an undertaking compared with other undertakings competing in trade between Member States, the latter must be regarded as having been affected,[30] irrespective of whether the recipient actually exports goods and regardless of the relatively small amount of aid and the recipient's moderate size.[31] The fact that the aid strengthens the recipient's position

---

[27]2016 Notice, paras 156–184.

[28]Case C-156/98 *Germany v. Commission* ECLI:EU:C:2000:467, para 26.

[29]Commission 1998 Notice (n 10), para 10.

[30]Case C-730/79 *Philip Morris v. Commission* ECLI:EU:C:1980:209, para 11.

[31]Case C-280/00 *Altmark Trans and Regierungspräsidium Magdeburg* ECLI:EU:C:2003:415, para 81.

compared with other competing firms in the Union is sufficient.[32] The Court has also consistently held that, in principle, operating aid, that is to say aid that is intended to release an undertaking from costs it would normally have to bear in its day-to-day activities, such as fiscal advantages, distorts the conditions of competition.[33] Overall, therefore, this criterion is relatively easy to satisfy.

**Selectivity or Specificity** An advantage that favours certain undertakings or the production of certain goods is 'selective' or 'specific', although selectivity can be justified by the nature or general scheme of the system[34] (this is a question distinct from whether the measure is or may be compatible with the internal market under Article 102(2) or (3) TFEU). Examples of such potential justifications include the progressive nature of tax rates by reference to income or profit, which can be justified by the redistributive aim of tax measures. Likewise, special rules for small and medium-sized enterprises and tax exemptions for non-profit-making undertakings, or cooperatives that distribute all profits to their members, can be justified by the nature of the tax system. Also, taking account of tax paid in the State in which an undertaking is resident can be justified by the internal logic of the tax system and avoiding unfair double taxation, although this justification becomes more complex where it results in more favourable treatment of non-resident companies or company head offices or treasury entities within a group.[35] These justifications have rarely been accepted and may be purely theoretical in practice.[36] Determining whether an advantage is selective is the most challenging criterion, when it comes to fiscal measures, some of which are explored further in Sect. 3.3 below.

Finally, as regards the determination of the existence of State aid, if a tax measure is regarded as constituting State aid, as with all aid measures, it can nevertheless be deemed to be compatible with the Treaty, in accordance with Article 107(2) and (3) TFEU. For the purposes of the present paper, it is sufficient to set out the relevant provisions.

Under Article 107(2) TFEU, the following will be regarded as compatible with the internal market:

> *(a) aid having a social character, granted to individual consumers, provided that such aid is granted without discrimination related to the origin of the products*

---

[32]Commission 1998 Notice (n 10), para 11; Case C-280/00 *Altmark Trans and Regierungspräsidium Magdeburg*, para 92.

[33]Case C-301/87 *France* v. *Commission* ECLI:EU:C:1990:67; Case C-86/89 *Italy* v. *Commission* ECLI:EU:C:1990:373; and Case C-156/98 *Germany* v. *Commission* ECLI:EU:C:2000:467, para 30.

[34]Commission 1998 Notice (n 10), para 12. Case C-143/99 *Adria-WienPipeline and Wietersdorfer & Peggauer Zementwerke* ECLI:EU:C:2001:598, para 41; Case C-308/01 *GIL Insurance and Others* ECLI:EU:C:2004:252, para 68; and Case C-172/03 *Heiser* ECLI:EU:C:2005:130, para 40.

[35]Commission 1998 Notice (n 10), para 26.

[36]Luts (2014/2015), p. 263.

*concerned; (b) aid to make good the damage caused by natural disasters or exceptional occurrences; (c) aid granted to the economy of certain areas of the Federal Republic of Germany affected by the division of Germany, in so far as such aid is required in order to compensate for the economic disadvantages caused by that division. Five years after the entry into force of the Treaty of Lisbon, the Council, acting on a proposal from the Commission, may adopt a decision repealing this point.*

Under Article 107(3) TFEU, the following measures may be deemed compatible with the internal market:

*(a) aid to promote the economic development of areas where the standard of living is abnormally low or where there is serious underemployment, and of the regions referred to in Article 349, in view of their structural, economic and social situation; (b) aid to promote the execution of an important project of common European interest or to remedy a serious disturbance in the economy of a Member State; (c) aid to facilitate the development of certain economic activities or of certain economic areas, where such aid does not adversely affect trading conditions to an extent contrary to the common interest; (d) aid to promote culture and heritage conservation where such aid does not affect trading conditions and competition in the Union to an extent that is contrary to the common interest; (e) such other categories of aid as may be specified by decision of the Council on a proposal from the Commission.*

### 3.2.1   Challenges in Determining the Selectivity of Tax Measures

Where a tax advantage is conferred by an ad hoc, individual measure that applies to a single undertaking or to a specific sector, or a tax measure favours national products or only those that are exported, determining selectivity is fairly straightforward.

However, the analysis of selectivity becomes more complex in the case of measures of general application that apply to an entire region or Member State. If it can be shown that the advantage conferred is effectively available to all[37] economic operators operating within a Member State, it will not be selective. Nor will it be so merely because some firms or sectors benefit more from a tax measure than others.[38] However, if the application of a general measure results in a *de facto*

---

[37]It is not sufficient that the measure is available to a wide range of operators and sectors. Therefore, neither the large number of eligible undertakings nor the diversity of the sectors to which they belong provides grounds for concluding that the measure constitutes a general measure of economic policy: *Adria-WienPipeline and Wietersdorfer & Peggauer Zementwerke* (n 34), para 48.

[38]Commission 1998 Notice (n 10), para 14.

restriction of the scope of the measure to certain undertakings, by way of the exercise of discretion by tax authorities or otherwise, it may be selective.

### 3.2.2 Derogatory or Exceptional Tax Measures: Identifying the Comparator Reference Framework

In order to determine whether certain undertakings receive a benefit, in derogation or by way of exception to the normal tax rules, the starting point is to determine what the 'normal' tax rules are.

In *Portugal* v. *Commission*, a Grand Chamber ruling of the Court of Justice of the European Union (CJEU), the Court pointed out that the determination of the reference framework has a *"particular importance in the case of tax measures, since the very existence of an advantage may be established only when compared with 'normal' taxation"*.[39] In such cases, it held that it is first necessary to identify and examine the common or normal tax regime applicable in the Member State concerned and then assess and determine whether the tax measure in question grants an advantage by derogating from the common or normal tax regime, inasmuch as it differentiates between economic operators that, in light of the objective assigned to the tax system of the Member State concerned, are in a comparable factual and legal situation.[40] However, where the measure concerned applies generally to an entire region within a Member State, the question that arises is whether the regional measure must necessarily be compared to the regime applicable in the Member State as a whole; in other words, whether the Member State regime is the correct comparator reference framework.

The measure at issue in *Portugal* v. *Commission* concerned a scheme of reduced rates of income and corporation tax adopted by, and applicable in, the Autonomous Region of the Azores. Portugal claimed that this was a general measure applicable throughout the relevant reference framework area, namely the Azores. However, according to the Commission, the correct reference framework area was Portugal, making the reduced tax rates a measure that conferred a selective advantage, specific to the Azores. The Court held that in circumstances where the fiscal measure in question confers an advantage in only one part of the national territory of a Member State, the reference framework need not necessarily be the Member State as a whole but may be restricted to the part of the territory that benefits from the measure. This applies where the measure was adopted by a regional or local authority that has, from a constitutional point of view, a political and administrative status separate from that of the central government; the measure was adopted without the central government being able to directly intervene as regards its content; and the financial consequences of a reduction of the national tax rate for undertakings in the region is not offset by

---

[39]Case C-88/03 *Portugal* v. *Commission* ECLI:EU:C:2006:511, para 56.

[40]*Portugal* v. *Commission* (n 39), para 56; Joined Cases C-78/08 to C-80/08 *Paint Graphos and Others* ECLI:EU:C:2011:550, para 49.

aid or subsidies from other regions or the central government.[41] These cumulative criteria were not met in this case because the Azores tax measure was offset by a financing mechanism that was managed by the central government. Therefore, the correct reference framework was held to be Portugal as a whole, with the result that the measure was found to be selective.[42]

### 3.2.3   Generally Applicable Tax Measures That Are *de Facto* Selective

In a subsequent ruling of the CJEU, again sitting in Grand Chamber formation, the Court was called upon to apply its ruling in *Portugal* v. *Commission* in the context of a measure that was not derogatory, in that the tax system did not lay down general rules from which a derogation was made for certain undertakings. In *Commission and Spain* v. *Government of Gibraltar and United Kingdom*,[43] the measure at issue was a proposed tax reform applicable to all companies established in Gibraltar, consisting of payroll tax, which was dependent on the number of employees employed in Gibraltar, and business property occupation tax, which was dependent on the occupation of property in Gibraltar for business purposes. The combination of these bases of assessment, and the absence of other bases of assessment, excluded from the outset any taxation of offshore companies since they have no employees and also do not occupy business property.

The Court held that, while it had admittedly ruled in *Portugal* v. *Commission* that the determination of the reference framework has a particular importance in the case of tax measures, contrary to the ruling of the General Court, the classification of a tax measure as selective was not conditional upon it conferring an advantage by way of a derogatory mechanism.[44] In essence, it held that, irrespective of the regulatory technique used, a tax measure could be regarded as selective where it achieves the same result by adjusting and combining the tax rules in such a way that their very application results in a different tax burden for different undertakings.[45] This requires more than a finding of a different tax burden resulting from the application of the general tax regime:

> the criteria forming the basis of assessment which are adopted by a tax system must also, in order to be capable of being recognised as conferring selective advantages, be such as to characterise the recipient undertakings, by virtue of the properties which are specific to them, as a privileged category, thus permitting

---

[41]*Portugal* v. *Commission* (n 39), paras 67–68.

[42]*Portugal* v. *Commission* (n 39), para 79.

[43]Case C-106/09 P *Commission and Spain* v. *Government of Gibraltar and United Kingdom* ECLI: EU:C:2011:732.

[44]*Commission and Spain* (n 43), paras 90 and 91.

[45]*Commission and Spain* (n 43), para 93.

*such a regime to be described as favouring 'certain' undertakings or the pro-*
*duction of 'certain' goods within the meaning of Article [107(1) TFEU].*[46]

In this regard, the Court held that by combining these bases of taxation, even though they are founded on criteria that are in themselves of a general nature, in practice discriminates between companies that are in a comparable situation with regard to the objective of the proposed tax reform, namely to introduce a general system of taxation for all companies established in Gibraltar. The fact that offshore companies were not taxed was not a random consequence of the regime at issue, the Court held, but the inevitable consequence of the fact that the bases of assessment were specifically designed so that offshore companies, which by their nature have no employees and do not occupy business premises, have no tax base under the bases of assessment adopted in the proposed tax reform. The fact that offshore companies, which constitute a group of companies with regard to the bases of assessment adopted in the proposed tax reform, avoided taxation precisely on account of the specific features characteristic of that group was sufficient to conclude that those companies enjoyed selective advantages.[47]

The result of this ruling appeared to be that in order to conclude that a tax measure that is ostensibly of general application is in fact selective, it is essential that the criteria applied under the regime result in an advantage being conferred on a group that can be identified by reference to properties that are specific to the group.

While this test appears fairly unambiguous, its application is potentially problematic. This is because there can be a fine line between a tax measure that benefits a group that is capable of identification by reference to properties specific to it and a tax measure that leads to a differential tax burden for different companies. This could potentially be the case for many, if not all, generally applicable tax measures. Therefore, if the line between the two is not respected, this could lead to an erosion of the sovereignty of Member States to design their tax regimes. An illustration of this can be found in cases *Banco Santander and Santusa v. Commission*[48] and *Autogrill España v. Commission.*[49] These cases concerned a provision introduced into Spanish tax law in respect of the amortisation of foreign shareholding acquisitions of at least 5%. The Commission found that the provision conferred a selective advantage in that it constituted a derogation from general tax rules and only benefitted certain groups of undertakings that carried out certain investments abroad. The General Court disagreed. It held that the fact that the measure in question was derogatory in nature was not, in and of itself, sufficient. It found that the measure in question was open to all economic operators and was targeted not at any particular category of undertakings but at a category of economic transactions, which did not, a priori, require the acquiring undertaking to change its activity. It also involved only limited responsibility with regard to the investment made (5%) and, implicitly, was

---

[46]*Commission and Spain* (n 43), para 104.

[47]*Commission and Spain* (n 43), paras 101, 106 and 107.

[48]Case C-399/10 *Banco Santander and Santusa v. Commission* ECLI:EU:T:2014:938.

[49]Case T-219/10 *Autogrill España v. Commission* ECLI:EU:T:2014:939.

therefore not restricted to a certain category of undertakings making significant overseas investments.[50] Significantly, the Court observed that the approach proposed by the Commission could lead to every tax measure, the benefit of which is subject to certain conditions, being found to be selective, even though the beneficiary undertakings would not share any specific characteristic distinguishing them from other undertakings, save for the fact that they would be capable of satisfying the requisite conditions to benefit from the relevant measure is;[51] in those circumstances, a tax measure could not be found to "[favour] certain undertakings or the production of certain goods" within the meaning of Article 107(1) TFEU. It is submitted that that was sound reasoning.

Unfortunately, the Commission successfully appealed these rulings before the EUCJ.[52] In a ruling of the Grand Chamber of the EUCJ the General Court's approach in the rulings in *Banco Santander and Santusa* and *Autogrill España* was overturned. Instead, the EUCJ ruled that it is sufficient that the measure *"irrespective of its form or the legislative means used, should have the effect of placing the recipient undertakings in a position that is more favourable than that of other undertakings, although all those undertakings are in a comparable factual and legal situation in the light of the objective pursued by the tax system concerned"*. It is submitted that this effectively undermines the requirement of selectivity and, with it, the ability of Member States to choose how to allocate the tax burden across various economic operators. If a finding that a general tax measure applicable to certain transactions or assets benefits some undertakings more than others is sufficient to establish that it is selective, irrespective of the sector in which those undertakings operate, and the goods they produce, it is difficult to envisage how a tax measure could avoid being regarded as selective. In those circumstances, whether a tax measure falls foul of EU State aid rules could effectively depend on whether it is deemed to lead to a risk of distortion of competition and affects trade between Member States, for which the evidential threshold is very low, as outlined above, and may be met by demonstrating that the recipient exercises an economic activity involving trade between Member States.

**The Case of Patent-box Regimes** The Commission's recent investigations into patent-box regimes raise interesting questions as regards selectivity, similar to those addressed in the appeals in *Banco Santander and Santusa* and *Autogrill España*. These regimes generally apply favourable tax rates to various IP assets, including

---

[50]This can be contrasted with the ruling in Joined Cases T-227/01 to T-229/01, T-265/01, T-266/01 and T-270/01 *Diputación Foral de Álav and Gobierno Vasco v. Commission* ECLI:EU:T:2009:315, concerning a tax credit available to undertakings in the Basque region in respect of investments in new fixed assets exceeding ESP 2 500 million. The General Court held that the Basque authorities had thereby restricted the tax advantage in question to undertakings which have at their disposal significant financial resources, and that the measure was therefore selective.

[51]*Banco Santander and Santusa* (n 48), para 72; Case T-219/10, *Autogrill España* (n 49), para 68.

[52]Case C-20/15 P *Commission v. Autogrill España*; Case C-21/15 P *Commission v. Banco Santander and Santusa*.

patents, by derogation from the normal tax rules. They can have harmful tax competition consequences, as highlighted in tensions between Germany and the UK following the latter's introduction of new patent-box tax rules in 2013.[53] For example, they can be harmful to the extent that they lead to an artificial shift in the place where patents are registered and other IP assets are held, away from the place where the underlying R&D takes place, to the jurisdiction with the most favourable tax treatment. The Commission's opening of informal State aid investigations into the ten Member States that have patent-box regimes, namely Belgium, Cyprus, France, Hungary, Luxembourg, Malta, the Netherlands, Portugal, Spain and the UK, brought those regimes under close scrutiny in informal State aid investigations launched since June 2013.[54] While such regimes are usually open to all economic operators, multinational corporations that tend to have large IP portfolios, especially in certain hi-tech sectors, such as pharmaceuticals, stand to benefit more than other undertakings. The delicate question, however, from a State aid perspective, is whether patent-box regimes confer an advantage on a category of undertakings that is identifiable by reference to properties specific to that group. The Commission already considered this question in 2008 in respect of an IP box regime in Spain. The Commission concluded that the regime was not selective in light of the fact that it was genuinely open to all economically active persons and did not strengthen the position of any particular class of undertakings, observing that the fact that some undertakings benefited more than others, and not every undertaking decides to self-develop a qualifying intangible asset and therefore benefit from the measure, merely reflected an economic reality.[55] While it would have been interesting to see how the Commission would address the current patent-box regimes, it seems that the need to do so may have been avoided, given that Germany and the UK, alongside other States, reached a multinational political consensus on the reform of patent-box regimes in the context of the OECD – BEPS project, in 2015.[56]

### 3.2.4 Discretionary Practices of Tax Authorities

Another area of complexity in determining selectivity relates to discretionary practices of tax authorities. Measures of general application, which, *prima facie*, apply to undertakings in general, may be selective insofar as the administration called upon to apply them has discretion as regards their application.[57] According to the 1998 Notice, an administrative decision that departs from the general tax rules to the

---

[53] See Financial Times, 13 June 2013.

[54] European Commission Press Release 2014b IP/14/663.

[55] Commission Decision C(2008)467 final of 13 February 2008 on State Aid N 480/2007, Spain – The reduction of tax from intangible assets [2008] OJ C 80/1, paras 14 to 18.

[56] OECD (2015).

[57] Case C-241/94 *France v. Commission* ECLI:EU:C:1996:353, paras 23 and 24.

benefit of individual undertakings leads, in principle, to a presumption of State aid, and the opacity of those decisions and the room for manoeuvre that the administration sometimes enjoys support the presumption of selectivity.[58] Similar guidance can be found in the 2016 Notice, in which the Commission describes the application of general measures to individuals on a discretionary basis as potentially selective where the exercise of the discretionary power goes beyond the simple management of tax revenue by reference to objective criteria.[59]

By way of illustration, as the CJEU has held, it is not necessary to demonstrate that the conduct of the tax authority is arbitrary but only that the discretionary power enjoyed by the tax authority allows it to vary the amount of, or the conditions for granting, a tax concession according to the characteristics of the investment project submitted for assessment.[60] In a case concerning a company's request to the tax authorities for the authorisation of deduction of losses, the CJEU held that the application of an authorisation system that enables losses to be carried forward to later tax years cannot, in principle, be considered to be selective if the competent authorities have, when deciding on an application for authorisation, only a degree of latitude limited by objective criteria that are not unrelated to the tax system established by the legislation in question, such as the objective of avoiding trade in losses. However, it held that if the competent authorities have a broad discretion to determine the beneficiaries or the conditions under which the financial assistance is provided, on the basis of criteria unrelated to the tax system, such as maintaining employment, the exercise of that discretion must then be regarded as favouring certain undertakings or the production of certain goods.[61]

In recent years, two practices of tax authorities involving the exercise of discretion have come under the spotlight, namely, advanced pricing arrangements (APA) or tax rulings and tax settlements, which are summarised below.

**Tax Rulings** Tax rulings or APAs can be obtained by companies from tax authorities to establish, in advance, the criteria, method, adjustments and assumptions that the company will apply to calculate and determine the price of its intra-group transactions, for tax purposes. Generally, these rulings effectively authorise the company to apply those arrangements over a certain number of years in the future. This is why they are sometimes referred to as 'comfort letters'.

The price charged for those intra-group transactions can increase or decrease the profits achieved by the relevant subsidiaries, thereby increasing and decreasing their taxable income. Multinational groups tend to have taxable liabilities in multiple jurisdictions with different tax rules and rates. This creates a financial incentive to

---

[58]1998 Notice, para 22.

[59]Commission 2016 Notice, paras 123–125.

[60]*Diputación Foral de Álav and Gobierno Vasco* (n 50), para 154.

[61]Case C-6/12 P *P Oy*, ECLI:EU:C:2013:525, paras 26 and 27.

allocate maximum profits to low tax jurisdictions and minimum profits to high tax jurisdictions, to inflate the prices paid for intra-group transactions or artificially allocate profit to various subsidiaries through transfer pricing. If profit allocation within a corporate group is artificial or exaggerated, it can grant that corporate group an unfair advantage vis-à-vis other operators in the market that do not have the ability to allocate profits across a network of multinational subsidiaries.[62] The methods for calculating and determining the price of intra-group transactions that are endorsed in an APA or ruling are therefore crucial and may result in a substantial reduction of tax liability for the group. This is why they are also pejoratively referred to as 'sweetheart deals' or 'tax sweeteners'. While the Commission does not consider that tax rulings in themselves are necessarily problematic, it is the degree of discretion afforded to the tax authorities in granting tax rulings that can give rise to State aid.[63]

Since June 2013, the Commission has been investigating tax ruling practices. At first, the Commission focused on three Member States, Ireland, the Netherlands and Luxembourg, but in December 2014, it extended its investigations to all Member States.[64] In parallel, the EFTA Surveillance Authority (ESA) started its own investigation into tax ruling practices in the EFTA States, Iceland, Lichtenstein and Norway. While the ESA concluded its investigation in February 2016, finding no evidence of any State aid infringements,[65] the Commission has issued negative State aid decisions, condemning Luxembourg in respect of rulings to FFT and Amazon, the Netherlands in respect of a ruling to Starbucks, Ireland in respect of a ruling to Apple, and Belgium for rulings on at least 35 multinationals, and ordering the recovery of the aid. Meanwhile an investigations is ongoing concerning the tax arrangements applicable to McDonalds.

**The FFT Decision** On 21 October 2015, the European Commission decided that Luxembourg had granted State aid to FFT through a tax ruling issued in 2012 that conferred a selective advantage by unduly reducing its tax burden since 2012 by €20 to €30 million.[66] According to the Commission, the activities of FFT, which is based in Luxembourg, are comparable to those of a bank, providing financial services such as intra-group loans to other Fiat car companies. Its taxable profits are the return on capital deployed by the company for those loans. The Commission considered that the tax ruling of the Luxembourg authorities endorsed 'an artificial and extremely complex methodology that is not appropriate for the calculation of taxable profits reflecting market conditions' and that the ruling had the effect of artificially reducing taxes paid by FFT in two ways. First, it approximated the capital base much lower than the actual capital through a number of 'economically unjustifiable assumptions

---

[62]Commission Decision C(2014) 3627 final of 11 June 2014, State Aid SA 38375 (2014/NN) (ex 2014/CP), Luxembourg – Alleged aid to FFT, paras 11 to 13.

[63]See Commission 2016 Notice, paras 169 and 170.

[64]European Commission Press Release 2014a IP/14/2742.

[65]ESA Press Release 2016 PR(6)09.

[66]Case No SA 38375 (Fiat); European Commission Press Release 2015a IP 15/5880.

and down-ward adjustments'. Second, the estimated remuneration applied to the reduced capital base was much lower than market rates, contrary to the arm's length principle. The Commission therefore ordered Luxembourg to recover the aid granted to FFT. While the latter has reportedly paid €23.1 million to the Luxembourg authorities as a result of the Commission's Decision, Fiat Chrysler Automobiles has flatly denied having received any illegal State aid from Luxembourg, and both Luxembourg[67] and Fiat[68] have challenged the Commission's Decision before the General Court, contesting, *inter alia*, the finding of selectivity.

**The Starbucks Decision**  On 21 October 2015, the European Commission decided that the Netherlands had granted State aid to Starbucks Manufacturing EMEA BV (Starbucks Manufacturing), through a tax ruling in 2008, which unduly reduced its tax burden since then to the order of €20 to €30 million. Starbucks Manufacturing is the only coffee roasting company in the Starbucks group in Europe and sells and distributes roasted coffee and other products (e.g., cups, packaged food and pastries) throughout Europe, the Middle East and Africa. According to the Commission, the Netherlands' tax ruling artificially lowered taxes paid by Starbucks Manufacturing in two ways. First, it endorsed a very substantial royalty paid by Starbucks Manufacturing to Alki (a UK-based company in the Starbucks group, which is liable to pay corporate tax neither in the UK nor in the Netherlands) for coffee-roasting know-how. This could not be justified, according to the Commission, as it did not reflect market value, and no other Starbucks group company or independent roasters to which roasting was outsourced was required to pay a royalty for using the same know-how in essentially the same situation. Second, the Dutch tax authorities endorsed an inflated price paid by Starbucks Manufacturing for green coffee beans to Switzerland-based Starbucks Coffee Trading SARL. Starbucks has challenged the EC's decision, claiming, *inter alia*, that the APA or ruling was not selective and that the EC used the wrong reference framework for determining selectivity.[69]

**The Decision Concerning Belgium's 'Excess Profit' Rulings**  On 11 January 2016, the Commission decided that Belgium granted State aid of around €700 million to at least 35 multinational companies through tax rulings under the 'excess profit' tax scheme.[70] While, ordinarily, Belgian company tax rules require companies to be taxed on the basis of profit actually recorded from activities in Belgium, the Commission found that, through the tax rulings, the actual recorded profit of a multinational was compared with the hypothetical average profit of a stand-alone company in a comparable situation. The alleged difference in profit is deemed to be

---

[67]Case T-755/15 *Luxembourg v. Commission* [2016] OJ C 59/48.

[68]Case T-759/15 *Fiat Chrysler Finance Europe v. Commission* [2016] OJ C 59/49.

[69]Case T-760/15 *Netherlands v. Commission* [2016] OJ C 59/50.

[70]Case No SA 37667 (Excess profit exemption in Belgium); Commission Press Release 2016 IP/16/42.

excess profit by the Belgian tax authorities, and the multinational's tax base is reduced proportionately. This is based on a premise that multinational companies make excess profit as a result of being part of a multinational group, e.g. due to synergies, economies of scale, reputation, client and supplier networks, access to new markets. According to the Commission, the scheme reduced the corporate tax base of companies by between 50 and 90%. The Commission reasoned that even assuming that a multinational generates such excess profits, under the arm's length principle, they would be shared between group companies in a way that reflects economic reality and then taxed where they arise. However, under the Belgian excess profit scheme, such profits are simply discounted unilaterally from the tax base of a single group company.

**Arm's Length Principle** One of the key issues in the Commission's decisions concerning Luxembourg, the Netherlands and Belgium is whether the values allocated to intra-group transactions or the manner in which taxable income is calculated in the rulings reflect market value, in conformity with the 'arm's length principle'. In *Belgium and Forum 187 v. Commission*, where one of the questions at issue was whether the flat-rate assessment of income under the cost-plus method conferred an economic advantage on certain undertakings, the Court ruled that in order to determine whether a method of assessment of taxable income conferred an advantage, it is necessary to compare that regime with the ordinary tax system based on the difference between profits and outgoings of an undertaking carrying on its activities in conditions of free competition.[71] The Commission takes the view that the Court thereby confirmed that if the method of taxation for intra-group transfers does not comply with the arm's length principle, leading to a taxable base inferior to one that would result from a correct implementation of that principle, it provides a selective advantage to the company concerned.[72] Thus, according to the Commission, the latitude afforded to tax authorities to endorse a particular tax method in a tax ruling can give rise to a selective advantage. Indeed, while the methods endorsed by tax authorities in a tax ruling ultimately determine the overall tax liability and the amount of any advantage, they also go to the question of selectivity insofar as they effectively allow a taxpayer to use alternative or more favourable tax methods for calculating taxable profits than those that would ordinarily apply to taxpayers in a similar factual or legal situation or that a prudent independent operator acting under normal market conditions would accept.[73] This type of analysis is extremely time-consuming and fact specific, and one wonders whether this is workable in practice. Indeed, policing tax rulings to determine whether the taxable methods endorsed by the tax authorities are appropriate would require a substantial amount of sophisticated resources. In reviewing the legality of the Commission's selectivity analysis in the FFT and Starbuck Decisions in the pending appeals, it is to be hoped that the

---

[71]Case C-182/03 *Belgium and Forum 187 v. Commission* ECLI:EU:C:2006:416, para 95.
[72]Commission Decision C(2014) (n 62), para 61.
[73]See Commission 2016 Notice, para 174.

General Court will provide some clearer and more workable guidance as to when tax rulings will be deemed selective. Failing this, the enforcement of State aid rules against individual tax rulings may ultimately be sporadic and piecemeal because the Commission is unlikely to have the resources to carry out these assessments throughout the EU.

**Tax Settlements** Where there is a dispute between a taxpayer and the tax authorities concerning outstanding tax liability, one of the ways in which the dispute can be resolved is through a tax settlement between the two parties. Tax settlements can save tax authorities time, effort and legal fees while optimising the recovery of taxes. However, if the tax authorities have wide discretion to reach a settlement that reduces the amount of tax liability without objective justification, this can give rise to a selective advantage. The 2016 Notice foresees two circumstances where this can arise: (1) where the tax authority makes a disproportionate concession to a taxpayer, which appears to constitute a more favourable discretionary tax treatment, compared to other taxpayers in a similar factual and legal situation, and (2) where it appears that the settlement is contrary to the applicable tax provisions and has resulted in lower tax liability.[74]

In January 2016, the UK's Chancellor of the Exchequer announced a tax settlement between the UK tax authorities and Google, requiring Google to pay £130 million in back taxes to the UK treasury. According to some press reports, the settlement could represent an effective tax rate of 3%.[75] Given the Commission's recent high-profile enforcement of State aid rules against fiscal measures, it was unsurprising that calls have been made for the Commission to investigate.

Should the Commission decide to open a formal investigation into the UK/Google tax settlement, this would represent a further example of the Commission's ambitious use of State aid rules to address sensitive questions regarding the taxation of multinationals.

# 4 Conclusion

State aid enforcement against tax incentives has placed Member State fiscal regimes under heavy scrutiny in recent years. Given the competence of the Member States in the field of taxation, this is a sensitive topic. The fact that major multinational companies have been implicated in the Commission's investigations has only increased the political importance of these enforcement initiatives.

In seeking to tackle discretionary practices by European tax authorities in their tax dealings with major multinationals, the Commission has embarked on an ambitious

---

[74]Commission 2016 Notice, para 174.

[75]Financial Times, 26 January 2016.

endeavour. The appropriateness and legitimacy of the use of State aid rules as a tool to achieve these goals aside, the Commission's recent enforcement efforts have raised some important questions concerning the interpretation of the selectivity criterion under EU State aid law. This criterion will continue to be tested before the EU courts in pending cases in the near future, and this could have far-reaching consequences for the reach of EU State aid law enforcement and ultimately the scope of Member States' sovereignty in the field of taxation.

# References

Commission Press Release (2016) State aid: Commission concludes Belgian "Excess Profit" tax scheme illegal; around €700 million to be recovered from 35 multinational companies, 11 January 2016, IP/16/42

Desai K (2014) A development in State aid practice – tax rulings and settlements become a focus of attention. Eur Competition Law Rev 35(12)

ESA Press Release (2016) 24 February 2016, PR(6)09

European Commission Press Release (2014a) State aid: Commission extends information enquiry on tax rulings practice to all Member States, 17 December 2014, IP/14/2742

European Commission Press Release (2014b) State aid: Commission investigates transfer pricing arrangements on corporate taxation of Apple (Ireland), Starbucks (Netherlands) and Fiat Finance and Trade (Luxembourg), 11 June 2014, IP/14/663

European Commission Press Release (2015a) Commission decides selective tax advantages for Fiat in Luxembourg and Starbucks in the Netherlands are illegal under EU state aid rules, 21 October 2015, IP 15/5880

European Commission Press Release (2015b) State aid: Commission investigates transfer pricing arrangements on corporate taxation of Amazon in Luxembourg, 7 October 2014, IP/14/1105

European Commission Press Release (2015c) State aid: Commission opens formal investigation into Luxembourg's tax treatment of McDonald's, 3 December 2015, IP/15/6221

European Commission Press Release (2015d) State aid: Commission opens in-depth investigation into the Belgian excess profit ruling system, 3 February 2015, IP/15/4080

Financial Times (2013) UK under pressure from Berlin over tax competition, 13 June 2013

Financial Times (2016) Experts probe Google tax payment, 26 January 2016

Luja R (2003) Harmful tax policy: when political objectives interfere with State aid rules. Intertax 31:484

Luts J (2014/2015) Compatibility of IP box regimes with EU State aid rules and code of conduct'. EC Tax Rev 2014/15:258

OECD (2013) Action plan on base erosion profit shifting. OECD Publishing

OECD (2015) OECD/G20 Base Erosion and Profit Shifting Project, Action 5: Agreement on Modified Nexus Approach for IP Regimes. OECD Publishing

Quigley C (2015) European State aid law and policy, 3rd edn

# State Aid and Gambling Services

Ana Pošćić

**Abstract** The combination of public goals and fiscal interests collides with the need to harmonise and liberalise the gambling market. Although the trend of market liberalisation is omnipresent, liberalisation is not an imperative. Member States are, in principle, free to regulate these issues, provided that they comply with the principles of EU law, especially competition and State aid rules. The focus of this paper is on the possible application of State aid rules in the field of gambling. Though the debate on State aid in the area of gambling has gained momentum, it has not been followed by a proliferation of corresponding case law. So far, the Commission has adopted only a few decisions, some of which have been challenged before the General Court. These will be analysed in this article. Special attention is given to the controversal OPAP decision, which has been subject to a lot of discussion.

## 1 Introductory Remarks

The trend of market liberalisation is omnipresent, but when it comes to gambling services, the situation differs significantly. In this segment, liberalisation is not an imperative. Striking down unnecessary and unjustified restrictions on the free provision of services is important, but it does not mean that Member States are required to liberalise gambling markets.

This area is not harmonised at the level of the European Union and remains within the competence of Member States. National regulations in this field differ widely. Member States are free to choose a regulatory model themselves. While some of them have opted for a total ban, others have decided to completely liberalise the field. Certain Member States have established monopolies or very restrictive, licence-based systems, depending on the type of game of chance. For the most part, however, the market is very fragmented.

Opening up gambling services to competition could raise demand. Stimulating greater demand in this segment is not particularly desirable for various socio-ethical

A. Pošćić (✉)
Faculty of Law, University of Rijeka, Rijeka, Croatia
e-mail: aposcic@pravri.hr

© Springer-Verlag Berlin Heidelberg 2017                                      273
V. Tomljenović et al. (eds.), *EU Competition and State Aid Rules*,
Europeanization and Globalization 3, https://doi.org/10.1007/978-3-662-47962-9_13

reasons. Member States are therefore entitled to limit competition by creating monopolies, as confirmed in case law, but only if they establish 'effective and strict control'. This means that other providers will have only limited or no access to the market. Thus, even if monopolies limit the freedom to provide services and the freedom of establishment, they can be justified by reasons of public interest, as long as the principle of proportionality is satisfied. Exclusive rights may be justified only if state control is 'effective', 'consistent' and 'systematic'. On the other hand, Member States that decide to open the market up by issuing licences or concessions must create a system based on 'objective and non-discriminatory criteria'.[1] According to the established case law, the fact that a state chooses a regulatory model that differs from that adopted by another Member State cannot affect the assessment of the proportionality of the measure in question.[2]

The gambling market is specific. The stakes are high, and extremely large revenues flow into state budgets. The fact that gambling is associated with sociological as well as cultural phenomena, such as addiction, illegal gambling and money laundering should also not be forgotten. Member States' freedom to frame their own restrictive systems is circumscribed primarily by their moral, religious and socio-economic heritage and traditions and also by the principles of EU law. Member States enjoy a wide margin of discretion in this area. They are free to set the objectives of their gambling policies and an appropriate level of consumer protection and protection of public policy on their sovereign territory, i.e. to restrict the number of operators, the type and scope of gambling services and the manner of their provision. They are also free to decide whether they wish to allow or prohibit gambling, impose criminal or other sanctions on unlicensed operators or limit the advertising opportunities for gambling. The gambling market is therefore far from being a single market, and it seems that there will be no significant improvements in the near future. Given that there is no shortage of monopolies in this sector, it is often referred to as their last bastion in the European Union.

Although Member States are, in principle, free to regulate these issues, they must comply with the principles of EU law, especially fundamental freedoms and competition rules. However, the concerted practices of state providers or situations in which the state tends to favour particular providers are particularly challenging, and a certain degree of competition must be present.[3]

The development of new technologies constantly opens up new possibilities for providing and organising various games of chance. It is a dynamic, commercially promising and extremely fast-growing market. Every type of aid or incentive given by the state to particular companies is liable to distort competition. In principle, State aid is prohibited, unless justified by reasons of economic development.

---

[1] For more on this issue, see: Nicolaides (2013), p. 282.

[2] Judgment in *Markku Juhani Läärä, Cotswold Microsystems Ltd and Oy Transatlantic Software Ltd* v *Kihlakunnansyyttäjä (Jyväskylä) and Suomen valtio (Finnish State)*, C-124/97, EU: C:1999:435.

[3] Arendts (2007), p. 42.

## 2 Application of Competition Rules *Sensu Stricto*

In some situations, national gambling regulations may be observed through the prism of competition and State aid rules. The possibility of applying competition rules in general was first invoked by individual advocates general in the earliest case law dealing with games of chance. In the 1999 Läärä case, for example, Advocate General La Pergola considered their application predominantly in the context of fundamental market freedoms. Contrary to the appellants' arguments linking competition rules to the concept of an undertaking, he argued that the existence of a monopoly in the field of the provision of services had to be judged from the aspect of the free movement of goods and the freedom to provide services. The problem arises if the monopoly is organised and exercised in a manner contrary to fundamental economic freedoms, especially the free movement of goods and the freedom to provide services.[4] According to Advocate General La Pergola, rules should be scrutinised within the context of not only fundamental economic freedoms but also other provisions, notably competition rules. However, the Advocate General mentioned competition rules only in passing and did not find it necessary to examine this aspect any further.[5]

Competition rules *sensu stricto* primarily include Articles 101, 102 and 106(2) of the Treaty on the Functioning of the European Union[6] (TFEU). These provisions regulate prohibited agreements, abuse of a dominant position and the position of public undertakings and those vested with special or exclusive rights. They apply equally to private providers of services and state monopolies.

State monopolies in the field of games of chance generate revenues that usually belong to the state budget. It is not uncommon to allocate these to various charity purposes. As such, they can be subject to Article 106(2) TFEU. This provision is applicable to undertakings entrusted with the operation of services of general economic interest or having the character of a revenue-producing monopoly. These are subject to rules on competition, but only in so far as the application of such rules does not obstruct the performance, in law or in fact, of the particular tasks assigned to them. This is a very complex area, which strives to bridge the gap between legitimate national public interests, on the one hand, and free movement, competition and state rules, on the other.[7] Since this is an exception, it should be interpreted very narrowly. This provision tries to balance the non-economic

---

[4]See AG La Pergola, Opinion delivered on 4 March 1999 in judgment *Markku Juhani Läärä, Cotswold Microsystems Ltd and Oy Transatlantic Software Ltd v Kihlakunnansyyttäjä (Jyväskylä) and Suomen valtio (Finnish State)*, EU:C:1999:435, para 16.

[5]See AG La Pergola, Opinion in judgment *Markku Juhani Läärä, Cotswold Microsystems Ltd and Oy Transatlantic Software Ltd v Kihlakunnansyyttäjä (Jyväskylä) and Suomen valtio (Finnish State)*, EU:C:1999:435, para 24.

[6]Consolidated versions of the Treaty on European Union and the Treaty on the Functioning of the European Union, OJ C 326, 26.10.2012, pp. 47–390.

[7]Hancher and Sauter (2012), pp. 281 and 282.

interests invoked by the Member States with economic concerns.[8] Member States determine the services of general economic interest themselves. However, this reasoning hardly applies to the gambling sector because the argument that operators of games of chance provide services of general economic interest is simply not convincing. Nevertheless, as will be shown, some Member States have tried to avoid the application of State aid rules, arguing that certain gambling services fall under this concept.

## 3  Application of State Aid Rules in General

State aid generally distorts competition. Granting aid to individual undertakings affects the allocation of resources, which can have adverse consequences on investment and development in the long run. State aid can also influence the market production-wise and disturb the balance among competitors.[9]

While various State aid concerns occupy an increasingly important place in the segments of media, environmental protection and problems associated with the financial crisis, they seem to have kept a low profile in the gambling sector. Lately, however, the situation has begun to change. It has become more than clear that potentially prohibited aid could arise in the context of tax incentives to domestic operators. One possible example is the system of selective tax reduction.[10]

It is debatable whether a liberalised sector needs control. General principles, though, teach us that control is the same and necessary in every area because a certain amount of competition needs to be preserved. Favouring domestic service providers can trigger the application of State aid rules. In EU law, any aid that distorts or threatens to distort competition by favouring certain undertakings or the production of certain goods is prohibited in so far as it affects trade between Member States. Even though State aid is prohibited in general, in some cases it may be found compatible with the internal market if it promotes legitimate goals and satisfies the principle of proportionality.

In order to be characterised as aid, an advantage granted to the recipient has to be of an economic nature and such that it could not be realised under normal market conditions. The measure must imply actual or potential use of public resources, and be selective, i.e. directed specifically at a certain undertaking or type of goods. The last condition that needs to be determined is whether the measure distorts competition or affects trade between Member States. In principle, the prohibition of State

---

[8]Hancher and Sauter (2012), p. 283.

[9]Hancher and Sauter (2012), p. 262.

[10]In the contested Commission Decision, it was determined that a selective lowering of taxes could be justified by exceptions to prohibited State aid. However, this did not apply to the system of selective lowering of taxes in the financial sector. The Court confirmed the Commission's Decision in judgment in *Portuguese Republic* v *Commission of the European Communities*, C-88/03, EU:C:2006:511.

aid almost always focuses on the distortion of trade between Member States. It is interesting that under the existing case law, it is not necessary to prove that the granted aid actually caused a distortion or disturbed the position of consumers. The most important thing is to show that the position of the undertaking has been reinforced in any manner whatsoever which would otherwise not have been possible. The mere possibility of this having happened suffices. An increasing number of critics insist, however, that there should be a stronger analysis of the impact in terms of restriction of competition.[11]

Basic principles are found in Articles 107 and 108 TFEU, as well as in the abundance of case law. Article 107 TFEU structurally consists of three parts. The first paragraph provides a general definition of aid contrary to the internal market, the second paragraph enumerates so-called automatic exemptions, while the third paragraph prescribes certain categories of aid that can be declared compatible with the internal market. Therefore, any aid that distorts or threatens to distort competition by favouring certain undertakings or the production of certain goods is prohibited if it affects trade between Member States. However, certain situations are considered acceptable.[12]

There are two possibilities of justifying aid that has been found incompatible with the internal market. The prohibition in Article 107 TFEU is never absolute or unconditional. Exceptions are contained in Paragraphs 2 and 3 of the article. Paragraph 2 enumerates types of aid that will always be exempted. However, this provision is of minor importance, given its limited scope. Paragraph 3, on the other hand, is more interesting because it describes situations in which the Commission is entitled to authorise certain types of aid. As always, all exceptions are interpreted very strictly.

Pursuant to Article 107(3) TFEU, the Commission is granted wide powers to exempt certain aid. A significant number of block regulations in this segment facilitate the Commission's job. When certain aid is not covered by the regulations, the Commission may grant an exception by referring to guidelines and instructions. In other words, a general prohibition of aid is complemented by the provisions of Article 107(2) and (3) TFEU, which give the Commission a certain amount of flexibility. Economic and social aspects are investigated, and the arguments for and against the aid are weighed against each other. There are several questions that the Commission always seeks to clarify.[13] In the end, it all boils down to compliance with the principles of necessity and proportionality.

---

[11]Bacon (2013), p. 13.

[12]Article 107(2) TFEU enumerates examples of aid which are always deemed compatible with the internal market. These include: (a) aid having a social character, granted to individual consumers, provided that such aid is granted without discrimination related to the origin of the products concerned; (b) aid to make good the damage caused by natural disasters or exceptional occurrences; (c) aid granted to the economy of certain areas of the Federal Republic of Germany affected by the division of Germany, in so far as such aid is required in order to compensate for the economic disadvantages caused by that division.

[13]See State aid action plan: Less and better targeted state aid: a roadmap for state aid reform 2005–2009 (Consultation document) {SEC (2005) 795}, COM/2005/0107 final.

Article 107(3)(a) TFEU refers to aid to promote the economic development of areas where the standard of living is abnormally low or where there is serious underemployment. It is interpreted jointly with sub-paragraph (c) of the same provision, which points out that aid to facilitate the development of certain economic activities or certain economic areas may be considered to be compatible with the internal market. These provisions are the basis for granting regional aid.[14] Although sub-paragraph (a) does not mention EU interests, the case law determines that the Commission must always be guided by the Union's interests when granting certain exceptions. Claiming that the measure has a positive impact on a certain region is not sufficient; what matters is the impact on trade between Member States. Therefore, even though aid falls under the category of aid described in paragraph 3, the Commission has the final say. This sub-paragraph may be linked to sub-paragraph (c), but the main difference lies in the criterion of 'underdevelopment'. The comparison under sub-paragraph (a) is made taking into account the entire Union, whereas under sub-paragraph (c) the comparison is made in relation to the national average. Such aid should be granted in a manner that develops less advantaged regions and that supports investment and the creation of new jobs. The scope of this sub-paragraph is very limited and specific as the Commission is the one that evaluates the problems existing in certain regions. It is therefore not surprising that this provision has rarely been applied.

Sub-paragraph (b) contains exceptions for aid to promote the execution of an important project of common European interest or to remedy a serious disturbance in the economy of a Member State. In order to assist the recipients and providers of aid, the Commission has developed additional criteria to help in its assessment.[15] The economic crisis in recent years has heated up the debate on potential aid to resolve serious disturbances in the economy of a Member State. In order to satisfy this criterion, the disturbance must affect the entire national economy. It is said that this provision has thrived after the great economic turmoil in certain Member States.[16]

Pursuant to sub-paragraph (c), the Commission is entitled to grant aid to facilitate the development of certain economic activities or certain economic areas, where such aid does not adversely affect trading conditions to an extent contrary to the common interest. It covers a wider spectrum of aid than sub-paragraph (a). This exception is also the one that is most commonly used. All sector and regional aid falls under this provision. The Commission's policy is directed more at granting horizontal aid used in certain activities or areas. In one of its judgments, the CJEU determined that all decisions in which the Commission adopts regional aid charts for each Member State should be interpreted so as to represent an integral part of the Guidelines on regional State aid and are considered binding only if accepted by Member States.[17]

---

[14]Bacon (2013), p. 110.
[15]Bacon (2013), p. 108; Liszt and Petrović (2011), p. 40.
[16]Bacon (2013), p. 109.
[17]Bacon (2013), p. 47.

When it comes to granting aid to promote culture and heritage conservation (Article 107(3)(d) TFEU), it is important to highlight that the concept of culture is also interpreted narrowly. The commercial factor must not be neglected because it can be a decisive element. Although sport is relatively closely linked to the notion of culture, it is sometimes difficult to determine whether it falls under this exception. Heritage conservation is, in principle, covered by this sub-paragraph. Cultural activities are therefore subject to the Commission's control. In other words, culture enjoys no special status when it comes to State aid.

# 4 Application of State Aid Rules in the Field of Gambling

State aid rules have so far not played an important role in the field of gambling. The relatively recent Commission action plan 'Towards a Comprehensive European Framework for Online Gambling' of 2012 does not even mention State aid rules.[18] The accompanying Staff Working Document partially covers this void as it contains a separate chapter on the application of State aid rules in the field of gambling. However, it only briefly mentions two cases decided on by the European Commission. Although debates about State aid in the field of gambling have gained momentum, they have not been followed by a proliferation of corresponding case law. So far, the Commission has adopted only a few decisions, some of which have been challenged before the General Court. They will be analysed later.

## 4.1 The *Dansk Automat Brancheforening* Decision

In this case, the Commission initiated proceedings against Denmark.[19] The Commission's Decision[20] has recently been confirmed by the General Court.[21]

---

[18]Communication from the Commission, Towards a comprehensive European framework on online gambling, /2012/0596 final/.

[19]Decision of the EU Commission to initiate formal investigation procedure provided for in Article 108(2) TFEU about Denmark Duties for Online Gaming in the Danish Gaming Duties Act, OJ C 35/2010 (ex N 302/2010).

[20]Commission Decision 2012/140/EU of 20 September 2011 on measure C 35/10 (ex N 302/10), OJ 2012, L 68, p 3.

[21]Judgment of 26 September 2014, *Dansk Automat Brancheforening* v *European Commission*, T-601/11, EU:T:2014:839. The applicants' claim was dismissed on account of a lack of legal interest, because State aid was justified in accordance with Article 107(3) TFEU, and was declared compatible with the internal market. Case *Dansk Automat Brancheforening* v *Commission*, C-563/14P. An appellate procedure is pending before the Court. On the same day, the General Court rendered an identical judgment of 26 September 2014, *Royal Scandinavian Casino Århus I/S* v *European Commission*, T-615/11, EU:T:2014:838, not yet published, which is also pending before the Court, judgment in *Royal Scandinavian Casino Århus* v *Commission*, C-541/14P.

The facts are as follows: in 2007, the Commission delivered a reasoned opinion to Denmark about obstacles to the freedom to provide sports-betting services in Denmark. Based on the opinion, Denmark decided to amend the existing gaming legislation and to replace the public monopoly in this sector with a regulated and partially liberalised system. In 2010, Denmark notified the Commission pursuant to Article 108(3) TFEU about the draft Gaming Duties Act, which was part of a wider legislative package.

In accordance with the Gaming Duties Act, the provision or arranging of gambling is subject to the payment of duties. The Act sets different tax rates, depending on whether the games are provided online or in land-based casinos. Therefore, holders of a licence to provide games on slot machines in amusement arcades and restaurants are subject to a charge of 41% of their gross gaming revenues. An additional 30% is paid on gaming machines in public houses, bars, etc. on gross gaming revenues exceeding DKK 30,000, and on gaming machines in amusement arcades on gross gaming revenues exceeding DKK 250,000. Holders of a licence to provide games in land-based casinos are subject to a basic charge of 45% of gross gaming revenues, less the value of tokens held, and an additional charge of 30% on gross gaming revenues exceeding DKK 4 million, calculated on a monthly basis. In contrast, holders of a licence to provide games in online casinos are subject to a charge of 20% of gross gaming revenues.

The Commission scrutinised the tax calculation method and found that the measure that Denmark intended to apply in the form of a tax on online gaming in the Gaming Duties Act represented State aid, which was, however, compatible with the internal market within the meaning of Article 107(3)(c) TFEU. The Commission based its conclusion on three arguments. All of them supported the existence of State aid. The Commission found that the notified measure, i.e. the setting of a minimum charge on online games for all operators established in Denmark, represented State aid within the meaning of Article 107(1) TFEU. It was considered that the notified Act provided a tax advantage to gaming operators, granted through state resources.

The notified measure could *prima facie* be considered selective because it differentiates online gaming operators from gaming operators in classic land-based casinos, although their situation is comparable in law and in fact. The Commission took the view that the Danish authorities had failed to establish that the apparent selectivity of the notified Act could be justified by the logic of the tax system.[22] After determining that all the criteria for State aid existed, the Commission examined the potential justifications. It concluded that the aid fulfilled the conditions required for it to be considered compatible with the internal market pursuant to Article 107(3)(c) TFEU.[23] In support of this conclusion, the Commission first stated that the Gaming Duties Act, given that it leads to market

---

[22]Commission Decision 2012/140/EU of 20 September 2011 on measure C 35/10 (ex N 302/10), OJ 2012, L 68, paras 72–101.
[23]Commission Decision 2012/140/EU, para 145.

liberalisation and allows Danish and foreign online gaming operators to provide their services to Danish residents, while guaranteeing that they satisfy the necessary licensing conditions, serves a well-defined objective of common interest.[24] Second, the Commission found that the aid is proportional because the tax rate of 20% of gross gaming revenue for online gaming operators is not lower than is necessary to achieve the objectives of the Act.[25]

However, an explanation as to how the Commission concluded that a lowering of taxes by more than 50% satisfies the proportionality test is lacking. The probable reason why it was considered necessary can be found in the fact that online gaming is one of the fastest growing segments of the gaming market. The tax reduction is aimed at attracting foreign service providers to apply for a licence in Denmark. Third, the Commission assessed the impact of the measure on competition and trade between Member States. In this regard, it stated that setting the tax rate for online gambling at the same or a similar level as the one applicable to land-based gambling would have created a situation where the industry and players would not have responded to the possibility of legally providing online gambling services on the Danish market.

The decision was justified because online providers face powerful global competition. Their business setting is completely different from classic, land-based casinos, which operate in a certain geographical area. Neither should the existence of monopolies in this segment be forgotten. According to the usual economic indicators, the total amount of collected taxes applying a higher tax rate would eventually be lower than the amount collected under a lower rate. It is well known that anti-competitive regulations and disproportional licensing systems do not increase revenues but rather push consumption to the black market.[26] It should also be mentioned that the majority of EU Member States apply a different tax rate, depending on whether online or classic gambling services are provided.

Dansk Automat Brancheforening, an association of undertakings and companies licensed to install and operate gaming machines, applied for the annulment of the Commission's Decision. The applicant has 80 members and represents approximately 86% of the operators of games played on slot machines in Denmark. The Judgment of the General Court is not directly relevant to this paper since it mostly deals with the applicant's *locus standi*, i.e. whether the contested Decision is of direct and individual concern to the applicant. However, pursuant to Article 263 (4) TFEU, any natural or legal person may, under the conditions laid down in the first and second paragraphs of that article, institute proceedings against an act addressed to that person or that is of direct and individual concern to them and against a regulatory act that is of direct concern to them and does not entail implementing measures. This provision is of vital importance when it comes to

---

[24]Commission Decision 2012/140/EU, paras 106–123. On State aid and taxes in general, see: Micheau (2011), pp. 193–218.

[25]Commission Decision 2012/140/EU, paras 124–137.

[26]Lignè (2011).

competition cases, especially in the field of State aid. It is deemed that a decision regarding State aid adopted in formal investigation proceedings individually concerns applicants if that aid substantially affects their market position. In this regard, it was established that the Commission's decision to close formal investigation proceedings affected not only the aid recipient but also its competitors that had an active role in these proceedings, if the aid from the contested decision had had a substantial impact on their market position.

After a detailed inspection, the General Court concluded that the applicant had failed to establish, on the one hand, that the consequences of the contested aid measure had affected its members in their objective capacity of classic, offline gaming operators in Denmark in the same way as any other economic operator in the same situation or, on the other hand, the importance of the potential impact of the contested aid measure on the economic situation of its members, i.e. that the measure could substantially threaten the position of one or more of its members on the relevant market. The contested decision therefore did not individually concern the applicant or its members. Thus, the General Court dismissed the action as inadmissible, given the applicant's lack of *locus standi*.

## 4.2 The Commission's Decision on the French Proposal for a Parafiscal Levy on Online Horse-Race Betting

The Commission's Decision of 2013 approving the French proposal for a parafiscal levy on horse-race betting is very interesting.[27] The intention was to pay the entire revenue from the levy to horse racing companies.

France notified the Commission of its proposal for a parafiscal levy to the amount of 8% of the betting stake in order to financially support horse racing associations. France initially sought to include the measure under services of general economic interest so as to avoid its assessment under State aid. After an investigation was initiated in 2010, the Commission expressed its doubts about the possibility of invoking the status of services of general economic interest. The question was whether the tasks performed by horse racing companies could be treated as a public service mission. France responded by sending an amended proposal to the Commission, modifying the system so as not to present the new measure as one used for financing public services. In other words, the Commission's doubts as to whether this sector implies services of general economic interest, i.e. about the application of Article 106(2) TFEU, became irrelevant. The new system was presented as an aid to the economic sector based on the common interest. Only those costs directly related to horse racing organisations

---

[27]Commission Decision of 19 June 2013 on State aid No SA.30753 (C 34/10) (ex N 140/10) which France is planning to implement for horse racing companies (C(2013) 3554) (2014/19/EU).

were part of the calculation of the level of the tax. Thus, the initially planned rate of 8% was decreased to approximately 5.6%.

The background to introducing this levy was as follows. At that time, France[28] had decided to liberalise online horse-race betting. The intention was to suppress the fast-growing trend of illegal online gambling. Three types of games of chance were opened up to competition: online horse-race betting, sports betting and poker games. Before liberalisation, an exclusive horse-race betting monopoly was held by the economic interest grouping PMU (Pari Mutuel Urban). Eighty per cent of its extremely large revenues were used to fund horse racing and the equine industry. Given the importance of PMU funding, the French authorities were concerned that opening up the industry to competition would threaten its sustainability. Opening up the market would logically lead to a decrease in the PMU's revenues, and players might consider switching to other types of games of chance.

Without a doubt, the measure fulfils all the elements of State aid,[29] as it is granted by the state. The PMU's activities are partially funded by collected levies, thereby creating a certain economic advantage for it. The levy on online betting benefits horse racing and the equine industry. Its intention is to prevent potential economic destabilisation as a consequence of opening up to competition. The entire revenue is aimed at horse racing companies. In other words, horse racing companies undeniably stand to receive an economic advantage. Company activities are partially funded from state resources. Revenues collected by the economic interest grouping are transferred to horse-race betting operators to finance their development.

The Commission examined whether the measure could be exempted under Article 107(3) TFEU.[30] Pursuant to its earlier practice, the Commission had granted financing aid to certain sectors several times before, especially if its purpose was to promote technological development and increase quality, competitiveness and productivity, as well as to adjust to market needs. The measure satisfied these conditions. It represented aid to the equine sector, which benefited all horse-race-betting operators. However, it was important to examine whether it also contributed to the achievement of common interest. Given the close connection between the levy and the aid, it was important to assess whether the levy complied with fundamental economic freedoms, i.e. the freedom to provide services.[31] In addition, the Commission examined if the measure was contrary to the prohibition of introducing a discriminatory tax system.[32]

Through its four-step approach, the Commission established whether the measure strove to achieve a well-defined common objective, whether the measure represented an adequate instrument for achieving that goal, whether an incentive

---

[28] See also Brassi and del Frederico (2005).

[29] Commission Decision of 19 June 2013 on State aid, paras 115–129.

[30] Commission Decision of 19 June 2013 on State aid, paras 130–149.

[31] Commission Decision of 19 June 2013 on State aid, paras 150–152.

[32] Commission Decision of 19 June 2013 on State aid, paras 153–157.

existed and whether the measure was proportional to the desired objective. This last element was intended to establish the extent of distortion of competition and trade, i.e. whether positive impacts prevailed. The aid complies with the principles of liberalisation of online betting in France and certainly tries to contribute to the development of the equine industry. Apart from attempting to achieve a well-defined objective, the aid is adequate for accomplishing this objective, which is to ensure the continuity of horse racing and fair competition in a newly liberalised sector. In addition, the measure promotes the development and continuation of existing activities in the field of horse racing.

It can be concluded that the true purpose of the aid is to redistribute the burden of financing among all online betting providers on the French market, i.e. to guarantee their sustainability and fair competition in a liberalised market.

## 4.3   The *OPAP* Decision

It is impossible not to mention the Commission's decision of 2012 finding that the Greek sports betting association OPAP (Organisation of Betting on Football Matches) did not receive State aid. According to the Commission,[33] the crucial element for the existence of State aid was lacking: the criterion of economic advantage.

Before proceeding with a detailed analysis of this decision, it is important to note that the CJEU had already (on 24 January 2013) ruled in a case concerning OPAP that the organisation's exclusive rights were contrary to internal market provisions, more precisely the freedom to provide services, because competition was excluded from the market.[34] Although this judgment is not directly relevant to this paper, it should be taken into consideration because it seems, as will be shown here, that the Commission's and the Court's views diverge. Despite the fact that these are two separate cases, it is interesting to observe them as parts of the same context. Thus, whereas in the Commission's view the key element for proving an advantage was missing, the Court clearly found that the monopoly prevents other competitors from entering the market for games of chance in Greece.[35] In order to explain this divergence, the Commission's decision will be carefully analysed.

In essence, the Commission's decision concerns two measures in favour of OPAP that were taken by the Greek authorities. One of them involved a prolongation of an exclusive right granted to the organisation to manage 13 games of chance

---

[33]State aid SA.33988 (2011/N) – Greece, Arrangements for the extension of OPAP's exclusive right to operate 13 games of chance and the granting of an exclusive licence to operate Video Lottery Terminals, Brussels, 03.10.2012, C(2012) 6777.

[34]Judgment in *Stanleybet International Ltd and Others and Sportingbet plc* v *Oikonomias kai Oikonomikon and Ypourgos Politismou*, C-209/11, not yet published in Reports.

[35]Nicolaides (2013), p. 272.

for an additional 10-year period (until 2030). This prolongation was granted in an addendum to the concession agreement. There was no public tender for the prolongation of the existing exclusive rights. The factual setting of this measure deserves closer attention. OPAP had already been granted a monopoly for certain games of chance in the year 2000, for which it paid an extremely large amount to the Greek authorities (EUR 323 million). The Addendum extended the monopoly for another period of 10 years. It should not be disregarded that OPAP employs a substantial number of workers. OPAP agreed to pay a lump sum of EUR 375 million for the extension of the monopoly, along with a levy of 5% of gross gaming revenues in the period from 2020 to 2030, but only on amounts exceeding a defined daily revenue threshold. Greece undertook the obligation to examine the gross gaming revenues over a 3-year period so as to be able to set the threshold for the future calculation of gross gaming revenues. This obligation appears important because it deals with additional revenue, which was not part of the previous 20-year monopoly concession.

The other notified measure concerned the granting of an exclusive licence to operate 35,000 video lottery terminals (VLTs) for a period of 10 years, which was contained in a separate agreement. The licence was granted for a consideration of EUR 560 million. There was no public tender for this exclusive licence either.

When the Commission started to examine the notified measures, it clearly stated that the investigation procedure would not affect any other procedure involving OPAP in any manner whatsoever. The problem was that OPAP's revenues were considerably higher because of the exclusive VLT operating licence than they would have been had there been other competing operators. The question is: why do competition principles exist in the first place? All the information was declared confidential, and no one could precisely quantify the extent of the potential economic advantage. It is even possible that Greece would have earned more had there been a public international call for tenders for allocation of more than one concession to operate VLT services.

The Commission focused on establishing whether OPAP had been granted a certain economic advantage. It examined both agreements jointly. Following the standard calculations, the Commission determined that OPAP would end up paying more than it would benefit from the exclusive rights. It was crucial to determine whether the price paid by OPAP corresponded to the value of the exclusive rights. If the price was lower, then OPAP would benefit, the state would lose certain revenue and the aid would be qualified as State aid. The Commission determined, however, that OPAP did not gain any advantage that would not be granted to an average operator in a situation of normal competition. The question remains: how is it possible to compare OPAP to average operators when they do not even exist?

It boils down to simple economic calculations. According to the Commission, an advantage is represented by a certain return exceeding the amount that an average operator would achieve in a situation of normal competition. That was the criterion. There would be no advantage if OPAP maintained the minimum return required by an average operator to cover its operative capital expenses. It is questionable who would be considered an average operator in a situation where there is only one provider and what would be considered a situation of normal competition when the market is completely closed. Only the minimum anticipated return was referred to because anything above it would represent an economic advantage. One can only speculate whether such an approach was intentionally rather lenient towards Greece.

The factual background to the previously mentioned judgment of the Court in the Stanleybet case could help clarify the situation. In this case, three companies considered that the exclusive right granted to OPAP was incompatible with the freedom to provide services and freedom of establishment. One should also not forget that Greece reduced its initial 51% share in OPAP to 34% in 2005. According to the explanation provided by the referring authority (the Council of State), this meant that the state maintained only superficial control over OPAP.

The Court first determined that exclusive rights are not compatible with Articles 49 and 56 TFEU. However, it stated that restrictions may be justified by overriding reasons of public interest, but they must be proportional.[36] Granting exclusive rights to a single entity may be justified only if the state's supervision is effective, consistent and systematic. However, the information available to the Court showed that the state's supervision was merely superficial. This seems to suggest that the consistency and efficiency of consumer protection rules can be guaranteed only through strict control by public authorities. Although the removal of restrictions in the gambling market is necessary, it does not mean that the market should be liberalised. The existence of competition in this field could encourage gambling. In other words, states are free to keep a monopoly, but only if they can ensure strict and efficient supervision. Otherwise, if they decide to open up the market, the system must be based on objective and non-discriminatory criteria.

One of the possible objectives of a monopoly is to prevent illegal gambling and keep the area under supervision. This, in turn, has a considerable impact on the profit of a single operator that is granted a licence to manage and operate games of chance. It is well known that the existence of competition creates risk. Where there is no competition, the risk factor is certainly reduced. A monopoly clearly increases profit, but in the case of gambling it should not be so because one of the objectives of such a monopoly is to prevent opportunities for gambling, addiction and the pertaining risk of criminal activities. OPAP was exposed to lower risk because there was no competition.

On the other hand, the Commission started its investigation by comparison with an average operator in normal circumstances. The problem was that normal circumstances did not exist in Greece and that OPAP was certainly no average operator because it held a monopoly. The Commission usually takes into account market circumstances and risks in its practice, but this was not the case this time.

Maybe those leaning towards the Commission's and the Court's views might argue that the economic advantage, which has to exist for Article 107 TFEU to

---

[36]Judgment in *Stanleybet International Ltd and Others and Sportingbet plc* v *Oikonomias kai Oikonomikon and Ypourgos Politismou* , para 21.

apply, is not the same as the one arising from a monopoly. The Court did not refer to such a differentiation in its judgment. It did not even discuss it. Inevitably, each holder of a monopoly stands to benefit from the lack of competition. If such an advantage exists, it can easily be offset by imposing heavier burdens on the holder of such a right. In other words, when the existence of State aid is examined, one should take into account the fact that the existence of a monopoly is in principle incompatible with the internal market. When trying to prove an economic advantage, it is important to take into consideration the potential profit that can be acquired by the holder of a certain right. Of course, if someone has a monopoly, then his profit exceeds that which could be earned by an average company, and it is precisely the profit of an 'average' company that the Commission took into account.

The logic behind this is as follows. If the market is closed due to a monopoly, the risk faced by a single operator on the market is much lower than in a situation of competition. It is precisely this risk that should be taken into account when examining the rate of return on investment by such operators. The amount of the licence determined in comparison with an average undertaking can represent an advantage and thus State aid. If examined in relation to the provisions on fundamental freedoms, the question is whether a measure contrary to the freedom to provide services or the freedom of establishment could be exempt from State aid rules. This is possible because it has been established that all four criteria have to be met in order for Article 107 TFEU to apply.[37] Thus, it is just a matter of verifying whether such activity represents an 'advantage' within the meaning of State aid rules. Nevertheless, a situation in which a company holds exclusive rights without thereby acquiring a corresponding economic advantage that it would otherwise not have under normal market circumstances is highly improbable.

It is settled case law that restrictions in the gambling market may be justified by overriding reasons of public interest, but it also has a significant impact on investigations in the context of State aid.[38] This mainly concerns the question of whether an undertaking enjoys a certain economic advantage. The point is that any examination of a potential advantage should also include an assessment of market specificity. In this situation, it is impossible to refer to an average undertaking. What should be taken into account is the market specificity, which in such a case is closed.

The Commission's decision has recently been confirmed by the General Court.[39] According to its judgment, Greece did not grant illegal aid by prolonging the existing exclusive right and at the same time issuing new licences for 35,000 VLTs for a period of 10 years. In the General Court's view, which corresponds with the Commission's standpoint, OPAP had overpaid for the prolongation of the

---

[37]Nicolaides (2013), p. 273.

[38]On the possible combined application of the rules on fundamental economic freedoms and State aid rules, see Staes (2015), pp. 106–121.

[39]Judgment of 8 January 2015, *Club Hotel Loutraki AE and Others* v *European Commission,* T-58/13, EU:T:2015:1, not yet published in Reports.

existing exclusive right. The General Court reaffirmed the Commission's calculations that OPAP will end up paying the Greek authorities far more than the value of the exclusive rights.[40] This element has drawn hefty criticism. It was deemed that no rational investor would accept such a deal. It is clear that OPAP's profits were substantially higher as a result of the exclusive licence than they would be in a normal market with competing operators.

The applicants in this case claimed that these two agreements should not be examined together because they concern two separate markets. It is crucial, as argued by the applicants, to assess the advantage separately for each market. According to the applicants, an examination of both markets together results in an incomplete protection of competition because measures representing an anti-competitive advantage within the meaning of Article 107(1) TFEU might escape prohibition. Thanks to its monopoly, OPAP is in a position to lower prices on the slot machine market and subsidise its operations by raising prices on the market for 13 games of chance.[41] However, the Commission failed to take into account this element, given its joint assessment of both markets. The problem was that the applicants did not substantiate their claims with concrete evidence because even though they argued that these measures should be observed together, they also referred to the connection between prices on the VLT market and the monopoly market.[42] Both agreements were concluded at the same time, even though they cover different periods. The General Court found that the Commission was right to consider both agreements as part of a single privatisation package, as they were made in the same economic context, and so should be assessed together.[43] In the General Court's view, they relate to a single market as they involve similar activities on the gambling market.

Pursuant to the established case law, the Commission does not have to determine the relevant market to establish the existence of State aid. It always examines the context of a transaction, taking into account the entire economic reality. One of the reasons for the conclusion of these agreements might lie in the increase of OPAP's market value, to make it more attractive to potential buyers. It seems that the background to this case was largely influenced by the Greek financial crisis. One might even suspect data tampering or 'dressing the bride' to increase the short-term value of the undertaking, making it more attractive to invest in and sell.[44] The fact that Greece decided to sell one-third of its holding in OPAP at about this time in order to service its debts should not be overlooked. As stated by the General Court, the Commission was familiar with the fact that both agreements were part of a single 'privatisation package', they referred to the same economic context and it

---

[40]Judgment in *Club Hotel Loutraki, para 39 above*, EU:T:2015:1, paras 17 and 18.

[41]Judgment in *Club Hotel Loutraki, para 39 above*, EU:T:2015:1, paras 79–81.

[42]Judgment in *Club Hotel Loutraki, para 39 above*, EU:T:2015:1, paras 94–96.

[43]Judgment in *Club Hotel Loutraki, para 39 above*, EU:T:2015:1, para 92.

[44]Von Danwitz (2009), p. 118.

was justifiable to consider them together.[45] In other words, it seems that the Commission's decision was guided by the notion of not in any manner threatening the financial capacity of Greece to service its outstanding obligations.[46] This decision and the General Court's position open up a series of questions. One of them relates to the future of the gambling market. The current situation makes its future development extremely hard to predict. The other question concerns the extent of the benefit of competition in this sector. Does this decision affect the business efficiency and productivity model, i.e. does it promote more efficiency on the Greek gambling market? One thing is certain: the political dimension of this case is clear.

# 5 Concluding Remarks

The combination of public goals and fiscal interests collides with the need to harmonise and liberalise the gambling market.[47] It is certain that liberalisation is still not in sight. Member States will keep their competence to regulate this sector. This is also a political question, and if the Union intends to make some changes in this area, then, as argued by Bogaert and Cuyvers, it has to make an offer that the Member States will not be able to refuse.[48] One should insist on fairer regulations in this segment, but it is less than likely that Member States will do something about it.[49] The Member States will certainly not give up the large revenues this market is known for.

It is important to set clear rules to control illegal State aid, whether it is by decreasing or setting different tax rates or by granting exclusive rights that imply economic advantages for certain operators. This is especially so in the context of new forms of games of chance. Online betting is a fast-growing industry that should be subject to clear rules. Transparency is crucial for achieving social benefits. Since the market is developing very quickly, it is hard to foresee all the possibilities and potential benefits for future operators. It is certainly important to open up the market and for the state to set clear and transparent rules to facilitate the provision of services while maintaining an adequate degree of supervision. This is also related to the concept of the digital economy, which has recently appeared high on the agenda. The digital economy is a new form of the economy based on digital technologies and represents one of the most attractive growth possibilities for the majority of states. It is based on online connectivity and accessibility and thus enables completely new business models. The Internet facilitates simple and cost-

---

[45]Judgment in *Club Hotel Loutraki,* para 39 above, EU:T:2015:1, para 92.

[46]Similar arguments are expressed in the commentary of Amsel (2015).

[47]Doukas and Anderson (2008), p. 266.

[48]Van den Bogaert (2011), p. 1211.

[49]Arendts (2007), pp. 51–52.

effective linking of distant and previously inaccessible markets. This phenomenon embraces much wider areas than business and markets. It includes individuals, communities and society. It is therefore important that all decision-makers and stakeholders in this sector are familiar with the trends and potentials, as well as the challenges, that lie ahead.

# References

Amsel P (2015) European Union court says no foul in Greek Government's fattening of OPAP, 9 January 2015. http://calvinayre.com/2015/01/09/casino/european-commission-rules-opap-vlt-monopoly-deals-legal/. Accessed 6 Mar 2015

Arendts M (2007) A view of European gambling regulation from the perspective of private operators. In: Littler A, Fijnant C (eds) The regulation of gambling, European and national perspectives. Martinus Nijhoff, Leiden, pp 41–53

Bacon K (2013) European Union law of state aid. Oxford University Press, Oxford

Brassi M, del Frederico L (2005) The notion of tax and the different types of taxes. In: Peeters B (ed) The concept of tax, 2005 EATLP Congress, Naples, 27–29 May 2005. IBFD, Amsterdam, pp 59–79

Doukas D, Anderson J (2008) Commercial gambling without frontiers: when the ECJ throws, the dice is loaded. Yearb Eur Law 27(1):237–276

Hancher L, Sauter W (2012) EU competition and internal market in the health care sector. Oxford University Press, Oxford

Lignè S (2011) Online gambling: competitive tax rate for online gambling is compatible with EU State aid rules. Press release. http://pr.euractiv.com/pr/online-gambling-competitive-tax-rate-online-gambling-compatible-eu-state-aid-rules-91422. Accessed 24 Jul 2015

Liszt M, Petrović S (2011) Kriteriji za dodjelu dopuštenih državnih potpora. In: Čulinović Herc E, Jurić D, Žunić Kovačević N (eds) Financiranje, upravljanje i restrukturiranje trgovačkih društava u doba recesije. Pravni fakultet Sveučilišta u Rijeci, Rijeka, pp 27–68

Micheau C (2011) State aid and taxation in EU law. In: Szyszazak E (ed) Research handbook on European State aid law. Edward Elgar, Cheltenham, pp 193–218

Nicolaides P (2013) Competition and advantage under internal market and State aid rules: is there a gap in the law? Leg Issues Econ Integr 40(3):271–290

Staes M (2015) The combined application of the fundamental freedoms and the EU State aid rules: in search of a way out of the maze Intertax 42(2):106–121

Van den Bogaert C (2011) Money for nothing': the case law of the EU Court of Justice on the regulation of gambling. Common Mark Law Rev 48(4):1175–1213

Von Danwitz T (2009) State aid control over public services: a view from the Court. In: Krajewski M, Neergaard U, Van de Gronden J (eds) The changing legal framework for services of general interest in Europe, between competition and solidarity. T M C Asser Press, The Hague, pp 117–129

# Certain Aspects of State Aid to Services of General Economic Interest

Marijana Liszt and Edita Čulinović Herc

**Abstract** This paper tackles postal services as one of the most widespread examples of services of general economic interest (SGEI) in order to highlight the specificity of the network industries and their contribution to EU harmonisation in this field. It also tries to position the notion of universal services in relation to the notion of SGEIs. The paper addresses the different views of various Member States on the perception of a public service and stresses the divergences that are inherent in the topic since different legal cultures, traditions and social and historic features affect the subject matter. In the absence of sectoral Union rules governing the matter, the Member States have a wide margin of discretion in defining services that could be classified as services of general economic interest. The Commission's task is to ensure that there is no manifest error with regard to the definition of SGEIs. The paper further analyses the role of the Commission's soft (law) approach, which has ended up in quite a coherent SGEI legal framework, including especially the SGEI package, but also primary law instruments such as Articles 14 and 106 TFEU, Protocol No 26 and the Charter on Fundamental Rights. This paper also presents the applicable rules that the Commission has applied in its recent Post Office Decision.

## 1 Introduction

In March 2015, among the headlines on the website of the European Commission – Competition, there was a press release on how the European Commission had endorsed £640 million compensation for the United Kingdom postal network for the period from 2015 to 2018. The UK Post Office Ltd has been granted compensation for delivering a whole range of public services in its entire network, that is, for providing services of general economic interest (SGEIs). The Commission found the measure to be in line with EU State aid rules, in particular because the

M. Liszt (✉)
Liszt & Posavec Law Firm, Zagreb, Croatia
e-mail: marijana.liszt@prl.hr

E. Čulinović Herc
Faculty of Law, University of Rijeka, Rijeka, Croatia
e-mail: edita@pravri.hr

© Springer-Verlag Berlin Heidelberg 2017                                             291
V. Tomljenović et al. (eds.), *EU Competition and State Aid Rules*,
Europeanization and Globalization 3, https://doi.org/10.1007/978-3-662-47962-9_14

compensation paid to Post Office Ltd was limited to the additional costs that the Post Office faced to fulfil its public service mission. So was this measure State aid in the sense of Article 107(1) TFEU or mere compensation for a public service in line with the Altmark Trans legacy? What services did it encompass? On what grounds did the Commission authorise the aid and with the help of which tools? How was the compensation calculated? Is there a similar public service provider in Croatia, and would such a service also have been considered beneficial for citizens by the public authorities in Croatia, as was the case in the United Kingdom? On that note, how are public services perceived in various Member States?

Through these questions and possible answers and through a brief analysis of this recent case before the Commission, as well as some comparative cases from the postal sector, we would like to shed light on the current (indeed, in the last couple of years very much advanced) EU legal framework for providing and financing services of general economic interest and the administrative practice of the Commission. However, in spite of the large amount that has been said and written on this topic in the last 15 years, this part of State aid law is still quite open-ended and still leaves plenty of room for debate. With this in mind, we will try to consider the issues that have still not been settled, including the challenges of defining SGEIs, bearing in mind the sensitivity of public services in general, as well as their importance for the public authorities of sovereign Member States.

## 2 The *Post Office* Case and Beyond

Post Office Ltd owns a nationwide network of around 11,700 post offices and provides a wide range of services to the public. The services it provides include access to postal services (but, curiously enough, not universal postal services[1]), basic banking and cash facilities, public utility payment facilities and governmental services such as handling of social benefit payments and passport and vehicle licence applications. Post Office Ltd is a subsidiary of Royal Mail, the United Kingdom's main postal service provider, which used to be state owned until 2013,[2] and which is the one that provides the universal postal service in the UK, in accordance with EU postal legislation.

Previously, the Commission authorised State aid measures in favour of Post Office Ltd in 2007 and 2011 as it concluded that such post office counter outlets act as 'focal points for the communities they serve'. In 2012, the Commission authorised the UK plans to grant a £1155 million network subsidy to Post Office

---

[1]Universal postal services refer to the provision of basic postal services to the UK population, including delivery to any address throughout the UK six times per week, and a sufficient network of letter boxes and post offices or postal partner offices.

[2]On 15 October 2013, Royal Mail became a quoted company with shares traded on the London Stock Exchange.

Ltd, aiming to keep open and modernise non-commercially viable offices. In January 2015, the UK notified plans to grant £640 million to Post Office Ltd for providing public services from 1 April 2015 to 31 March 2018 to the Commission for State aid scrutiny. Post Office Ltd has and will continue to have a public service mission to carry out and maintain a set of public services over a larger network of post offices than would be commercially optimal. The Commission's assessment showed that the compensation to Post Office Ltd was designed to ensure that it would not exceed the cost of the public service mission. The payment of the compensation is made dependant on Post Office Ltd reaching certain annual milestones regarding the scope and size of its network. This has been envisaged to give an incentive to Post Office Ltd to be efficient in the provision of public services. Moreover, the award of the public service mission complied with EU public procurement rules. The Commission therefore concluded that the measure was compatible with Article 106(2) of the Treaty on the Functioning of the European Union (TFEU), which governs the assessment of services of general interest under the State aid rules.

*'Today's decision will make sure that those UK citizens who live in more remote areas will also have access to a post office...' (Margarethe Vestager, Commissioner for Competition)*

In Croatia, there is no public service provider such as Post Office Ltd. The universal service is provided by Croatian Post (HP Hrvatska pošta d.d.). The universal service obligation (USO) is a notion very close to the notion of a service of general economic interest, and in a way is concurrent to it.[3] USO is also a type of public service obligation (PSO) that sets the requirements designed to ensure that certain services are made available to all consumers and users in a Member State, regardless of their geographical location, at a specified quality and, taking account of specific national circumstances, at an affordable price.[4] Flynn and Rizza (2001) provide for a good overview of market development in the postal sector with regard to liberalization and deregulation. According to Popović (2013), the term universal service is used to depict the concept of a service of general economic interest in the legal framework of a network industry. So the USO for Croatian Post means that this service must be available to all citizens of the Republic of Croatia over the entire territory of Croatia at the same time and at an affordable price. On the other hand, other providers of postal services may choose which services to

---

[3]As Advocate General Tesauro opines in Case C-320/91 *Paul Corbeau* of 19 May 1993[1993] ECR 1-2563: 'in the context of postal services, the concept of universal service obligation is founded on a basic principle of fairness, according to which it is the State's duty as far as practicable to create equal opportunities and living conditions for all its citizens, including the provision of a means of inter-personal communication, in order to promote social cohesion'.

[4]The definition of a specific USO is set at EU level as an essential component of the market liberalisation of certain sectors, such as electronic communications, post and transport.

provide and in which cost-effective areas. For example, Croatian Post must deliver postal items to the most remote and most inaccessible areas of the Republic. It needs to deliver a letter within Zagreb for a price of HRK 3.10, but it should also deliver a letter from Zagreb to one of the farthest islands, to the island of Lastovo, at the same price. Regardless of the number of postal items for some sparsely populated areas, these postal items must be delivered by Croatian Post within the prescribed deadlines.

Were it not for the public service obligation, Croatian Post would be able to act as any other provider of postal services, that is, it could close hundreds of postal offices and several hundreds of courier offices in less densely populated areas and on less accessible islands that prove commercially unprofitable. Therefore, in this hypothetical case, it could choose users and offer only profitable services (known as 'cream skimming' or 'cherry picking'), as do other postal service providers operating exclusively in accordance with market principles. This unfair burden and the related costs of Croatian Post result from its obligation to provide the service in question over the entire territory of the country in compliance with high quality standards.[5]

Croatian Post can be compensated for this unfair burden or net cost of the universal service obligation according to EU law. The right of a universal service provider to compensation is foreseen in the national legislation of all EU Member States, where, in many cases, a financing mechanism for this compensation is also foreseen. In accordance with EU rules, or, more precisely, EU rules on services of general economic interest (SGEIs),[6] Croatian Post submitted a request for compensation of the unfair financial burden[7] to the Croatian Regulatory Authority for Network Industries (HAKOM) for the first time after the accession of the Republic of Croatia to the EU. Upon the authorisation of HAKOM, the money paid to Croatian Post for the net cost will be used for the further maintenance of the accessibility and sustainability of the postal network in order to ensure the availability of and accessibility to a universal service, as a service of general economic interest and of interest to all citizens of the Republic of Croatia, to everybody under identical conditions on the entire market.

---

[5]'Services of general economic interest would not be provided if pure market economy logics were applied. This is why they are linked to the notion of – market failure' (Popović 2013).

[6]As the Commission itself admits in its 2011 'Quality Framework for Services of General Interest in Europe', the debate on services of general interest suffers from a lack of clarity of terminology. Communication from the Commission to the European Parliament, the Council, the European Economic and Social Committee and the Committee of the Regions – A Quality Framework for Services of General Interest in Europe, Brussels [2011] COM(2011) 900 final.

http://ec.europa.eu/services_general_interest/docs/comm_quality_framework_en.pdf.

Accessed 8 Jun 2015, Concepts are used interchangeably and inaccurately. The basic concepts are: Service of General Interest (SGI), Service of General Economic Interest (SGEI), Social Services of General Interest (SSGI), Universal Service Obligation (USO), Public Service Obligation (PSO) and Public Service. All these concepts will be explained further in the text.

[7]At its session of 14 November 2014, the Council of HAKOM adopted a decision on the amount of net cost representing unfair financial burden on the universal service provider, Croatian Post.

Similar to this subject, in the field of services of general economic interest in the postal sector and universal postal services, there were four State aid cases before the Commission in 2012: Deutsche Post, Bpost, La Poste and Hellenic Post. The Commission approved compensation of EUR 5.6 billion granted by Germany to Deutsche Post from 1990 to 1995 to cover the cost of the universal postal service. However, the Commission ordered Germany to recover from Deutsche Post incompatible aid between EUR 500 million to EUR 1 billion resulting from a combination of high regulated prices and pension relief subsidies, which put Deutsche Post in a better position than its competitors. Similarly, in the Bpost case, the Commission ordered Belgium to recover EUR 417 million of incompatible aid from Bpost since the yearly compensation received in the period 1992–2010 for public service missions resulted in some overcompensation. In the case of La Poste, the Commission reaffirmed its objective of high-quality public services by approving EUR 1.9 billion of aid paid by France to La Poste to finance part of the cost of the public services of delivering press items to citizens and being present in remote areas for the period 2008–2012.

Finally, the Commission approved aid of EUR 52 million granted by Greece to Hellenic Post (ELTA) to contribute to financing the modernisation of its public postal services until 2021. This was aimed at broadening the range of services offered over the whole territory of Greece, in particular in the peripheral regions. However, in 2014, ELTA found itself again under the Commission's scrutiny. ELTA is a Greek state-owned postal operator entrusted with the universal postal service and additional SGEIs, such as basic banking services (receipts, payments of social benefits and pensions, payment of bills, cash payments) or the issuing of licences, certifications and certificates sent by the state to citizens. ELTA operates on a market that has been fully liberalised since 1 January 2013 by the Greek Postal Law but has never before received compensation for the delivery of universal postal services. Only in 2014 did the European Commission find the direct subsidies granted by Greece to ELTA for the delivery of the universal service over a 2-year or three-year transitory period to be in line with EU State aid rules on SGEIs. The Commission concluded in particular that the grants only compensate ELTA for the extra costs of carrying out public service obligations. It is interesting to note that ELTA has been receiving compensation for both the universal postal service and the additional SGEIs it has been providing.

We can see from the above cases that some Member States may entrust the same undertaking with both SGEIs and the universal postal service, as in the case of ELTA, or can entrust one undertaking with SGEIs and another with the universal service, as in the UK case. Accordingly, some Member States classify certain postal services as SGEIs apart from the universal postal service that is provided mostly by incumbent operators. Here we have to point out that EU law does not create any obligation to designate formally a task or a service as being of general economic interest, except when such an obligation is laid out in the Union legislation,[8] such

---

[8]'The sectoral legislation adopted at EU level has always carefully balanced the need to increase competition and the use of market mechanisms with the need to guarantee that every citizen continues to have access to essential services of high quality at prices that they can afford. This has

as a universal service in the postal and telecommunication sectors, due to the liberalisation of the market on one hand and legal harmonisation on the other.[9] Actually, the relevance of SGEIs has grown apace with the scope of liberalisation in the EU (Sauter 2008), and SGEIs are now broadly applied in the network industries and increasingly in the social sphere.

## 3 The Challenges of Defining SGEIs

Some Croatian scholars see services of general economic interest as a new concept of public service in which the existing model of public services has been gradually transformed (Klarić and Nikolić 2011). In the Commission's soft law, services of general interest (SGIs) are commonly defined as services that public authorities of the Member States classify as being of general interest and, therefore, subject to specific public service obligations (PSOs[10]). The term covers both economic and non-economic services. The latter are not subject to specific EU legislation and are not covered by the internal market and competition rules of the Treaty. SGEIs are economic activities that deliver outcomes in the overall public good that would not be supplied at all or would be supplied under different conditions in terms of quality, safety, affordability, equal treatment or universal access by the market without public intervention. It should be noted that the word 'economic' in SGEIs refers to the nature of the activity concerned and not to the public interest, which may be non-economic in nature (e.g., the promotion of public health). The notion of 'economic' services indicates that the exemption of Article 106(2) TFEU applies to undertakings only. Public authorities acting as such are not subject to competition rules.[11] At the same time, it should be stressed that public services can be owned and operated publicly (or through public undertakings)[12] or privately and that the structure of ownership does not determine the application of EU rules, all in line

---

been the case, for instance, in the network industries from telecommunications and postal services to transport and energy' (Quality Framework for Services of General Interest in Europe 2011).

[9]Where EU harmonisation rules refer only to certain specific services, the Member States have considerable discretion in defining additional services as SGEIs. For example, in the electronic communications sector, Member States are required to lay down the universal service obligations provided for by the Directive, but they have discretion to go further than the Directive in defining electronic communication services as SGEIs.

[10]The public service obligation (PSO) represents a common mechanism for the provision of services of general economic interest throughout the Member States of the European Union, but is not a thoroughly defined concept of law within the EU and its legal framework (Henning 2011). Henning argues that the concept has received significantly less attention from law practitioners and academia than the terms SGEI or USO. Indeed, the term PSO is mostly discussed in connection with Article 93 TFEU with regard to EU transport law.

[11]It is possible to draw a conclusion that a certain entity is an undertaking with regard to the fact that the activities concerned could be performed in competition (Sauter 2008).

[12]Such services can also be performed in-house, as explained in the 2011 SGEI Communication.

with the principle of the neutrality of the system of property ownership.[13] The PSO is imposed on the provider by way of entrustment and on the basis of a general interest criterion that ensures that the service is provided under conditions allowing it to fulfil its mission.

Social services of general interest (SSGIs) include social security schemes covering the main risks of life and a range of other essential services provided directly to the person and that play a preventive and socially cohesive or inclusive role.[14] While some social services (such as statutory social security schemes) are not considered by the European Court as being economic activities, the jurisprudence of the Court makes it clear that the social nature of a service is not in itself sufficient for it to be classified as non-economic. Therefore, the term social service of general interest covers both economic and non-economic activities.

To sum up, SGEIs are services of an economic nature that public authorities identify as being of *particular importance to citizens* but that are not supplied by market forces alone or, at least, not to the extent and under the conditions required by society (Pesaresi et al. 2012a). The jurisprudence of the Court of Justice has established that SGEIs are services that exhibit special characteristics as compared with those of other economic activities.[15] The concept may apply to different situations and terms, depending on the Member States. Namely, there are differences between one Member State and another and between one sector and another in the design, scope and organisational approach of services of general economic interest, owing to different traditions and practices (Aviani and Đerđa 2008). The public authorities in the Member States, whether at national, regional or local level, depending on the allocation of powers between them under national law, have considerable discretion when it comes to defining what they regard as services of general economic interest. The only limits are those imposed by EU law (in harmonised sectors at the EU level) and manifest errors of assessment. Namely, the freedom of Member States to define SGEIs is subject to review by the Commission and to the Union's courts to check for manifest errors of assessment.

As has been pointed out above, the examples of SGEIs can be large commercial services such as postal services, energy supply, electronic communication services or public transport that are provided to the entire population under affordable conditions. But further examples of SGEIs can also be a wide range of health and social services, such as care for the elderly or people with disabilities or even

---

[13]As set in Article 345 TFEU.

[14]The 2006 Communication Implementing the Community Lisbon programme, 'Social services of general interest in the European Union', identified two main groups of SSGIs in addition to health services: statutory and complementary social security schemes, organised in various ways (mutual or occupational organisations), covering the main risks of life, such as those linked to health, ageing, occupational accidents, unemployment, retirement and disability and other essential services provided directly to the person. These services that play a prevention and social cohesion role consist of customised assistance to facilitate social inclusion and to safeguard fundamental rights.

[15]E.g. Court judgment in Case C-179/90 *Merci convenzionali porto di Genova* [1991] ECR I-5889, para 27.

childcare. Services in the areas of social security, healthcare and education may be SGEIs only if they are considered economic activities. It is also important to stress that SGEIs must be addressed to citizens or be in the interest of society as a whole as services addressed only to businesses do not normally qualify as SGEIs.[16]

Looking deeper into the Commission's case law, it could be found that there is a whole range of further sectors that the Member States wish to present as SGEIs, such as sea and coastal freight water transport, sea and coastal passenger water transport, air transport, land transport, television programming and broadcasting activities, radio broadcasting, financial and insurance activities (occupational pension schemes), telecommunications (broadband), renting and operating of own or leased real estate (social housing), hospital activities, news agency activities, electric power generation, transmission and distribution, and pension funding. It is also possible to provide a list of sectors where the Court or the Commission has accepted the existence of a service of general economic interest in the past. These include the following: river port operations, establishing and operating a public telecommunication network, water distribution, operation of television services, electricity distribution, operation of particular transport lines, employment recruitment, basic postal services, maintaining a postal service network in rural areas, regional policy, port services, waste management, ambulance services and basic health insurance. However, this does not mean that these services should be regarded as services of general economic interest in all Member States, at all times.

In our view, one of the most interesting issues within this subject is how the Member States perceive what is to be classified as a public service (SGEI). Certainly, there must be differences in the perception of the notion of public service in a country at the south of Europe, or at its north. A British Labour Party politician, Peter Hain, once said that 'public services are an intimate part of the relationship between national governments and their citizens and so individual Member States should have the right to define their own services of general economic interest and the way in which they are delivered'. In their Fourteenth Report on European Union, the European Committee of the House of Lords of the UK Parliament stated that European societies are committed to the general interest services they have created that meet basic needs. In their view, these services play an important role as social cement over and above practical considerations. They also have symbolic value, reflecting a sense of community that people can identify with. Finally, they form part of the cultural identity of everyday life in all European countries.

SGEIs have not been defined by the Treaty. It may be that the reason to leave open the definition of SGEIs was to give Member States wide freedom to define missions of general economic interest and to establish the organisational principles of the services intended to accomplish them. The concept of SGEIs is also a dynamic one. Perceptions of what such services comprise, or what they do not

---

[16]'If the services are not supplied to the general public, as in the case of GEMO, then there may be an indirect granting of state aid due to the distortion of competition among the users of the services in question' (Nicolaides 2003).

comprise, vary in time and place (Sauter 2008). It sometimes also has to do with the historical, cultural, sociological or national heritage of a certain Member State or its part. This adds to the complexity of the subject. At the same time, as pointed out by Jääskinen (2011), social, health, education or training services may, depending on the situation, display characteristics of normal market services, and SGEIs may have an economic or non-economic or social character, or they may be exercised by a public authority.[17] For example, the services provided by a psychiatric hospital may fall under all of these categories. Not even this perspective makes for a clear delimitation of notions.

The divergent perception of the content of SGEIs of various Member States may be one of the causes for the rather late attempts of legal harmonisation in this area,[18] except for sectoral legislation in the liberalised network industries such as telecommunications, postal services or energy.

# 4   The Divergences

Divergences in the perception of the public service mission may be only one aspect of the ongoing debate on the common denominator of services of general economic interest. The real palpable tension is the one that used to be present between the sovereign Member States and the European Commission as the supranational body entrusted with control of State aid and at the same time the chief policy maker of the Union. The Member States wish to obtain a broad public service exception on one hand, and the European Commission, on the other hand, seeks to avoid opening Pandora's box, which could threaten the application of the market freedoms and the competition rules (Sauter 2008). As Rusu and Kekelekis (2011) explain, for Member States, the financing of SGEIs is a means of achieving the social and cohesion objectives set out in their constitutions. However, for the European Union, this may constitute a distortion of competition between Member States and is subject to close scrutiny. This terrain is therefore one where a clear definition of the services and the national interests concerned and the delimitation of national and EU competences are of crucial importance.

According to Sauter (2008), the parties in this debate, fearing liberalisation and privatisation based on EU law (notably the public sector unions and their political

---

[17]Sauter (2008) notes that vertically integrated services provided by public authorities tend to be ignored by the Treaty, whereas 'introducing even a modicum of competition among undertakings providing the same services can lead to the competition rules being applied to the point where legitimate national public interest may be threatened' which, in his view leads to the 'central paradox' where the same services are provided by undertakings on one hand (then the competition rules apply in full) or, on the other hand, by entities which are not considered as undertakings but are 'solidarity based' (they are excluded from competition rules altogether).

[18]Cremona (2011) states that the fragmented nature of EU rules on services of general economic interest is probably inevitable given the diverse nature of these services in themselves and their regulation in different Member States.

allies), campaigned to give public services a sound basis in the Treaty itself.[19] France was a Member State that often acted as a standard bearer for such efforts. Slot (2008) makes reference to the political importance of the notion of public services, mentioning that it was highlighted during the French campaign for the referendum on the Constitutional Treaty in the spring of 2005. One of the arguments of the 'No' campaign was that the 'Community was gradually undermining the public services!' So the debate here is not only about the balance between state control and market freedoms but also about the relationship between EU regulation and national policy choices (Cremona 2011). Schweitzer (2011) mentions the 'persistent friction' between EU law and the Member States' public service traditions and concludes that these are the result of 'fundamentally different conceptions of the role of markets and the role of the states'.

For the above-mentioned reasons, the provisions of EU law relating to services of general economic interest are not only fragmented but are also controversial. There are conflicting pressures either to protect public services from competition or to subject them to competition. This tension and the latent conflict between the stakeholders in this area have been reflected in EU law all along. All this has been apparent from the initial interference with Member States' control over their public services in the original Article 90[20] of the Treaty of Rome, which created an exemption from the full application of the Treaty rules for such services,[21] to the introduction of Article 16 EC by the Treaty of Amsterdam in 1997, which reaffirmed the importance of SGEIs, their position inherent in the shared values of the Union and their role in promoting social and territorial cohesion.[22] It is also apparent in today's version of Article 14 TFEU, which recognises explicitly the competence of the Member States to provide, to commission and to fund such

---

[19]Illustrative in this sense is also the writing of a former Commissioner for Competition, Mario Monti, in 2010: 'Since the 1990s, the place of public services within the single market has been a persistent irritant in the European public debate.'

[20]This is today Article 106 TFEU. Its paragraph 2 sets out as follows: 'Undertakings entrusted with the operation of services of general economic interest or having the character of a revenue-producing monopoly shall be subject to the rules contained in the Treaties, in particular to the rules on competition, in so far as the application of such rules does not obstruct the performance, in law or in fact, of the particular tasks assigned to them. The development of trade must not be affected to such an extent as would be contrary to the interests of the Union.'

[21]According to Szyszczak (2011) services of general economic interest were for a long time derogations from the European rules of competition and internal market. New concepts have gradually been introduced into the framework of EU law and official documents, firstly through the liberalisation processes starting in the 1980s and, secondly, through the Commission's soft law.

[22]Szyszczak (2011) explains that the increased attacks on public services using the competition and free movement rules of the Treaty led the Member States to give services of general economic interest greater prominence in the Treaty by the insertion of a new article 16 EC. 'This Article was a melting pot of different preferences from the Member States. Its purpose is to define a shared competence between EU and Member States and the need to integrate, or harness, the important roles such services play in European integration, ensuring social and territorial cohesion as well as ensuring that national patriotism does not offend the principles of a competitive and integrated market.'

services in compliance with the Treaties and which creates an explicit legal base for secondary legislation in the form of regulations, involving the Council and the Parliament in the co-decision process.[23]

Protocol No 26 to the Treaties introduced by the Treaty of Lisbon establishes, for the first time at the primary law level, the fundamental principles that apply to services of general interest.[24] According to the *Quality Framework*, the Protocol makes clear that the principles need to be adapted to the different services at stake and, therefore, no 'one-size-fits-all' approach is possible. It also confirms that the provisions of the Treaties do not affect the competence of Member States to provide, to commission and to organise non-economic services of general interest. However, the need to distinguish between economic and non-economic activities remains, and a case-by-case analysis continues to be necessary since the nature of these activities evolves constantly.

The Treaty of Lisbon established another cornerstone of the revised SGEI position in the framework of EU law: apart from amendments to Article 16 EC (now Article 14 TFEU), and Protocol No 26 annexed to the Treaties, the Treaty of Lisbon has also given Article 36 of the Charter of Fundamental Rights,[25] which recognises the concept of access to SGEIs, the same legal value as the Treaties. All these legal acts clearly underline the importance of services of general interest in the EU and set out the principles that guide the EU approach to these services. As stated in the *Quality Framework for Services of General Interest in Europe*, they provide a sound basis for pursuing a flexible and pragmatic approach, which is essential in this field since the differences in needs and preferences stem from different geographical, social and cultural situations.

The above-described diverse and fragmented institutional setting for the concept of SGEIs[26] has, however, proved beneficial for the subsequent development of the Commission's soft law and policy documents concerning SGEIs. It appears that the Commission has been successful in neutralising dissent by drawing out a decade-long sequence of consultation exercises and generating a series of papers that might

---

[23]Until that moment the only appropriate legal base for the SGEI legislation was today's Article 106(3) TFEU ('The Commission shall ensure the application of the provisions of this Article and shall, where necessary, address appropriate directives or decision to Member States.') This legal base was used for the 1991 Telecommunications directives, but as the Court held that Article 106 (3) does not give the Commission general legislative power, but only a specific one to deal with State measures concerning legal monopolies, the Commission was reluctant to use it more often.

[24]At the same time, Sauter (2008) sensed that the fact that it was felt necessary to adopt the Protocol highlighted the deep concerns held by the Member States that something essential may slip from their control on that issue. He added that, in reality, the Protocol appeared to add little of substance as regards SGEIs themselves.

[25]The Charter of Human Rights was proclaimed in December 2000. Article 36 of the Charter: 'The Union recognises and respects access to services of general economic interest as provided for in national laws and practices, in accordance with the Treaty establishing the European Community, in order to promote the social and territorial cohesion of the Union'.

[26]The concept of SGEIs now appears in Articles 14 and 106(2) TFEU, in Protocol No 26 and in Article 36 of the Charter of Human Rights.

charitably be defined as 'harmless' (Sauter 2008). Indeed, on a general note, the Commission was of the opinion that a softer approach would be appropriate for this area of law. Since 1996, the Commission has published a barrage of communications.[27] It seems at first that the Commission had chosen soft law instruments due to weak legal competence to legislate in this area, but it is curious that once new EU legislative competences were granted through Article 14 TFEU, the Commission, as the one holding a monopoly on legislative initiative, has still opted not to introduce hard formal legislation but instead continues to use soft law techniques. A more thorough investigation of the philosophic concerns of such a soft law approach on one hand and the realistic conditions of the turbulent times on the other would be outside the scope of this article. Nevertheless, such an analysis deserves to be made as the status and development of these Commission soft law and policy documents concerning SGEIs would be worth exploring.

## 5 The Current Legal Framework for the *Post Office* Case

Now let us go back to the Post Office case, which served as our starting point, and let us present the current material and procedural rules of EU law applied in this particular matter. The United Kingdom obviously notified the measure to the Commission. It did so pursuant to Article 108 TFEU,[28] which is the principal article dealing with the procedural facet of the control of State aid. This article

---

[27]Services of general interest in Europe (1996), Services of general interest in Europe (2001), Report to the Laeken European Council – Services of general interest (2001), Green paper on services of general interest (2003), White paper on services of general interest (2004), White paper on services of general interest (2004), Implementing the Community Lisbon programme: Social services of general interest of the European Union (2006), Communication on 'Services of general interest, including social services of general interest: a new European commitment' (2007), Commission staff working document - Guide to the Application of the European Union Rules on State Aid, Public Procurement and the Internal Market to Services of General Economic Interest, and in Particular to Social Services of General Interest (2010), Communication from the Commission to the European Parliament, the Council, the European Economic and Social Committee and the Committee of the Regions of 23 March 2011 – 'Reform of the EU State Aid Rules on Services of General Economic Interest' (2011), Communication from the Commission to the European Parliament, the Council, the European Economic and Social Committee and the Committee of the Regions – A Quality Framework for Services of General Interest in Europe (2011), Communication on the application of the European Union State aid rules to compensation granted for the provision of services of general economic interest (2012), Commission Staff Working Document – Guide to the application of the European Union rules on state aid, public procurement and the internal market to services of general economic interest, and in particular to social services of general interest (2013).

[28]The procedure regarding notified aid is set by Council Regulation (EC) No 659/1999 of 22 March 1999 laying down detailed rules for the application of Article 93 of the EC Treaty as amended in 2013 and Commission Regulation (EC) No 794/2004 of 21 April 2004 implementing Council Regulation (EC) No 659/1999 laying down detailed rules for the application of Article 93 of the EC Treaty.

gives the central powers to the Commission and appoints it as the alpha and the omega of State aid control. The fact that a Member State notified a certain measure actually means that the Member State sees this measure as State aid, so it allegedly, in the eyes of the notifying party, fulfils the conditions foreseen by Article 107(1) TFEU. In the tenor of that provision, a measure can be deemed to be State aid if it has been granted by a Member State or through State resources in any form whatsoever that distorts or threatens to distort competition by favouring certain undertakings or the production of certain goods and it affects trade between Member States. It follows that, in order for a measure to be qualified as State aid within the meaning of Article 107(1) TFEU, the following five cumulative conditions have to be met: (1) it has to be imputable to the Member State and granted out of State resources, (2) it has to confer an economic advantage on undertakings, (3) the advantage has to be selective, (4) the measure has to distort or threaten to distort competition and (5) it has to affect trade between Member States. In addition, such State aid is, in principle, incompatible with the internal market.

However, every rule has its exceptions, so paragraphs (2) and (3) of Article 107 provide for possible exemptions, in which cases a measure can be deemed compatible with the internal market, either automatically[29] (paragraph 2) or upon the discretionary assessment of the European Commission[30] (paragraph 3). At this point, we have to add the third legal basis for possibly compatible aid foreseen by the Treaty. This is the above-mentioned Article 106(2) TFEU. Precisely, this article has served as a legal basis for the Commission decision authorising State aid for Post Office Ltd.[31]

Let us see how this case looks from the procedural point of view. As good practice, the procedure started informally on 2 May 2014 with pre-notification contacts between the Commission and the authorities of the United Kingdom, followed by several exchanges of information. Pre-notification contacts provide the Commission services and the notifying Member State with the opportunity to discuss the legal and economic aspects of a proposed project informally and in confidence prior to notification and thereby enhance the quality and completeness of notifications. In this context, the Member State and the Commission services can also jointly develop constructive proposals for amending problematic aspects of a planned measure. This phase thus paves the way for the more speedy treatment of notifications once formally submitted to the Commission.[32]

---

[29]'...(s)hall be compatible with the internal market'.

[30]'...(m)ay be considered to be compatible with the internal market'.

[31]Decision of 19.03.2015. C(2015) 1759 final, State aid SA.38788 (2015/N) – United Kingdom Compensation to Post Office Limited for costs incurred to provide SGEIs 2015-2018.
http://ec.europa.eu/competition/state_aid/cases/256622/256622_1651530_118_2.pdf. Accessed 6 Jun 2015.

[32]The Pre-notification phase is described in the Code of Best Practice for the conduct of State aid control procedures, 2009/C 136/04.

The UK formally notified compensation to Post Office Ltd for costs incurred to provide SGEIs 2015–2018 by State aid notification software (SANI[33]), and the case was registered under number SA.38788.[34] The Commission first of all noted that the UK accepted the State aid qualification under Article 107(1) TFEU of the notified measure but still verified if the measure was indeed State aid. It concluded that it was. The compensation granted to Post Office Ltd for the delivery of public services was imputable to the state and was given through State resources. Since the annual compensation under the funding agreement benefited only one undertaking and granted additional funds exclusively to that undertaking, this measure was also selective.

To constitute State aid, a measure must confer an economic advantage on its recipients. The Commission recalled here, in paragraphs 65–68 of the Decision, that compensation for SGEIs granted to a company might not constitute an economic advantage under certain strictly defined conditions. Public service compensation is deemed not to grant any economic advantage where the four cumulative Altmark conditions are met. In particular, in its Altmark judgment,[35] the Court of Justice held that where a state measure must be regarded as compensation for the services provided by the recipient undertakings in order to discharge public service obligations, so that those undertakings do not enjoy real financial advantage and the measure thus does not have the effect of putting them in a more favourable competitive position than the undertakings competing with them, such a measure is not caught by Article 107(1) TFEU.[36]

For such public service compensation to escape qualification as State aid in a particular case, the four cumulative criteria (Altmark criteria) summarised below must be satisfied: (1) the recipient undertaking is expected to have public service obligations to discharge, and such should be clearly defined; (2) the parameters on the basis of which the compensation is calculated must be established in advance in an objective and transparent manner; (3) the compensation cannot exceed what is necessary to cover all or part of the costs incurred in the discharge of the public service obligations, taking into account the relevant receipts and a reasonable profit; (4) if the undertaking that is to discharge public service obligations is not chosen pursuant to a public procurement procedure that would allow for the selection of the tenderer capable of providing those services at the least cost to the community, the level of compensation needed should be determined on the basis of a cost analysis that a typical undertaking, well run and adequately provided with means to meet the

---

[33]State Aid Notifications Interactive (SANI) has been developed in order to facilitate the electronic transmission of notifications as required by Regulation 794/2004.

[34]It is important to stress that the UK fully respected the stand-still obligation laid down in Article 108(3) TFEU and did not grant the aid until the Commission reached a decision authorising the notified measure.

[35]Case C-280/00 *Altmark Trans GmbH and Regierungspräsidium Magdeburg v Nahverkehrsgesellschaft Altmark GmbH* [2003] ECR I -07747.

[36]In that case, if the measure is not State aid in the sense of Article 107(1), there is also no notification obligation according to Article 108 TFEU.

public service obligations, would have incurred, taking into account the relevant receipts and a reasonable profit from discharging the obligations (a 'typical undertaking').

The Commission concluded that this compensation was not Altmark compliant.[37] The UK authorities have not provided information substantiating that the Post Office was being compensated according to the costs of a typical well-run undertaking within the sector. In the absence of this information, the Commission was not in a position to consider that the fourth Altmark condition had been met.[38] Therefore, the Commission concluded that the selective measure must be considered as conferring an advantage to the Post Office, which can be qualified as economic advantage within the meaning of Article 107(1) TFEU.

Furthermore, it is clear that any State measure conferring on the Post Office an economic advantage may distort competition within the internal market and affect trade between Member States, given that the Post Office operates in sectors that are open to competition, and that the measure potentially makes the entry and the development of other retailers or retail financial services providers in the UK more difficult. In light of the above arguments that proved the involvement of State aid under Article 107(1) TFEU, the Commission decided to assess the lawfulness and compatibility of the measure with the internal market.

As previously mentioned, the Commission approved the measure, invoking Article 106(2) TFEU. Namely, under certain conditions,[39] Article 106(2) allows the Commission to declare compensation for SGEIs compatible with the internal market. Additionally, the SGEI Framework[40] adopted by the Commission in 2011

---

[37] As in a number of other cases. E.g. Bartosch (2006) criticises the Altmark judgment and especially the Commission's response to the judgment. In his view, the Altmark criteria are 'completely out of touch with reality', so, in the eyes of the Commission, hardly any aid scheme fulfilled the requirements set by the judgment. In his view, the benefits of the Altmark ruling itself are, for these reasons, highly questionable. The practical impacts of the Altmark judgement and its theoretical implications are also discussed by Gromnicka (2005) and Louise and Vallery (2004).

[38] Klasse (2013) shows that the criteria laid down by the CJEU for public service compensation to be free of State aid elements have been met only on rare occasions in the case law. He notes that this is a consequence of the difficulties the Commission has faced when applying the Altmark test which resulted in a very strict reading by the Commission of the Altmark criteria. Klasse notes that the main challenging factor remains the assessment of the fourth Altmark criterion. Save for in exceptional circumstances, the benchmarking exercise has never been successful. He argues that it is difficult to reconcile the Commission's approach emanating from its case law with the jurisprudence of the European Courts.

[39] Article 106(2) provides for an exception from the rules contained in the Treaty insofar as the application of the competition rules would obstruct, in law or in fact, the performance of the tasks assigned. This exception only applies where the development of trade is not affected to such an extent as would be contrary to the interests of the Union.

[40] Communication from the Commission, European Union framework for State aid in the form of public service compensation [2011] OJ C 8/15.

http://eur-lex.europa.eu/legal-content/EN/ALL/?uri=CELEX:52012XC0111(03). Accessed 7 Jun 2015.

as part of the new and revised 'SGEI package'[41] sets out guidelines for assessing the compatibility of SGEI compensation, which exceeds €15 million per year.[42] Namely, at the current stage of development of the internal market, State aid falling outside the scope of the SGEI Decision may be declared compatible with Article 106(2) of the Treaty if it is necessary for the operation of the service of general economic interest concerned and does not affect the development of trade to such an extent as to be contrary to the interests of the Union. The conditions set out in sections 2.2 to 2.10 of the SGEI Framework must be met in order to achieve that balance.

According to the 2011 SGEI Framework, the Commission checked the compatibility criteria in the Post Office case in the following manner. Firstly, the Commission examined the entrustment of the SGEI, which was granted as required through a formal act. Considering the features of the entrustment letter, as well of the funding agreement, the Commission considered that the entrustment and duration criteria of the SGEI Framework had been satisfied. With regard to the existence of the genuine service of general economic interest, as verified through public consultation, which had been duly carried out, the Commission considered that the SGEI in question did constitute a genuine SGEI and that the UK had not committed a manifest error in its definition.

As the 'aid will be considered compatible with the internal market on the basis of Article 106(2) of the Treaty only where the undertaking complies, where applicable, with Directive 2006/111/EC on the transparency of financial relations between Member States and public undertakings as well as on financial transparency within certain undertakings' and the UK confirmed that the financial relations between Post Office Ltd and the UK are transparent as required by the Transparency Directive and that the public funds provided to Post Office Ltd and the use made of these public funds will continue to be identified clearly in the Post Office's published statutory accounts, the Commission established compliance also in that regard.

---

[41]The 2011 SGEI Package replaced the 2005 SGEI Package (also called the 'Monti-Kroes Package'), which has been very much inspired by the Altmark case law. Following a public consultation and a thorough revision process, the Commission adopted the first three texts of the new SGEI package (the SGEI Decision, the SGEI Framework and the SGEI Communication) on 20 December 2011 in order to define the conditions under which State aid in the form of public service compensation can be considered compatible with EU rules, and on 25 April 2012 the Commission adopted, as the final pillar of the package, the *de minimis* Regulation for the field of SGEIs.

[42]This threshold is determined by the SGEI Decision which sets out the conditions under which State aid in the form of public service compensation granted to certain undertakings entrusted with the operation of services of general economic interest is compatible with the internal market and exempt from the requirement of notification laid down in Article 108(3) of the Treaty (in a way functioning as a block exemption regulation). Commission Decision of 20 December 2011 on the application of Article 106(2) of the Treaty on the Functioning of the European Union to State aid in the form of public service compensation granted to certain undertakings entrusted with the operation of services of general economic interest (notified under document C(2011) 9380) [2012] OJ L 7/3.

http://eur-lex.europa.eu/legal-content/EN/ALL/?uri=CELEX:32012D0021. Accessed 7 Jun 2015.

Considering that the current SGEI Framework makes the compatibility of the compensation conditional upon compliance with Union public procurement rules, whenever applicable, the Commission was satisfied that the EU public procurement compliance criterion was met in this case. Furthermore, the Commission checked for absence of discrimination in the measure at hand and deliberated on the amount of compensation, as well as the absence of overcompensation. It found that the net avoided cost methodology implemented by the UK authorities was robust and in line with the SGEI Framework. When examining reasonable profit, it also concluded that the resulting profit figure was not excessive. At the same time, it found that the entrustment letter contained sufficient efficiency incentives for the provision of the SGEI, that the Post Office complied with the requirement for separation of accounts and that it could be concluded that the UK had taken sufficient measures to closely monitor the Post Office's funding over the new funding period in order to prevent any overcompensation of the Post Office.

Finally, the Commission concluded that the potential additional remedies to avoid undue distortion of competition had not been proven necessary, that the transparency requirements had been complied with and that the notified measure, being in line with the conditions set out in the SGEI Framework, was compatible with the internal market.

# 6    The SGEI Legal Framework Not Applied in the *Post Office* Case

After having mentioned and briefly described the Commission's soft law instrument that was applied in the Post Office case (the SGEI Framework), it also seems appropriate to touch upon the rest of the current SGEI legal framework since all these instruments together form a unique SGEI package that is now the best and by far the most elaborated set of rules for the SGEIs since the notion was born. The interplay between these rules is neither simple nor very user friendly, but it does provide some legal certainty, and it forms a credible legal source to be referred to in each specific SGEI case. Among the referent instruments, the crucial piece of legislation seems to be what is known as the SGEI Decision.

Commission Decision 2012/21/EU of 21 December 2011 on the application of Article 106(2) TFEU to State aid in the form of public service compensation granted to certain undertakings entrusted with the operation of services of general economic interest[43] declares certain types of SGEI compensation constituting State aid to be

---

[43]This Decision replaced SGEI Decision 2005/842/EC. Given the development of intra-Union trade in the provision of services of general economic interest, demonstrated for instance by the strong development of multi-national providers in a number of sectors which are of great importance for the development of the internal market, the Commission has deemed it appropriate to set a lower limit for the amount of compensation which can be exempted from the notification requirement in accordance with the 2011 SGEI Decision than what was set by the 2005 SGEI

compatible with the Treaty pursuant to Article 106(2) of the Treaty and exempts them from the notification obligation under Article 108(3) of the Treaty. Provided that a number of conditions are met, limited amounts of compensation granted to undertakings entrusted with the provision of services of general economic interest do not affect the development of trade and competition to such an extent as to be contrary to the interests of the Union.[44] An individual State aid notification should therefore not be required for compensation below a specified annual amount of compensation, provided the requirements of the Decision are met.[45]

The Decision applies to State aid in the form of public service compensation, which falls within one of the following categories. The first category is compensation not exceeding an annual amount of EUR 15 million for the provision of services of general economic interest in areas other than transport and transport infrastructure. Where the amount of compensation varies over the duration of the entrustment, the annual amount shall be calculated as the average of the annual amounts of compensation expected to be made over the entrustment period. The second category is compensation for the provision of services of general economic interest by hospitals providing medical care, including, where applicable, emergency services (the pursuit of ancillary activities directly related to the main activities is permissible, notably in the field of research). The third group is compensation for the provision of services of general economic interest meeting social needs with regard to health and long-term care, childcare, access to and reintegration into the labour market, social housing and the care and social inclusion of vulnerable groups.

The fourth category refers to compensation for the provision of services of general economic interest with reference to air or maritime links to islands on which the average annual traffic during the two financial years preceding the year in which the service of general economic interest was assigned does not exceed 300,000 passengers. Similarly, the fifth group refers to compensation for the provision of services of general economic interest concerning airports and ports for which the average annual traffic during the two financial years preceding the year in which the service of general economic interest was assigned does not exceed 200,000 passengers in the case of airports and 300,000 passengers in the case of ports.[46]

---

Decision, while allowing for that amount to be computed as an annual average over the entrustment period.

[44]The Decision only applies where the period for which the undertaking is entrusted with the operation of the service of general economic interest does not exceed 10 years. Where the period of entrustment exceeds 10 years, the Decision only applies to the extent that a significant investment is required from the service provider that needs to be amortised over a longer period in accordance with generally accepted accounting principles.

[45]If, during the duration of the entrustment, the conditions for the application of the Decision cease to be met, the aid shall be notified in accordance with Article 108(3) of the Treaty.

[46]The Croatian example of SGEIs exempted through the SGEI Decision is the State Aid Scheme for the period between 2005–2012 in the form of compensation for the services of general economic interest concerning line maritime transport on national lines 338 Valbiska – Lopar and return, 501 Brodarica – Krapanj and return, and 612 Komiža – Biševo and return.

However, in the field of air and maritime transport, the Decision only applies to State aid in the form of public service compensation, granted to undertakings entrusted with the operation of services of general economic interest as referred to in Article 106(2) of the Treaty, which complies with Regulation (EC) No 1008/2008 and, respectively, Regulation (EEC) No 3577/92, where applicable. At the same time, the Decision does not apply to State aid in the form of public service compensation granted to undertakings in the field of land transport.

The Decision sets out the special rules regarding entrustment and compensation, which cannot exceed what is necessary to cover the net cost incurred in discharging the public service obligations, including a reasonable profit. It also foresees that control of overcompensation is supposed to be ensured by the Member States. The Member States are also required to keep information on the beneficiaries transparent and to provide periodic reports to the Commission or, should it be required by the Commission, to provide ad hoc information on certain compensation measures.

The third piece of the 'package' is the Communication from the Commission on the application of the European Union State aid rules to compensation granted for the provision of services of general economic interest,[47] that is, the so-called SGEI Communication. It is a totally new instrument without a counterpart in the 2005 SGEI package. The purpose of the Communication is to clarify the key concepts underlying the application of the State aid rules to public service compensation. It focuses on those State aid requirements that are most relevant for public service compensation. It explains the concept of aid, starting from the concepts of an undertaking and economic activity as, based on Article 107(1) TFEU, the State aid rules apply only where the recipient is an 'undertaking', and the Court of Justice has defined undertakings as entities engaged in economic activities, regardless of their legal status and the way in which they are financed.[48] To put it simply, there would be no application of the State aid rules unless the provider of a service of general economic interest is to be regarded as an undertaking. And there is no undertaking unless the services that a certain entity provides are considered economic activities. However, the Treaty does not define what an economic activity is. This has been done by the case law of the EU courts instead.

In this sense, Article 107 TFEU would not apply where the State acts by 'exercising public power' or where some authorities act 'in their capacity as public authorities', such as in the examples of the army or police, air navigation safety and control,

---

[47]Communication from the Commission on the application of the European Union State aid rules to compensation granted for the provision of services of general economic interest [2012] OJ C 8/4.

http://eur-lex.europa.eu/legal-content/EN/ALL/?uri=CELEX:52012XC0111(02). Accessed 7 Jun 2015.

[48]The Court of Justice has also held that any activity consisting of offering goods and services on the market is an economic activity. However, the question whether a market exists for certain services may depend on the way those services are organised in a certain Member State. So, if the service is provided in a market environment, then the service would fulfil the condition to be regarded as an economic activity, which would make its provider an undertaking and which would trigger the application of the State aid rules.

maritime traffic control and safety, anti-pollution surveillance and the organisation, financing and enforcement of prison sentences. Also, Article 107 would not be applicable in the case of social security schemes that do not involve an economic activity, depending on the way they are set up and structured.[49] Similarly, in the healthcare sector, the involvement of economic activity depends on the level of competition in a market environment of a certain Member State, which differs to a great extent between the Member States. General education systems are also predominantly non-economic, which would again imply the inapplicability of State aid rules.

The State aid rules would also not be applicable if public service compensation does not affect, or threaten to affect, trade between Member States. Still, according to the Altmark case law, there is no threshold or percentage below which trade between Member States can be regarded as not having been affected, even considering a relatively small amount of aid or the small size of the recipient undertaking. On the other hand, it is interesting to point out that the SGEI Communication expressly mentions that the Commission has in several cases concluded that certain activities were of a purely local character and, in that regard, did not affect trade between Member States (as in the case of a swimming pool facility used predominantly by the local population, local hospitals, local museums that were unlikely to attract cross-border visitors and local cultural events...). However, the SGEI Communication is without prejudice to the relevant case law of the Court of Justice, as only the Court may interpret the Treaty,[50] so the lack of effect on trade as a trigger to the inapplicability of Article 107 must be interpreted narrowly.

Additionally, the SGEI Communication provides the conditions under which public service compensation does not constitute 'advantage' as one of the requirements of the notion of State aid. Thereby, it does not constitute State aid if the Altmark criteria, described earlier in relation to the Post Office case, have been fulfilled. From that perspective, the Communication elaborates on the existence of a service of general economic interest and its specific features, the importance of the entrustment act, the parameters of compensation and instructions on how to avoid overcompensation. One of the true innovations of the Communication (Pesaresi et al. 2012a, b) is the issue of the selection of the provider 'at the least cost to the community' and the clarification of the interplay between public procurement and State aid rules. It also elaborates on the amount of compensation where the SGEI is assigned under an appropriate tendering procedure and the amount of compensation where the SGEI is not assigned under a tendering procedure, all related to the still contentious 'fourth' Altmark criterion.[51]

---

[49]In general, EU courts distinguish between the schemes based on the principle of solidarity and economic schemes.

[50]The Commission is bound by the Treaty and the Court's interpretation of the Treaty provisions, so the Communication can only describe and interpret, to the extent possible, what the case law has left unclear (Pesaresi et al. 2012a, b).

[51]As Klasse (2013) explains, even though public procurement is the main rule under Altmark, the Court of Justice has been reluctant to impose an obligation on the Member States to perform tenders every time. Instead, in Altmark, the Court created an alternative test based on the efficiency of the

Finally, the last piece of legislation in the latest SGEI package is Commission Regulation (EU) No 360/2012 of 25 April 2012 on the application of Articles 107 and 108 of the Treaty on the Functioning of the European Union to *de minimis* aid granted to undertakings providing services of general economic interest (the SGEI *de minimis* Regulation[52]), which exempts from EU State aid rules aid of up to EUR 500,000[53] per company, over a three year period. It is considered that such compensation is not problematic as it is too low to have any impact on trade and competition, and thereby the effect on trade requirement of the concept of State aid would not be fulfilled.

# 7 Summary

In this paper, we found it interesting to tackle postal services as one of the most widespread examples of services of general economic interest in order to highlight the specificity of the network industries and their contribution to EU harmonisation in this field. We have also sought to position the notion of universal services in relation to the notion of SGEIs since the Post Office itself, although a member of the postal sector, is an SGEI provider different from a universal postal service. After addressing the different views of various Member States on the perception of a public service, we drew the general conclusion that divergences and tensions still exist and that they are inherent in the topic since different legal cultures, traditions and social and historic features affect the subject matter. Namely, in the absence of sectoral Union rules governing the matter, the Member States have a wide margin of discretion in defining services that could be classified as services of general economic interest. The Commission's task is to ensure that there is no manifest error with regard to the definition of SGEIs. On that note, we found that the role of the Commission's soft (law) approach has proven in general and ultimately to be

---

provider of the service and the least cost for the community. However, the Altmark judgment did not specify what constitutes a typical, well-run undertaking. The concept has been criticised for being virtually impossible to accomplish in practice because of a lack of comparable undertakings that could be used as benchmarks. Klasse concludes that the Commission's practice appears to be based on the premise that the fourth criterion can only be met in its first alternative, i.e. if the provider is chosen on the basis of a competitive tender. However, even in those cases where the choice of undertaking to be entrusted and the amount of compensation are affected by way of a procurement procedure perfectly in line with competition and public procurement rules, the compensation may fail the Commission's necessity test (or the 'least cost' criterion).

[52]Commission Regulation (EU) No 360/2012 of 25 April 2012 on the application of Articles 107 and 108 of the Treaty on the Functioning of the European Union to *de minimis* aid granted to undertakings providing services of general economic interest [2012] OJ L 114/8. http://eur-lex. europa.eu/legal-content/EN/ALL/?uri=CELEX:32012R0360. Accessed 7 Jun 2015.

[53]The threshold is higher than the general *de minimis* thresholds in the field of State aid (EUR 200,000 over 3 years) because it can be assumed that the support measures at least in part compensate for the extra costs incurred for the provision of a public service.

beneficial. Although it has suffered from a great deal of criticism all along, we now do have a somewhat coherent SGEI legal framework in place, including especially the SGEI package, but also primary law instruments such as Articles 14 and 106 TFEU, Protocol No 26 and the Charter on Fundamental Rights. From the State aid law perspective, the financing of SGEIs is in principle allowed if this is necessary to ensure the proper functioning of the markets for the benefit of consumers.

This paper has analysed the applicable rules that the Commission has applied in its recent Post Office Decision, and at the same time the opportunity was taken to present the rest of the instruments contained in the 2011 SGEI package. The paper has briefly tackled some of the issues raised, among others the issue of economic activity as a prerequisite for the application of competition rules, the follow-up on the Altmark legacy and the still hot topic of the private procurement rules within the scope of the State aid battlefield.

**Acknowledgements** This paper was supported by the Croatian Science Foundation project no 9366 'Legal Aspects of Corporate Acquisitions and Knowledge Driven Companies' Restructuring'.

# References

Aviani D, Đerđa D (2008) Europska regulacija gospodarskih službi od općeg interesa. Zbornik radova Šestog međunarodnog savjetovanja Aktualnosti građanskog i trgovačkog zakonodavstva i pravne prakse. Pravni fakultet Sveučilišta u Mostaru, Neum, pp 141–149

Bartosch A (2006) Compensation for public service obligations: post Altmark reflections. In: Sanchez Rydelski M (ed) The EC state aid regime: distortive effects of state aid on competition trade. Cameron May, London, pp 55–68

Cremona M (2011) Introduction. In: Cremona M (ed) Market integration and public services in the European Union. OUP, Oxford, p 4

Flynn L, Rizza C (2001) Postal services and competition law – a review and analysis of the EC case-law. World Competition 24(4):475–511

Gromnicka E (2005) Services of general economic interest in the state aid regime: proceduralisation of political choices. Eur Public Law 11(3):425–458

Henning M (2011) Public service obligations: protection of public service values in a national and European context. In: Szyszczak E, Davies J, Andenaes M, Bekkedal T (eds) Developments in services of general interest. TMC Asser Press, The Hague

Jääskinen N (2011) The new rules on SGEI. Eur State Aid Law Q 10(4):599

Klarić M, Nikolić M (2011) Ustrojstvo javnih službi u Europskom pravnom poretku. Zbornik radova Pravnog fakulteta u Splitu 48(1/2011):89–102

Klasse M (2013) The impact of Altmark: the European Commission case law responses. In: Szyszczak E, van de Gronden JW (eds) Financing services of general economic interest: legal issues of services of general interest. TMC Asser Press, The Hague

Louise F, Vallery A (2004) Ferring revisited: the Altmark case and the state financing of the public service obligations. World Competition 27(1):53–74

Nicolaides P (2003) Compensation for public service obligation: the floodgates of state aid? Eur Competition Law Rev 11:561–573

Pesaresi N, Sinnaeve A, Guigue-Koeppen V, Wiemann J, Radulescu M (2012a) The new state aid rules for services of general economic interest (SGEI). http://ec.europa.eu/competition/publi cations/cpn/2012_1_9_en.pdf. Accessed 6 June 2015

Pesaresi N, Sinnaeve A, Guigue-Koeppen V, Wiemann J, Radulescu M (2012b) The SGEI communication. http://ec.europa.eu/competition/publications/cpn/2012_1_10_en.pdf. Accessed 6 June 2015

Popović N (2013) Horizontal approach to network industries in Croatia. Croat Comp Public Adm 3:859–894

Rusu IE, Kekelekis M (2011) The implications of the Europe 2020 Strategy for Services of General Economic Interest (SGEI). http://www.eipa.eu/files/repository/eipascope/20110912111229_ EipascopeSpecialIssue_Art9.pdf. Accessed 8 June 2015

Sauter W (2008) Services of general economic interest and universal service in EU law. http://ssrn. com/abstract=1136105. Accessed 7 June 2015

Slot JP (2008) Recent developments in EC state aid law. Referat im Rahmen der Vortragsreihe "Rechtsfragen der Europaeischen Integration". Zentrum fuer Europaeisches Wirtschaftsrecht, Vortraege und Berichte, Nr 172. http://www.zew.uni-bonn.de/publikationen/schriftenreihe-des-zentrums-fuer-europaeisches-wirtschaftsrecht/heft-172-slot.pdf. Accessed 7 June 2015

Schweitzer H (2011) Service of general economic interest: European law's impact on the role of markets and of member states. In: Cremona M (ed) Market integration and public services in the European Union. OUP, Oxford, p 11

Szyszczak E (2011) Introduction: why do public services challenge the European Union. In: Szyszczak E, van de Gronden JW (eds) Financing services of general economic interest: legal issues of services of general interest. TMC Asser Press, The Hague

CPSIA information can be obtained
at www.ICGtesting.com
Printed in the USA
LVHW082136060619
620471LV00007B/421/P

9 783662 569092